SMART SIGNS, FOOLISH CHOICES

———•———

An Astrological Guide to Getting Smart in Affairs of the Heart

ROBIN MACNAUGHTON

CITADEL PRESS
Kensington Publishing Corp.
www.kensingtonbooks.com

To Mary,

a wonderful agent and a wonderful person.

———◆———

CITADEL PRESS BOOKS are published by

Kensington Publishing Corp.
850 Third Avenue
New York, NY 10022

All Kensington titles, imprints, and distributed lines are available at special quantity discounts for bulk purchases for sales promotions, premiums, fund-raising, educational, or institutional use. Special book excerpts or customized printings can also be created to fit specific needs. For details, write or phone the office of the Kensington special sales manager: Kensington Publishing Corp., 850 Third Avenue, New York, NY 10022, attn: Special Sales Department; phone 1-800-221-2647.

CITADEL PRESS and the Citadel logo are Reg. U.S. Pat. & TM Off.

First printing: May 2004

10 9 8 7 6 5 4 3 2 1

Printed in the United States of America

Library of Congress Control Number: 2004100538

ISBN 0-8065-2504-5

Contents

iv CONTENTS

    The Capricorn Woman   110
    The Capricorn Man   115

12. Aquarius: January 21 to February 19   120
    The Aquarius Woman   120
    The Aquarius Man   125

13. Pisces: February 20 to March 20   130
    The Pisces Woman   130
    The Pisces Man   136

14. The Moon Signs and Emotional Choices   142

    Finding Your Moon Sign   144

    The Moon Signs   145
       Moon in Aries   146
       Moon in Taurus   147
       Moon in Gemini   148
       Moon in Cancer   150
       Moon in Leo   152
       Moon in Virgo   154
       Moon in Libra   155
       Moon in Scorpio   157
       Moon in Sagittarius 159
       Moon in Capricorn   161
       Moon in Aquarius   163
       Moon in Pisces   165

    The Four Lunar Elements   168
       Moon in Fire   168
       Moon in Air   169
       Moon in Earth   170
       Moon in Water   171

Introduction

So many people now are desperate to find love. From the personal ads to the Internet matchmaking services, there is white-hot activity among singles to find that perfect someone. However, while everyone is caught up in scrutinizing the qualities of the prospective other—is he or she good-looking enough, powerful enough, thin enough, built enough, rich enough, young enough—they're not looking at *themselves* in the deeper sense. They are not looking at why, in their previous relationships, they made the choices they did in the first place, and why they stayed long enough for it to turn from a few dates into a relationship.

When we don't examine why we got into relationships that deeply affected our lives, we will repeat that same dynamic with someone else. And someone else after that.

There is a woman I know who has been married four times, each time divorced because she fell out of love with her husbands. When she started dating number four, she told everyone she knew that he was her true soul mate. When she dumped him after one year of marriage, she told everyone that he was boring. Now, of course, this man was the same on day one of their first meeting as he was on the day their marriage ended. This woman has no clue that any of her failed attempts at marriage have anything to do with her.

People come to me all the time, asking me if they will ever meet their soul mate. And it is so clear to me that they don't even know their own soul. When people bring up the issue of soul mate to me, what they are really saying is, "Will I find the right person to fill up the emptiness that I have inside of me?" Of course, the answer can only be no. Starting a relationship with such high expectations that it will fulfill an inner emptiness is a bad choice, which will reveal itself to be illusory, historically and maybe hysterically speaking.

These choices have nothing to do with love. Love is a sacred, spiritual experience issuing out of an alive soul, not a hungry, desperate soul. There is a most wondrous Sanskrit word that comes from the Hindu religion. It is *Namaste* and it means: "I honor the light within you that is within me." The light it refers to is the light of God, the God that is already in our souls—and that is love. All the rest is psychological projection, attachment, addiction, and piteous need.

Only when we become aware of the old, undermining tapes in our own head that come to define us—the fear tapes, the need tapes, the self-pitying tapes, the anger tapes—can we start moving beyond that which we have already created and become conscious so that we can start to make new choices, smart choices. It may still seem that an initial romantic meeting is about magic; however, the course of the relationship is about choice.

The following chapters illustrate classic, archetypal issues pertaining to each of the sun signs that, if left unconscious, tend to play themselves out repeatedly. As a tool for emotional, psychological awareness, astrology is invaluable for depicting, with clarity, the inner story of a romance. It shows what we have to learn and how we have to grow to attain the emotional power that will release us from old pain-producing patterns. Different astrological signs point to different emotional issues and lessons that influence our choices. The unfolding of these issues sheds light on such questions as why certain signs always choose a certain type of person, why certain people tend to be disappointed repeatedly, why certain people suffer from such soulful loneliness, and why certain people never learn their lessons—or even realize there is a lesson to be learned. Every love pattern in a person's life has a psychological cause that can be revealed through astrology.

The outer is always a reflection of the inner. However, until we become aware of these dynamics, we can't change them and ascend to a higher place where we will be able to make wiser choices.

Whether we realize it or not, the deep love experience involves a journey. This journey brings us back to ourselves in the deepest, most affirmative sense. From this place, we can derive the meaning, the lessons from these invaluable growth experiences, and then go forward, hopefully more conscious and more enlightened in the ever-mysterious experience of love.

How to Use This Book

In the following chapters, we'll be looking at each of the twelve sun signs. For each sun sign for both men and women, "The Smart Scoop" provides an overview of its distinctive personal and emotional strengths. "The Feeling Scope" gives a picture of what each sun sign is like emotionally, and how the emotional makeup of each sun sign tends to play itself out in various situations. Next, "Fatal Attractions" describes the kinds of attractions that typically set that sign up to fall into difficult relationships, and what various behaviors ensue in given circumstances. "Foolish Choices" will describe the initial romantic choices each sun sign characteristically makes. Finally, "Fated Lessons" and "Getting Smart in Affairs of the Heart" describe the unique emotional lessons each sun sign must learn to grow from experience and turn a troubled relationship into one of promise and potential.

We will also examine the moon signs, which determine our emotional side, and the rising signs, which influence how we show ourselves to the world. Read the sun sign material first to get a basic overview, then go to the moon sign material to get a deeper emotional context. Finally, look at the rising sign material to get a sense of how the outer personality can differ from the inner.

1. THE COSMIC QUALITIES AND THE FOUR ELEMENTS

———◆———

Before we actually get into the sun signs themselves, we need to discuss two essential ingredients integral to each sign. These essential ingredients are the Cosmic Qualities and the four elements. The Cosmic Quality of a sun sign determines the nature of the sign, or how it tends to function, and the element defines the sign's basic temperament.

The Cosmic Qualities and Conscious Choices

Every sign and every planet in astrology has its own unique nature. The nature of a sign is based on a number of things, but one of the most crucial is the Cosmic Quality. The nature of a sign is important, especially in relationships, because people behave according to their unique nature and it is very difficult for them to do anything else. How many times have you heard someone say, "I don't understand why she makes those choices. I would never do that!" Well, of course, because the person speaking is not that person she is judging and does not share the unique nature that prompts that person to behave in a certain specific way. So often in relationships, deep problems arise

1

because people come together who are very different by nature, and instead of trying to adjust to those differences, they expect their partner to give up who they are and behave just like them. When conflicts arise because that immediate transfiguration doesn't occur, power struggles and tug-of-wars occur that can eventually erode the entire connection. However, with awareness, difficulties can be worked out and smoothed over. The following is a key to the Cosmic Qualities associated with each sign that play a big part in determining how we go about living our lives.

Cardinal Signs: Aries, Cancer, Libra, Capricorn

Cardinal signs are self-starters. They are often leaders who feel the need to initiate things. They put a strong emphasis on doing. While another Cosmic Quality may sit and ponder a problem and need time to think it through, the Cardinal sign is up and running and has no patience for putting anything off. Cardinal signs are great at starting a business, but sometimes they take on more than they can chew. They often have many irons in the fire, even if the irons tend to burn themselves up. Cardinal signs love the newness of things, and have an incandescent enthusiasm for new projects, new relationships, new people, and new ideas. They can get bored and annoyed by people who move at a much slower pace. Because they are so action-oriented and not given to analyzing things, they can be lacking in compassion and understanding for other people who are very different from them. They need to learn patience, tolerance, and, often, follow-through. Since they also tend to move only to the beat of their own drummer, they need to polish their listening skills.

Mutable Signs: Gemini, Virgo, Sagittarius, Pisces

Mutable signs are adaptable, flexible, and changeable. These signs are generally easy to get along with since they can go in any direction without any problem. The strength of mutable signs is that they are generally tolerant, and instinctively understand that there are other sides to a situation than their own. They don't get locked into a position, but tend to take the attitude that everything is relative and everybody's position is valid to them. This understanding quality often makes them excellent at dealing with people. (The one exception is Virgo, which does tend to be critical and intolerant. Nevertheless, the mind of a highly developed Virgo can be an extraordinary thing when it comes to intellectual assimilation and understanding.)

When mutable sign people come up against a wall or hit a snag, they do not lament. They look for another solution and another solution after that, until they find the one that works best. Instinctively they know that, just as there are many different ways of seeing the world, there are many different workable ways of doing something. Likewise, the flexibility that mutable signs bring to a relationship works so well that they can take the relationship to another level by helping their partner see another point of view.

The weakness of a mutable sign is that they often lack staying power, having a hard time finishing the projects, and sometimes the relationships, they start. Because these people can so easily move in different directions, they are the most likely of the Cosmic Qualities to have affairs, and are actually capable of sustaining a double life where they move back and forth between two people. They need change and movement far more than stability, and so when they feel bored by being locked in, they tend to look around to discover what's more interesting.

Fixed Signs: Taurus, Leo, Scorpio, Aquarius

Fixed signs are fixed in their thinking. Deeply resistant to change, they are the opposite of the Mutables. The strength of fixed sign people is that they have staying power and can accomplish any task they set their mind to. Of all the Cosmic Quality types, the fixed signs tend to be the most faithful. However, they can also suffer from tunnel vision, and tend to compartmentalize in their thinking. Once a fixed sign gets in a groove, they don't look to the right or left. They can be very stubborn, terrified of change, and locked in to a way of thinking that both cuts them off from the rest of the world and creates a rut that only gets deeper with time. Fixed sign people are so entrenched in their rules and routines that they have a hard time understanding the differences that other people present. They often try to bend the world to their will, and, caught in a relationship conflict, want to win more than they want to communicate and move on. Because of their rigidity, fixed signs have a hard time learning from experience. Presented with the same lessons again and again, they tend to have the same responses, responses that, in their minds, ensure a sort of security. They have a deep fear of the unknown that is the key factor for their refusal to open up and take some risks.

The Four Elements and Foolish Choices

Another important factor in the fate of a relationship is the elements. The elements define our basic temperament and what we are most spontaneously apt to do. Sometimes we act unconsciously, blindly, and impulsively because of the strength of our element. In this chapter we will discuss the elements and the chemistry that they create.

The Four Elements

The twelve sun signs fall into one of the four basic elements: fire, air, earth, and water. These elements indicate the essential personality temperament, which profoundly influences many of a person's choices. For instance, the element earth is security oriented on both a material and emotional level. And when earth signs enter into a relationship, it is with expectations around their security needs being met. Their criterion for commitment is rooted in security, and this can be so important that it completely effaces the individuality of the other person. In other words, the partner is seen less for who he or she is as a person than for whether he or she measures up to elemental earth standards. In this section we will examine the expression of each of the four basic elements.

Fire

Fire is pure, undiluted energy. Fire sign people (Aries, Leo, Sagittarius) have energy plus. They are energetic, impatient, impulsive, and spontaneous. Fire sign people are full of life, vim, and vigor and are highly self-expressive. Often childlike in their attitude, they tend to want what they want when they want it. Most of all, they want to have fun. The world is their playground and their mission is as much pleasure as can be had.

Fire signs seek excitement, hate being bored, and love to be entertained. Likewise, they are often entertaining since they have such an expansive view of life. Dramatic, romantic, and expecting experience to be larger than life, they are often prone to love-at-first-sight situations that can quickly burn out should things get boring. Passionate, enthusiastic, and very impulsive, they often act before they think, sometimes getting themselves into some serious emotional stews. However, self-centered, restless, and somewhat detached, they never let anything get them down for long. Their need is to drop the loss, take the gain, and move on to what's around the corner.

Although fire signs do like a lot of attention, they also tend to need a challenge. Therefore, they especially run from anyone clingy, weepy, and wanting more of their time than they're willing to part with. Always having many friends and many irons in the fire, they prize their freedom. Fire signs need to feel unfettered and able to do their own thing without anyone tugging at their leg. Their emotional memory is fleeting and fueled by the fun that is in front of them. Therefore, with great zest, they can have a love 'em and leave 'em attitude that implies no sense of responsibility toward the person they are supposedly loving. Instantaneous gratification is their ticket to heaven, and when they no longer feel gratified, they have got to get going—fast.

Air

Air sign people (Gemini, Libra, Aquarius) are mental and analytical, and sift all experience through their minds. Typical air signs trust their logic above their intuition and are forever trying to figure things out with their head. They are emotionally detached, changeable, sociable, cerebral, and need a lot of stimulation and space. Air signs gravitate to smart people, who are mental turn-ons and make them think. Verbal communication is their mainstay; so in a relationship, they like to talk, exchange ideas, try out new ways of looking at life, and share thoughts with someone who both stimulates and understands them. Because of their emphasis on the written and spoken word, air signs make natural writers, journalists, television personalities, problem solvers, teachers, and scientific thinkers. However, emotionally they can be superficial and difficult to pin down. Of all of the elements, the fire and air signs have the hardest time with commitment and are the most capable of being unfaithful. Both of these elements, which are compatible with each other, have an overwhelming restlessness in their personality, which has to do with a fear of being trapped and of missing out on something which the single life might provide.

Air sign people enjoy brief, superficial interactions that other elements might consider foolish and shallow. They are often heavy partygoers, who, like the fire signs, just want to have a good time in the moment. Air signs have a horror of feeling tied down and can be very fickle should a situation start to take that direction. Of all of the elements, they are the most capable of switching gears in midstream and suddenly disappearing. Because their heads rule their hearts, they can get terribly confused about what they are feeling, can change their feelings frequently, and sometimes simply not feel at all. Often funny, charming, and highly socially skilled, they can have a magnetic, superficial allure that makes them appear irresistible. However, under the surface they can also be cold, self-centered, and completely aloof. Air signs can be very hard to read because they always appear so friendly and convivial. They can seem to be an overnight best friend, when in the light of day the connection gets completely forgotten.

Air signs have poor staying power and can only seem to commit as long as their minds let them. They approach relationships with rational analysis, not feeling. Therefore, while good at understanding underlying dynamics, they have great difficulty understanding under-the-surface raw feeling. Emotional displays frighten them and make them feel like they can't breathe. Air signs are easily suffocated, and when they get frightened, run, hide, and completely disappear. And should they get discovered in their hiding place by some driven, determined, and emotionally obsessed individual, would coolly offer some rational excuse for their behavior that might not have anything to do with the real reason. Sometimes air signs are so out of touch with their feelings that they don't know why they do things. Sometimes they have a vague idea so they jump on that, and add to it, convincing themselves as they go along. These are the talkers of the zodiac and some air signs can talk their way out of a prison ward. Therefore, the best advice for dealing with them successfully: Don't listen to everything they say but watch everything that they do.

Earth

Earth signs (Taurus, Virgo, Capricorn) are the practical, pragmatic types who have two feet on the ground and need to know where they're going. Earth signs are the most security-oriented, both on a material and emotional level. They go for the concrete, stable, and enduring experiences that promise both security and longevity. Earth signs are earthy people. They need what is tangible, not what is most exciting or ideal. Whether it is a contract or a table, they need to be able to reach out and touch something before they trust it is real and secure. Whereas the air signs often couldn't care less if something is real or not as long as it appears terribly unusual and interesting, earth signs immediately question how well it works and its practical value. If there is really no practical value, the earth sign will think that the whole thing is just terribly silly. Their attitude is basic such as what good is a chair if you're supposed to use it as a kind of art object and not sit in it comfortably?

Earth signs are very sensual; therefore, touchy-feely comfort is most important to them. So is utility. Everything must have a purpose and a practical goal that will bring about a desirable concrete situation. They are the builders of the zodiac, focused on material creation. They put themselves forth in a plodding, methodical manner to get the job done—regardless of how boring the job may be. Fire signs who love to burst forth with bright, new creative concepts always try to get the earth signs to do their dirty work after their initial enthusiasm has worn off. And the thing of it is, the earth signs don't mind because they are totally organized, task-oriented, perfectionistic performers. Highly focused and completely tenacious, they climb the mountain one step at a time and make steady progress that eventually gets them where they want to go. Often, they come to own the mountain because of their amazing patience and fortitude in the face of obstacles. Painstaking and steady, they leave no stone unturned and no matter how hard, boring, frustrating, and infuriating their task, they keep going until their goal is achieved.

This same attitude brought to relationships can make the other elements find them boring. However, typical earth signs don't consider excitement. Their focus is simple and linear: in a relationship they want security and stability that they can trust. Earth signs are most conservative, and so their life designs are very much geared around values of the status quo. Loyal, loving, and usually trustworthy, they want a partner they can depend on, not a playmate. They also expect a situation that will last forever, regardless of subtle problems that are being played out. Earth signs tend to be blind to subtlety and to seeing situations that are underneath the surface—or sitting right in front of them. Their minds don't go there. They go to material details in which they dwell. When these day to day details take over, they drown out passion through which some elements seek to live. When too earth bound, earth signs can put out fire, suffocate air, and with water, become mud. However, they don't see it. What they see are their lists, their tasks, their duties and responsibilities and they give themselves fully to this call. Such earth signs believe that as long as they make money, handle it well, and show up day after day to share it with a partner, they are doing their job. But a relationship isn't a job. It is a much more subtle, deep, and comprehensive thing. And all of those subtleties are the ever-elusive challenges and stumbling blocks for the classic earth sign.

Water

Water signs (Cancer, Scorpio, Pisces) are the emotional signs of the zodiac. Sensitive, intuitive, and subjective, the water signs are emotional introverts who often live in their own world. Usually aware and even psychic, the water signs see human subtleties and instinctively understand them. They are comfortable in a nonverbal realm where they feel things, and they trust their feelings as a source of truth. Water signs are often psychic sponges and need to be self-protective in negative situations because they can absorb the vibrations and experience them as moods. Water has a way of picking up on what is beneath the surface and staying there in that emotional environment. Their own feelings are often so intense that it is difficult for them to deal with the day-to-day frustrations of life. Intense emotions stay with them and can hold them back. Water signs are emotionally retentive and especially slow at moving on.

These signs are the most enigmatic of the zodiac. Complex, deep, sometimes supersensitive and needy, they carry within them a bone-deep insecurity that is existential. Likewise, these signs often project their own complexities onto simple situations, which makes everything more complicated than it ever should be. Their perspective can be utterly subjective, so that their sense of reality sometimes distorts the facts of a situation. Part of their subjectivity is that they cannot be persuaded that it is possible their perceptions might be somewhat askew. Water signs live and die by their feelings and so if they strongly feel something, without question they feel they know it to be true.

Water signs can be misunderstood because they can have a hard time communicating what is deep inside of them. They also need a long time to process experience so that they can come to understand it in their own terms. Water sign women often want men to be mind readers, and water sign men are often introverts who don't communicate their deepest feelings at all. Sometimes they can't communicate them because passing moods are overwhelming them and they need quiet time alone to crawl into their shell and sort things out. Often, the world is too much for them, since they feel they tend to be surrounded by insensitive people who get on their nerves and who can't possibly see and feel all that they can. Water signs are the most perceptive. That is their gift and it is also their curse. Living day to day in a superficial world when you have such amazing emotional depth is not an easy thing. And water signs battle with their moods and emotions on a daily basis.

Water signs are romantic and, more than all the other elements, need love in their life. They seek close, intimate connections that reflect and affirm their inner sensitivities. Most water signs seek a soul mate and would be the last element to marry for money. Without inner connections they can be deeply lonely and even despondent. Although Scorpio men can cut off from their feelings or sublimate them into work, money, and power situations, water signs generally crave love in order to feel complete. When lost in love, it can consume them.

Water signs can be obsessive-compulsive regarding their emotional needs, and they usually have a great deal of emotional need. Of all the elements, these people are the most fearful because they have vivid emotional imaginations which allow them to conceive of anything that might happen—from the purely positive to the most disastrous. Water signs seek meaning and an understanding of the purpose of life. They also need to feel spiritually inspired and are the most inclined to spiritual studies and psychological vocations. When coming from compassion instead of emotional subjectivity, they can be brilliantly intuitive counselors and spiritual healers who have the power to help empower others.

The Elements in Combination

Certain elements in combination are very incompatible and create constant friction in the give and take of a relationship, while other elements flow together and energize each other. Therefore, the compatibility of the elements can be a crucial factor in determining the ease or lack of ease that one feels in the presence of another person.

Because the elements have to do with energy and the kind of energy field one gives off, one can actually feel physically that specific energy of the person, especially if more than one planet falls in a given element. This accounts for some of those times when one is tempted to say, "I just feel uncomfortable around that person and I don't know why." Certain energy fields pull on the energies of an incompatible field, or irritate it, or even put out your energy and make you feel tired or drained. Needless to say, this can become a serious problem if, in other ways, you are compatible with the person and you like them and care for them, but can't be in their presence for too long before feeling physically uncomfortable. However, being aware of this in advance, there are ways to work this problem out without anyone taking anything personally. It can be as simple as saying, "We both know that we have incompatible elements even though we care very much about each other so let's take little vacations from each other where we give each other the chance to energetically recharge." In this section we will examine the compatibility levels of the four basic elements in combination.

Fire with Fire

A fire sign (Aries, Leo, Sagittarius) with a fire sign flows. Having the same element, they have the same essential temperament: impatient, impulsive, fast, fun loving, and excitement seeking. Fire is the most intensely alive element and it expects others to run at its pace. Fire signs don't want to be held back, hate the word no, and adore burning the candle at both ends. Together they make great partners in crime who, when they put their heads together, can turn anything into a party. This is a most successful combination for friendship, business, and love. Inspired, enthusiastic, creative, and forever looking for the most fun way to do something, they instinctively fire each other up and the incandescent energy is contagious!

Fire with Air

Air fans the flames of fire while fire inspires air. A fire sign (Aries, Leo, Sagittarius) with an air sign (Gemini, Libra, Aquarius) is an excellent combination with instant chemistry and great emotional compatibility. Fire and air complement each other in such a way that they bring out the best in each other's temperaments, stimulate each other's minds and spirits, and energize each other in their chosen directions. Fire and air are intensely alive together. This is a great choice for friendship, marriage, or just having loads of fun.

Fire with Earth

A fire sign (Aries, Leo, Sagittarius) with an earth sign (Taurus, Virgo, Capricorn) is a challenging choice at best. A good combination for business, as the different headsets can both complement and compensate for each other, it is often a losing struggle for love. Fire tends to feel smothered by earth, and earth is often irritated by the energy of fire. Fire signs and earth signs look at life in completely different ways. Earth is slow, practical, deliberate, methodical, and motivated by the need for security and stability whereas fire is impulsive, freedom loving, easily bored, and impatient if things are too slow or stable for too long. Fire signs and earth signs seem to be coming from such completely different parts of the universe that they often have a hard time communicating. This combination is so irritating that it is not a smart choice.

Fire with Water

Just as water will put out a fire, fire signs (Aries, Leo, Sagittarius) often feel extinguished by water signs (Cancer, Scorpio, Pisces). Fire signs hate the feeling of being curbed or contained. They want to feel free to move in whatever direction takes their fancy, and they often feel slowed down by the emotional water signs. Fire can get impatient with all of the emotional displays of water, while water can look upon fire as shallow and insensitive. On very close contact, fire makes water even more insecure, and fire may feel, especially with the intense energies of Scorpio, that there is a subtle energy pull that puts out the fire. At the same time, however, it can be a sexually passionate connection that can sizzle both emotionally and sexually.

Air with Air

An air sign (Gemini, Libra, Aquarius) with another air sign is completely at home. Communication is a thing of ease here and since air signs are naturally curious, they like to carry on conversations about how things work and why. Air also has strong space and freedom requirements that they mutually respect. Air with air is a built-in comfort zone that requires little work but offers endless satisfaction. Because air's number one need is to have mental stimulation, two air signs can fulfill that for each other effortlessly. Long talks and lots of quality time make this the kind of connection that has strong staying power. Air signs tend to become friends first and lovers later, building a strong foundation that can form a lifetime of meaningful experiences. This is a smart choice where relating is easy.

Air with Earth

Air signs (Gemini, Libra, Aquarius) and earth signs (Taurus, Virgo, Capricorn) are highly incompatible and approach life in very different ways. Earth is practical and grounded, always focused on the pragmatic view of a situation whereas air can get lost in ideas that can be theoretical rather than practical. The slow, plodding, methodical ways of earth can annoy air who is mentally agile and quick to come up with answers without hours of footwork. On the other hand, earth may see air as undependable, unreliable, capricious, and up in the clouds. Both of these elements are grounded in completely different spheres, which could make communication arduous and challenging. Because both view the world through their own perspectives, which are completely antagonistic to the other, this combination is fraught with such problems that it could lead to eventual breakdown. This is a most difficult choice at best.

Air with Water

Air with water is another challenging combination that requires patience on the parts of both people. Air signs (Gemini, Libra, Aquarius) are emotionally detached while water signs (Cancer, Scorpio, Pisces) are purely emotional. Air signs live in their heads while water signs live in their emotions. Water may see air as cold and removed while air may see water as utterly subjective. Water is highly intuitive while air relies on reason, logic, and analysis to get to truth. Water can drown air in their emotions while air can hurt water's feelings with their emotionally remote attitudes. This combination makes for great communication problems. However, both elements are highly intelligent in their own unique ways, and if they can manage to just sit down, try to talk things out, and listen to one another's viewpoints, this is a choice that could promote growth.

Earth with Earth

An earth sign (Taurus, Virgo, Capricorn) with an earth sign is a most compatible combination where both people are temperamentally alike and share the same world view. Earth signs want to feel they have both feet planted firmly on the earth and they know exactly where they are going. Security-oriented, sensual, practical, and material, they speak the same language, physically and emotionally. This is not an exciting combination, but it is durable and lasting. Since earth signs want things to last forever, this is a very wise choice.

Earth with Water

Earth signs (Taurus, Virgo, Capricorn) and water signs (Cancer, Scorpio, Pisces) complement each other. Therefore, this could be a very compatible combination. Water signs find security in earth signs while earth signs find sensitivity and caring in water signs. Both need stability to feel safe and both want enduring relationships, not one-night stands. Since both are sensual, there is usually sexual compatibility. There is also a mutual support system based on an intrinsic understanding that both are there for each other. This combination usually makes for a lasting relationship that feels like a comfort zone. It could be a very smart choice.

Water with Water

A water sign (Cancer, Scorpio, Pisces) with a water sign is a common combination where there is emotional and sensual compatibility. Although each water sign is different in its individual approach to the world, all three are emotional, intuitive, and ruled by feelings. Water signs can intuit each other and often can read each other's minds. They all have a need for emotional security that is an overriding factor in their life. And they also have a need for intimacy that some of the other elements don't have. Although water signs are the most complex and can be moody, they have an essential intuitive basis for understanding each other. Such a deep affinity often makes this a very smart choice.

2. ARIES
MARCH 21 TO APRIL 20

Ruling Planet: Mars
Element: Fire
Cosmic Quality: Cardinal
Essential Quality: Masculine, positive
Planetary Principle: Action
Primal Desire: Leadership
Material Factor: Enterprise

The Aries Woman

The Smart Scoop

The Aries woman is pure energy and drive, verve and white-hot ambition. She is the captain-of-the-cheerleaders type who never learned how to sit still. Nor would she want to. At any given point in time she has so much on her plate that an efficiency expert would not be able to divine how she does it.

Well, first of all she is a lively fire sign with a temperament that jumps in first and thinks later. Second, she is ruled by the warrior planet Mars, which rules speed. She walks fast, talks fast, thinks fast, and seems to come out first in anything she undertakes. A born leader, the Aries woman walks tall in most situations.

Positive, enthusiastic, powerful, and full of steam, she breathes fire. A commanding presence with strong take-charge ability, she can put a man to shame. The minute the Aries woman makes up her mind, the job is done. She was born being active and can be like a forest fire out of control.

Strong, willful, self-conscious, and impatient with anyone who tries to slow her down, she is direct and to the point in all her dealings. Subtlety is not her saving grace. Nor is nonchalance. Her style is to streak through life and come out winning. Therefore, she may walk on any man too passive to assert himself. He won't even know what hit him.

The Feeling Scope

She is passionate and hot, inspired and full of feeling. The Aries woman wants to live life to the fullest, and she does. Courageous, impulsive, and sparked by a sense of adventure, she needs new challenges to charge her interest but is often bored by the prizes that come too easily. She loves razzle-dazzle, success, exciting things to look forward to, and getting her own way as often as possible.

Wildly romantic, she loves love in all its guises, illusions, and magical trappings. Strongly sexual, with an overwhelming *joie de vivre*, she needs an equally exciting man to both challenge and entice her. She gravitates toward men who are stars—dynamic and romantic with a touch of heroism. The Aries woman can be a fool for love when it manifests in larger-than-life terms with all the grand touches of a great movie.

Fatal Attractions

She can fall in love in ten minutes—and out of love in about five. The Aries woman loves the idea of a fatal attraction because it sounds so utterly daring. She loves romantic love, maybe even more than success. However, for her attraction to be so intense it qualifies as fatal, her partner must be successful—and a little status and fame could never hurt.

Hot romance is the way to her heart. And it greatly helps if the road is strewn with daily armfuls of flowers and a few little luxury items. Her fatal attraction should have great taste, sophistication, and believe in fine dining as a way of life. When the champagne flows like tap water, the deal is closed.

Foolish Choices

When passionately in love, the Aries woman can lose her head. Then, lo and behold, there is nothing to protect her. Because she takes her passions so seriously, they can control and undermine her.

Easily infatuated, she can fall for a line that flatters her ego, since, basically, she wants to believe it. The Aries woman takes things at face value and does not read between the lines. Since she heavily invests in the big picture, she is not alert to subtleties that can be signals of trouble down the road.

Sometimes she looks for love in all the wrong places and is so swayed by the superficial that she sees the situation through a distorted lens. Failing to delve beneath the surface, she can be at a loss when it comes to understanding her partner's deeper feelings. At times the Aries woman can be consummately self-centered and focused on how life revolves around her. Her difficulty in discriminating between realistic expectations and rationalizations, can lead her to operate both blindly and from impulse. When she is compelled to operate from fantasy and to neglect fact, the Aries woman can end up angry, alone, and clueless as to how she got there.

Fated Lessons

The Aries woman has to learn to slow down and see beneath the surface. Certainly, a romantic extravaganza can be great fun. However, it may not be able to become "happily ever after." The fate of some romances is to remain romances, and not transform into eternal love.

When the Aries woman gets angry and disillusioned she becomes dark and loses her signature sparkle. And when she becomes obsessive-compulsive, she is crazed, able to think and talk of nothing else but her obsession. Although this can alienate anyone within hearing range, she is the last to notice.

All fire signs need to grow up and learn that life is not always the drama of their dreams. Caught up in the glamour of the romance, the Aries woman can completely forget the feelings of the man. She needs to learn to get beyond herself and be more sensitive and insightful.

Finally she needs to learn that real love is about sharing and caring, not roses and champagne. When a situation disappoints her because it doesn't work out, she needs to learn how to take stock instead of blaming. Treating it as a learning experience instead of a loss will aid her immeasurably the next time. It will also make her a wiser and better woman.

Getting Smart in Affairs of the Heart

Like all the fire signs, the Aries woman wants passion and excitement, sometimes to the exclusion of actually wanting the person. Once she has taken the fatal plunge, she is floundering emotionally and has lost her power. Getting smart means using her head, not losing it.

When a man has sexual or emotional power over her, she can lose her self. Normally strong, headstrong, and very much a dynamic individual, she can throw caution to the wind, putting herself completely at his disposal. She needs to know when to pull back in order to move ahead. She also needs to look at the entire picture, not just the exciting parts, to assess what she is doing, where she is going, what is really happening, and what kind of person she is getting caught up in. When she has answers to all these questions, she has a measure of control. However, when she doesn't think beyond the moment, she is compromising herself.

Even though she comes on as completely independent, when she loses her mind to the heat of passionate love, she becomes needy. In other words, the Aries woman is extremely smart and self-possessed as long as you keep her out of the bedroom. Her all-or-nothing approach can do her in if she doesn't take some provisional self-protective measures. On a good day, she is a survivor and a warrior; on an emotionally distraught day, she is a mess. Therefore, she needs to be able to use her sharp brain to see what's coming. Normally perceptive, she needs to look underneath the surface at both the substance of her connection and the psyche of the man to whom she has surrendered. If she doesn't, she will do it all over the next time. Her search for romantic happiness will be in vain unless she allows her brain to back up her heart.

The Aries Man

The Smart Scoop

He is wild and restless, ready for a challenge, a warrior who wants to set the world on fire. The Aries man is energy personified and ever prepared to take charge. Confident, competent, and a born leader with an aura of excitement and a charismatic presence, the Aries man is a force to behold. Ambitious, successful, and sometimes a little too full of himself, he burns with drive and determination, focused on getting what he wants and always creating new goals to aspire to. With a mind that moves in overdrive, he is so enterprising and resourceful that he can turn a quick idea into a multibillion-dollar business.

The Aries man rushes in where angels fear to tread, and takes full advantage of his impact. A passionate romantic who can be the undisputed king of conquest, he adores the challenge of the chase but can sometimes get a little bored with the prize. The Aries man is an impressive force who fears nothing but who can inspire terror in the faint of heart. With invincible courage he can move mountains and make the most aloof women lose their cool. His masculine appeal is stellar. But his ability to be faithful leaves a lot to be desired.

The Feeling Scope

He is fiery and full of steam, a fulmination of explosive power. The Aries man can cause chaos when his temper overtakes him. Hot, passionate, and always prepared to rise to the occasion, he is a winner who takes all. And he always wants it.

Something of a lothario who loves women, sex, romance, and passion, he comes even more alive with conquest, and can be so direct and to the point as to give one windburn. Not used to compromise, he commands at will, and his will has a way of getting the job done. He can be both brash and bold, winsome and wildly romantic. When caught up in the passion of the moment, he can start a fire in his partner's soul. The Aries man is hot in the moment, but burns too fast to feel deeply. Impatient and a bit of a bully, he likes to get to the point as quickly as possible and then move on to what's next. Yet, in the moment he can make time stop with his fervent intensity and he can also provide all the props to generate a great love.

Vain, egotistical, and used to having life bow down before him, he can make a woman feel like a queen since he is so confidently kinglike. However, how long before the fire burns out remains to be seen. He can be quite a playboy but also a very committed lover—if only for a time. But if the time is right, some woman may just get lucky.

Fatal Attractions

Since the Aries man is prone to love at first sight, he is capable of a lot of fatal attractions. And for many women, falling in love with him can prove to be fatal. The erstwhile lady-killer Marlon Brando is an Aries, and in his day had a deranging effect on continents of women.

The sex appeal of the Aries can make other attractive men seated at the same table seem to vaguely disappear. Ardent, and focused formidably when he heeds the call, he is a most intense pursuer who puts his all into his conquests.

The Aries man's most fatal attractions are women who look hot, and are. Not one for subtlety or complications, he steers strongly to the purely superficial—which spells sex appeal: the stronger, the better; the more obvious, the more divine.

Foolish Choices

He can be a fool for sex, never considering consequences. When an Aries man is mature, he can be an exciting, dynamic, even devoted partner. However, many miss that mark and tend to be spoiled little babies at heart. Selfish, demanding, temperamental, and totally egotistical, he can be most difficult to deal with and makes a good case for living alone.

Caught in the throes of some impulsive action, he can be completely blind to the fact that this is a person upon whom he is treading. As a matter of fact, he doesn't even hear the squeaks. Since his attitude tends to be "Me first and perhaps you later," he can—and will—operate at someone else's expense, without hesitation. He can be a bully, especially when it comes to winning a strongly desired prize. However, it is his capacity for caprice in the area of romance that can make him a kind of *enfant terrible*. Notorious for flings just to alleviate a bout of boredom, he can break some woman's heart in a flash. Since he does have feelings, he may repent his ways once snared. However, in the right moment would he—*snap! flash!*—choose to do it all over again? You bet.

Aries men can be chronic womanizers who want what they want when they see it. Having poor self-control and even less propensity for selfless thinking, they are tricky to deal with, not to mention a potential disaster for a partner's heart.

Fated Lessons

In his early years, the Aries man's fiery nature may be impossible to tame, but once he grows up and calms down he can be capable of learning through love—given enough patience and fortitude on the part of his partner. However, headstrong and emotionally hard-of-hearing, learning lessons is difficult for him because he never wants to assume blame. The secret is that this strong world-conquering man has a fragile ego, and needs lots of stroking. Therefore, it is hard for him to admit to being wrong, and harder yet to change his wild, impulsive ways.

However, the truth is that when an Aries man truly loves, he is all aflame, and that passion in his heart can help him hear that his selfish, foolish ways are in the way of what he wants most. As opposed to some signs who can be cut off and indifferent, he suffers from excess feeling, which undirected, can undermine him. His fated lesson is the power that can come from being able to get beyond himself to be more conscious of how he is treating the other person. There was an Aries man I once knew who used to demand, "Don't confuse me with the facts!" And he meant it.

For this man who can easily achieve so much, the lesson of emotional objectivity is his greatest challenge. He has to understand that when he chooses to do only what he wants to do when he feels like doing it, regardless, he is undermining a relationship predicated on *two* people. And when he is undermining his relationship in the long run, he will only get less, or perhaps nothing. When all one's self-talk begins with *I* and ends with *me*, it is time to change. However, he has to learn that, and often the hard way.

Getting Smart in Affairs of the Heart

The Aries man can have a big heart when he stops being a baby or a bully. And when he chooses to put his head to use to be more sensitive, he can be as powerful a partner as he is a corporate boss. This hard-earned sensitivity enables him to see beyond himself and to act on what he is seeing. The more that he sees, the more choices available to him because now he can simply say to himself, "I don't like that. I can do much better." And being a man of action, he will.

Getting smart is about having this sort of self-control that can make a bad situation better and a fair one fantastic. Instead of being at the mercy of impulses that can cause both himself and his loved one pain, his choices can free him to be far more than he ever thought he could be. Being smart in affairs of the heart is about being conscious, not contemptible, and about having the control to tell the difference. Like all the fire signs, the Aries man wants to have it all but has to understand that if he settles for asking less of himself, he is choosing a glass half full. He must learn to live up to the big picture of how he wants life to be, and realize he has everything to create it.

3. TAURUS

APRIL 21 TO MAY 21

Ruling Planet: Venus
Element: Earth
Cosmic Quality: Fixed
Essential Quality: Feminine, negative
Planetary Principle: Production
Primal Desire: Stability
Material Factor: Prudence

The Taurus Woman

The Smart Scoop

Warm and earthy, sensuous and sensual, the Taurus woman wants tangible and lasting beauty in life, and all sorts of pleasures that speak well to the senses. An old-fashioned romantic who was born to be married, she lives for love that is stable and secure. The queen of creature comforts in all their forms, she can create an environment that is breathtaking and luxurious or simple, embracing, calm, and serene. Sporting the spirit of the eternal feminine, the Taurus woman bears the gifts of her ruler Venus: creativity, beauty, love, and kindness.

Loyal, caring, sincere, and unassuming, she contributes to life through her quiet thoughtfulness. Steady, enduring, solid, and trustworthy, the Taurus woman is the true friend and devoted partner who will be there during the bad times.

A formidable cook and elegant entertainer, she shines in the kitchen and can make magic of a mundane meal. Uncannily creative, a decorator *cum laude*, and often a singer with an unearthly voice (Barbra Streisand is a Taurus), the Taurus woman is, in many ways, born gifted and great at making life fun.

Her problem is that she can take her talents for granted while giving her total power to men. Her need for security can consume her and cause her to make very bad choices. The Taurus woman needs to value her life outside of a relationship instead of choosing a relationship as a crutch.

The Feeling Scope

The Taurus woman wants an enduring relationship above all else and often feels that life is lacking without it. Being a fixed earth sign who is slow to change, when she gets hooked on a certain someone, she stays hooked, regardless of the quality of the connection. Extremely sexual, sensual, and highly security-oriented, she can be obsessive-compulsive about some character who is doing her in, even though another part of her can admit that she's miserable. Nevertheless, she holds on, tenacious and true to the end, hoping that things will change despite repeated negative circumstances.

Stubborn and somewhat lacking in self-esteem, she can diminish her whole potential by refusing to stop the rationalizations and just move on. Instead, with time, she tends to intensify her grasp, diminishing herself further and further. I have so many stories on the Taurus woman's predicatment that it is hard to choose one to illustrate my point. However, what first comes to mind is what I will call the "Dinner Story."

There was a Taurus woman I once knew who was involved with a flashy, successful, self-centered Aries man for seven years. He worked on Wall Street and was supposedly so overcompromised by his work that he could only manage a quick stop by her place for sex and then a quick jaunt back to work. Feeling bad for him because he was always working so hard, so hard that he only once had the time to take her out in seven years, she cooked him dinner every time they got together. Finally, the time came when she gave him an ultimatum for marriage, and he disappeared. She later found out that his breathless busyness was because he was wining and dining other women. Shocked and dismayed, she told a friend who said, "Well, after seven years what did you *think* he was doing?" She replied in a tiny voice, "Well, he told me he had a lot of meetings."

So often the Taurus woman chooses men with fire sign planets who can be completely capricious and totally unfaithful. Although she needs stability and security, it is as if another part of her has to first drag herself through the fires of hell. Having "feelings" for the wrong person will bring her to that hell in a blazing chariot. However, when she starts to have positive feelings for herself, it can all change. And that can be a choice.

Fatal Attractions

The most fatal attractions for the Taurus woman are men who are liars and infidels. And the galvanizing kicker is usually created by either money or sex.

There are Taurus women who believe that their fast ticket to bliss is someone who will pay for them—big time. When talk comes up of jewelry, big trips, or lifestyle luxuries, she can be bought—and wants to be!

Another type aspires only to the bedroom and can't get out the door. Taurus has an animal sexuality that can be so consuming that they are completely controlled by their instincts. When the instincts rule, the mind doesn't see, the ears don't hear, and the body takes over. Both types of Taurus women are owned by their attractions. And the result can be fatal. (Keep in mind that Nicole Simpson was a Taurus.)

Foolish Choices

When she chooses someone on the basis of sex or materialism, the Taurus woman is shooting herself in the heart. However, to her mind it seems that she is getting something she can't do without. That is where she starts to get foolish. Choosing to let herself be enslaved by primitive needs is a fundamental mistake. In doing so, she is saying no to herself and is shutting down her own possibility.

There are some Taurus women whose security needs make them crave a relationship at all costs. They often will put up with the wrong person, who they trust will get better—or is better than nothing. That need for someone else to fill up her inner emptiness rather than relying on her own inner resources can result in choosing a cell mate, not a soul mate. This can lead to a kind of limbo. And at its worst, can lead to a life that becomes deadened and devoid of meaning.

Fated Lessons

Because the Taurus woman is a poor judge of men, looking at them from the outside instead of seeing what's beneath the surface, she has a lot of lessons to learn. Her most essential lesson is not to give herself up and lose herself to the relationship. Because Taurus is also tradition-minded, she can also lose herself to the idea that marriage will save her and bring her an everlasting emotional and financial security. Basically, she wants to believe that all things last forever. A few things do. On the other hand, in the progression of life, the only real stability is change. And the gorgeous June wedding can be a fleeting seduction into a very big trap. In the meantime, she will pay for her dependencies. They will claim her spirit, and because she can hold on with such tenacity, she can lose years of her life to them.

The Taurus woman also needs to learn how to look beneath the surface at a man and be honest with herself about what she sees. She needs to learn how to admit to herself that she is in a situation that is beating her up—emotionally, spiritually, and/or physically. And she needs to learn that she has to stop making excuses for bad behavior. Finally, she has to learn how to be more independent so that she is not owned by her needs—for sex, money, security, or romantic illusion. Taurus tends to repeat the same story over and over. One outrageous example of this was Nicole Simpson. And look where that got her.

Getting Smart in Affairs of the Heart

I know a Taurus woman who got smart and who went from a history of two abusive marriages to the most successful relationship she could have. I know another Taurus woman who has the most exalted marriage of thirty years that I have ever seen in my life. Both value and express selfhood, and their partners value that, too. Both come from preference instead of need and dependency. And both are conscious, value their own lives, and value where those lives can bring them. One of these women has come a very long way to get where she is. It can be done. However, before she began her journey, she made typical foolish Taurus choices and suffered terribly for it.

Both women know that you can only have a great relationship when you first have an affirmative relationship with yourself that is spiritual and creative. Both look down the road of their lives and say "Yes!" to themselves in all of their own spiritual, creative, and material potential. Both make positive individual choices. Both are smart.

The Taurus Man

The Smart Scoop

He's a stolid sort of guy who stays straight on his path and seldom strays. The Taurus man is motivated by money and all the goodies it can bring. Practical, conservative, plodding, and prepared to go the distance, he has a stick-to-it-ive nature that, in many ways, serves him both well and ill.

Simple in his outlook, he also expects life to be simple and very satisfying. The Taurus man craves his creature comforts and little luxuries. Materialistic and motivated by the concept of *more*, he is geared to *more* money, *more* sex, *more* security, and *more* material trappings. The Taurus man is owned by the tangible. If he can touch it and own it, it is real. Security, stability, and sex are his mainstays. Philosophical conversations don't go far, especially if he is hungry. One can maintain his attention through food and appealing to his senses. However, the attention has more to do with the quality of the cooking than the meaning of life.

The Feeling Scope

Pragmatic but also romantic, the Taurus man is slow to come round. Shy, insecure, cautious, and self-protective, he keeps to his turf until completely sure. He is the master of commitment—but on his timing. Realistic about all the bad that can come from risk-taking, he wants to feel a relationship can really work because it could mean forever. Since security in every sense of the word is his driving force, the Taurus man holds himself back through pragmatic considerations. Slowly considering all the blacks and the whites and then coming up with a clear picture, he arrives at a conclusion that will allow him to go forward. Calm, caring, methodical, and on his own timetable, he cannot be pushed—except through sex.

When committed, he can be loyal, loving, romantic, and thoroughly dependable. His character is like clockwork and his ability to care is sincere and solid. No fly-by-night, fool-around sort, he simply loves to settle into his nest surrounded by his creature comforts and be cozy. At his best he is highly supportive, sensuous, and creative, a bastion of strength during the bad times and an endearing, uplifting partner during the best times. The Taurus man has an enduring quality that can be counted on. And unless the sexual relationship has gone bad, he will be around forever. However, he also tends to be emotionally dense and needs expectations spelled out clearly and with no innuendo.

Fatal Attractions

Stellar sex appeal is what cements his attention. The Taurus man is sexual, earthy, uncomplicated, and very much a slave of his senses. He loves sex, even more than he loves food and maybe even as much as he loves money. A fool for a pretty face and a great body, he is the classic Playboy peruser and is fatally attracted to anyone who fills the bill. However, deep conversation is a detriment. The Taurus man does not want to speculate on the nature of the universe. Rather, he is seduced by the simplest of pleasures. A woman who appeals to that sexual, sensual side of him is a woman who will not only get his attention but keep it.

Foolish Choices

The lower Taurus man can be cold, selfish, and insensitive, tuning out everything but his own basic setup. Rigid and uncompromising, he can get stuck in ruts that make his life a boring, repetitive exercise that never deviates from form and only further insulates him in time.

Shutting out the world as it fails to apply to him, he makes it get smaller and smaller as he gets more and more cut off. This sort of Taurus man can see only his own game plan but can't hear who is in front of him. Impervious to what is external to his own being, he walls himself up in himself, completely unconscious of the effect this is having on his partner. Petty-minded, grudge-bearing, and consumed with only his own gratifications, he alienates others without even knowing it. Also, jealous and possessive, when truly angry he can be unspeakably cruel. At the same time, he is self-righteous, unrepentant, and unaccountable for what he feels is just and deserved.

This kind of Taurean man does not understand himself or other people. Nor does he desire to. Never analyzing himself or his situation, he plods along on the surface and remains unconscious of the deeper feelings of the person sitting before him.

There was a Taurus man I once knew who was extremely successful and a complete workaholic. His life was completely compartmentalized and packed with projects as well as political involvements that left him no time for any kind of close communication or spontaneous interaction. In a truly obsessive manner, he happily went from one involvement and interest to another, always planning newer, more consuming ones. One day his deeply emotional Scorpio wife joyfully left him for another man and he was shocked and devastated. It was always right there in his face, but he never saw it coming. Neither could he see, nor comprehend how, his completely self-absorbed ambition left her utterly lonely. She needed a person and for so long all she got was a routinized robot in a rut. The irony of the selfishness of the Taurus man is that out of all the people he injures, in the end he often suffers the most.

Fated Lessons

The Taurus man has to learn to be less rigid and self-centered if he isn't going to contaminate his relationships. His lessons are simple and to the point. He has to learn how to get beyond the small enclosure of self to extend himself to another person if he wants a relationship to work. He has to learn how to perceive, which means really see and hear the other person. He has to learn how to see himself so that he becomes aware of the effect that his behavior is having on someone else. Finally, he has to learn how to get beyond the surface minutiae to a place of emotional compassion that allows him to take in the feelings of another person while he keeps his own selfish needs out of it. In essence, he has to learn how to become more conscious if he isn't ultimately going to suffer the loneliness that he is so afraid of.

Getting Smart in Affairs of the Heart

The Taurus man who has lost or suffered needs to look at the pattern of his life and stop blaming. Instead, he needs to do some serious soul searching and ask himself questions, beginning with "What was my part in this failed situation?" Since his tendency, when hurt, is to resort to rage and seek revenge, he needs to reverse this process immediately if it isn't going to happen all over again the next time. His absolute refusal to take responsibility for his part in the situation, as well as his refusal to try to see how he could have possibly brought something on by specific behavior, is stupid.

Getting smart means that he lets self-reflection replace recriminatory behavior. That he attempts to communicate so that he can get a better understanding of things that baffle him. It means that he tries to go deeper and have some respect and consideration for feelings outside of his own. It means that he realizes that he must get out of his own way and stop living unconsciously in a little cocoon that closes him up and off. Finally it means that he focuses on his own heart, not his ego, to hear what it is trying to tell him. All of this will mean a great departure from the way of life he may have trusted so far. It also means change, which is extremely frightening to a Taurus. But this is about the joyful potential of his life.

I know of a couple of unattached, highly successful Taurus men who, outside of work, won't leave their living rooms. Their prior connections have been completely shallow, and from time to time they despair their plight but do nothing about it. They could both have so much but they won't extend themselves, and in the meantime they are only getting older. It takes a very big bonfire to ignite the sedentary Taurus. Unfortunately, some have seen to it that all their material needs are set, and so they can complacently settle back and be lulled day by day by their own superficial, meaningless existence where the only thing changing is the color of their hair. These men will not risk. They will not go forward, and when they come close to a connection they see it only in sexual terms. They do not see the person. They only see the part that that person can play in their life. And so each encounter self-destructs and they are none the wiser. Getting smart means actually valuing their encounters, not merely their own gratifications. And so many Taurus men have such a long way to go.

4. GEMINI

MAY 22 TO JUNE 21

Ruling Planet: Mercury
Element: Air
Cosmic Quality: Mutable
Essential Quality: Masculine, positive
Planetary Principle: Versatility
Primal Desire: Communication
Material Factor: Invention

The Gemini Woman

The Smart Scoop

She is sharp, quick, clever, cunning, and a most creative thinker. At her best, the Gemini woman can divine a world of possibilities from one small coincidence. Always thinking, analyzing, abstracting, and extrapolating, she thinks in overtime—with little sleep in between.

There are times when her thoughts get the better of her. When her mind won't turn off, she can be battered by her brain. But it's also her ticket to greatness. With a wit that runs circles around stars, she has only to get grounded and focus.

Amusing, adaptable, and highly persuasive, she is often popular and, at the least, very likable. Conscious and curious, with a childlike love of learning, she is a sponge for information and needs constant stimulation. Knowing a little about a lot is her trademark and it often proves useful. The grand dame of a dinner party, she can converse with everybody about something. Glib, witty, and never without the last word, her gift and her signature style is communication.

The Gemini woman loves to be mentally intrigued and to engage in fascinating conversations. Change, variety, and exciting new experience make her come alive. Boredom, routine, and too much predictability wilt her.

Restless and ever ready to move in new directions, she needs to feel that she is going somewhere that's much more exciting than where she has been before. Her choice in a man often revolves around this expectation, which sometimes saddles her with the wrong person— who seemed so right at the time.

The Feeling Scope

The Gemini woman is a complex character, often at odds with herself and her feelings. As a woman, she wants to feel; as a Gemini, she tends to think. When in love, her mind can overrun her.

She can be a butterfly and a flirt who is footloose and fancy free. She can also be a detached game-player who makes everyone crazy. Contradictory, changeable, fickle, and forever analyzing, she can be a big nemesis to some simple unsuspecting male. Running hot and cold, changing her mind in midstream, and fighting off boredom in between, she scorns any man who can't meet her challenges.

She is repulsed by sensitive souls who crave her company. It's too confining. She also hates men who wear their heart on their sleeve. She finds them weak. The Gemini woman wants space and a challenge. Therefore, she gravitates to cool, often selfish, disconnected men, who, by omission, can be quite controlling.

Too much emotional intensity disgusts her. Not enough leaves her longing for more. Not only is she contradictory, she can also be critical. When no one meets her criteria, she cuts off her feelings and forsakes the game. Until she finds that marvelous meeting of the minds, she would rather be alone.

Because the Gemini woman is so caught up in her ideas, she can be a bit like a dog chasing its tail. To listen to her forays is to wonder where feelings come in. The truth is: when she finally is awed by a mind more dazzling than hers, then she starts to feel.

Fatal Attractions

Like a moth to a flame, she loves men who challenge her. The Gemini woman likes to verbally spar. She also likes to lose her head to someone so commanding that he makes her forget herself. Competence and smarts mean so much to this woman that she can be completely swept off her feet by accomplishment and dazzling quick-wittedness.

However, a brain does not a person make and this is where she falters. Amusing and talented only go so far, just as all charm and no soul wears thin in time. When the worm turns and the real person appears out from under the veneer, problems often develop that are too deep to successfully deal with.

What makes the Gemini woman's attractions fatal is that she looks at the surface and fails to probe for the entire picture. A big bank account, prestigious title, presents flying her way, or a blindingly huge diamond ring can close the deal. When many glorious factors seem to be there, she tends to jump headfirst and find out the truth much later. Yet, with some nice guy without the surface flash, she will grill, audition, play head games and hard-to-get. That's because she is. Her head turns her in her romantic directions. And if her focus fails to be completely captivated, she will be like a reluctant cat slowly killing a half dead mouse. In truth she would rather lose or be in love with longing than be bored.

Foolish Choices

When she chooses the flashiest man for the wrong reasons, she is being very foolish. Many Gemini women just want someone to talk to and they stop there. Talking is one thing, commitment quite another. Deeper communication should show whether a deeper relationship is possible.

The classic foolish choice is when she gets caught up in her idea of a person and completely misses who that person really is. The Gemini woman tends to go for snippets of a person. This might make them wonderful candidates for a job description, but not necessarily a person with a heart.

On the other hand, Gemini needs far more stimulation and space than emotional reassurance. And this can create problems. She can go for a long time before actually looking at the quality of her partner. For a long time, each time seems like the first time. Then one fine day when her emotional, drug, or alcohol problems have to be faced because they prevent her from going forward, crises ensue. And it is time to ruefully wake up to the entire picture.

Fated Lessons

Her quintessential lesson is to learn to go deeper and not plunge in headfirst because of a fabulous, glittery surface. The Gemini woman can be very superficial and needs to be aware of how that can undermine her.

A brilliant brain or a big diamond ring does not mean that this is a good person. Telling the good guys from the bad guys takes a lot more criteria than simply his accomplishments or bank account.

When the Gemini woman feels she has found her twin, she is quick to plunge in. With all other contenders, she is quick to criticize. Her most difficult lesson is to look at a man with her heart, not merely her head, and to cultivate compassion. As she develops deeper spiritual values, she will magnetize to her a man who reflects this deeper level, a man with both a brain and a soul. And there will be a sense that they can go somewhere together, instead of merely retreading experience, experience that is sure to get old.

Getting Smart in Affairs of the Heart

As detached and independent as she can be when uninvolved, once the Gemini woman feels that she has found her other half, she starts to lose herself. This is when her thinking really starts to falter. Rationalizing away tell-tale signs of serious problems, she takes to analyzing and making excuses. The more excuses she makes, the more deeply embroiled she becomes until it starts to feel that she is breaking in half.

Marilyn Monroe was a Gemini, and the drama of her doomed love life consumed her. However, what lay at the core was that she lost herself to talented, self-confident men who became a substitute for an inner self she could never feel.

The Gemini woman needs to look for a partner, not an icon or a hero. For a man, not a mythic being. To be smart, she needs to develop a relationship with her own depths or else she will continue to project her unconscious onto a dream lover. This is about process and it takes time and work. The more psychological work she does in which she becomes more conscious of the patterns of her choices and why they don't work for her, the faster she will be able to spot key situations that she might have fallen into before. Likewise, the more—through books, courses, or groups—that she works with her own soul, the more she will feel inspired by the magic that is already inside her. At this point, she won't be projecting magic on a man. Instead she will be magnetizing an equal who reflects her own inner sense of possibility unfolding.

For the Gemini woman, to be smart in affairs of the heart is to be conscious—of where she has been and why, as well as where she can no longer afford to go. The more she grows in consciousness and begins to live through the intelligence of her heart as well as her head, the more she will become whole, and a new, more interesting world will open up to her.

The Gemini Man

The Smart Scoop

His smarts are his trademark. The Gemini man is an amalgam of mental impulses changing minute by minute. He is clever, quixotic, witty, and never at a loss for words. He can be a charmer who can steal your heart away. He can also be a fast-talking trickster who can wheel and deal his way through life, laughing all the way.

If he is a typical Gemini, not much gets him down. He also doesn't go that deep or stay that long to get seriously compromised or hopelessly entangled. His mind is ever on the move and he can think circles around most people.

He is restless, changeable, and always ready with a retort. The Gemini man is a great game-player looking for a partner who won't bore him. The problem is that everything begins to bore him if it hangs on too long. That is why he needs a heavy dose of novelty and mental stimulation.

A gregarious people-person, he is a born entertainer who can be many personalities in the smallest period of time. All he needs is the chemistry of the crowd. Alternately clever, madcap, or the cool surveyor of a situation, he plays all his roles with verve and panache. The Gemini man can light up a room with his sparkle and get all the attention that the Leo man craves. However, he is not one to be captured. The way to his consciousness is to captivate him. Novelty, challenge, and a mind as clever as his own are best for starters. After that, an endless flourish of fun will keep him coming back for more.

The Feeling Scope

He is a born flirt and it's nothing personal. It's just the personality of this man who might be caught in a corner making a little old lady giggle. The Gemini man loves to verbally engage. Yet, ask him what he's feeling and he'll probably say he doesn't know. His mind is so crowded by a confluence of thought.

The Gemini man doesn't like to think about feelings. He's a mental, not emotional, creature and very much a duck out of water in the feeling realm. Heavy emotional scenes are anathema since he finds them both suffocating and confining while emotional demands drown him and make him run cold. How he knows he's in love is that he thinks more than a lot about a certain person. The mental spigot is fully on and it won't turn off.

In love, the Gemini man can be so mentally obsessive that it can drive him crazy. It brings him sleepless nights, fantasies, smoking, fretting, and planning. However, lurchings of his heart he does not have. This man's mind moves in such overdrive that he can function as two different people in a five-minute period. That's easy. However, falling in love and having things called "feelings" is so far from his beaten mental track that it can only hit him hard. Thus, it can be quite confusing for the Gemini man, caught, when he least expected it in the nefarious feeling realm. Some Gemini men avoid this altogether and just play around on the surface. However, when Cupid calls quite mysteriously, the call demands to be heeded, and once again the Gemini man splits in two: the thinking man and the feeling man who doesn't know what to do with his feelings.

Fatal Attractions

He knows he is fatally attracted when he thinks of her twenty-four hours a day. However, he probably still doesn't have a name for it. As smart as he is, the Gemini man can be completely clueless in emotional matters.

The kind of woman who makes his mind move has a mind as exciting as his is. Or she is completely different from anyone that he has ever met before. But basically, he needs to feel intrigued and that he is having more fun than he can ever remember having. Gemini men love to enjoy life and to share it. They also love scintillating communication sparked with lots of laughter. Beauty only goes so far with this man, who needs to feel mentally transported. It may work for the first five minutes. After that, the encounter either thrives or fails to survive based on the quality of chemistry and communication.

Foolish Choices

He can be a butterfly with a tongue like quicksilver. Gemini men can be faithless lotharios who lust for novelty and neverending conquest. A game player who is in it for the sport, he can play with feelings and flee from face-to-face. Something of a trickster, he can be capricious and erratic, fickle and afraid of going deeper.

The Gemini man can say one thing and do another. A shape-changer, his chameleon nature belies all trust, as does his tendency toward lying. Emotionally ambivalent, he can pretend to be in one relationship while seeing someone else on the side and then cavorting with a third in between.

The Gemini man can be so emotionally detached that he is mindless of the mess that he is making. When he goes on disconnect, he can be a blight to the brain of any woman. Often dazzling and persuasive, his charm can disarm and his cleverness can make him irresistible. However, he just doesn't get the damage that can be done to a great person.

Fated Lessons

As a dual sign, the Twins, the Gemini man does need a mate, but in the sense of someone to complete him. He may marry, divorce, and go through life never finding that person until, much later, serendipitously, she suddenly emerges. All mutable signs are unconsciously seeking their other half, and the Gemini man is no exception. However, at the moment when that twin appears, so too do the lessons.

The sign that has traveled through life trusting logic, reason, and the fruits of thought, now is in a situation where none of that will help him. His fated lesson is to feel his feelings without tearing them apart with his mind. The Gemini man is cruel only when he is cut off from his heart. Living in his head alone, he is living as a fragment. At the moment he starts to live in his heart, he will know that if he cheats, lies, and lives only on the surface, he will never experience the joys of what lies beneath. When the Gemini man allows himself to feel, life opens up in a way that his intellect cannot imagine. He is no longer a shell of a man. He is a miracle in progress.

Getting Smart in Affairs of the Heart

Like the Tin Man in *The Wizard of Oz*, the Gemini man doesn't realize he has a heart. Locked up in his head, he just can't stop thinking.

Cut off from his heart, he can't see the chaos he can create. Nor can he care. However, when touched by love, he starts to extend himself in a way that goes way beyond thinking.

The Gemini man can be considerate, giving, romantic, and thoughtful when his heart has come alive. Now the frozen thinking pattern has been replaced with a sensibility that honors the other person. Impulsively he follows his feelings like he once followed only thought. His behavior says, "I think of you, I feel you, I care for you," where heretofore typical Gemini behavior cried, "I'm cut off and I don't care."

Following the promptings of his heart, he is now smarter than he ever knew himself to be. He is becoming a whole person, as opposed to a thinking mouthpiece. He is becoming a caring person as opposed to a compartmentalized, eccentric character. And finally, he is finding meaning where there was only surface amusement. At first, going deeper may be frightening, but feelings have a way of making him forget time.

5. CANCER
JUNE 22 TO JULY 23

Ruling Planet: The Moon
Element: Water
Cosmic Quality: Cardinal
Essential Quality: Feminine, negative
Planetary Principle: Love
Primal Desire: Security
Material Factor: Tenacity

The Cancer Woman

The Smart Scoop

She is sensitive and sweet, a truly feminine female. The Cancer woman
might be the most emotional sign of the zodiac. Born under the ruler-
ship of the mysterious moon, she can be a mystery unto herself.
Moody, changeable, and sometimes hard to predict, she ebbs and flows
with the influences that surround her. Like all the water signs, the
Cancer woman is a psychic sponge, intuitively soaking up surrounding
moods and feelings, and sometimes confusing them with her own.

Loving, nurturing, and needing lots of love in return, she lives for
intimate contact. She dates to marry, not merely to have a good time.

The Cancer woman is serious about love. For her it has to be lasting. It also has to provide the sort of stability that makes her feel secure.

Home, family, and domestic bliss are the bastion of her well-being. On her own out in the world, dark moods may overtake her. Depression is a familiar stopping place for this woman who follows her feelings around. She needs beauty, comfort, and lots of closeness to keep her demons at bay. Subjective as well as supersensitive, she thrives in an atmosphere that nurtures her sensibilities. The Cancer woman is an old-fashioned romantic in a cold, hard, modern world. That is both her beauty and her albatross, and has an annoying and persistent way of getting in her way.

Intuitive, empathetic, and more than willing to give the world to those she loves, she is a woman of pure feeling, wrestling with ineffable fears and forever seeking peace and comfort in the atmosphere she creates around her. At home, the Cancer woman can create the kind of creature comforts that make dinner party guests want to move in. Instinctively, she knows how to turn a room into a nest where the furniture alone has a nurturing effect. Creative in both cooking and decor, she can bring magic to moments by conjuring a commanding experience of the quaint and cozy. Even her most goal-oriented guests suddenly forget their plans, sink into the depths of the overstuffed sofa, and want to be taken care of for life.

The Feeling Scope

She is a creature of pure feeling. There are days when it seems that she is eternally PMS-ing. Moody, weepy, cranky, sad, and sympathetic is her style. The Cancer woman might have created moods. However, she also understands them and how easily they can overtake what might otherwise be a beautiful day.

She lives to love. Success alone would never bring the sort of meaning that could make her heart feel warm. In an increasingly cold, depersonalized world, the Cancer woman is both personal and caring. Likewise, she is insecure and vulnerable until she feels her love returned.

This is one woman who was made to be married. Giving to a fault, she gets joy from the sort of shared experience that speaks of partners who are equals. Even if she plays defensive and aloof and conjures up a self-protective shell, close encounters are her only kind.

Fatal Attractions

The Cancer woman is dominated by the notion of love everlasting, picket fence and all. She believes in forever and nothing can sway her in the direction of a less intense approach to love and life. Therefore, someone who consistently tells her what she wants to believe will win her heart, hands down.

Security, both emotional and material, are in her guidelines to a great life. The Cancer woman needs to feel that she can depend on key people. Otherwise, the self-protective shell will surface and take over the person. The Cancer woman can be quite frosty if she feels in danger of being left out in the cold. Rejection is the bane of her existence, and the very thought of it can bring a blight upon entire periods of her life.

Therefore, she sets her sights only on someone she thinks she can trust. However, there are always some flashy, dangerous dudes who pop up to divert her and run havoc with her system of natural selection. In these instances, she can become obsessed. However, because she is so intuitive, something deep inside her knows from the start that she could be burned. Nevertheless, the excitement posed by the passion fuels her fantasies and makes her forget, if for the moment, that she may not be moving along the prudent path.

The irony of the Cancer woman is that although she is so self-protective, she has also been known to make choices that are downright destructive. However, being as emotional as she is, at the time she just can't help herself. I know of one very savvy and sophisticated Cancer woman who took up with someone who increasingly became a madman who began to physically resemble Ted Bundy in his final stages. This all-out obsession was almost beyond comprehension.

Nevertheless she threw all of her emotion into it and it completely controlled her life. The good news was that she lived, despite one frightening incident where the outcome could have been otherwise.

Cancer is a cardinal sign and cardinal signs like challenge. On occasion, this can be true as well of the Cancer woman whose mind's eye creates a prism of passion and potential. Although she is normally cautious, she can get caught up in crazy-making situations that overtake her sanity and entangle her in a web of wanton despair.

Foolish Choices

With the tenacity of her symbol, the crab, the Cancer woman can hold on to the wrong people for too long. Due to wishful thinking, insecurity, and deep emotional need, she can cling to the wrong person or relationship for what might seem an eternity to someone else.

The greatest challenge for a Cancer woman is to let go. Emotionally intense, willful, and unwilling to change, she can endure a great deal of emotional hardship unnecessarily. It appears that the pain of the present is better than the fear of the unknown. And it is this psychology which keeps her in place.

To those looking in from the outside, such emotional tenacity may seem terribly masochistic. However, to comprehend the levels of fear and sensitivity that hold her in place takes more understanding than most people are capable of. Cancer women are terribly intense and often drown in their own emotion. Like the tides of the mysterious moon, Cancer's ruler, these forces are powerful and cannot easily be put aside. However, the Cancer woman needs to be aware that she does have choices about who she loves. And given her intense, tenacious nature, this prudent choice could be the most important in her life.

Fated Lessons

The Cancer woman needs to trust her own power, instead of giving it away to those outside of her. She has to value herself, her gifts, her intuition, and her caring ability, instead of looking for affirmation from the outside world. She must also stop looking at men as security bastions that will rescue her from her aloneness. Once the Cancer woman values herself as an individual, she will make better choices, which will enable her to operate from a self-empowered position instead of from a sense of secondary value that is reactive rather than proactive.

Getting Smart in Affairs of the Heart

The head will never rule the heart for the Cancer woman. However, there is an awareness that she can develop that will serve her well.

Given her difficulty at letting go, she needs to stay away from "bad boys" who will only break her heart. Since mindless passion may lead her in the direction of such bad boys, when choosing a partner she needs to be aware of her needs—and that she does have needs.

One, for instance, is that she needs someone to hear her. Another is that she needs someone who wants to hear her and wants to understand her. She also needs someone demonstrative, someone who can show her patience, kindness, and tenderness—even on her moody, gloomy, cranky, witchy days.

The Cancer woman can easily get caught in the trap of giving love to get it. Give her half a chance and she will become the woman who does too much. It is not that she is driving an insidious psychological bargain, but it is her nature to love to nurture. However, it all does becomes a problem when she loses herself in the process.

At this point, enter seething resentment and a sudden shift of feeling. Suddenly she wants to take it all back. "Boy am I sorry that I took care of you when you were sick, you creep! Where were you when I felt like jumping off the Empire State Building? You don't even understand suffering, much less care!"

In all this turmoil who suffers most? Of course the Cancer woman. One thing she always forgets is that she often counts on mind-reading and doesn't know how to express her feelings openly and constructively like: "Dear, I am sorry to tell you but I am having a very bad day today. I feel weepy and insecure and I'm sure my boss hates me but not as much as I hate my job. I really need you now. Could we just talk for a while?"

Such talking can be so cathartic that she might come to realize that it's not her job per se that she hates, but some part of her job that she has the power to change. It can also improve her relationship by deepening it through the care and trust and insight that can come out through such communication. However, if she just goes inside the shell and starts slamming dishes it all just gets worse, she goes downhill, and everybody hates being around her.

The most fundamental issue for the Cancer woman is to consciously honor her own needs. She need not apologize for being more sensitive and intense than most people. However, she needs to realize that she must communicate that in the right way. Stuffing everything in, grimacing, and bearing it will only bring her down. The Cancer woman is a very feeling person and she has a right to her feelings. They can, in fact, be her conduit to truth and transformation—as long as she doesn't try to cut off from them and in the process, cut herself off from the world.

Until she conquers this problem, she will repeat the pattern. From this perspective, all her relationship experiences will go down the same inconsequential road. To be emotionally smart, she has to own her heart and take conscious responsibility for how she handles all that passes through it.

The Cancer Man

The Smart Scoop

Without a doubt, the Cancer man is the most sensitive in the zodiac. Ruled by the moon, the mysterious female planet that rules emotions, his is not a simple journey in what everyone knows is still a "man's world."

Underneath his outward veneer, which may be cool, controlled, impeccable, and polished, he may feel like a woman PMS-ing on her worst day. The moods come and go with the Cancer man and while there are often outer catalysts, on the inside there is no sense of serious control.

At his best, the Cancer man is sensitive, tender, loving, and kind. He will spoil those closest to him. However, he shows no interest in particular for those people on the periphery who have not proved themselves. Although he is perceptive and intuitive, he is also emotionally subjective. He prefers to keep his world small and populated only by those he trusts who love him.

When the time is right, he wants a marriage with unquestioned loyalty. In turn, he is the king of commitment. The woman to whom he has given his heart need never worry that he will wander. The Cancer man does best with an old-fashioned home and family and to these he will give his all. However, the woman who always works overtime and doesn't know how to bake apple pie need not apply. Chances are that after a couple of dinners he will have screened her out anyway. Nice, but a little too ambitious. And doesn't want children!? Not a consideration on the coldest day in August.

He is extremely serious about his life and how he wants the scenario to unfold. Cautious, careful with money, security-oriented and very conventional, he scrupulously lives within these bounds. The woman he marries must be the mother of his children. The family must come first. There will not be excessive non-family involvements like demanding careers, social life, future ambitions, or worldly pursuits. Mr. Cancer may seem a little shy and quiet if you don't know him. However, the truth is that he has a will of steel.

One-pointed and tenacious concerning everything that is important to him, he will break up in multiple parts before he will give up. Once his mind is made up, there is no talking him in or out of anything. The jury is closed, although there wasn't one from the start. Mr. Cancer rules his own roost and doesn't need anyone to run interference. He hates conflict, which means anyone saying *no*. His form of creativity is about conjuring a life that suits his needs and to that end he will single-mindedly pursue his dream with both delight and dedication.

The Feeling Scope

He is insecure and moody and makes up for it with routine and self-discipline. Life in the outer world is not always that easy for the inner life of the Cancer man. He takes his blows on the inside and deals with fear privately.

This is not a man who will sit down in some bar and tell strangers his feelings. His is a secretive, sacred world where, very often, he lets no one in. In his mind he is a sort of emotional survivor against the oceanic moods and emotional fluctuations that he has felt all his life and which can control him. It is these moods and past hurts, which are still a part of him, that haunt him. That is why he is so focused on emotional and material security as a buffer against the stress of the outer world.

Security is his keyword. In money he can trust, and with the right woman he can create the right kind of life: a cozy, comforting life that will allow him to go into the future with trust. This is a man who needs calm, not excitement; a quiet dinner at home, not a night on the town; tender affection, not erotic invention. Still, there will be times with even his chosen woman when he may seem cold, aloof, and closed off.

The Cancer man can be as difficult as he can be a darling. There will be times when he shuts out the world completely and goes into an emotional stew. It is likely at such times that even he doesn't know what is bothering him. He can be a kind of conundrum that changes like a kaleidoscope, and it is impossible to predict which end is up and when. This man is motorized by a fluctuation of feelings. The wise woman knows she can't get too caught up in them. At such times it is best to give him his space and maybe leave a cup of tea by the computer. In time he'll come around and soon forget he was such a crabby guy that everyone decided to go shopping. Now, all alone, he'll get annoyed that everyone left him. There are times when it is completely impossible to please the crab. Like the moon in its moving phases, his emotional changes bring subtle fluctuations, but never a self that is completely the same, day to day, week to week.

Fatal Attractions

Although in finding the perfect marriage partner, the Cancer man is calculating and cautious, he has his fatal attractions along the way. Deeply insecure and impressionable, he is often galvanized to striking, self-confident, vivacious women who make him feel even more insecure. There is a touch of masochism in this man who can get hooked on someone who sends out loud signals that she doesn't even see him. Such women are usually free-spirited, high-flying fire signs and, ironically, the last type that he would ever marry. Such women may become an obsession. The core of the obsession, of course, is the proof of his own self-worth. In winning over what he deems to be a prize, his own value soars. Cancer is a cardinal sign, and all cardinal signs like challenge. So too, the younger Cancer man looks to highly attractive women as a challenge to his self-esteem.

Such contacts seldom, if ever, work out. However, they can be valuable learning experiences providing he is willing, at some time, to go deep enough. Usually that is not the case. Security priorities far outweigh self-scrutiny, and so the Cancer man moves sedulously in his self-appointed direction: marriage with the right mate.

Foolish Choices

The Cancer man's choices all reverberate back to his insecurities. Basically, he tests his self-worth with beautiful women, but chooses a woman who will make his entire domestic life feel secure.

To look at women as if they are completely role-defined is indeed rather immature and dehumanizing. To make crucial life choices on the basis of such a worldview is emotionally shallow, and leaves out the spiritual element of love. There are Cancer men who go about the prospect of marrying like a new college grad in search of an economy car. One man explained it to me; A certain job level had been achieved, there was now enough money in the bank, all the debts were paid off, dating a million women had become boring. He was "going wife shopping" and was getting ready to have a family.

When a man announces that he is ready to have a family but there is no particular woman in sight, it can only make one wonder how important the wife will be as an individual as opposed to a symbol. Although he would never see it that way, the Cancer man's choices can be very depersonalizing. "Why," he would exclaim, "I will be a great father. And loyal husband." As long as the chosen lives only for him.

Fated Lessons

Alas there is trouble in paradise if the Cancer man's wife one day decides she wants more. Individuality is seriously discouraged, as are ambitions, artistic aspirations, and humanitarian pursuits. Guess what: that guy who seemed so sweet and insecure in the dating phase is very controlling. Once married, it is his world.

The Cancer man would reply: "But I love her!" He cannot separate his need for control from his own sweet feelings. It is all the same stew, and his wife must partake of it fully. Many women get so buried in the nest and the domestic obligations that they go along with this subtle scenario without questioning why they feel so tired, so lonely, and so completely unheard. Her Cancer man may come home, be in a mood, and not speak to anyone. But he'll compliment her on dinner and, at the table, turn his attention to the kids. He loves his family.

Although he might never see it this way, the Cancer man can be very self-centered. He needs to learn that marriage is a deep, ideally spiritual union that is more than a domestic setup that serves his security needs. If he doesn't, he is depersonalizing and dehumanizing the person he is marrying, and the results of this may be sorrowfully felt down the road.

Should his wife develop a burning desire to get out from the confines of the nest long enough to do her own thing, this would seriously conflict with "the plan." One such woman had to engage in a fight to just have a Sunday lunch with a friend when her Cancer husband didn't want to leave the house. On the way to lunch her cell phone rang and he whined, "Do you still love me?"

The Cancer man needs to learn the difference between love and dependency. Yes, there are times when he can be tender, loving, warm, and affectionate. But does he really know whom he is being tender to? Who that person is apart from the role in his life that she is playing? The Cancer man often gives love to get love because he needs love. His hardest lesson is to distinguish between dependent love and healthy love that honors and respects the individuality of the partner.

The great psychologist Carl Jung once said that "character is fate." The more that the Cancer man operates from control and turns a deaf ear to anything but his own needs and expectations, the more he is setting himself up for fated lessons that his own character has created.

Getting Smart in Affairs of the Heart

Being a truly tenacious sort, it is terribly hard for the Cancer man to realize he has lessons, never mind learn them. In his subjective world, he is always doing the right thing but is in danger of being hurt from the outside. For his own good and the good of anyone in the future, I once informed a Cancer man that his behavior to a certain woman had been terribly disturbing and that he needed to be more conscious of other people's feelings. He laughed.

Most Cancer men do not want to be more conscious. They want to get what they want and they want it to continue. However, their prescription is simple: they need to understand that women have feelings and needs too, and sometimes those needs require things like personal freedom, individuality, creativity, spirituality, and growth—all the activities that are deadly to his nesting contract.

If the Cancer man can learn to really listen, not merely hear, but listen, he just might begin to open up to that person he professes to love. I know one woman who is married to a Cancer man who says he refuses to listen to any of her dreams or future ambitions and simply says, "I'm not interested in that. I thought you wanted to be with me."

The key is in listening. The hard part is in wanting to. The Cancer man has to realize, hopefully before it's too late, that if he truly doesn't want to listen to his partner and only values that partner for the gratification of his own needs, he is in an unconscious, shaky connection that will only deteriorate with time. He also has to realize that he owes it to himself to get smart. If he never gets smart, he will ultimately suffer from his marital choices. It is only a matter of time.

6. LEO

JULY 24 TO AUGUST 23

Ruling Planet: The Sun
Element: Fire
Cosmic Quality: Fixed
Essential Quality: Masculine, positive
Planetary Principle: Creativity
Primal Desire: Joy
Material Factor: Power through effort

The Leo Woman

The Smart Scoop

She is the incandescent queen of the zodiac. Magnetic and alive, she radiates a light that long precedes her. The Leo woman has a charisma that can captivate a crowd. Positive, popular, charming, and persuasive, she is often put on a pedestal by her peers.

The Leo woman wants to live life to the fullest, but never forgets those less fortunate. Warm, loving, and generous to a fault, she might be the most giving girl in the zodiac.

Smart and savvy, with a razor-sharp sense of humor, she has a personality that could tame serpents. Success is her birthright, and it seems to the world that all she has to do is show up. However, in truth she is a tireless worker who is willing to go a long distance to get what she wants.

When she loves, she is a luminous force who is dramatic, romantic, and full of *joie de vivre*. A sun goddess who sees life in the largest terms, she is a glamour queen who engages in grand schemes, yet still always carries the light of an invincible, childlike charm.

The Leo woman's outlook is that life should be perfectly divine and love must be legendary. Each big romance starts out as a larger-than-life affair. However, as the color fades and all the flaws emerge, she is increasingly clouded by a sadness that swells deep inside her. The Leo woman is a big child at heart, and she is all heart. Therefore, her love lessons hit her hard and deep down, and can dull her light for a while. However, in time she heals and turns her attention to what turns her on in life.

Positive, powerful, and ever open to all the possibilities of life, she is always prepared to go forward with a new sense of expectancy. Popular because she is so alive and inspiring, the Leo woman loves to love—everything and everyone around her. Like no other sign, she shares her warmth with the world in a way that makes her galvanizing and unforgettable. She is the sign of the sun, and like the sun she radiates an energy that comes straight from the heart.

The Feeling Scope

The Leo woman is ruled by her heart, which can make her head go out the window. When her heart is deeply touched during the course of a connection, she can leave reason to the gods and go forth to follow her dream despite the consequences. A full-blown romantic when Cupid rushes in, she is lured by words of love accompanied by upscale gestures.

However, needy she is not. She sets her sights high and is blind to any fool ignorant enough to think he could win her with half-hearted efforts. The Leo woman must be won over, and initially will cast a very cold shoulder on a presentation that falls below her expectations. After all, to her mind, life should be a banquet and has taught her along the way that she is a queen who should be catered to—or at least given very careful consideration.

Having a great deal of pride and a lot of self-confidence, she could not conceive of pursuing a man, no matter how attractive. Men must come to her—and with the right attitude. Men who don't call might as well doze in their coffins. She doesn't tolerate bad behavior—unless of course she is blindly in love.

In that case, she can make some very foolish choices, fueled by her need to see only the best. When hurt, the Leo woman can be cold and imperious; when deeply disappointed, she can become quietly obsessed. She is a woman to never be taken for granted, for when she gives her heart she gives the gift of her highest ideals.

The Leo woman is moved by emotional superlatives. Deep inside she wants a man to feel grateful to be graced by her. In turn, she can change his life by the grandness of her love and the splendor of her glorious light.

Fatal Attractions

Leo women are wooed by the grand and the glamorous. Excitement, sophistication, and high-pitched romance resonate a high-profile desirability. Leo women often fall prey to their cinematic sense of what seems larger than life. Their taste in men tends to be upscale. Therefore, they look at the glossy overview of the big picture and in the process can blind themselves to some of the critical particulars.

Leo women are galvanized by men of great success, power, and ambition. In all respects, appearance counts and can get in the way of really getting to know the person. When the star quality shows off its luster, the fatal attraction can turn to love. Down the road, when the initial razzle-dazzle wears thin, she might feel doomed by the downside. Leo women loathe darkness, bad manners, thoughtlessness, and inconsiderate, selfish, low-down behavior. All become fatal and force her to change from a woman of fire to one of ice.

Foolish Choices

Fiery, passionate, prideful, and ruled by her heart rather than her head, the Leo woman has been known to rush headlong into romantic situations that might best be avoided. She can be a fool for love who feeds off flattery, fantasy, and high expectations. At all times she must realize that she does have choices and is not a pawn propelled by fate.

When falling in love, the picture that she paints for herself is grandiose and often greatly divorced from reality. The Leo woman mythologizes her romance and imbues it with mystery and the mark of destiny. Often, she actually needs that experience more than the man himself. The more a situation closely resembles a Metro-Goldwyn-Mayer production, the more she makes the choice to throw herself into the fires.

Although the Leo woman has a strong sense of self, curiously she loses it when she falls in love. To keep the aura of excitement glowing, she will give of herself to the point of emotional bankruptcy. Gracious and generous to a fault, she will allow herself to be taken advantage of, and even cruelly used, until the pain in her heart becomes so unbearable that she has to back off. Idealistic to the extreme, she can't believe that someone she loves might be incapable of loving her back in the same intense way. Therefore, her most foolish choice is in trusting too quickly and giving her heart away to men who are all charm and no soul.

Fated Lessons

When it comes to love, it seems that the Leo woman learns the hard way. Idealistic and trusting to a fault, she wants to believe what someone is presenting to her, especially if the picture puts the boring, mundane, tedious reality at bay. Deep inside she yearns for a great love that will transport her to a fairy-tale dimension devoid of darkness and mediocrity. Her need to mythologize romance, to make it into an experience of wonder never before known to man, can get her into deep emotional difficulty. When she truly gives away her heart, she also gives her mind. And it is the giving of her mind that makes rational, healthy, objective thinking impossible.

When a Leo woman loses her divine, heavily invested dream, she can become heartsick, and it takes her a long time to recover. Her fated lesson is that she is a fool for love and is often more carried away by the grandiosity of the experience than by the actual person. Under deep scrutiny, the person who has made her heartsick can be seen to have fatal flaws that speak of death to any serious connection. He is often emotionally compartmentalized, says one thing and does another, is fearful of intimacy, and is often frightfully selfish. What she has seen in him is what she wanted to see, and no amount of input from any outside source can interfere with that vision. In a sense she has to bottom out on her own wishful thinking before reality dawns. When that happens, she swears she will never do it again—of course until the next time.

Getting Smart in Affairs of the Heart

The Leo woman needs to look before she leaps, even if the situation is oh-so-tempting. Lots of experience should make her see that although roses and romantic dinners can be divine, they are entertainment and not necessarily the stuff of the heart.

Because her heart is so powerful and can metaphorically overtake her, she needs to protect it with her head and not be so quick to throw all into the ocean of emotion. It is critical that she start to become conscious of how she has helped to create the disappointment that has ensued by refusing to see signs that were there from the start. Fairy tales are fun to read, but they are not the stuff of life. Therefore, the higher she brings herself though her own imagination, the farther there is to fall.

The Leo woman needs to look at love in a deeper spiritual context that prompts such key questions as: Is this a sensitive, caring person or a self-centered character who is only concerned with his own expectations?

Does he ask questions and, even better, remember the answers? Is he consistent in his behavior? Does he have a heart, or only an ego? Does he have a history of splintered relationships that say something about him? Is he as considerate as one of my best friends and if not, why am I making allowances? (And she has to look hard at the fact that she is making allowances.) Has there been a subtle shift in his behavior from the romantic beginning to a slight cooling and perhaps some not too cool assumptions? Am I putting more and more energy into waiting for things to get as great as they started out than I am in feeling peace, joy, and confidence?

The Leo woman has to learn that the greatest love is a spiritual love with a person who has a heart that is highly developed. Many men are cut off from their hearts even though they may come bearing gifts. Essentially the Leo woman has got to want to see the difference. If she wants something deeper than fun times, she has to be responsible enough to herself to sit back and sort it all out from the start.

She has to learn how to enjoy the party but not throw her heart, mind, and soul into the production. She also has to hold parts of herself back for herself, and take the time to watch, wait and listen and never want anyone more than she wants herself. The heart of the Leo is a gift. The right man will respect that and it will open his heart.

The Leo Man

The Smart Scoop

I remember a Leo man I once knew saying, "I'm a very spoiled person and the person who spoils me is me." No truer words were ever said. However, Leo men have such a special knack for pulling off their razzle-dazzle that they can be great fun—unless, of course, they are also very childish.

The Leo man is smart, funny, fun-loving, and loves the greatest things in life. And he uses it all to put himself center stage. At his own party he wants to be the star and captivates the crowd with grand gestures. When the Leo man gets total attention, his exuberance flies. As he revels in his own anecdotes and dramatizes his daily life, there is no one as commanding in the crowd. The Leo man comes alive when he feels all faces upon him and that's his fuel. However, a performer with a silent phone and no audience is a different animal. His mind twists inward—until some new audience appears and all the lights once again go on.

The Leo man is exceedingly smart about self-presentation. So smart that his date will think she is with the Baron de Rothchild. That's the point. The flashiest car, the most expensive clothes, the most upscale restaurant, champagne by the buckets. Mr. Leo is more powerful than a noncompete clause. I know a woman who was seeing a multimillionaire Leo man who brought her to the most exclusive New York restaurants and each time would boom at the waiter so that everyone in the room could hear, "Just give her anything she wants!" This is many women's dream. He knows that and he's buying. The payoff comes when he gets anything he wants. And the fascinating thing about the Leo man is that he does usually get it.

I know one Leo man who is tall, good-looking, extremely well educated, very successful, funny, and fun (when you don't know him). When he was a boy, his mother cut up his food for him. When he grew up and married, his wife cut up his food for him. By the end of the marriage, she tried to cut him up.

And so it goes. The irony to this man is that for someone who tends to be so attractive to the opposite sex, he also tends to have more relationship problems than some dumb dufus who tries too hard. Why? It's simple. In relationship he forgets that there are two people.

The Feeling Scope

The Leo man is a romantic showman. He wants his world to be picture perfect and his woman to be the fantasy of all men. The Leo man's feelings revolve around himself: his goals, his dreams, his ambitions, and his ego.

He feels that he should get what he wants immediately, if not sooner. Instantly infatuated with beautiful bodies, he becomes smitten with sexy babes who make him look good. (Keep in mind that Mick Jagger is a Leo.) At all times the Leo man has to look the part. Because he puts such huge stock in what people think of him, he is under constant pressure to perform. It takes the Leo man a very long time to grow up. Some never do. Until that time comes, his feeling scope is narcissism, plain and simple.

Fatal Attractions

The Leo man is galvanized by a great body and a face to go with it. Beauty, glamour, charm, sex appeal, and a personality that is supportive to his ego is his recipe for bliss. The Leo man needs to see his best self reflected in the eyes of his lover, who in turn has to make him look good by her appearance, power, personality, and position. However, if she looks too good, suddenly no one is paying attention to him—and that could become a problem.

The Leo man is also jealous, possessive, controlling, and demanding. The play has to go his way or it won't go on. When he is caught up in the throes of a fatal attraction, he will probably think he is in love. This instills the instantaneous need for even more control, since now he has something to lose. And so on comes the onslaught of flowers, gifts, fine wines, and fancy places. The Leo man knows that no woman in her right mind will walk away from luxury, and so, with the most resplendent luxuries, he buys love.

Foolish Choices

In love, Leo men can make a lot of foolish choices. I know of one Leo man who married and divorced the same woman four times! The last marriage lasted because his wife finally learned she had to cater to him. This man had horrific temper tantrums like a two-year-old; however, his very attractive Sagittarius wife charmed him into a gurgling

Gerber baby. Nevertheless, was he faithful to her? Not on your life. He had a particular preference for prostitutes.

Often, Leo men worry so much about their sexual performance that they can't perform or focus on the woman. In such cases, prostitutes can solve the problem. Now, when that is a choice, is intimacy an option? The Leo man is often so caught up in himself and his expectations that deep emotional intimacy is something he doesn't really get. He goes for gratification, and often lacks both the time and the inclination for anything deeper. Highly ambitious, he tends to be a constantly compromised and very busy man. Chances are that he is so overloaded running a company, producing a movie, or starring in it that he can only focus on his woman of choice for so long. Like many men, he compartmentalizes his time and his emotions. When she is with him, he is grandiose. One hour later he will be taking a conference call. Two hours later he will be taking a meeting and may completely forget to call.

One typical foolish choice of the Leo man is that when the newness wears off, he starts to take his woman for granted. This is greatly enhanced if she gives too much. He starts to expect the attention like mail. Eventually, he even becomes annoyed by it when her phone call announcing the special dinner she has planned interrupts his train of thinking or his sit-ups or his flirtation with his secretary.

So that brings us to the next foolish choice: infidelity. Because the Leo man's attitude is basically that the best counts for everything and more counts for better, he does not struggle with himself too much when temptation prevails. However, foolish and arrogant as he is, he is always found out. Then the self-pitying suffering he goes through outdoes the spectacle of the crucifixion.

There was a Leo man I once knew who took his lovely, giving girlfriend for granted for several years, never taking her on the sun-drenched island trips he got from work because he didn't think she was sexy enough. One day he took up with his new secretary. Since he did not bother to hide his tracks, his girlfriend found out. Like a quick brush with death, he found his clothes and laptop in the street and she proceeded to land another boyfriend who was more powerful, successful, and very wealthy. Mr. Leo almost took to his bed—alone. He lost a lot of weight, begged, pleaded, and sobbed, and bought her a huge diamond ring. But the years of being treated like an afterthought all came back to her, and she never forgave him.

This woman was my client, and in the long course of their relationship there had been a couple of these breakups in which she had suffered immeasurably because during the course of it all she had lost herself. Each time, when she recovered enough to get another boyfriend, he wanted her back. When he finally got her back, it wasn't long before he once again took her for granted. She said to me, "He wants what he can't have or shouldn't have and it will only happen again."

I agreed with her. I had seen this pattern many times with very attractive, very successful Leo men. Regardless of their age, deep inside they are little bitty boys who want to own and rule the sandbox. Unless they can get beyond self, they will stay stuck in self, and all the romantic choices from there on in are bound to be foolish.

Fated Lessons

Mr. Leo does not learn his lessons well, and tends to repeat them. His ego is an albatross that impels him toward immediate gratification and blinds him to the feelings of others. One friend I once had who was married to a remarkably difficult Leo man would utter perfectly neutral statements like "Did you take out the garbage?" or "Are you taking your car or mine?" And the response was invariably "I have feelings *too.*" He was so caught up in his feelings and so overextended in his ego needs that he couldn't really hear anything but himself.

All of the popular astrology books go on at great length about all the gifts the Leo man comes bearing when he falls in love. That can be true. And that may be wonderful for five minutes for women who want to be bought. However, after the novelty wears off and the relationship has settled into a secure, predictable phase, this man is interested in no one's feelings but his own. He wants what he wants when he wants it and has no interest in lessons. And when he comes bearing gifts, it is to please himself playing the grand role of gift bearer. He loves the spectacle of himself as grandiose and generous, making life heart-stoppingly sparkling and dramatic.

Getting Smart in Affairs of the Heart

Of course, not all Leo men are as monstrous as the classic caricature. Some Leo men, depending on influences in their individual chart, have a depth and a will for growth that puts them light-years ahead of their brothers who merely want to win. For these latter individuals there is no getting smart unless they really want to. Before this happens something has to register of the hurt they have created. And they have to realize that in hurting, cheating, and lying to their partner they are also hurting themselves.

It is as if this sort of man is lost so far down in himself that he can barely peep over the edge. And he doesn't want to. Getting smart for the Leo man means developing compassion and caring. Doing a kindness for the sake of kindness, not for compliments. And, most of all, acting from the heart and not the ego.

It usually takes a crisis for the typical Leo man to even begin this process. What invariably happens is when the crisis is over, he goes back to his old self-serving ways. Actor that he is, he is remarkably adept at getting his partner to feel sorry for him after he has almost completely done her in. When she sees the tears and the suffering of that sad little boy underneath who is hurting so badly, she forgets her own hurts and how many times they have come to haunt her.

A woman came to me who was married twenty years to her second Leo husband. Both husbands had abused her severely emotionally, and because the present husband was so characteristically controlling and domineering, it had taken away all her confidence, even though she was very intelligent and highly educated. Now, this man, who had lost one of his businesses, demanded an enormous amount of money from her—which she was to obtain from a second mortgage on her house from the first marriage. I said to her, "I give people options. I never take such a strong stand as I am taking now, but you must get away from this man, totally, completely. I don't mean merely get a divorce, but move very far away where he won't be able to control you." She replied that she knew that and had even gotten divorce papers and was contemplating moving to another state where she had relatives. But she was afraid. The more that I encouraged her, I felt her fading away and her eyes becoming blank. Finally I said to her, "I am also psychic and things come through me very strongly in a reading, and I have something very difficult to tell you. If you don't get this man out of your life you are going to get sick, very sick." Still she stared at me impassively. Then I said to her, "Okay, I will tell you how you will get sick because it is coming through clearly. You will get cancer." Her reply to me was "You can't tell I'm wearing a wig?"

So much for making the same bad choices. In her case, she kept choosing the same astrological sign. In following up with her, I found out that she did indeed give him the money, and stayed with him because she felt sorry for him. This woman has two small, adopted children with this man who is emotionally abusive even to her ninety-two-year-old mother. I asked her, "Don't you want these children to have a mother?" However, she was too far gone to want to grasp what I was saying. Deep down, she didn't believe that she had any choices.

7. VIRGO

AUGUST 24 TO SEPTEMBER 23

Ruling Planet: Mercury
Element: Earth
Cosmic Quality: Mutable
Essential Quality: Feminine, negative
Planetary Principle: Purity
Primal Desire: Crystallization
Material Factor: Service

The Virgo Woman

The Smart Scoop

Self-possessed, refined, and so very sensible, the Virgo woman rules through her ability to serve. Dedicated, efficient, and highly systematic, she can take on tasks that others shrink at. That is because she is so capable. From counseling to nursing to organizing to knowing instinctively how to give care, the Virgo woman is a power behind the scenes. Fastidious and full of ideas on how to improve an already successful enterprise, she can do amazing things with a mess and make magic in the midst of disorder.

Humble, self-effacing, and the last to boast about her abilities, she quickly becomes indispensable at whatever it is she chooses to do. More interested in a job well done than in accepting praise, she has a down-to-earth, no-nonsense approach that puts self-important personalities to shame. Selflessly loyal, giving, and nurturing, she needs quality in life—not quantity. A no-frills personality who puts her performance above all else, she is dependable, responsible, sensible, reliable—and always in the driver's seat. Always thinking, reflecting, reading, and studying self-improvement, she is a walking resource on how one can be better.

Considered cool by some, she has, in fact, a strong sense of decorum and such a dignified self-presentation that it precedes her. The Virgo woman is actually shy and unassuming. Not consumed by ego needs, she is a woman of substance who deals with what is really important and doesn't waste time with trifles.

The Feeling Scope

She is loyal and empathetic, nurturing and never-complaining. A best friend during bad times, the Virgo woman is always there. Practical, rather than sentimental, she puts her feelings to use by doing good deeds and acts of kindness.

Thoughtful, discriminating, sincere, and self-protective, she takes love seriously and fears being hurt. Insecure and not completely sure of herself where love is concerned, she sometimes gives too much to be loved in return.

Fatal Attractions

There is always one in her past: some scoundrel who took her heart and had no idea what to do with it. The Virgo woman is sincere, and so trusting that early on she can be taken in by some bad boy who seemed so right from the start. When the Virgo woman is hurt, her entire world shatters and for quite some time after she won't let herself feel.

Brilliance and passion can bring her to the brink of heaven. But when it blows apart, it's like every part of her is bleeding. From that time on, she becomes cautious and critical and will only go forth if she feels she's found a friend.

Foolish Choices

As the sign of service to others, the Virgo woman can give too much and specifically give to get love. In her foolish phase, she can be self-effacing, putting her lover on a pedestal and herself way down beneath. Idealistic and longing for someone perfect to look up to, she glorifies him in her imagination and then silently suffers his bad behavior. The more selfish he is—and he is always selfish—the more selfless she becomes. The more he takes, the more she gives. The colder he becomes, the more compulsive she gets—until, finally, an agonizing emotional trap has been created.

At this point, torn between gut-wrenching pain and murderous resentment, she is hardly able to live with her own feelings. Anger is a horrible thing for this woman who wants to be nice. Many Virgo women repress it until they find themselves committing little violent acts. For dark behavior is the shadow of this sign that wants to be so black-and-white perfect and proper.

For some, the rage will manifest physically through psychosomatic symptoms such as headaches, stomach problems, and skin eruptions. For others, it will become depression. However, the longer they stuff it down to preserve their situation, the more likely it can turn into disease. When a Virgo woman makes a very serious emotional commitment, it is made forever. Therefore, to break such a bind can also break her spirit—if only for a time.

Hopefully the rage and pain will hit a critical point and release her. Then she will be able to call her spirit back from this emotional investment that has become so costly, an investment predicated on an unaffirmed self that could only see so far at the time.

Fated Lessons

Her fundamental lesson is not to psychologically project and create a false god of some intelligent man, but to own her own talents. Ruled by the planet Mercury, the planet of intelligent thinking and communication, she needs to honor her own intelligence. For when a Virgo woman does not honor her own intelligence and treats herself as a mere servant, she then becomes neurotic and an oral compulsive, a chatterer, a compulsive eater, and a worrier about minutiae who cannot shut off her mind.

She needs to learn to use that mind and to go to exciting places with it instead of attributing that power to a man she puts above her. Wherever the positive place that that mind takes her, there she should reside and grow. In that growing she becomes more and more her unique self, and becoming a complete unique self, not a servant, is her life lesson, her challenge, and the secret of why she incarnated in this lifetime.

The symbol associated with Virgo is the virgin. However, virgin in ancient Greece in the time of the divine secret rites of Eleusis did not mean what it does today. It meant a self-containment based on a flowering within by connecting to one's higher, divine spirit which is the outpouring source of life. This is the fated lesson of the Virgo woman: to flower from within herself first and to never give herself away.

Getting Smart in Affairs of the Heart

Of all the signs, the Virgo woman seems to get smart in affairs of the heart so much faster than her astrological sisters. She tends not to make the same mistakes over and over, but uses her inherent critical faculties to discriminate. She also has the primordial virgin archetype deep within her psyche, which makes her more self-sufficient and self-contained than so many women who look to men to fill them up. The wise Virgo woman values her own mind and spirit enough not to lose it. She also knows that losing it is not a function of love. In love, as in everything else, the Virgo woman has values that uphold her and determine a great deal of her fate. The purity of her vision makes her an impressive voice of intelligence and integrity, while her instinctive insights set her apart from someone who is merely intellectual. The Virgo woman learns her lessons well. At her best she is in touch with both the inner and outer worlds and gains truth from both as well as a life meaning that increasingly comes to define her.

The Virgo Man

The Smart Scoop

He is intelligent and critical, disciplined and dependable. The Virgo man is cool and controlled on the surface but shy and insecure underneath. He puts reason before passion and work before pleasure. Efficient, responsible, and emotionally reserved, he is the taskmaster of all time who treats work like a religion. Highly organized and extremely perfectionistic, his setups are so anal that they can terrorize someone creative.

The Virgo man is orderly, and that is how he has to live. The contents of his freezer are alphabetized and the contents of his closet look like an architect arranged them. He is so meticulous that he probably vacuums his ceiling and cleans the back of the refrigerator. His desk has nothing on it except furniture polish and his house looks like he just rented it for the afternoon. Is it a wonder that so many people think the Virgo man is cold?

Yet far from it. He can be very sexually passionate and he can be very caring. But, at the same time, when upset, this complex man can run ice cold. The Virgo man can turn his feelings on and off like a water faucet. And when caught up in work, his clear priority is that that should come first.

Although his controls can make him boring and constrictive when they rule him, the Virgo man still does have a heart. However, unassuming and insecure, he relies on this outer order to calm him down and keep his feathers smooth. The most cool, attractive Virgo men are nervous Nellies underneath and must compensate for that to gain control. At the same time, he can be a true friend in need who will give you the shirt off his back—but don't dirty it.

The Feeling Scope

He is pragmatic rather than romantic, and emotionally cautious and tentative as opposed to someone who will sweep you away. Nevertheless, the Virgo man does feel his feelings. Deep under the surface and under all his controls, he is like a shy, gangly adolescent who is calculating his way through his first date. Nevertheless, the mind still rules, and it tells him watch out!

The Virgo man has to be completely certain that everything is on his side before he opens up. One thing that will deter him is overwrought emotional displays. He finds hyperbolic emotional scenes and/or acts of rage disgusting and vulgar, and they leave him cold. Not one to trust easily, there is also no way the Virgo man will risk rejection. However, when he does allow himself to love it is deadly serious and he is faithful, sincere, and completely committed.

However, he is not the wining and dining type. It is more likely he will offer to cook and have a quiet evening at home. In general the Virgo man likes simple pleasures and clean, healthy, wholesome food. He will also not wax rhapsodic about a woman's beauty. He didn't pick her for that; it's too superficial. Instead, he will offer some helpful suggestion about how she can greatly better her life by giving something up (that probably is an essential pleasure). For instance: "I know you don't want to hear this but wine kills brain cells." Instead of grabbing her, taking her into his arms, and kissing her, he'll first go brush his teeth. Kissing comes later. With the Virgo man it's always first things first.

Fatal Attractions

Attractions are not fatal for the Virgo man. They are well thought out and carefully considered. He is a perfectionist. That does not mean that he has to have the most beautiful woman in conventional terms. It means that he is looking for the perfect person who fits with him and makes him feel stimulated, completed, and secure.

Essentially, he is a purist who hates make-up and anything fake. The Virgo man wants the true person, free of cosmetic illusions. He also wants to be free of the masquerade of romantic invention where games come into play and people pretend to be who they are not.

The Virgo man is most attracted to someone he can really talk to and whom he respects. Physical attraction comes into play through that perspective. The Virgo man first has to find a woman attractive on the inside. The outer facade fails to enchant him, although he may admire it in a detached fashion from across a crowded room.

As he is a mental type, the Virgo man likes to find a woman intellectually impressive and, hopefully, accomplished. That's for starters. Intense rapport and a sense of compatibility that is like chemistry would be the deciding factor that would motivate him to move forward.

Foolish Choices

When he gets angry he runs cold, cuts off, and treats someone as if they've become a corpse. The Virgo man has a hard time with the feeling side of himself. The spiteful, negative shadow can control him, and when that happens its very unfortunate.

When the Virgo man becomes cold, cruel and vindictive, it is a foolish choice. This is a man who is capable of caring, kindness, compassion, loyalty, understanding, and love. When he chooses to operate from the lowest part of himself, he thereby diminishes his own potential for emotional happiness. With such white-hot anger comes a price, and the price is a closed-off heart that can't feel.

The Virgo man sometimes operates from behind such bone-deep defenses that people mistake that for the whole person. At the bottom of that defense is fear, and this can contaminate his whole life, leaving him in an emotional limbo where he can only think and not feel.

When the Virgo man is cut off from his feelings and lives only through his work, dictated by his disciplines, rules, regulations, and systems, he creates a sterile, lifeless world where love has no chance. Self-controlled, cynical, cold, and often angry, he is fueled by self-righteousness, which perpetuates the continuum. Seeing life only through the perspective of the small and the petty, he becomes imprisoned in himself. And that is not only foolish, it is tragic.

Fated Lessons

The Virgo man's lesson is to open up and feel his heart, not just live in his head. Like all of our fated lessons, it is a towering and painful challenge. And that is because he often has to attract and live through what he fears most to get beyond his fears and resistances. However, the slightest dent in his armor awakens the conditioned response, and he tends to retreat in self-protection.

His most essential lesson is that he has to love life, not just think it or escape from it into dull routines that are like a kind of subtle madness. When he completely denies the vulnerable side of himself—and all Virgo men have one—he is completely diminishing his ability to feel. Taken to the extreme, this deadness can bring on disease. And the *dis-ease* has to do with the fact that he has not a clue as to what to do with his heart.

Getting Smart in Affairs of the Heart

Instead of cutting off his feelings when a situation gets uncomfortable, the Virgo man needs to talk them out. He needs to understand that if he refuses to trust, he will be creating a tiny, dead little world that will never offer him any possibility. He needs to have the courage to rise above his defensiveness and develop the will to get beyond the self-righteous anger that keeps him locked in place.

With any confrontation or emotional challenge, the Virgo man develops negative expectations that multiply into a self-fulfilling prophecy. His knee-jerk response of "See, I told you so, I know you're going to do it again" inevitably does elicit the very same behavior.

Part of his inherent smarts is his analytical ability, which will enable him to grasp the dynamics of a situation without destructive recriminations. If he can detach from his tendency toward seething resentment in order to analyze the big picture instead of pointing a finger, he can achieve a clear grasp that can allow him to go forward. Then, talking things out in a calm, nonconfrontational manner with his partner, he has the possibility of coming to such a better understanding that the relationship can grow.

However, fundamentally, he has to value his own heart and all the joy that can come from feeling with it. Even if he can't readily experience this, he should be able to ask, from within the confines of his limited, cut-off existence, "Is this all there is?" Being smart is admitting to himself that he wants more than mere routine and that he is willing to take the risk that feeling involves. And then take it.

8. LIBRA
SEPTEMBER 24 TO OCTOBER 23

Ruling Planet: Venus
Element: Air
Cosmic Quality: Cardinal
Essential Quality: Masculine, positive
Planetary Principle: Balance
Primal Desire: Harmony
Material Factor: Creation

The Libra Woman

The Smart Scoop

The Libra woman is very smart, sporting a steel-trap mind and an uncanny analytical ability. She is also socially savvy and has a natural grace and demeanor that draws people to her. Born under the planet Venus, beauty is her *raison d'être*, and whether it is in her personal style or in the details of her environment, she creates it with an élan that is tasteful and arresting.

The Libra woman loves the best things of life and her tastes tend toward the lavish. Whether entertaining or being entertained, she has high expectations of the perfect scenario. A true romantic who is in love with romance in all its potential splendor, she is capable of falling in love many times, unfortunately however, each time not necessarily any the wiser.

Despite her cerebral smarts, the Libra woman is emotionally innocent, impressionable, and somewhat adolescent. In love she doesn't use her head unless to overanalyze. In the long run, all of this analysis usually proves useless, as she never arrives at any convictions, only more confusion. At this point she implores the opinions of her friends, with whom she continues to analyze. When the Libra woman's emotions are completely stirred up, she loses the power of her mind. However, the face she shows to the world is the picture of grace and charm.

The Libra woman might be the most charming in the zodiac. She is certainly the most pleasing, and knows exactly how to make a man feel like a king as she caters to his needs. However, as the sign of fairness, equality, and justice, she fully expects her efforts to bear rewards. The Libra woman needs to be showered with all the luxuries of romance: fine champagne, fresh flowers, frequent phone calls, and, of course, fine restaurants. No last-minute phone calls or Chinese take-out for her.

Her taste is impeccable and so is her timing. The Libra woman seeks to live in a perfect world where manners count and people behave with politeness and decorum. She is one woman who is so pleasing to be around that she is ridiculously popular. The Libra woman was born knowing how to make her world a more beautiful place, and lives with the joy of sharing.

The Feeling Scope

Although she can appear to be very emotional, the Libra woman is still an air sign, which has to do with thinking. Therefore, it is her thoughts which control her and her emotions.

The Libra woman can get very emotionally caught up in her mental picture of life. A perfectionist who is insecure if she feels she falls short of her own ideal, she can get down and depressed and let little things bother her. Her mind tends to work overtime with worry, fear, and fretting about the future. All of this plays havoc with her emotions, which are really thoughts. Librans are often very much out of touch with how they really feel. In love, they look at the other person but they don't feel them. They listen to what they are saying but they often don't hear them. Consequently, they miss cues and clues, and often have a hard time comprehending the true direction of their relationship.

It is not uncommon to see a Libra woman lamenting her lost love one week and then being perfectly cheerful about a new prospect the next. She would be the last to admit that she is detached emotionally; however, like all air signs, with incomprehensible coolness she can move on.

Fatal Attractions

The Libra woman is mentally in love with the idea of grand love. In her mind's eye, she longs for a handsome hero who knows how to do the most precious things. He is sophisticated and showy but graceful at the same time. He also has exquisite taste and timing and treats her as a beautiful princess for whom he cannot do enough. He comes bearing gifts: the finest of wines, champagne, rooms full of roses, and, of course, jewelry. There are sun-drenched vacations on his yacht and dancing in the moonlight. In short, he presents the scenario of the most romantic movie.

Unfortunately, such fantasies fail, and so many attractions do prove fatal. And when the champagne starts to look like stale beer, the Libra woman's raptures of emotion have the personal warmth of a cold call. What happened to this phantasmagorical drama that could not be outdone? "Oh, he was a bore," she mutters as she throws his clothes in the street and makes dinner plans with her friends. Now she is ready for the real thing; now she knows what to really look for.

What she looks for and gets is the superficial. I knew one Libra woman who married her ex-husband because he was a great dancer. I know another Libra woman who married her ex-husband because he was the best-looking in his high school class. The Libra woman's fatal attraction is what looks good. And when she thinks she has found it she does not delve beneath the surface. All those fancy dance steps, good looks, great restaurants, and fun seemed like a life that would last forever. It certainly should have, had he not had flaws that were so fatal.

Foolish Choices

Libra women usually marry early and divorce at least once in their life. When immature, they do tend to choose a husband based on his being a good dancer or great-looking. Looks and lifestyle mean more than a lot to them, and they don't look beyond or delve beneath the surface.

Consequently, they are prone to form shallow connections based on superficial values. Because Librans don't like to live alone, marriage is always the goal of dating, and, over time, becomes an empty shell with no communication or depth.

The Libra woman marries to satisfy her needs and superficial expectations. She believes the words of old-fashioned love songs that speak of secure nests, and love that is sublime and everlasting with a dream man who adores her. On these ideas she bases her foolish choices. When they fail her, she still tends to think she got the concept right but just messed up by choosing the wrong person.

At a certain point, if she is going to move beyond making foolish choices, the Libra woman has to go deeper and realize that relationships are about more than image. Image alone will always fail her and leave her wanting.

Fated Lessons

Many Librans seek out relationships because they are desperate not to be alone. Time and again, Librans look to others to feel whole. A relationship born from need instead of preference starts out with a strike against it. There is a strong tendency toward codependency in this sign, and a sense that life is intrinsically meaningless unless it is shared with a certain someone. Looking to another to validate self is a sure-fire way to diminish individual potential and constrict the entire out-look on life.

Libra is a deeply insecure sign, and therefore has huge lessons around developing a healthy self-esteem. There is often little or no value put on self, regardless of the many gifts and talents that are often associated with this sign. Putting huge expectations on another as a safeguard against a devalued self is not only dangerous but usually also self-defeating.

The Libra woman also puts more emphasis on outer things than on her inner growth and development. Her values emphasize looks and beauty at the expense of spiritual considerations. Therefore, she often attracts to herself relationships and situations that are shallow and become increasingly empty. It is so important for this sign to work on growth and going deeper. Each failed relationship carries a lesson about self. An unaffirmed self can never have a healthy relationship. When, out of fear of loneliness she settles for a cell mate, she will never find her soul mate. In the end she must choose whether to give up and give in, or to consciously take on the responsibility for her own happiness.

Getting Smart in Affairs of the Heart

The sun is in its fall in Libra, which correlates to a weak sense of self. The first step for a Libra woman to get smart in affairs of the heart is to work on self-love and not look to a man as a substitute for her own relationship with herself. When she bases her self-worth on her relationship with a man instead of her relationship with herself, she is setting herself up in a very weak and dependent position that could become extremely self-sabotaging.

Libras tend to think that relationships are the be-all and end-all to personal happiness, and that without them they feel like nothing. Such undertakings as therapy, psychoanalysis, spiritual study, meditation, retreats, prayer, and affirmation can transform this attitude and open up the individual to themselves in powerful, growth-producing ways. Developing a grounding within the self that grows with experience means also developing a confidence within the self and a connection to a higher power that is personally sustaining. When a person comes from this place, they choose a partner on preference, not need, and should this relationship, over time, not work out, they are not devastated and are able to put it in perspective.

The Libra woman also tends to hold on to a bad relationship, thinking it is better than no relationship. Getting smart means learning to let go when it becomes clear that the relationship is not going to get better. At this point, having a healthy self-esteem to fall back on will enable her to move forward with the game of life and all the potentially wonderful things she may encounter along that journey.

When in a relationship, from time to time, she should take inventory on the relationship and herself by asking such questions as: Am I compensating through eating and drinking for the emptiness I feel in my relationship? Am I in this relationship only because I am afraid to be alone? Am I allowing my fears to control me so that I am giving in and putting up with conditions that are making me unhappy? Libras tend to go along with a situation until another better one comes along, and if that doesn't happen, they can stay stuck and miserable for years.

Finally, another foolish Libran trait is serial monogamy: going from one relationship to another with no breathing space in between. The Libra woman needs to learn to be alone and like it. She need to develop interests that are self-sustaining; to make friends who are independent and whom she can learn from, and to plan fun activities that divert her from the ringing of the phone. Finally, she must come to understand that a relationship, while a potentially meaningful part of life, is not a substitute for an individual life plan. However, the more she explores her own potential and gets joy from that, the more she is not only getting smart about why she is here on earth, but also getting smart and free in affairs of the heart. The Libra woman needs to learn how to be free in love and not so bound by fear that she remains fettered to a situation that so limits her that she has no vision of the potential of her own life.

The Libra Man

The Smart Scoop

He is a clever, witty, charming character with a cool facade and impeccable manners. The Libra man is a gentleman who was born to enjoy the finer things in life and would love to be to the manner born. The larger-than-life writer and sybarite F. Scott Fitzgerald was a Libra, and put in just as much time living the grand life as he did on his career.

The Libra man has a refined sensibility and an overwhelming sense of fairness. He is also very smart, sharp, eloquent, and persuasive. Therefore, it is not surprising that many lawyers are born under this sign. The Libra man loves beauty and can be quite creative in conjuring it. A beautiful woman in a candlelit setting sets the tone for his mood. An old-fashioned romantic who brings flowers and remembers anniversaries, he enjoys all the little touches that set a woman's heart aflutter. However, she in turn must keep up all appearances, not only in her looks but also in her behavior. The Libra man loathes discord, crudeness, quarrels, and disharmony of any kind. Ideally, he wants life to be picture-perfect and his love life to uplift him on his darker days.

Sentimental, yet also cerebral, he has an uncanny knack for thinking out his feelings. Therefore, if aspects of a relationship start to appear rather unattractive, he is capable of quietly thinking things through and then politely disengaging. One day, the man who had appeared so romantic has disappeared and it is a cool, distant fellow who is walking out the door.

The Feeling Scope

As a heady air sign, the Libra man is less emotional than romantic. Caught up in the pleasure of appearances, he can be completely disengaged from the depths of the person he professes to love. Passionate, complex, or intense he is not. His feelings float on the surface and tend toward the superficial. Above all, the Libra man relies on reason, not compassion or intuition, to sort out life's complexities. Therefore, he is acutely uncomfortable with intense, tear-jerking emotional displays. It is harmony that makes him happy, and pleasantness that he wants to have at all costs.

Born under the sign of partnership, he is not happy going it alone and needs a relationship for sharing and security. Mr. Libra is most definitely a marrying man who needs to live his life *a deux*. When dating seriously, he talks in terms of "we" instead of "I" and looks to a future of never being lonely.

Fatal Attractions

Great beauty leaves the Libra man breathless, and a magnetic personality to go along with it can put him over the edge. This is not a man who is going to probe deeply into character. He wants to have fun and to feel good about himself at the same time.

He is prone to infatuation, so if he encounters a stellar someone, suddenly it is the right time, the right place, and the perfect face. There are Libra men who marry for security and a cozy nest; however, their fatal attractions are the women who sweep them off their feet in the first five minutes. Down the road, of course, the dizzying love spell usually wears off and there is trouble in paradise. However, even in hindsight it can't be denied that it all felt so fine at the time.

Foolish Choices

The Libra man can be a big flirt and prone to be blinded by his fatal attractions. Self-indulgent and determined to satisfy all his desires, he is capable of having a lot of desires a lot of the time. There is a type of Libra man who can be serially unfaithful, completely failing to comprehend the intense pain this can cause his partner. This is a sign for whom immature desires can direct the entire course of life. Making superficial and shallow choices instead of trying to go deeper and exercise some compassion, Libras can lose out on a lot of great things in life, including their relationships.

The dark side of Libra is cold and conniving, cut off and prone to self-pity. During such episodes, they often salve their wounds with empty sex and alcohol. This is the result of numerous foolish choices that have made them numb. The lower Libra man is completely self-centered and has come to live a life where everything is about him. Instead of developing emotional perception, he operates from psychological projection and renounces all responsibility for a life that has become increasingly meaningless. As in the case of F. Scott Fitzgerald, too much pleasure has turned into pain with tragic results.

Fated Lessons

When the Libra man is enslaved by his senses, he becomes emotionally fickle. One day he is madly in love; three weeks later he has lost all feeling. Of course, these "feelings" were no more than adolescent fantasies.

Although this is the sign of balance, balance is actually the archetypal lesson for Libra. In truth, when he is negative and foolish, his life is seriously out of balance and he is cut off, living in his own world. Since Libra is actually a dependent sign, needing relationships and people, this is the saddest, loneliest choice. A Libra man alone because of his own foolish choices is usually chronically depressed. At this point, he expects the world to do something for him. Unfortunately, his hardest lesson is taking responsibility for what he has created. His immaturity often shows itself as a victim attitude. In truth, he is a victim of himself. The sun is weak in the sign Libra, which means weak ego strength, deep insecurity, and the tendency to look to others for meaning, satisfaction, and relief. Therefore, his most profound lesson comes in going deep enough into himself, past the fear, the self-pity, and the damaged expectations from the wrong choices, to develop a constructive, affirmative, spiritual relationship with himself. Until he is willing to make that commitment to himself, he will be forever looking for a self in all the wrong places, and the emptiness will own him.

Getting Smart in Affairs of the Heart

Many Libra men are smart in affairs of the heart, valuing their partner and partnership. However, they are not the ones who have affairs. This latter type has to see the pattern in his life and the cause and effect of his behavior. This type may also take a long time to grow up, and not even want to get smart. Often, it is his women who have to do the work, asking themselves, "What am I doing with this cold, cut off, noncaring person who doesn't even try to know me?"

This sort of Libra man needs to wake up, stuff the self-pity, and realize that if he really wants to share his life with someone, he needs to be less needy. The dark Libra man needs to stop lamenting his lot in life and look at the sorrow he has created through his selfishness. Libra is a very creative sign; however, he has to become aware of what he is creating. Is he creating misery or meaning? He has a choice. If he doesn't like what he is creating, the Libra man has to stop, halt his thought processes, and focus his attention on what he wants to create. The "poor me" plan will only push him deeper into his own wallowing.

For the Libra man, getting smart in affairs of the heart means realizing that he does have a heart, not just a brain—and honoring it. It means feeling feelings, not just thinking thoughts. It means focusing on where he wants to be, not just on where he has been. And, fundamentally it means he has to be honest with himself and his partner. The smooth, fast-talking playboy will one day grow old and alone. And, if he is to be smart, he has to not take a partnership for granted, but to contemplate the joy of a positive give-and-take. Finally, he has to want to love, not just to be loved. It all begins there.

9. SCORPIO

OCTOBER 24 TO NOVEMBER 22

Ruling Planets: Pluto and Mars
Element: Water
Cosmic Quality: Fixed
Essential Quality: Feminine, negative
Planetary Principle: Power
Primal Desire: Control
Material Factor: Transcendence

The Scorpio Woman

The Smart Scoop

She is a woman of mystery—often quiet and serene on the surface, yet seductive and sexually magnetic. With the Scorpio woman there is always so much more than what you see. Passionate, intense, and extremely complicated, she is an irresistible conundrum to most men. However, it is not most men who interest her. Highly intelligent and intuitive to the point of being psychic, she is attracted to men who have at least an equal amount of power. Power is her birthright and her Achilles' heel. Knowing how to use it wisely may be the greatest challenge of her lifetime. Many Scorpio women unconsciously shirk love in their drive for sexual and psychological power. The problem is they get that power. Then what to do next? Get more.

Power can become an obsession to this woman who was born with so much that it's like giving a loaded gun to a baby. However, her secret is that deep underneath the surface, insidious insecurities swirl, and on any given day she does not feel herself to be the formidable woman or femme fatale that she appears to the world. Deep, intense, and more than a trifle moody, the Scorpio woman feels safe burying herself in the superficial. When people or situations start to touch her depths, she is in for it. Another side of her takes hold, which can be beautiful, passionate, loving, fearful, dark, angry, obsessive, or compulsive. Unless she trusts totally—and there are less than a few people she trusts totally—the worms come out with all those words of love.

Her complicated nature usually makes it easy for her to see through other people's complications. Instinctively she understands and intuits hidden levels of feeling in people. The Scorpio woman is so smart she can be dangerous—to others as well as herself. Since her all-or-nothing personality can easily bring her over the edge, self-control is a *sine qua non*. Her megawatt, under-the-surface intensity is not to be equaled. Cool as a cucumber on the surface, the Scorpio woman can burn up a big city with her brain. At her best she is a courageous, uncontrollable force. Either way, one thing is true: You don't want to be on her bad side. It's just not worth it.

The Feeling Scope

Her feelings are as deep as deep gets. Next to the Scorpio woman, everyone looks superficial. It is not easy being crowded by such an overpopulated underworld of fears, feelings, fantasies, insecurities, bouts of anger, resentments, obsessions, compulsions, and contortions of passion, pain, love, and longing. Who has the energy just to go to work? Sometimes Scorpio women don't. They sometimes just want to be left alone because they have to be. Next to all that is going on in their inner world, who cares about revising clauses in some contract? To the mind of the true Scorpio woman, it seems that she is always being drowned out by the demands of the quotidian.

Some surrender to the most mundane aspects of the superficial to completely avoid their feelings. Ask this sort of Scorpio, "Do you ever get depressed?" She will look at you blankly. "Me? No." Wait till she goes through a bloody divorce or her husband leaves her. After descending into the depths of hell as only a Scorpio would experience it, she'll hire a killer and watch him do her bidding. No, you do not want to be on her bad side.

Betrayal is the worst that can happen to her—whether it's by God, man, or the impersonal forces of nature themselves. It doesn't matter which exact source inflicted the hurt; she takes it personally. And guess what—she wants to hurt back.

The Scorpio woman believes in revenge, not in turning the other cheek. Despite her high-octane intelligence and intuition, forgiveness is something she cannot comprehend. Neither will she ever forget a wrong done to her. It will be written on her grave, along with the date and the time and what the weather was like that day.

When provoked, her feelings can be so intense that they can completely overtake her. It's a little like waking up a nest of snoozing cobras. You don't want to do it.

It's not like an enraged Scorpio woman would necessarily yell and scream and threaten, although some do give quite a performance. There is also the deadly silent treatment where you're made to feel as if you're dead—or should be. What should be said here in her defense is, whether she realizes it or not, she suffers just as much as she is making someone else suffer. In that sense there is never any real justice for this woman because she so loses herself to the darkness of the plot. Try telling an enraged Scorpio woman that in giving out the poison, you are also drinking of it. She'll never get it. And she'll never give up or let go the gauntlet.

On the other hand, this is one woman who is fiercely, totally loyal—and loving. Have a Scorpio woman as a best friend, and you don't need a crowd. She will give her all, be self-sacrificing, devoted, and dauntless. However, she also has a great deal of pride and will not be walked on.

Neither will she be taken for granted. Once it appears that there are no "thank you's," she will pull herself back from the burning grounds and let her friend fight her or his battle alone.

The Scorpio woman is a complicated amalgam of fire and ice. One faithless provocation may strike a conflagration in her soul; several will make her run completely cold. And so this woman, who has a memory that would defy a computer, can become so coldly disengaged through such gutwrenching disgust that she completely kills off a person in her mind. And that is the end of that. Down the road, throw out this person's name and she will say, "Who? Oh, him. Ugh. Ancient history." No feelings. Just a vague impression like some idea she had once in the second grade.

The Scorpio woman wants to love, but also wants to be absolutely sure that she will be loved back. Completely, totally, and without question. She also wants love to be as intense as she is, not merely, "Oh dear, I have a great idea. On Sunday, let's clean out the refrigerator together." No, no, no, no. She needs sparks flying, and if things get too dull, she'll make them fly. She also needs passion, not boring time spent. Some man who attempts to listen to the news while making love will soon find himself on the floor—and out in the cold without his overcoat. When it comes to her intense feelings, she will not compromise. Weak, passive, well-meaning men need not apply—and shouldn't, in defense of their mental health. The intensity of her feelings can push a man to the brink of madness. She's probably been there herself several times. Oh, well, it's better than being boring and feeling nothing at all.

Fatal Attractions

Although she is labeled as the sex siren of the zodiac, the Scorpio woman is less interested in sex *per se* than she is in passion. Her entire feeling self is aroused in the act of passion. Passion transports her to another realm of beingness where she psychologically dies and is reborn. The French call the orgasm *la petite mort*, "the small death." For the Scorpio woman, the entire act of sexual passion is a small death. With the right man, it is also a spiritual experience where her spirit unites with his spirit.

Therefore, perhaps of all the signs, it is the Scorpio woman who is most vulnerable to fatal attractions. She also has a penchant for danger. Dangerous men are wild, fearless, driven, indifferent to shame and blame, make their own rules, and can be very exciting. Whether with dangerous men or dangerous situations, the Scorpio woman can get fatally entangled before she knows it's too late.

She is also attracted to men of power. The Scorpio woman sees power as sexy, and before she learns the life lessons such enthrallment can teach, the compulsions that it can arouse can be psychologically fatal.

The Scorpio woman is an obsessive-compulsive personality, and when passionately transported, is completely controlled by this instinctive side of herself. Therefore, what she may deem to be love can be extremely painful. This is one woman who definitely throws herself into situations where angels fear to tread. Often, the men who arouse the intensity of her passions are as personally desirable as an inmate in death row. But they're not boring. And they don't appear to be weak. (The truth is that they are always weak in the feeling function, but fake it well at the time.)

The Scorpio woman needs to feel. She may hum along coolly on the surface, completely efficient, setting all her ducks in a row. However, that cerebral realm is only a small part of her. When a man comes along who is smart, sexy, self-confident, or just crazy enough to open her up, watch out! There she goes, taking all her demons with her. A Scorpio woman never passionately loves a man she doesn't also, on some level, want to kill. There is always murder brewing in paradise. So objects of her great passion, a word to the wise: Always know where she keeps her knives.

Foolish Choices

When caught up in the throes of a grand passion, the Scorpio woman throws all caution to the winds—and with it, her smarts, psychic awareness, and self-protective armor. She doesn't care. She feels alive, and in that moment even the news of imminent nuclear attack wouldn't penetrate.

As strong as she is, there is also a slightly masochistic streak in the Scorpio woman's personality. She often attaches to losers who leave a lot to be desired overall. Let's put it this way: the Scorpio woman is extremely intelligent as long as you keep her out of the bedroom. Once in there with her fatal attraction, she doesn't have a chance.

Coming from this *non compus mentis* place, she can make a lot of foolish choices, attracting uncaring men who are often married, in love with their own power, or who so emotionally compartmentalize that she is left sad and lonely in the long run. When the Scorpio woman completely gives away her power to a man it is a sad sight to see. However, it is a choice. And it is her life challenge to see that.

Fated Lessons

The only way a Scorpio woman is going to learn her lessons is through experience. At a certain point, when she sees where such mindless passion has left her—heartbreakingly lonely—she can begin to stand back from the situation and start to see the truth of it all. However, this is a process and takes time. At first there is a great deal of rage against the man who showed up but gave nothing. If and when she is able to get beyond that, she might look to herself and realize the truth of her own part. She wanted it, she encouraged it, and at first she didn't expect more.

At first, such passion feels like life. The truth is, it can take away life like any addiction. Hopefully, with time, she will learn where these rhapsodic entanglements will lead and make the choice that she is no longer willing to pay the price. As a matter of fact, memories of past ghosts and grievances, which still haunt her, will serve to diminish the attractiveness of a situation that once would have felt irresistible.

The great psychologist Carl Jung once said, "There is no growth without pain." This is particularly true of Scorpio, who suffers deeply over her emotional lessons. And, ironically, the shrewd, psychic Scorpio woman, who in other areas sees all, must learn the emotional lesson that in these mind-blowing, passionate forays, from the very beginning, what you see is what you get. Do you see a sensitive, caring person, or a powermonger; do you see someone who connects to your soul, or someone who spells danger from the start; do you see someone single, or a married man with three kids. The beginning, middle, and end of the affair is obvious from the start, and the Scorpio woman who has become wise will come to learn that she chose it.

Getting Smart in Affairs of the Heart

The Scorpio woman has to come to a place deep within herself that knows that sensation in the moment may not be emotionally fulfilling down the road. Until she comes to that place, she will repeat the old, ultimately self-defeating patterns.

She also has to understand that high-octane sexual passion cannot replace a real love that gets deeper and richer with time. Since she is so smart already, what she needs to do is take serious stock of her experience and then do some soul-searching concerning what she really wants from her life. If she has suffered enough from involvements with the wrong kind of people, she will do this willingly, and may even choose solitude and celibacy for a while. This is the time to focus on her real power: her spiritual depths, her potential for a connection that is meaningful and a love that issues from the soul. No matter how negative she may feel, she must have faith that it is out there in the universe, waiting for her when she is ready.

In the meantime, she should pray. Praying puts her in touch with her higher self and the powers of the universe. When she assiduously aligns herself with the higher power of the universe, she starts to become so much more than her problem. She becomes her own possibility—and from there, miracles can happen.

The Scorpio woman must use her power in the right way—not to control, dominate, or manipulate, but from within, as love and gratitude for the highest reaches of herself that in time will magnetize the right person who affirms that choice.

It is part of the mythic Scorpio legacy as the sign of death, rebirth, and transformation that they often have to go down into the depths of hell before they slowly come back, see the light, and emerge as a stronger, wiser person. The suffering and deep, inner loneliness often so inherent in this sign, which seems like such a curse, is also its gift. Scorpio is the sign of death; something old and no longer useful must die off for something new and wondrous to be born.

The Scorpio woman must realize that this will be born when she is ready and tends to her soul in the right manner, through prayer, affirmation, meditation, and reflection. Through all of these she will come to realize that she can no longer go back to those old, familiar, unconscious patterns. Now, every day, she has choices. And those choices are going to move her forward, first brighter and then more brilliant in her own light—and then closer and closer to the mystery of love.

The Scorpio Man

The Smart Scoop

He might be the smartest man in the zodiac. Intuitive, aware, shrewd, and savvy, he has an uncanny ability to see through people and to read in between the lines. Complex, crafty, and very cunning, he operates on many levels simultaneously. While emotional, kind, and caring, he can also be cold and cut off. A cool, smooth, emotional conundrum, the Scorpio man has a searing mind and a forward-thinking imagination. Often achieving the best while imagining the worst, he approaches life like a warrior ready for action. Composed, calculating, observant, and cautious, he can outwit his opponents with one precise word.

The Scorpio man is about power, pure and simple. It is in his eyes. One laser-beam look, and his contender has lost the challenge. Such is the essence of Scorpio control. First in the fast-track of megawatt success, he remains cool under fire in corporate killer forays. Focused on winning with slow-burn intensity, his formidable mind disarms dragons and demons, and dethrones complacent kingpins.

With a steel-trap memory and endless emotional energy, so much goes on inside him that he needs to disconnect. Deep, sometimes dark, and ever alert to the worst that can happen, he controls his emotions like a mastermind. To some he may seem cold, to others, unnerving, while the few he lets close know he has fathoms of feeling. However, nothing ever shows on the surface of the Scorpio man except a scrutinizing stare and an enigmatic smile.

The Feeling Scope

He is the most emotionally enigmatic man in the zodiac. Complicated, contradictory, and most definitely mysterious, the Scorpio man's reputation precedes him in a crowded room.

He has a sexual magnetism that makes women tremble. And like his power, it centers in his eyes. Intense, penetrating, and provocative, they gleam with passionate potential. Passion, like power, is his *raison d'etre*. It races endorphins to his brain and keeps the blood flowing to his heart.

Everything he does of import is fueled with the energy of passion. His megawatt emotional energy could light up the entire state of California—with lots left over. Add to that bottomless, churning emotional depths, and you have a person who has need for his legendary emotional control. There is so much swirling around inside him that he needs to compartmentalize. If he is pure Scorpio, there are more facets to his personality than are mathematically possible. However, the best kept secret is that under all the sexual magnetism and steely control is a raw core of vulnerability that needs its quota of protection. Private, aloof, and heavily defended, he is not a man easy to know or to love—until he decides to open up, value love, and let down the barriers.

Trust is a towering issue with this man who suffers from bone-deep fears of rejection, abandonment, and betrayal. The second that he surrenders emotionally to a woman, he also imagines the worst. Hence, the legendary Scorpionic jealousy, suspicion, and cunning mind games. For many Scorpio men the fear can be too great to deeply love and so they go through a lifetime cut off. However, those who do give in to those hissing demons in the primordial depths know that their emotions can make them madmen.

Despite their reputation as loners, Scorpio men don't like to live alone, so they marry for security and stability. A secure living situation provides a comfort zone as well as distractions from their consuming depths, while too much time alone makes them moody.

As the sign of sex, death, and transformation, Scorpios are prone to deep ruminations that are profound, unutterable, and often fearful. The mind of the Scorpio man can make the most simple situations complex, as he takes nothing at face value and looks for hidden meanings.

When passionately in love the Scorpio man is possessed and obsessed, his mind can become so overrun with thought that he often loses his power to it. When passionately in love, his control crumbles and he starts to both come alive and to die a little. To be so carried away is to be vulnerable to loss, and this prospect can be so crazy-making that it can make him feel like he is dying. This man is a myriad of contradictions. However, one thing holds true: opening up to deep feeling is as difficult as trusting. In truth, once the door to his depths is sprung by passion, desire, and need, his fear demons also pop out.

This man, so often feared and criticized for having no feeling, is largely misunderstood. Just as one can't envision all the creepy creatures crawling on the bottom of the ocean floor, one cannot begin to imagine what can go on in the Scorpio man's depths. Love, hate, lust, fear, need, rage, sadness, and raw vulnerability are all stuffed into deep, dark places while he sits up straight, cool, and inscrutable, ready for action in a competitive world.

Fatal Attractions

He doesn't have to go looking. Women find him and follow him anywhere. The sexiest man in the zodiac, all he has to do is take advantage—and he certainly isn't dull in that department. The classic Scorpio man mesmerizes with one long look. His magnetism is so strong that it isn't fair for the rest of the male population.

The Scorpio man thrills to the prospect of passionate encounters. However, he is not one to chase a woman down. His style is to coolly circle around and send out signals. In record time, she comes willingly to the seduction.

When the Scorpio man is in love, he can be deeply, emotionally passionate. But if he is only acting out a momentary escapade, he can leave behind a chill that can penetrate bone. A man of both fire and ice, his is an all-or-nothing person. Therefore, when he lacks respect for someone, he can be cold, cruel, and cutting with that person.

It is easy to wonder how a man who seemed so hot can turn so glacial. The Scorpio man can turn his feelings on and off like a water faucet. The determining factor to his emotional barometer is his level of emotional involvement.

Scorpio men resonate to challenge. That does not mean cat and mouse games of hard-to-get, but rather a galvanizing attraction with a woman who radiates her own sense of power. He comes alive to the sort of intelligent personality and sex appeal that speaks of taking him somewhere exciting. His most fatal attraction is a sexy woman as deep as he is, with whom he can talk for hours without even realizing that he's talking.

Foolish Choices

A secret of the Scorpio man is that he knows he has a soul. He may not know what to do with it, but he can feel it as it interferes with his rational functioning. It raises its claim in a plethora of ways, through moods, fears, funks, and an underlying sensitivity that can occasionally overwhelm him. Because this inner sanctum can be so severely threatening, he tries to snuff it with drive, discipline, goals, and lots of self-control.

A classic Scorpio control is minimal disclosure. The Scorpio man holds everything inside and will rarely express his deeper feelings. As a result, he often suffers a deep, inner loneliness that is like a carefully concealed wound.

The average wife of a Scorpio man usually has no idea of what is going on inside him. A complete emotional introvert, he will conceal his fears and communicate only on a superficial level. When deadness starts to define the marriage and boredom overtakes him, his classic solution is a sideline affair. However, this recreation is never a panacea for the spiritual emptiness that starts to haunt him. The more that he cuts off from what his own soul is trying to tell him, the more he shuts down on his life.

Meaning is a profound need of this sign, and the more conscious he is, the more he requires it. This is a man who can be both enlarged and empowered by deeply meaningful, emotionally intimate love. However, to attain it he must first come to terms with the truth of his negative choices. The foolish choice of a superficial and secure rather than soulful union will only leave him lonely in the long run. Since Scorpio is the deepest sign of the zodiac, the sign of sex, death, and transformation, a special power of this sign is spiritual power and rebirth. When he chooses to honor the wisdom of his soul instead of steely control, the entire course of his existence can be transformed from the profane to the sacred. He can then leave his foolish choices behind him and lead a life enlightened by his higher power.

Fated Lessons

Although the Scorpio man's secretive nature often sabotages the closeness that could bring him an emotionally intimate connection, it is not an easy thing for him to open up. He has compartmentalized and concealed parts of his life for so long, it seems only natural to continue. What he doesn't realize is how intensely he is sabotaging himself and pushing away a woman he may really want to be close to.

When he has lived his entire life according to such strict, inner controls that, at a certain point, have become unconscious, the walls don't crumble overnight. However, the relationship affected by it may. His fated lesson is that he can bring about the abandonment he fears most when he refuses to grow beyond his old, self-defeating defense mechanisms.

When the Scorpion is completely trapped, it will sting itself to death. Likewise, when Scorpio men create their own emotional traps, a part of their life dies to them. When his choices bring death to the spirit of his relationship, he suffers grim lessons of depression and loneliness. Some Scorpio men resort to alcohol to escape their traps. Others become workaholics or turn to empty affairs. However, the only effective way out of the trap is for him to fully face himself and be prepared to do what it takes to change.

Unlike some signs who can breeze through life and bounce quickly back from bad times, Scorpio suffering runs deep. Because he never forgets, pain lingers like a curse and can haunt him until he understands its truth and meaning. For a sign of such stunning awareness, it is ironic that the Scorpio man tends to not get what the universe keeps telling him. He often replays the same tape in the second marriage that made the first die a slow death. Until he bottoms out hard on his own behavior so that nothing is left but burning motivation for growth, his fated lesson will bring him back to the same places with only a change of partner.

Getting Smart in Affairs of the Heart

The Scorpio man needs love probably more than any other sign. Many are not conscious of this because they have made power such a priority. However, the fact remains that love is the greatest challenge of their lifetime.

A Scorpio man can run a corporation with his eyes closed or build an empire single-handedly, but loving successfully remains a far more elusive matter. There are men of many signs who can live superficially and never crave deeper meaning. However, the Scorpio man who does slow down knows that he needs a higher love that lights up his life and affirms the possibility of his soul.

Getting smart means that instead of stuffing down his feelings and making emotional choices motivated only by security, he has to start living consciously through his total being. He has to go deep down into himself instead of running away from himself, and in the process connect with his heart. The Scorpio man needs a soul mate, not a cell mate, to live and love to his true potential. That means so much more than choosing some person with whom to have sex, children, and a yearly vacation. It means choosing a partner who can be a best friend and share his depths, fears, frailties, and spiritual feelings. Ideally, that person would be wise when he would be dark, inspiring when he would be uncertain, and always understanding of the nuances of his inner world. Likewise, he would open up instead of cutting off, and let someone in instead of compartmentalizing. In the process he would learn the joy of letting go and talking out his troublesome feelings, gaining a sense that with every deep sharing and sacred moment that he is going somewhere deeper in spirit.

I remember a rich and powerful Scorpio man I once met who was newly married. I asked him why he chose to marry his wife and he replied that he had to travel a great deal for work, and while he was away his first two wives had been unfaithful. He said that he needed a wife that he could trust, and had felt when he met his present wife that she was reasonably attractive and intelligent but not someone who would threaten his security.

The decision for a marriage based on a "secure home base" instead of a soul-based love has its predictable soulless consequences. Over time, this connection becomes a functional unit with two people passing in the kitchen. Because most adult Scorpio men do, at some point, look at life in terms of meaning, a merely material existence will never ultimately suffice and in the long run will emotionally under-mine them.

The Scorpio man must develop a relationship with his own soul before he can have a sacred relationship with a woman. He needs to hear his soul, heed his soul, feed his soul, and honor his soul as the sacred part of him that holds the real power. In-depth astrological analysis, meditation, contemplation, Jungian psychoanalysis, prayer, and shamanic soul journeys—in which a guide leads him into the deepest parts of his psyche—are the most obvious ways to begin to forge this inner relationship. He then can bring this wise, growing consciousness to his outer relationships, illuminating them. If, in time, he comes to understand that that relationship is no longer meant to be, he will make a different choice for the next relationship based on the life of his spirit.

Finally, he must realize that everything is a matter of choice. When we are fear-based we think we don't have expansive choices, like the controlling Scorpio man on his "reasonably secure" third marriage. The controlling Scorpio man needs so much control because he is so fear-based. However, the fact remains that whatever he chooses from fear becomes a dead area. Relationships based on fear swiftly deaden, trapping the partners in their own creation The only way out of such potential traps is through conscious, courageous, creative choice.

I know a powerful Scorpio man who has done his time with fear, control, compartmentalization, and success-obsessed drivenness, and who now prays, uses affirmations, and contemplates issues in higher ways. He recently told me with pride that he sees the necessity of work-ing on the inner, not the outer, because if you work hard enough on the inner, the outer will take care of itself. He knows that this is his ticket to true power, wherever that takes him.

Scorpio is the sign of transformation, and what Scorpios are aware of, they have the power to transform. But it is all fueled by choice. Hopefully, one day the controlling Scorpio man will wake up, get really smart, and make his most important choice—courageously going where his wise old soul wants to take him.

10. SAGITTARIUS

NOVEMBER 23 TO DECEMBER 21

Ruling Planet: Jupiter
Element: Fire
Cosmic Quality: Mutable
Essential Quality: Masculine, positive
Planetary Principle: Expansion
Primal Desire: Liberty
Material Factor: Growth

The Sagittarius Woman

The Smart Scoop

She bubbles over with *joie de vivre* and a restless need for excitement. The Sagittarius woman wants to live life to the fullest, and she does. She is expansive, adventurous, impulsive, and impatient. She loves to travel on all levels—physical, emotional, and spiritual. A free spirit, (she wants to feel the wind in her face with the joys of the unknown coming to claim her). To her mind, life is an endless series of adventures, explorations, and never-ending possibilities. The Sagittarius woman needs change, variety, and constant stimulation to keep her from feeling bored. She has a short attention span that quickly takes in so many people and things that she can sometimes spread herself too thin. Yet it is all a part of the magic of living life. She has her visions and her rhythms and she can't slow down.

Independent and forever flying around with her head in the sky, she is a law unto herself and woe to the one who tries to constrain her. The Sagittarius woman has a fear of feeling restrained by anyone or anything. Likewise, she respects others' freedom. Not romantic in the traditional sense, she rebels against stereotypes and rigid thinking. She does what she does only because she wants to do it. When others' expectations don't gel with her course of action, she can quickly take flight.

The Sagittarius woman is an idealist who thinks big and wants the best because she believes she deserves it. No shy violet about voicing her thoughts, she is quick to assert her rights about her way of doing things. At times a trifle harsh in her handling of people, she compensates with her generous spirit and superb sense of humor. The Sagittarius woman loves to laugh, just as she expects to be happy. Positive, optimistic, and defined by powerful thinking, she makes her own luck and never lets a rainy day get in her way.

The Feeling Scope

As Sagittarius is a mutable sign, she is changeable, adaptable, and sometimes unpredictable. Except when it comes to her great love of animals, the Sagittarius woman is detached and removed. She moves fast in many directions simultaneously, but doesn't go very deep with anything in particular. Midstream, her interest usually wanes and she becomes attracted to another person, place, or pursuit. Friendly to everyone but impersonal to most, she can be quite difficult to really get close to.

A social queen with far more acquaintances than friends, unless she has strong Scorpio influences she doesn't seek the intensity upon which other women depend. The Sagittarius woman is far more interested in having fun than in fretting over failures or the future. More flighty than faithful and committed, she is also more mental than emotional and can cut off from close ties with ease.

Fatal Attractions

Men who are notable, brilliant, or highly accomplished are first to fascinate her. Wanting to be or at least be seen with someone "in the know" is as exciting to her mind as actually accomplishing something. The Sagittarius woman has a need to feel she stands out from the masses, whether that means being judged terribly trendy or terribly brainy, or being with someone who is.

Extravagant, and needing to feel free to spend lavishly whenever she likes it, she often gravitates toward wealthy men who feel grateful to indulge her. When the Sagittarius woman turns on her light and uses her guile, she can charm an intelligent man into a state of stupidity. And she often does.

Yet such attractions often prove fatal down the road. There is always a price to be paid for all those trips and gifts, and usually that price is her freedom. When she feels confined or compromised the Sagittarius woman runs cold. She can cut out without a backward glance and doesn't even smell the trail of blood behind her. If she did, she wouldn't care. She'd just let someone else clean it up.

Foolish Choices

The Sagittarius woman can be just as capricious in her choices as she is flighty in her commitments. She may choose a man for purely self-serving reasons and then, when he gets boring, drop him without a good-bye. Her out-in-the-cold man may feel crazy at the thought of this charming woman who went through him like the wind. However, while he is shaking and shuddering, she has moved on to her next seduction.

The Sagittarius woman tends to fly though life, riding high on her dreams only to change her mind midstream. Caught up in the whirl of her most wonderful visions, she is impervious to any pain she is creating. What is worse is she doesn't care.

The lower Sagittarius woman is cold, cut off, and uses her connections for self-serving purposes. Easily bored and very impersonal, she travels through life with a forward-thinking attitude that caters to the goal of instant gratification. Her choices are about freedom, fun, and finding a quick way out when things get too overpowering.

Fated Lessons

Responsibility is her dirty word, but its lessons still follow her. The Sagittarius woman's greatest lesson is to learn that there is great freedom and power in the ability to take responsibility.

Her problem is that she never sees any problems, only people who annoy her. The sign of the Archer, she is forever moving ahead to a future world where everything will be better because it will be completely of her own choosing.

Lessons are what she thinks she gets from books. They empower her to think she is smarter and superior. Her fated, real life lesson is to realize that she is the creator of her life and her destiny and that the cruelties she has created will circle back on her. She can choose to either feel or forget to see or ignore the pattern in her life of people she has hurt, dropped, or ignored. Whatever she does, the choice is hers as well as the lesson.

Getting Smart in Affairs of the Heart

There is no doubt about it. The Sagittarius woman is both smart and invincible. However, she is not invulnerable. At a certain point, her past will catch up with her. There are many Sagittarius women who are serious about their lives and their commitments. However, there is a classic Sagittarian personality that is so impersonal that there is no conception of authentically connecting.

This woman can be so out of touch with deeper feeling that she is deafened to the sound of sobs. Many marriages and friendships later, she still does not comprehend her contribution to the end. Smiles that last for miles pave only the way for further forays.

To get smart in affairs of the heart, she has to do inventory on herself, starting with dropping that self-righteousness and asking many probing questions about her past. The classic Sagittarian approach is to slough off every broken relationship because it either bored or annoyed her, and to never see that a relationship is about two people who have choices. She also has to spend some time meditating on the feelings of other people, as opposed to only the dreams of her future endeavors. Finally, she has to realize that she has to go deeper—for herself; that she has to take responsibility—for herself; that she has to develop compassion—for herself. And that as truly wonderful as books, courses, and travel can be, there is so much more that her own heart can tell her. To want to move through her heart in all experience and see how well that serves her, is to become far more than smart. It is to become truly wise. And it is her choice.

The Sagittarius Man

The Smart Scoop

The Sagittarius man is often brilliant or simply very, very smart. A mental explorer who is interested in a little bit of everything, he is on a perpetual quest to understand how the world works and why he's here. The Sagittarius man gets caught up in his "things"; whatever they are—studying philosophies, ecology involvements, writing projects, mountain climbing, treks to totally untraveled terrain—he is always busy. His mind is like a vast warehouse of all kinds of information that he has been collecting since he was a kid. The Sagittarius man loves to learn because of where it might take him mentally. Life to him is an endless adventure that challenges him to learn more and more.

Sometimes he seems to be going in several directions simultaneously. Restless and freedom-loving, he is also impulsive and completely enthusiastic about each new involvement that consumes him.

However, when it comes to love, he is hard to tie down and usually has one foot out the door, headed in another direction. The Sagittarius man hates to feel confined, so commitment does not come quickly. He tends to treat love like a sport and often doesn't look beyond the moment. However, his ebullient personality, stellar sense of humor, and strong sense of self make him sought after by a bevy of females. Often he doesn't even know what to do with the attention—until someone comes along who is like a best friend and playmate rolled into one.

The Feeling Scope

He tends to be detached and lost in a world of thought and speculation. The Sagittarius man is self-involved and very much the center of his universe. Emotionally unconscious, and covetous of his time, he can easily do without a relationship—unless it fits into his unique framework.

Friendly with a plethora of people, he is casual and noncommittal, attached more to his interests than to any one person, and constantly afraid of feeling confined. Often late, seriously absent-minded, and sometimes a "no show," he is certainly not a romantic individual. Nor does he encourage such expectations being thrust in his direction.

Nevertheless, for those who value their own freedom, love to laugh, and favor a casual, friendly approach, he can be winsome and a lot of fun. For the right person he can also become an exciting companion, provided he remembers to show up.

Fatal Attractions

Attractions seldom consume him, and because he is so open, he may have more than many. However, because he is also so self-involved, he can get so caught up in his projects that he is attracted by no one.

The Sagittarius man likes independent women with lots of pizzazz who also love to do their own thing and would never think of tying him down. The more unusual, the better, and the more of a challenge, the more he is intrigued. Because he hates the feeling of being caged, he needs someone self-confident who is consumed by her own world; ideally a world that offers adventure, travel, intrigue, and new horizons.

The Sagittarius man gets on best with a best friend who is a mirror reflection of himself. However, that still does not mean that he will be sensitive or always faithful. To turn his back on a fleeting fun adventure would be, to his mind, a serious compromise. His footloose-and-fancy-free style is like a fanatical religion.

Foolish Choices

The Sagittarius man's self-serving ways can seriously work against him. Insensitive and deeply self-involved, he can undermine what might otherwise be a wonderful relationship. His emotional myopia can make a woman feel so left out in the cold that she eventually leaves him. In general, he needs a great deal of talking to to get his total attention. Will that turn him into a more sensitive, accommodating man? It's not very likely. His game plan does not include giving in. Life, to him, is a fascinating adventure and it must be lived on his own terms.

Additional foolish choices include stand-up routines, chronic lateness (as in days), and infidelity. Of course, he doesn't see infidelity as infidelity because he is being true to himself and the moment. And certainly, if his woman wants to do the same, he will be the first to remind her that she is completely free.

Fated Lessons

This is not a sign that learns emotional lessons readily. The Sagittarius man's lessons come from books, stimulating courses, fascinating travels, and perhaps a monastery sojourn. The keyword to the Sagittarius man is "getaway," whether that be mental, emotional, or experiential.

He cannot be told what to do. Even a polite suggestion would most likely go unheard. Therefore, he is about as easy to wrestle as an anaconda. If a woman cries, he'll laugh; if she threatens to leave, he'll wish her the best; if she screams, he'll walk out the door and never look back. Because basically his credo is "Take me or leave me but just don't bug me," asking forgiveness is just not his thing. Not at all romantic, he doesn't get the little gestures and nuances that go into any great love. Nor does he want to. The Sagittarius man's lessons are all around him. Does he get them? No. He's getting on a plane to go to some godforsaken distant land—all alone.

Getting Smart in Affairs of the Heart

Should the Sagittarius man grow up, he has great potential for an exciting relationship. However, he is a playmate, not a committed, stay-at-home soul mate. Women who want grand romantic gestures or constant emotional reassurance should best stay away. On the other hand, women who are as restless and adventurous as he is could do well with this man who is more like a friend than a lover.

To successfully maintain a love connection, he needs to be able to think beyond himself and actually want to accommodate the other person. Developing some emotional sensitivity is key for this man who is so committed to the life of the mind and the great unknown. This is more difficult than it could ever seem, for when he feels cornered by expectations, he can get quite cold, selfish, and perverse. His first love will always be his freedom, and if that feels threatened in any way, he grows wings and takes flight. At this point, his primal instincts are beeping self-protection and he is heeding only their call.

In marriage, the Sagittarius man will not compromise his comings and goings for the greater good of the relationship. As with the Sagittarius woman, it has to be "my way or the highway." Even in love, he has so much more on his mind than the marriage and has a very short fuse for listening to the fact that his behavior is selfish and inconsiderate. However, he can be funny, fun, entertaining, stimulating, and a wonderful travel companion who thinks up the most exciting trips. He can also be wildly generous and an impulsive gift giver of little luxuries. However, will he remember Valentine's Day and an anniversary or birthday? Probably not.

The Sagittarius man likes to take life as he finds it and there is only so far that he can be persuaded otherwise. However, he would be very smart to try to cross over the line in the sensitivity department and realize that there are things called feelings and other people have them. It is so hard for this man to get smart in affairs of the heart for two reasons. First he doesn't value his heart, only his brain. Second, he already thinks that he is as smart as anyone could be. Beyond that, life is about making the most of each new opportunity that pops up. And if they're not popping up fast enough, he's sure to create them.

11. CAPRICORN
DECEMBER 22 TO JANUARY 20

Ruling Planet: Saturn
Element: Earth
Cosmic Quality: Cardinal
Essential Quality: Feminine, negative
Planetary Principle: Manifestation
Primal Desire: Attainment
Material Factor: Materialization

The Capricorn Woman

The Smart Scoop

Serious, successful, and old at a very young age, the Capricorn woman is a born executive who could be chairman of the board or a partner in the biggest law firm. Ambitious, efficient, highly organized, and perfectionistic, she is impeccable in business and her business is to shine. The Capricorn woman is a classic superachiever who can be an overpowering masculine force in the boardroom, yet an utterly feminine and erotic feline in the bedroom.

A dynamic initiator and a born leader, she drives herself hard and with formidable force, focusing on her goals with tireless tenacity.

Determined to make it to the top since she was about ten, she stands out from her peers as a woman prepared to go the distance. The Capricorn woman knows how to make her mark in the world with nothing to back her up but her brain. Cool, confident, efficient, and hardworking, she will do whatever she has to do to get ahead—and then some.

The Capricorn woman glamorizes success. It has been in her bones since she was a baby. And she builds her empire brick by brick, always looking ahead at the big picture while at the same time leaving no stone unturned in taking account of all the petty details. Her bottom-line business attitude combined with her fast-track mind make her a star in a sea of ruthless competitors. Focused on the top and grounded in the complexities of the material, she moves to her own beat, always striving to do her best, ever becoming the authority figure she was meant to become.

The Feeling Scope

Cool, confident, controlling, and very poised, the Capricorn woman is a very different person deep underneath. Emotionally insecure and needing love as much as her opposite sign, Cancer, she can't be happy without a deep, intimate, committed relationship that mirrors her ideal self. Highly self-critical and deeply self-conscious, in her most intimate personal domain she can be a moody little girl needing love. Status-oriented and strongly fashion-conscious, she puts on a face to the world that is a mask of invulnerability. Yet the material realm is but one part of the picture of the Capricorn woman. She also has a dark side which takes the form of depression, melancholy, and deep inner loneliness. That is why a Capricorn woman must always keep busy. She is keeping the demons of fear at bay, and should she slow down too much, she could go into a slump that could cost her that cool and invincible facade.

Many Capricorn females are self-made women, highly ambitious and very smart from the start, but departing from a past of darkness that could still come to haunt them. Born under the planet of Saturn, the planet of darkness, constriction, and melancholy, she has a lot of life challenges to face before getting to the light. The early years are often very painful, but as she gets older and comes into her own as an accomplished, self-possessed, and independent woman, life lightens up and she increasingly feels her own power. As she progresses, accumulating society's rewards for being the poster girl for success, life seems to shed its light in her direction—until the day comes when she is again dark and depressed because nothing is enough. The Capricorn woman needs to be in love.

There are signs who are marvelously happy to flit about. The Capricorn woman isn't one of them. She couldn't flit if she tried. She is one sign who needs a committed partnership to feel complete. Living solo, she is prone to Saturnian bouts of melancholy that can make her question her entire life, where she is going, what she is doing, and whether, in the long run, it is all worth it.

Fatal Attractions

She is invincibly attracted to accomplished men who mirror her own level of self-realization. The Capricorn woman worships accomplishment. And it can make her blind to other critical qualities that may be missing.

The sense of a destined meeting of minds, or the experience of encountering a man whom she can feel extremely proud of is her version of the gates of romantic heaven clanking open. The man in her life must reflect her own enterprising spirit. This is all part of the seriousness with which she imbues her life plan. Even in romance she is ambitious to the end. However, it is this confusion of the inner needs with the outer goals that can precisely get her into trouble.

Foolish Choices

When the Capricorn woman fancies that her heart has been captured, the steel goes into meltdown and perfume fills the air. At this point she is like a nervous teenager in love. Such a transformation is something to behold. One woman I know who can be quite a terror in the business world took to, behind closed doors, doing her boyfriend's laundry. Of course, this information was top secret, only to be divulged on pain of death; nevertheless, she did indeed turn into a little accommodating crocus. Another top-notch trial attorney, who found her relationship failing, went into such a decline that she couldn't get out of bed. Love is extremely important to the Capricorn woman, so important that once she feels she has been touched by it, something in her will never be the same.

When she feels she is in love, she will extend her boundaries to do a lot of things that she would never consider doing otherwise—and, at times, can look quite foolish. What she will give and the degree to which she is willing to accommodate take her beyond herself. And that is quite an interesting concept. In taking on adulthood, first the Capricorn woman has to find herself. Then, in falling in love, she loses herself and finds a new kind of consciousness that takes her beyond her controlling ego.

These infatuations seldom last. However, they do have their value as learning experiences. They make her realize that there is a life beyond material achievement that bears experiencing. Even if it doesn't work out, and along its course she does foolish things to allay her insecurities and ensure love, hopefully she will come away with the sensibility that love is a value that bests material ambition.

Fated Lessons

Her greatest life lesson is self-love, despite the trappings of her achievements and passing feedback from boyfriends. Despite their outer facade, so many Capricorn women struggle with their self-worth and measure it in material and corporeal terms. Left to her own devices, she doesn't want to deal with deeper emotions. She simply wants to set her life up according to her highest superficial goals, and work to achieve the goods.

Rigidly self-critical regarding her physical aspects, the Capricorn woman keeps plastic surgeons in sports cars and private fitness trainers in fancy condos. Everything has to be perfect—or else someone might find out! What? That she's not perfect. And what does that mean? One glaring fact: that she's not lovable after all.

When involved in a relationship *that* is the terror of her insecurity—a secret she shares only with the mirror. She is so hard on herself, yet soft on the men with whom she falls in love. Because she has such a highly developed fear factor, she is overly alert to rejection signals. And since her pride is so strong, the fear sometimes turns to rage and she acts out, bringing on what she fears most.

As she gets older, she faces the challenge of treating herself as a self-affirmed individual as opposed to a carbon copy of society's most superficial values. The more that she does this, the less she is operating from a facade or a defense and the more she is beginning to operate from an authentic place that permits her to feel all kinds of positive emotions she was never capable of before. Therein she has come to encounter the power of her own light.

Getting Smart in Affairs of the Heart

When something starts to change deep inside the Capricorn woman and she begins to be conscious of a part of her that really needs and is capable of a high quality relationship, as opposed to some connection with some high profile boyfriend, she will magically attract a situation of real closeness, trust, and intimacy. However, this sort of love takes on a level of maturity that she couldn't conceive of before. Through this deeper, richer kind of love the Capricorn woman allows herself to be nourished for the first time. She is no longer the one who is waiting, giving, running, and scrambling frenetically to hold everything together. Now two people are sharing a trust and meeting halfway and this trust comes straight from the heart.

The Capricorn Man

The Smart Scoop

He is the megawatt success sign of the zodiac. The apogee of ambition, the Capricorn man is a climber born to make it to the top—and own it. Conservative, driven, hardworking, and obsessed with material security, his goal is to amass a fortune—or to get as close to it as possible.

A workaholic who probably had his first job at five, he was born believing that life is about a high profit margin and all projects should lead to substantial material reward. Money and status are so important to the Capricorn man that he can't imagine how people can live without them. Disciplined and tenacious, and terribly judgmental of anyone who isn't, he can achieve any goal he sets his mind on and won't allow temporary failure to faze him. (Keep in mind that Nixon was a Capricorn.) The Capricorn man keeps going forward, no matter what, and treats each setback as a challenge leading him to his final reward.

His singleminded pursuit of his goals is so powerful that in comparison other successful men fall by the wayside. The Capricorn man can outdistance the best. He can also outwait the opposition. He doesn't need to look like a flashy front-runner. Rather, his thing is to own the whole show. With the makings of a tycoon by the age of ten, he stood out as invincible. His bank account was set, his vision perfected, and his ducks all in a row. His only problem was he had to wait to grow up.

Since then, he can't get enough material reward. And, of course, he wants all the high-status toys that go with it. The Capricorn man thinks that other people care terribly about the kind of car he drives. Deeply insecure, he defines his self-esteem by such things as his gold Ferrari and his art collection. Controlled by the kind of role he plays to the world and how the world grovels back to him, he needs to fly high to feel great. Gravely serious about his self-image, he can never relax, even in his sleep. At all times, there is too much ahead of him and he has to keep up with himself.

The Feeling Scope

He can be cold and conniving, self-centered and insensitive. The Capricorn man relates to things like Swiss bank accounts, not people. When it comes to people he needs to be in full control. Power-oriented and always playing the boss, he is detached and determined to have his way at all costs. However, the cost is never to him, since he doesn't see the effects of the situations he sets up. Pulling all the strings, he puts everyone in their place and then proclaims the rules. The Capricorn man compartmentalizes full-time. Highly organized, he is like an efficiency expert even in the most intimate of settings. Both bossy and blatant, he tells; he doesn't ask. He is just too busy to listen.

Conventional and security-conscious, he always marries because he needs a wife. However, this move could be more of a practical matter than anything to do with love. The Capricorn man doesn't understand love and he doesn't need to. He understands money and what it will buy, and knows that this understanding is to his advantage. So, in a sense, he buys a wife who wants to be bought and who will play by the rules: that he is boss. Chauvinistic and emotionally myopic, the Capricorn man cannot deal with an independent woman. She needs to need him financially, comport herself properly, do her social and domestic duty, and be at his constant disposal.

Because he is highly sexual—not passionate or sensual, but sexual— a wife serves another practical function. He gets his needs met. The Capricorn man is highly pragmatic and it has always served him well. He runs everything like it's a business, and no one can really blame him because there are usually no complaints—only more cars in the driveway.

Fatal Attractions

Cautious, calculating, shrewd, and self-centered, the Capricorn man doesn't have fatal attractions. He has attractions and then stands back, tests them out, observes a while, and then decides whether they will work for his life. A self-made man from childhood, he has always made the decisions about his life. And all decisions have to work out according to a set plan. A fatal attraction is far too spontaneous for this man, who has never had an impulsive moment in his life.

A fatal attraction for him means that this is a woman who is marriage material and who must be carefully considered as if she were applying for a high-level security job. For starters, she must be highly attractive, well presented, socially acceptable, and must always compliment him with great enthusiasm. She must also know how to dress for success, give great dinner parties, and be able to impress his business associates to such a degree that he is envied. Finally, she cannot have any serious ambitions of her own that would interfere with his timing or expectations. For all this she will be materially compensated very well. However, she must also jump to his beat and be prepared to do his every bidding promptly.

Foolish Choices

The Capricorn man is a control freak who cannot see that his emotional choices could have far-reaching effects. An emotionally unconscious and egotistical individual who looks at life from the perspective of the gratification of his desires, he does not take feelings into account. His only consideration is getting what he wants—the sooner, the better. Treating his relationship with the same detachment as he would a staff meeting, he sets up a system where everyone knows their place and everyone knows their place is to serve him. For a woman who falls into this situation, the effect can become dehumanizing and even degrading, and one day she may wake up or be awakened by another man who treats her like a female instead of highly paid hired help.

The Capricorn man, being a tried-and-true chauvinist, has a very low tolerance for feminine energy where feelings need positive feedback. His is a masculine, competitive world predicated on cause and effect, profit and loss, and cost-benefit ratios. Essentially, the Capricorn man is all about business, and brings that with him through door the moment he arrives. Detached, preoccupied, overworked, and exhausted, yet still focused on the business of the day, he has no real energy for the life of the relationship. For all he cares it can wilt.

When years have passed and the marriage has wilted for so long it has collapsed, the Capricorn man may look elsewhere for sexual gratification. At this point, he is susceptible to his secretary, nurse, assistant, or receptionist who is younger, has long legs, and makes herself very available. The wife by this time is bitter. There's a divorce. A new wife. And no more consciousness on his part the second time around.

Fated Lessons

Because Capricorn men are emotionally clueless, they don't comprehend that there ever *is* a lesson. One such man, an extremely wealthy doctor, went through two wives in three years. Another, a multimillionaire, lost his girlfriend to another man. Neither understood how their plight could have arisen. Although the Capricorn man can be deeply insecure, when he makes enough money he feels completely invulnerable. That is because he equates his financial security with emotional security, and can never see the telling signs to the contrary coming straight at him.

For the Capricorn man, the fated lesson is about loving. It is not that he is incapable of loving. It is that he completely confuses the emotional with the material. His way of expressing love is through money. Moving from the bank account to the heart is so difficult for the Capricorn man that he just can't get it. His pattern has always worked so well in the past that he has become walled up in it, and those walls have come to define him. Because he doesn't get that there are walls and that they are closing in around him, his lessons usually hit him over the head. One such Capricorn man had a complete nervous breakdown. After he recovered, he still didn't understand how he got where he got—and so, sad and alone, he did what he always did. He just kept going.

Getting Smart in Affairs of the Heart

The Capricorn man's plight is a clear example of the old cliche that money isn't everything. However, don't ever tell that to a Capricorn man who is wealthy and winning. Wealthy or not, the control issues and lack of consciousness that the Capricorn man brings to his connections deadens them.

Because he doesn't take kindly to any kind of emotional communication, let alone constructive criticism, it is not easy to get through to this man. The Capricorn man is condescending, stubborn, and completely unaware. Nevertheless, for him to get smart he has to wake up and become conscious. How does that happen? It begins with his will. He has to care enough about his relationship that he is willing to listen. He has to care enough about his relationship that he is willing to put his business to the side to communicate about the relationship. He has to care enough about the relationship that he is willing to let down the wall and open up his deeper feelings. For that to happen, he first has to value his connection as much as his bank account.

Getting smart in affairs of the heart fundamentally means he presents to the relationship his heart, not merely his armor. He brings a person to the relationship, not merely a body that is so exhausted it falls asleep. And finally, he understands that a relationship is about a feeling exchange, not a material transaction. And that feeling exchange can make a great positive difference in his world. The smartest attitude of all is that he realizes that he really values that feeling exchange, and that he has a new ambition: to give it his conscious attention and gratitude.

12. AQUARIUS
JANUARY 21 TO FEBRUARY 19

Ruling Planet: Uranus
Element: Air
Cosmic Quality: Fixed
Essential Quality: Masculine, positive
Planetary Principle: Truth
Primal Desire: Knowledge
Material Factor: The Quest

The Aquarius Woman

The Smart Scoop

Quite often brilliant and ahead of her time, the Aquarius woman is an individual who thinks for herself and marches to the beat of her own drummer. A unique blend of mind and heart, she is a crusader for the underdog and a champion for the underprivileged. Independent, very aware, and highly conscious in her thinking, she is an idealist who does both big and little things to make this a better world.

A people person with a plethora of friends, she is loyal to the end and a rescuer even when it's most inconvenient. As a friend in need, she is incapable of the word "no" yet never expects a return favor. Caring, committed, and ever faithful to a friend or a cause, she is both dependable and reliable, honest and kind. True to the values she espouses, she often takes on more than her share and is the first to offer her time regardless of how she is compromised. With her high-minded ideals and altruistic attitudes, she sails high above the heads of many of her sisters. Ever alert to suffering and injustice in daily life, and ever desiring to make a bad situation better, she stands out as the most evolved of the three air signs. Her values go far beyond her own self-interest, and actively extend to the world around her. Sometimes accused of being cold and detached, she is actually detached from herself, just as she is distanced from selfish desires.

In love, she is a best friend who can play many roles while never sacrificing her identity. Unlike so many signs, she doesn't delude herself about aspects of her love, but looks at the partnership objectively. Because she is so independent and doesn't conform to stereotypes, she is free to simply be the person she feels like being in her relationship. As much as she may love her partner, she knows that in the end her happiness is dependent on her own choices.

The Feeling Scope

Cool by temperament and objective by nature, the Aquarius woman is often misunderstood. Because she doesn't wear her heart on her sleeve and is the last to do hand-wringing, crying, screaming, and breast-beating because of a broken heart, she can be considered cold. Actually, she is self-contained and may cry her eyes out to her pillow but is not about to share her emotion with the world. In the aftermath, she will analyze the situation objectively, and regardless of her bruised heart or ego, will manage to understand the entire situation in detail—even if it is most distasteful and going completely against her grain. Even if she would ideally love things to be different, she has the courage and the mindset to admit that they will never be.

If she is a typical Aquarius woman, she is uncomfortable with anger and tends to squelch it. However, she often has a calming effect on other people's violent emotions because she doesn't get personally involved.

In a relationship, she needs a lot of space and time to do her own thing. A little claustrophobic, she can't bear to be crowded and can be made deeply anxious by someone coming on too strong. Freedom-loving, and needing privacy and private alone time, she needs to feel that this part of her is respected.

When in love she wants a best friend, and she will be the same. Sensitive, caring, giving, and understanding, she gets joy out of sharing in an equal situation. The original liberated woman, she is free to be exactly who she feels like being, and she is usually a lot of things a lot of the time.

Fatal Attractions

For the Aquarius woman, attraction comes from the sense of connecting with a kindred spirit who is wonderful to talk to. Unless she is very young, the Aquarius woman tends to have fewer negative relationships than most other signs. And that is because she tends to look at the person instead of getting blinded by a fantasy that personifies some unconscious characteristic.

When young, and before her ego is fully formed, she can get caught up in some strong personality who browbeats her and lowers her self-esteem. Having little or no experience and a lot of openness, she can be diminished by some man who, through his strong confidence level, seems to have all the answers, even if he doesn't even know the right questions.

Later on in life, she often forms a meeting of the minds with someone who is a lover, pal, confidant, soul mate, and best friend. For the Aquarius woman, sexual attraction comes as a result of a deep rapport and high opinion of the other person. Add to that shared values and ideals, and therein is an Aquarian match that is as close to heaven as two people can get.

Foolish Choices

The Aquarius woman is always tempted to put herself last. And, of course, there are always those others who will gladly take advantage. Having a strong sense of justice for all, the Aquarius woman can forget her own needs and do too much in a given situation. At times, her boundaries can weaken and she can be walked on by selfish, heartless souls who are encapsulated in their self-serving schemes. Likewise, respecting someone's freedom who does not deserve it and who is, in turn, unfaithful, is another foolish choice that she could avoid with a little less idealism and a heavier dose of realism at the time.

Wanting to be all things to all people all of the time, the Aquarius woman sometimes suffers from seeing only the good because, basically, she wants to believe it. Discrimination is not her first impulse, and so she can make choices that undermine her best interests—if only for a time. It takes a great deal of life experience and sometimes a lot of hurt for her to realize that some seemingly "nice" men can do some very nasty things that are beyond her wildest imaginings. Trusting the wrong people can bring very painful lessons that break her heart. It is not that the Aquarius woman is naive. Rather, she is ever hopeful that she lives in a world where the people close to her are as trustworthy as she is. Sadly, that's not always the case. Yet her choice of coming from a guileless, open heart is perhaps less a foolish act than a purely unfortunate one.

Fated Lessons

The Aquarius woman's lessons usually come early in life, through a first marriage or some significant connection that has caused her to suffer markedly. Her fated lessons have to do with self and self-preservation. The sun is in its detriment in Aquarius, which indicates a weak ego and sense of self that must be strengthened through life experiences.

In the early years, she often devalues herself while at the same time putting a huge value on a significant other. With the arrival of children, there is a tendency to sacrifice for home and family to the exclusion of self, often resulting in the deeply alienating experience of being unappreciated and having a complete absence of positive feedback. Burying the hurt, anger, and resentment only pushes it down deeper until a point is finally reached where she must come to terms with the fact that she cannot go on as she has been, that she should not go on as she has been. Therein is the big breakthrough of her life.

Before the Aquarius woman can experience a man who truly values her, she must first come to a point where she starts to value herself, her soul, and what she may be as a person. In other words, she must learn what her opposite sign Leo was born knowing: the necessity of self-consciousness. So lost in others, she has to retrieve her spirit and lay claim to it. And when she does, she can be one powerful, wise woman. Such a process does not happen overnight. It is the course of her soul's sacred journey. This journey is intended to bring her further and further away from the fragment of self that she once was to greater wholeness, consciousness, and possibility. When she can experience the joy of giving without giving herself away, when she can value herself and her potential as she would another person, she has come a long way with her life lessons.

Getting Smart in Affairs of the Heart

The Aquarius woman must learn how to say no before the universe will say yes to her. That comes into being with developing a positive self-value that enables her to have boundaries that she faithfully maintains.

She can run amok when she values others to the exclusion of herself, and therefore gives in and puts up with situations that don't serve her well. Wanting to value everyone's freedom and personal priorities is a wonderful thing. However, she must consider whether this seriously interferes with her own priorities and personal happiness, because, if so, there will be consequences—sometimes even physical ones.

There is a wonderful Aquarius woman I know who, for years, played such a perfect role of wife and mother for her large family that

her husband jocularly called her a saint. She has also had many physical problems—including the removal of her gall bladder—all connected to repressed rage. As is so typical of the sign Aquarius, during
those years she had no idea that she was angry. It just seemed so natural to do what she had to do and forget about herself. Certainly, this
was easier than dredging up all her dark and dirty feelings. However,
her body forced her and still forces her to admit feelings that she
would simply rather not have.

For the Aquarius woman, getting smart in affairs of the heart means
listening to her own heart as it speaks its truth to her. If she listens
carefully, it will speak to her of the necessity of self-love. If she listens
often enough, she will hear it in the right moment and make the right
choice that could change the entire course of her life.

The Aquarius Man

The Smart Scoop

He's brainy, often brilliant, and can be a genius, eccentric, or lunatic.
Whatever he is, and perhaps it's a little bit of everything, the Aquarius man lives in his head.

Futuristic, theoretical, technical, and transpersonal, he is the thinking behind the throne. Independent, individualistic, and a fanatic
about liberty, he loves to speculate on progressive notions and engage
in intellectual debates. Curious and on a quest for truth wherever
he can find it, from high-end computer technology to what sounds
like science fiction, the mind of the Aquarius man can easily leave the
earth.

Mild-mannered and friendly to a lot of people, he goes his own way
and can be a kind of loner in perpetual motion. A law unto himself,
he likes to observe people but not get too close. Chafing at confinement and addicted to his freedom, he does best in relationships where
he can come and go according to his own needs and always feel the
wind right in his face.

Often ahead of his time, an inventor, creator, conveyor of visions beyond the normal range of the human mind, his ideals are pervasive in scope and often oriented toward human potential and positive social change. Broad in outlook and interested in everything from outer space to cyberspace, he loves space of every kind and could be an astronaut, airline pilot, or someone who jumps out of jets just because.

The Aquarius man lives in his mind and it serves him well. It often serves others well as well. Thomas Edison was an Aquarius, as was Abraham Lincoln. However, he needs a very special woman to appreciate that what little personal time he has tends to be taken up with causes—either real or imagined. For instance, when he has not said anything personal to his partner in weeks, he may be very concerned that we are not communicating properly with UFOs. The Aquarius man won't get too personal—unless it's for a quick five minutes and he's running out the door for a meeting with friends.

The Feeling Scope

He is mental, not emotional. Furthermore, he is completely uncomfortable with feelings, unless it's about something like saving the whales or how robots replacing manpower might hurt a lot of people.

The Aquarius man may talk about feelings theoretically. However, he hates emotional displays and wants everything emotional to be logical. Reason is his comfort zone. The more a situation strays into the realm of the irrational, the more he wants to flee—and probably will. Like all air signs, who have a cerebral approach to emotional problem solving, he can cut out in record time if matters become too emotionally compromising.

If cornered, he'll express himself in the cliches of a teenager, using stock phrases such as "You just want a commitment, blah, blah," forgetting that he once swore that this was the woman he was meant to be with for the rest of his life. The Aquarius man has a selective emotional memory. He hates to feel that his freedom could in any way be compromised; therefore, he will rigidly refuse to be accountable for anything compromising he might impulsively say.

Aquarius men don't do well with closeness. They are much more suited to impersonal conversations and passionless sex. Self-controlled, cerebral, and self-centered, they can be downright cold. Although he sees himself as the nicest guy in the zodiac, someone who will go over your contract, fix your computer, or help you move, he is the last person to have around if you happen to be crying. Feelings for the Aquarius man are like a case of the flu. They're not something he wants to be around. Better yet, he wants to believe that he is above and beyond them.

Fatal Attractions

The Aquarius man, who has his mind in the clouds, finds an attraction on the earth because he trips over it. However, even then, the woman has to be of a caliber all her own and no garden-variety human being. A woman who is brilliant, free-spirited, and eccentric, with a sense of mystery and the knack of making the most exhilarating conversation on the most outlandish subjects, is sure to get his attention—and even keep it. At all times, she must impart the impression that she is so completely consumed with her creative projects that she has no time and might even be moving to California (if she lives in New York). Now he feels comfortable.

It is necessary that she is as detached as he is, and even though she doesn't have to share his personal interests it helps if she indicates that she is too booked up to put any energy into emotional relationships, except, of course, for her millions of friends. Then, after offering her phone number, she should jump up and tell him she has to go.

A fatal attraction for the Aquarius man is one in which he feels mentally intrigued and simultaneously assured that he would never be trapped. The more a woman appears to be a free spirit who is her own fascinating person, the more he will feel drawn in her direction.

Foolish Choices

Many an Aquarius man has walked away from great women or lost them due to his insensitive, selfish behavior. Emotionally cut off and compartmentalized, he is capable of coolly walking out the door after twenty years of marriage and never looking back. Many an Aquarius man simply refuses to discuss his feelings, or, when asked why he is doing what he is doing, will reply he doesn't know. The feeling realm can be frightening to him and he often wants to avoid it altogether, immersing himself completely in thought.

And so he often makes emotional decisions based on rational thinking. A fixed sign, he is rather rigid and stubborn in how he goes about things, leaving little or no room for compromise. Once his decision is made, it tends to be a done deal. The Aquarius man simply lowers the boom and then he is on his way. There are corporate firings that have more compassion. Indeed, one client of mine was not only dumped by her Aquarius husband, but also fired!

Aquarius men don't know themselves. They are also not honest with themselves. If they were, their worlds would be a lot messier and their agendas inconvenient.

Fated Lessons

Like the Sagittarius man, the Aquarius man has very poor emotional learning potential. That is because each lives in his own world where nothing really matters outside of himself.

There are Aquarius men who are very nice, kind people. However, they still don't comprehend the feeling world or the repercussions of ignoring it. When it comes to emotional issues, things need to be spelled out for him and even then he probably wouldn't agree. Because he is wedded to logic and thinks in paradigms, he would probably never begin to understand why a woman would leave him, never mind the lesson to be learned from it. He sees himself as a perfectly harmless sort who is simply doing what he has to do.

There is always a built-in justification in his reasoning that can sound more like an analysis of an engineering plan than a person's intimate life issues. Therefore, what he would probably divine from the demise of any long-term relationship is just that it was no longer working. I think of one Aquarius man of my acquaintance who had, at one point, a highly compatible marriage. However, he traveled constantly, all around the world, and never called home. After years of loneliness, his wife cooled and the marriage crumbled. When explaining why it ended he said that his wife had grown cold and gained weight. Interestingly enough, he completely left himself out of the picture except for one small detail. One day she was going through his things, looking for a legal paper, and came across a book titled *How to Dump Your Wife*. He thought it quite amusing.

Getting Smart in Affairs of the Heart

The Aquarius man doesn't get smart because he won't change and he doesn't listen. He doesn't listen to life, his wife, or the implications of his own predicament. He simply goes his own way and starts over.

If he would listen, reflect, do inventory, connect the dots, and be willing to take some accountability, there is a potential that he could become more conscious. However, such a game plan can be very painful and promises no immediate rewards. It is easier and cozier to stay unconscious and continue along the timeworn path, pursuing life in his own style. Like the Sagittarius man, he values his freedom above love relationships and has a bone deep fear of being confined by anyone's serious expectations.

13. Pisces

FEBRUARY 20 TO MARCH 20

Ruling Planet: Neptune
Element: Water
Cosmic Quality: Mutable
Essential Quality: Feminine, negative
Planetary Principle: Sacrifice
Primal Desire: Merger
Material Factor: Love

The Pisces Woman

The Smart Scoop

She is the most intuitive sign of the zodiac. Hers is a mysterious, almost magical intelligence issuing from the depths of her unconscious mind. The Pisces woman knows things she has no way of proving logically. They come to her through subtle sensations, impressions, and fluctuating feelings.

She can't control the activity of her mind any more than she can control her moods. The stream flows forth in a confluence of impressions, inner dialogue, and vivid imaginings. Essentially, the Pisces woman has the mind of a visionary. With proper focus, she can manifest her dreams. Her problem is that she is too easily distracted and allows confusion and moods to overwhelm her.

If undisciplined, she gives her power away to passing influences. Needy, negative people, selfish men, completely insensitive superiors, minor disappointments that seem like major downers, and moods that make her weep—all drive her chariot over the cliff.

At her peak, she could win a Nobel Prize, become a paid intuitive, legendary painter, or healer who saves a significant piece of the world. In a million ways the Pisces woman can be brilliantly creative. Her problem comes when she doesn't value the gifts the universe has given her and unconsciously throws herself away.

The Feeling Scope

Sensitive, vulnerable, and in search of the sublime, she moves through life immersed in her emotions. Moody, changeable, dreamy, and fantasy-filled, the Pisces woman flourishes in incandescent romantic encounters. When not in love, she dreams of the day her prince will appear. When in love, she tends to get lost.

She needs to be swept up by the stirrings of her own wild heartstrings and be completely carried away—or she's cool and indifferent. The Pisces woman is an all-or-nothing personality, and quite complex. Magic and intensity are key to captivating her attention. Add a strong element of passion and she's a goner.

The Pisces woman can create her own poetry in motion through her active imagination. Probably the most purely imaginative woman in the zodiac, she thrives on what stimulates those creative recesses of her mind. She also responds to what appeals to the full range of her feelings, whether that be love, compassion, empathy, or pure, old-fashioned sympathy for the underdog.

Her feelings control her and can lead her to strange, wonderful and not so wonderful places. They can keep her connected to the codependent, command her to try to save the unsaveable, hold her as emotional hostage to the cruel and manipulative. They can also lead her down a primrose path to situations that are simultaneously ecstatic and painful because, like the Leo woman, she can easily lose track of her head. The Pisces woman is all about feeling. Listen to how she expresses herself and you will hear someone whose decisions are based entirely on feeling. "That just felt right to me" or "It just didn't feel right to me" or "I couldn't do it because my feelings told me to do something else." Whatever the situation, there is no arguing with her feelings. They are her beacon and light of truth. However, they can also be the bane of her existence. Although she accords them unquestioned power, they are by no means invincible and can lead her to have perceptions that are seriously askew.

Fatal Attractions

She can sense him from across a crowded room. There is always something about the attraction that feels compelling. If it doesn't feel compelling, she can be as cool and aloof as a census taker.

The Pisces woman is attracted to men who appear dazzling and magical. However, chances are that she also has had at least one man in her past who is downright dangerous. Initially, she was probably drawn to him like a moth to a flame, and then down the road was lucky to emerge with her purse. Many Pisces women have been victimized by men because they get so caught up in the moment that they are blind to the big picture. And this lack of foresight can create formidable situations that are not easy to recover from.

A classic fatal attraction for the Pisces woman is a man who needs to be saved. This woman has a big soft spot for birds with broken wings, and can follow a sacrificial path that leads her to play martyr to self-created victims. Alcoholics, drug addicts, and the weak-willed, down-and-out, and needy have their definite appeal to a certain type of Pisces woman whose feelings "say" that they would die without her.

When a fatal attraction takes over for this highly emotional woman, it can be such a powerful thing that she may put her life on hold—

hoping, waiting, giving, serving, and crying her eyes out because her vision cannot be redeemed and all she has left is a sense of doom.

Foolish Choices

She can be a fool for love. Driven by a romantic dream or the Technicolor contents of her own imagination, she can cling to false hopes until she is no longer dealing with reality.

A basic problem for the Pisces woman is that she can't distinguish what *could be* in all possible worlds from what actually *is* and from what *never* could be. In her head she edits, translates, and suffers from denial. In the process she makes the foolish choice of staying in a situation that she should have long been out of. Because she is immensely intuitive but emotionally subjective, she often scorns the cold, hard reason that could free her to move forward. An old-fashioned romantic, reveling in unrequited love, the Pisces woman is often in love with longing. Whether it's great bursts of feeling for her sentimental memories or an all-encompassing empathy for the sadness and potential of some soul, she often lives in a fantasy that both diminishes and undermines her. Getting caught up in an inner world that is divorced from reality is not only foolish but dangerous. This is a woman who has so many wondrous gifts to give. However, she must not give herself away in the process.

Fated Lesson

Because she is so emotional, she suffers hard from her lessons. And her lessons are always difficult because of her tendency toward denial.

The Pisces woman often has huge lessons around projections and expectations. For instance, she looks to a "soul mate" to connect to her own soul, which she doesn't truly value in the first place. Instead of reveling in the abundance of her own creative gifts, she puts her chosen man on a pedestal and gives up her power.

The Pisces woman often attracts men who are controlling and who delight in the power accorded to them. Caught up in the throes of her unfolding fairy tale, she won't lend herself to the voice of reason—until it's too late. Her great lesson is that she should maintain herself in a relationship, not lose herself.

There is an old cliche that we can't really love another until we first love ourselves. On any given day we can become infatuated with another person, fantasize about another person, obsess about another person—but those are all just states of mind that, if taken far enough, like some drug, will make the mind go crazy. Some people, and certainly many Pisces women, believe that the crazier they are, the more they are in love. However, love is not about emotional craziness and mental escape—which have more to do with addiction. Love is an elevated state of the spirit and the heart, and it requires consciousness. The most fundamental lesson for the Pisces woman is to love consciously, and not waste herself on someone who was clearly trouble from the start. She must learn that she always has choices and that her choices should be primarily based on self-respect, self-value, and self-protection.

Getting Smart in Affairs of the Heart

The Pisces woman has to get real. How, exactly, does this happen? It could start with questions such as "Do I really need this bad excuse for a relationship?" and "What do I need it for?" to be followed by "Do I want a shot at a happy life, or do I want to pretend I'm not miserable when I know I am miserable?" Questions such as these are critical for one reason: her answering them honestly means she knows she is making a choice.

The second that she realizes there is a choice, even if it is a very hard choice, she has taken a step out of the vicious circle of victimhood. When she is willing to relinquish the lie that she has something promising when, in fact, she has nothing but deep inner anguish, she is starting to get smart. The second step comes in getting clear. This means forgetting false hope and going down to the depths of the pain and the rage and looking at the behavior that caused it. For instance, she might ask herself whether her partner was selfish or controlling, whether he repaid her care with indifference, and whether he was perhaps afraid of experiencing deeper emotions. She might also look at his actions as opposed to his words: Did he say one thing and do another?

Processing this experience and putting it in perspective will take time, and for a while this time may feel unbearable. She has to cry it out, run it out, paint it out, or write it out. All of these endeavors will be cathartic and help her release from the grip of the expectations that are holding her back.

When she is finally able to let go of the illusion that this fragmented person is going to fill her up, she can begin to start to look at herself—perhaps for the first time in her life. She must then have gratitude for herself and her glorious gifts that she had heretofore been so willing to undervalue and ignore. At this point she must vow to honor her life, her uniqueness, and her sense of serendipity and magic that can bring her joy through its endless possibility. Finally, on a daily basis she must pray for the faith that she can have heaven on earth—in her own way, in her own time, with the right person who is an equal. Without such faith, she can fall back into her old, emotionally addictive patterns that will magnetize another man who repeats the same scenario.

The Pisces woman must come to a place where she consciously values and wants to celebrate her own life—even without a relationship. If she can come to that point where she feels self-fulfilled rather than needing to be filled up, and where she enjoys and takes pride in herself as she is, she will mysteriously attract a higher love when the time is right. The secret to her ability to attract and generate a successful love lies in a paradox: she has to be able to let her unhealthy need for fairy tale romance go before she is able to attain a deep, spiritual, meaningful, and lasting love. In other words let go the illusions and let in the faith that something real that is deep, wondrous, and joyful is on the way.

The foolish choice the Pisces woman makes is in giving her power away to romantic gesture as opposed to real love. The smart choice is to call her spirit back and to value that above all else. When she chooses to focus on the power of her own brilliant, creative spirit she will attract a man of spirit, not some emotional cripple who leaves her longing.

The Pisces Man

The Smart Scoop

In many ways he might be the most intriguing man in the zodiac. Changeable and often utterly charming, he lives through a confluence of feelings, thoughts, aspirations, dreams, fantasies, and far-out plans. The Pisces man is a paradox: often friendly, occasionally remote, sometimes spontaneous, other times elusive, he is a chameleon who no one can completely see through.

As the twelfth and final sign of the zodiac, he has a psychic accumulation of all the other signs in his mental data bank. And psychic he is. Many Pisces men can read your mind, see through to your core, and know in one flash your fears, needs, and expectations. The classic Pisces man has a pure, undiluted, intuitive brilliance that outdoes every other sign. (Keep in mind that Einstein was a Pisces.) He is highly imaginative and creative (many brilliant composers, including Chopin, were Pisces), a visionary, and often mystical. He is also magical, and can conjure an entire evening of such sparkling humor and whimsical innovation that the participants lose all sense of time. That is why I say it is Pisces, not Scorpio, who is the most seductive man in the zodiac. He can completely captivate your mind, soul, emotions, imagination, and love of life through a flicker of his own imagination.

Being a feminine water sign, he instinctively understands feelings and emotions. More important, he feels no need to apologize for them. Being highly creative, his feelings bring him to fascinating places. They are his connection with his own life and sense of possibility. That is why he relates more easily to women than to men, who tend to cut off and compartmentalize.

To a woman he can be the sort of best friend who understands all. Remarkably easy to talk to, he is also an acute listener who takes it all in. However, he can never be owned or possessed. The Pisces man needs his psychological space to dream his dreams and mull about all sorts of possibilities, many of which will never happen.

If he is a typical Pisces, he is not going to get cardiac arrest from climbing to the top. He is a dreamer. Things have to feel right and serendipitously happen in their own way. His attitude is that the top can come to him. Then he'll decide if he even wants to experience it.

The Feeling Scope

The Pisces man is a man of many, constantly fluctuating feelings. Feeling is intrinsic to his thinking process, and defines his sense of self in any environment. The Pisces man is extremely sensitive to environment, soaking up the vibrations like a sponge. I once knew a Pisces man who declared that he was one person in Greenwich Village, became a completely different person in Midtown, and yet another person on the Upper West Side. And he was a psychologist!

The feelings of a Pisces man can change many times in any given day, and with them change his moods, which color his outlook. He can seem like many different people in one body. He is. This man can be very unpredictable, at one point appearing warm, funny, and invincibly charming and at another, cold and completely disengaged. One day he may seem like a sensitive old soul, on another, hopelessly callous and immature. One week he may be totally inspiring, the next week wickedly cynical. One must take the Pisces man as one finds him and not expect perfection. Chances are that in a short amount of time his feelings will change again, and so will his personality.

When in love, he can be the wildest of romantics. The Pisces man loves love, and needs it. Going it alone is not his style. It makes him moody and even depressed. With the love of his life, the Pisces man wants to merge and feel the sort of connection that, if not soulful, at least brings him security and comfort. Whatever his feelings are, he knows he has to follow them. The Pisces man is too emotional to thrust forth a stiff upper lip and pretend that everything is sunny when it's not. He wants to be happy and do his thing without outer interference. When a Pisces man is dark, he is deeply cut off from himself.

Fatal Attractions

He is most readily attracted to vibrant women who bring out his own vibrancy. The Pisces man first likes to feel transported. However, his ideal playmate may not make the most stable and secure partner down the road. Therefore, he often marries someone solid who may even financially support him.

This man can be so dazzlingly witty and wonderful to be with that his insecurities go unnoticed. However, true chameleon that he is, he tends to lack the solid core from which would come the self-confidence that would strengthen and support him. Therefore, his insecure self looks to the outside, to an audience or a partner, for approval and affirmation that he is loved.

His fatal attractions are of two kinds: either an affair which could be as fleeting as the moment, or a partner whom he knows is right for him for the rest of his life. In any given lifetime, he tends to have both.

Foolish Choices

The Pisces man can be a big escapist and prone to excess, using drugs, affairs, and alcohol to self-medicate against the effects of a cold, cruel world. He tends to have a very hard time confronting what makes him uncomfortable, and withdraws deep into himself when feeling weak and insecure. Therefore, at such times it can be very difficult to know where he is really coming from since he will just clam up. This is also when he is at his most vulnerable to infatuations, seductions, and his drug of choice.

Predisposed to divine highs and emotional excitement, the Pisces man may make some rather foolish choices. One ultrasophisticated client I once had, who was also an attorney and owned her own restaurant in Paris, commented to me with jaundice, "There is a Pisces man in every woman's past." She was referring, of course, to the sort of Pisces men who are prone to make foolish choices. Unfortunately, those do number more than quite a few.

When bored or besieged with the darker aspects of himself, the Pisces man will have affairs. Many have serial infidelities and think nothing of it. I know of one Pisces man who flirted with his wife's maid of honor while his new bride was in another room. The Pisces man has an amazing ability to disconnect from his wrongdoings and looks askance at anyone who does point them out. During marriage, this man might have a more active love life than most men who are single. How do they seduce all these women? They have an intuitive trick. They start out funny and friendly and, once they have attained the total attention of the woman, turn completely passive. Frustrated by what seemed so potentially thrilling, now the woman moves forward and is forced to take over the seduction.

It is not sex *per se*, but sensation that makes his brain percolate. The Pisces man is more sensitive and sensual than sexual. He also hates to feel bored. And so, in that frame of mind, should a situation present itself, his sensibilities perk up and take over. By nature he is both secretive and fantasy-oriented and very much likes to have fodder for his fantasies. However, should a jealous wife try to kill him over his foolish choices, he would most likely look at her in shock. According to him such things should not be taken seriously. They were only passing panaceas for temporary ennui.

Fated Lessons

Yes, at his worst this man can be quite dangerous. However, at his best he is a pure delight. His lessons usually come in the form of divorce or mental cruelty at the hands of some infuriated female. However, does he ever learn them? Usually not. He lives in his own private inner sanctum, and there nothing can control him.

The Pisces man treasures his personal freedom and can't be told what to do. He is also an escapist who tunes out anything that attempts to confront or confine him. I knew one Pisces man who was married for many years to his true love, a beautiful woman. He had the most beautiful house as well as the most beautiful life. At one point many years into the marriage, he decided to take a vacation from work while his wife continued to work. As the vacation got longer and longer and his many creative projects kept changing to be replaced by other, more consuming, creative projects, his wife got increasingly edgy. One day she came home from work and found him writing poetry. And so she said, "You know, I could quit my job and write poetry, too." And he replied, quite cheerfully, "And you're perfectly welcome to." He told me this story himself and then said in a disarmingly cool and distant manner, "If she wants to divorce me she can, but I'm not giving up my freedom." I asked him, "Don't you love her anymore?" He looked at me, shocked, and said, "Well, of course I do! That has nothing to do with it." As an astrologer I knew this was classic Pisces stuff—scary and incomprehensible to most people, but typical nevertheless of the hot-cold climate in which this dreamy heart resides.

And so Pisces men do not suffer their fated lessons well. Keep in mind that their emblem is two fish, swimming in opposite directions. And likewise, so can this sign switch gears and run from hot to cold and out of your life the second they feel bored, squeezed, or trapped. It does no good to threaten them because they will go along with the threat. It is chilling to witness that a person who can be so emotional can also be so impersonal. In the mind's eye of the Pisces man, he lives in a universe with millions of fascinating options only limited by his imagination. And this is one imagination that never stops.

Getting Smart in Affairs of the Heart

Not all Pisces men are affair-prone, but without even trying they are flirts. Therefore, a very possessive, jealous woman should think three times before believing she can own this man. Ruled by the ineffable, ethereal planet Neptune, the affable Pisces man is a law unto himself who is easily seduced and ready to drop what he should be doing and take up with anybody—providing they're interesting enough. This man has more than a touch of irresponsibility in his character, but then again, he doesn't look at it that way. Someone else's sense of urgency is probably over a matter that he feels has no sense of urgency whatsoever. Furthermore, what he may consider important in the moment, like hanging out and having a few beers with his buddies, is something that does not exactly jibe with connubial expectation. In essence, he cannot be controlled; at most implored, and even that may be of no avail.

However, he is compassionate. And if he feels that he has truly hurt someone he loves, he will feel that person's pain. Will it stop him from doing the same sort of thing again? Probably not. His mind is a confluence of flowing feelings and imagination, and he just doesn't connect those kinds of dots.

And so the overall paradox of this unpredictable man is that in one respect he is very predictable. His choices, whether good or bad, come from his complicated, ever-changing, elusive character, which he can do nothing about. His morals are his and his alone, and he is completely detached from the judgments or scathing opinions of anybody else. This is a man who lives in his own world. He is willing to share it with the right person, but crowd him or cage him and you'll lose him. Even though he is living in this small, limited, earthly existence—as opposed to the eternal, limitless universe—he is not sure how he got here. However, from his perspective, he is sure that he is already smart in affairs of the heart because he knows that love is always completely relative.

14. THE MOON SIGNS AND EMOTIONAL CHOICES

While the sun sign has to do with our conscious personality and our ego needs, the moon sign has to do with the unconscious part of our personality and our deep emotional needs. It indicates our feeling nature and how we handle our emotions. For instance, are we cool and detached, or deep, complex, and very emotional? Do we hold on to grudges for a long time, or do we blow through experience with very little bothering us for very long? It is all there in the moon sign, which is a critical indicator of the sorts of emotional choices someone makes and the kinds of emotional needs they have.

The moon is the feminine principle source of not only feelings, but also higher intuition. The sun is the masculine principle, which has to do with reason, logic, and power urges. In our society, which is defined by masculine values, many men are uncomfortable with the lunar aspect of themselves so they stuff it down, putting all their focus into their power drive. They then choose a woman on whom they project. For instance, because they are not comfortable showing feelings or caring, they choose a woman who is very emotional, very giving, and who sometimes cares too much. It is very common to find women who psychologically carry the feeling nature of their husbands. In time, when the psychological projection wears off, as all psychological projections do, the man often gets sick of her but doesn't know why. He doesn't realize that she represents an aspect of his own psyche that he has never consciously integrated into his own personality, so he starts to feel as uncomfortable with her as he is with that deeper emotional aspect of himself. It is typical of this sort of man, who is cut off from himself, to have no idea why he does things. If one were to ask him his motivation for a certain action, he would reply he doesn't know. And shockingly enough, this behavior takes place among the most educated: doctors, lawyers, highly successful businessmen, and sometimes psychiatrists and psychologists who are so used to dealing with other people that they conveniently forget the deeper part of themselves.

The man who is not in touch with his moon sign sees sex as an erotic rather than a passionate act, and believes in power and reason as superior to sensitivity and feeling. He is usually emotionally shallow or cut off, and compartmentalizes his life into segments of experience, none of which connect on a feeling level. When a man is not in touch with his feeling side, his relationship becomes a sterile confinement based on "doing," not feeling. His sensitivity is tainted by a sense of logic, reason, and sometimes competition that is all-pervasive. Coming from this perspective, it is difficult, if not impossible, for him to honor, or sense his partner's feelings. Both people in the relationship instead relate through the role they play within the context of the relationship, and their relatedness ends with the nature of that role, whether breadwinner, mother, or chauffeur of children.

To have a relationship that is alive, one has to live through one's moon sign as well as sun sign. In Jungian psychology the feminine, lunar aspect of one's self is referred to as the anima, while the masculine reasoning part of one's self is referred to as the animus. As a man matures emotionally, his anima gradually becomes more integrated into his life and he becomes more in touch with his feelings. As he comes to value them and loses the fear of expressing them, he will be increasingly capable of loving a woman as a whole person, instead of being infatuated with a psychological projection. He will then be able to treat her as a complex individual instead of a missing part of his own psyche.

However, the immature man will go through life projecting his anima onto the woman who becomes the object of his infatuations. He is classically the playboy or puer (young male soul) who repeatedly falls in and out of love in about five minutes. A woman can often sense a man in this state through her highly developed intuition and can use it to her own ends to gain power over him. Most women love to be wined and dined, given presents, and deluged with long-stem red roses—which is often the initial behavior of a man who has encountered his anima woman and is temporarily possessed. He is in love overnight. However, often, down the road, disaster lurks. This sort of man doesn't know himself or his deeper feelings. All that he knows is that a part of him has come to life, maybe for the first time in his life—and it seems magical. However, when his reason is restored, everything may start to look remarkably different. The glow is gone and so is the sense of wonder.

For better relationships, both sexes should strive for greater consciousness and a balance of both the anima (lunar principle) and animus (solar principle). The result is a deeper relatedness and a dynamic relationship that can grow, rather than a static relationship based on sterile stereotypes.

In this chapter, we will discuss the moon signs and the emotional choices they cause us to make. We will also examine the four lunar elements.

Finding Your Moon Sign

Because the moon is the fastest-moving body in the zodiac, changing signs every two days, special tables are needed for determining what sign your moon is in. The moon sign tables presented in Appendix A at the back of the book will help you determine the sign of your moon if you know your time of birth. These tables, based on Greenwich Mean Time in England, indicate exactly what time the moon changed signs. However, even if you don't know your exact time of birth, just look up your date of birth. In many cases the sign will be clear. When it appears to be marginal, read the next closest sign and consider which of the two seems to fit you best.

The basic formula for people born in the United States to calculate their moon sign using the tables in Appendix A is:

1. Take your time of birth and add five hours if you were born in the Eastern Time Zone, add six hours if you were born in the Central Time Zone, add seven hours if you were born in the Mountain Time Zone, and add eight hours if you were born in Pacific Time Zone. Add nine hours if you were born in Alaska, and add ten hours if you were born in Hawaii.

2. Take your adjusted time of birth from step 1 and subtract one hour if you were born during Daylight Savings Time, World War One, or World War Two.

For instance, if you were born at 4:45 AM in the Eastern Time Zone, add five hours for the Greenwich Mean Time adjustment, which would give you 9:45 AM. Then, if you were born in the summer, which is during Daylight Savings Time, subtract one hour, which gives you 8:45 AM.

To determine your moon sign, turn to Appendix A, find the table for the month and year of your birth, and look for the moon sign during which your day of birth fell. If the moon sign changed on your day of birth, determine the sign using your adjusted time of birth.

The Moon Signs

Because the moon sign is a prime indicator of how we love, how we express our feelings, and whether we have problems with the feeling side of our nature, it is an all-important factor in the relationship realm. Hopefully, the following pages will offer some trenchant insights into self and significant others.

Moon in Aries

Element: Fire
Cosmic Quality: Cardinal
Key Action Phrase: I will.
Key Need Phrase: I need ego strokes and to feel like I'm winning.

The Moon in Aries type is highly motivated, restless, and impatient, with a passion for life and a penchant for succeeding at whatever they take seriously. Dynamic, competitive, quick-thinking, and ever on the go, they need challenges to spark their interest. They also need to come out on top in whatever they choose to take on. Courageous, aggressive, assertive, and enterprising, their enthusiasm carries them into uncharted regions and can bring them to terrains where angels fear to tread.

People with the Moon in Aries are leaders who love to conquer new territory and try the untried. However, entranced by novelty and caught up in the moment, they may be poor at follow-through and at honoring previous commitments. Freedom-loving and easily fired up by anything that fascinates them, they are equally bored by people with less vim and vigor, passion, courage, and propensity to take life on at all costs.

The Moon in Aries type can be cut and dried, impatient, insensitive, and not prepared to listen to lamentations or long explanations of why something won't work. Nothing annoys them like negativity of any kind. Ambitious, driven, and possessed of a deadly candor, they cut to the chase in record time and also cut through others' fears and resistances, all while on the run.

Sometimes tactless and taken to speaking before thinking, the Moon in Aries type can create their own kind of trouble through the sort of impulsive behavior that is best left at the door. Rarely looking before they leap, this moon sign is loath to slow down and see the entire picture. Fueled by the vision of their plan and putting all else to the side, when it comes to love they often choose unwisely. Often caught up in the chase and bored by the prize, they can be consumed by their need for conquest, which carries them into unsatisfactory situations and sometimes keeps them there.

However, once this headstrong sign makes up its mind that a certain madness is love, there is no dissuading them. The Moon in Aries person will not listen. Deep inside, all they hear is the voice of their own mind which says that they can make a bad situation better. Moon in Aries people believe that they can change a leopard's spots. And maybe they can. However, when it comes to love, it helps to be humble, look, and listen.

Moon in Taurus

Element: Earth
Cosmic Quality: Fixed
Key Action Phrase: I want.
Key Need Phrase: I need financial stability and preferably
*   prosperity.*

Conservative, practical, materialistic, and motivated by the financial picture, the Moon in Taurus type plans ahead with dollar signs in mind. This is the most simple, straightforward moon sign. Emotionally shallow, uncomplicated, and consumed with creating and maintaining a strong financial status quo, they put their focus on security, both material and emotional.

The Moon in Taurus person is stable, no-nonsense, and sees life in back and white. Living on the surface, they trust the tangible and can get tangled up in it. They devote their energy to such matters as maintaining their mutual funds account or buying a car as if they were to die tomorrow and security were the entire meaning of life. Patient, methodical, organized, and usually faithful, they follow along their path with tunnel vision, feeling they are growing as they accumulate goods.

Moon in Taurus people trust the tangible like a monk trusts God, and they need a lifestyle of routine that is predictable and enduring. Marriage is a must since it sets up a structure that can be counted on.

However, the relationship, which is usually based on doing, buying, and owning, stays very superficial and never strays from the straight and narrow. Should a Moon in Taurus person have a mate who, in time, grows spiritually or emotionally and wants more, there will be trouble in paradise. The Moon in Taurus person cannot understand that there is anything more, so this sort of communication falls on the deafest of ears—those of someone set in their ways who doesn't want to change.

Of all the moon signs, this one has the least potential to learn from experience. Not able to see beneath the surface, they cannot comprehend that there is anything *but* the surface. Therefore, all sorts of subtle feeling states of their partner fly by them, leaving them in the dark and alone in their new car. The Moon in Taurus type can benefit from crisis if they get counseling and have things spelled out for them that they could never grasp on their own. Then they have the potential of a new platform for living in which they can perhaps start to think, evaluate, and understand that it takes more than the material to make a good marriage. It takes a heart that can hear.

Moon in Gemini

Element: Air
Cosmic Quality: Mutable
Key Action Phrase: I think.
Key Need Phrase: I need mental stimulation and someone
exciting to talk to.

The Moon in Gemini person is ruled by their head and has a hard time connecting to their heart. These people need a lot of change, variety, diversity, and mental stimulation to keep the demanding cerebral side of their personality happy. They respond to humor, cleverness, quick-wittedness, and sparkling conversations. Emotionally detached and needing social sparks and mental challenges, they are most taken with others who are equal to their own personality—and who can dazzle and outdistance them with superior wit.

This moon sign can easily say one thing and do another. Consistency is not their strong point, unless it is social consistency, as in the need to constantly party. There are Moon in Gemini people who are intellectual; there are others who are merely social. There are still others who aspire to intellectual pursuits but have no staying power. Moon in Gemini tends to lose interest easily, and usually has a long trail of failed relationships, projects, interests, and undertakings from the past that bit the dust the minute they started to seem old. This quicksilver attention span needs what's new and sparkly and so whatever crosses their path under this guise becomes their most current subject of fascination—or object of infatuation.

Moon in Gemini people can be charming, witty, and maybe the most fun to be with. Until very old age sets in, fun is like a religious experience that they can never get enough of. That is why they tend to burn the candle at both ends and aim for quantity, not quality. They can run through so many people that it would give a normal person wind burn, but in their case they are simply assuaging their restlessness that fuels them forward. Emotionally fickle and hard to pin down, they are runners—from one thing to another, from one person to another, from one dream to another. Changeable, curious, and inquisitive, they come alive during the course of an interesting conversation, an exciting new study, or a convivial group of people who have all assembled for the serious purpose of having a very good time. The Moon in Gemini mind is always moving in overdrive, and so when bored by belabored points, long, drawn-out stories, or intense emotional scenes, they feel trapped and take flight.

This moon is independent, freedom-loving, and needs to feel the wind in its face at all times. Variety and diversity make them feel connected. Emotional demands drown them and do them in. Cool, detached, and emotionally superficial, they don't hold on to feelings for very long which often results in situations where life flies by them. Since they don't have the depth to really understand other people's feelings, they often have poor staying power in relationships, especially when the partner wants to do more than party.

However, Moon in Gemini can intellectualize feelings and rationalize away problems like no one on this earth. And because they are so superficially intelligent, it can appear that they are compassionate. However, their comfort zone is talking, not feeling. Talking is their ticket to anywhere, and they do it with such facility it is very difficult not to believe them. Moon in Gemini people can live by their wits, be great con artists, writers, communicators of all kinds, and public relations people who can talk you into anything. Their best relationship choices are with compatible friends who are as restless and detached as they are. They should definitely stay away from anyone deep, intense, demanding, and emotional since this relationship choices, doomed from the start, will become a disaster down the road.

This is one moon sign that does not grow up easily, if at all. However, should transformation take hold at some point, they will start to choose personal quality instead of social quantity, and learn the joys of a deep intellectual commitment instead of repeatedly scattering themselves in the wind.

Moon in Cancer

Element: Water
Cosmic Quality: Cardinal
Key Action Phrase: I feel.
Key Need Phrase: I need to be emotionally secure and loved.

Because the moon rules the sign Cancer, it is at home to express its own nature in this sign and is therefore, by sign, very powerful. This is the most sensitive of the twelve moon signs, emphasizing care, compassion, sensitivity, empathy, and nurturance. Closeness, intimacy, and the need for love are central to this sign, which always marries, usually has children, and is very much taken up with family life.

Moon in Cancer people are motivated by emotional security, and make choices around that. This could even go as far as marrying someone they don't love but who is stable, secure, and will help to create a harmonious home life. The domestic atmosphere is critical to the Moon in Cancer's sense of well being. So is trust. Somewhere in the psyche, old emotional wounds lurk, leading to choices that will ostensibly eliminate the possibility that they will ever be hurt again. Predictability and stability are their mainstays. This moon sign feels its hurts much more seriously and deeply than other signs. It may never go away. Ruled by their feelings, Moon in Cancer types don't forgive easily, either. All choices are made around self-protection and self-preservation. And if that is seriously threatened, in record time they retreat within their shell.

Moon in Cancer types are supersensitive, deeply emotional, sentimental, and very instinctive. They are also intuitive and often psychic, able to pick up on the feelings of others and often empathetically come to their aid. That is why this can be a very healing moon.

Moon in Cancer people are devoted parents who take a total approach to their children. Somewhere, they have memories from their own childhood of loneliness, criticism, and misunderstanding that left its scars. Therefore, in their own adult years, their overriding need is to compensate for their own past.

Because they are so sensitive and sometimes thin-skinned, some Moon in Cancer types are actually afraid of their own feelings and live behind a cool, aloof shell that protects them from the world. They can be very moody, with a tendency to brood over incidents that affected them deeply. They can also nurse slights, bear grudges, and cut off completely when they feel threatened or uncomfortable.

However, when they trust, they can be deeply committed, loyal, and very nurturing. Warm, sensual, loving, and affectionate, they flower in a loving situation. Once their base insecurity is banished and they begin to relax, lighten up, and trust that love will always be part of their life, they are at their best. Their life flourishes once they've found the right relationship. At that point, they benefit from a little less self-absorption and subjectivity, and a little more of a desire to get beyond the immediate family and to give of their heart in some way to the world around them. Once the Moon in Cancer makes that choice to move beyond personal emotional gratification to a transpersonal love where they help others, their sensitivity, empathetic powers, and psychic resources can be a powerful source of transformation on souls who haven't yet come to see the way.

Moon in Leo

Element: Fire
Cosmic Quality: Fixed
Key Action Phrase: I am.
Key Need Phrase: I need a grand love that supports my ego.

The Moon in Leo person is in love with their own individuality. Positive, expansive, and possessed of great *joie de vivre*, they also have a strong need to impress their own talents upon the world. Indeed, such strident individualists as Gloria Steinem, Barbra Streisand, and Jane Fonda have this moon sign.

Inherent to this moon sign is a sense of drama that plays itself out anywhere from the stage and movie set to the bedroom. Moon in Leo people are very romantic, and love the luxurious trappings that they associate with love. Champagne, candlelight, and the finest of wines are their metier. This is the sybaritic sign, and all their choices revolve around what is grand, glamorous, and beautiful. Pleasure-loving, prideful, generous, magnanimous, and, usually, ambitious, they want their world to shine and they want to be the center light in the midst of the blaze. Idealistic, a little showy, and forever conjuring scenes that are larger than life, Moon in Leo types put themselves on a pedestal, and only someone who proves his or her worth can win them over. However, once they have been seduced and conquered, they are loyal—as long as the praise and presents keep coming.

There are those born with this moon sign who are so full of themselves, their ego, and their expectations that their self-indulgence can be quite insufferable. This type thrives on flattery, since, basically, they want to believe it. And when the compliments slow down, they have a way of stepping up the pace and helping them along. Mae West had this moon sign and would spend hours staring at herself in the mirror above her bed, never getting bored with the view.

The more evolved Moon in Leo type brings their heart rather than their ego to everything they do. These people are generous, magnanimous, optimistic, and have a consciousness that extends beyond themselves. They also have a childlike sense of humor and a creativity that can open doors—in both their own lives and the lives of others. However, whatever they choose to do, they have to have their heart in it.

When a Moon in Leo type falls in love, it is with their whole heart. Romantic, passionate, and prepared to go to the ends of the earth for their chosen one, they can initially allow this love to take over their life, regardless of how consuming their career might be. A Moon in Leo in love is like a teenager infatuated for the first time. Blinded by this light and not wanting to see anything but their dream, they can become devastated and disillusioned if seriously disappointed. Moon in Leo types are so romantic and idealistic that they don't always make the best choices. Highly emotional, with a tendency to be all-or-nothing, they need to learn to discriminate as much as they anticipate the unfolding of their own script. Nevertheless, even when hurt, their strong sense of self always helps them recover. This is one moon sign who will keep going until they get it right, and with time they usually make the sort of smart choice that makes it all worthwhile.

Moon in Virgo

Element: Earth
Cosmic Quality: Mutable
Key Action Phrase: I work.
Key Need Phrase: I need someone who meets my critical standards.

The Moon in Virgo is the moon of the terminal taskmaster. Conventional, constrictive, duty-bound, and disciplined, it is the workaholic moon of the person who can never relax. Moon in Virgo people believe in business before pleasure, pragmatism before feelings, and petty details over spiritual or creative acts. Grounded in their responsibilities to the exclusion of every other consideration, they are usually critical, emotionally cut off, and completely out of touch with deeper feelings—theirs or anyone else's. This is a great moon for a lawyer, accountant, surgeon, or politician (many, many presidents and politicians have had this moon). However, when it comes to affairs of the heart, it does not fare well.

Shy, insecure, and often self-effacing, the Moon in Virgo type finds their comfort zone in taking care of details and in cleaning. Cautious, discriminating, orderly, and always tidying or organizing, they have a hard time letting go and can get so caught up in minutiae that they can make an otherwise lovely evening a miracle to get through. Moon in Virgo types tend to be control freaks who are rigid and small-minded. Judging others by the criteria they use to judge themselves, they create a world without possibility where no one has a ghost of a chance unless they live by formula. These people can be calculating, controlled, controlling, and worrywarts over the most petty matters. Because their authentic feelings are so deeply buried under superficial details, it is hard, if not impossible, to really connect to them.

Many Moon in Virgo people are simply cold and don't know how to feel. Their compulsiveness often impedes emotional intimacy, while their critical faculties can make another person feel very diminished. Emotional displays often disturb them and complexities confound them. However, it is a prevalent self-righteous attitude that preserves the entire setup, never allowing them to see themselves.

More evolved Moon in Virgo people use their discriminating faculties to create a beautiful environment or perfect an artistic talent. This can be a wonderful moon for an architect, interior designer, painter, musician, or writer who has transcended the petty realm and is using their higher faculties. On a spiritual level, this can be the moon of a healer who has a calling to serve. On a very high level, Moon in Virgo is about deriving meaning through service to others. However, to reach this level, a choice must be made that, while petty details may have their place they should not define the entire course of a life. When Moon in Virgo people have come to this realization and have made some fundamental choices about the importance of giving and taking love, they can be some of the most serious, dedicated, loving people to be found. However, sometimes they have to slowly grow into those choices and away from the superficial criticisms that only serve to keep them in the same place.

Moon in Libra

Element: Air
Cosmic Quality: Cardinal
Key Action Phrase: I need.
Key Need Phrase: I need a harmonious, sharing partnership.

The Moon in Libra personality was made for the good life. Beauty, harmony, and all the best that life has to offer feature in the picture-perfect life of which this moon sign dreams. Hating conflict, anger, and ugliness of any kind, this conciliatory moon finds comfort in that which is nice and proper and never poses a threat to the perfect flow of the perfect party, dinner, or day.

This is the social moon of the gala party planner/hostess who has it all, or date who knows how to do everything right. Moon in Libra people are gracious, have great manners, and go out of their way to be pleasing at all times. However, under all those smiles they are far more emotionally detached than they appear.

Libra is an air sign, and air is thinking, not feeling. And so people with this moon sign tend to think their way through experience rather than feel things deeply. Being more cerebral than emotional, this moon sign often distances itself from real feelings, staying on the surface where eveything is polite and put tidily in its place. In the attempt to distance themselves from intense emotions, they can be downright cold when faced with some messy emotional display.

Essentially, the Moon in Libra type is more comfortable with reason than with emotion. They make excellent lawyers and arbiters, as they can see two sides of a situation and can coolly negotiate a middle ground. They can also diffuse a sticky emotional situation that is going nowhere positive, through their ability to be rational, objective, emotionally detached, and intellectually insightful. These people are the most clever peacemakers. However, they don't want to feel forced to live in this role. Instead, they want to be with someone as conciliatory as they are, where they can trust there will no bumps in the road—or down the road. Like those with Moon in Gemini, these people think before they feel. Thinking is the comfort zone, and shared ideas can be the basis of a great relationship.

The Moon in Libra is highly relationship-oriented. They cannot be happy alone but need a partner with whom to share experience. While all air sign moons do seek space and a certain amount of freedom, Moon in Libra types need that space within the context of a relationship. That is why they need a cool, nonpossessive partner with whom they are compatible and can do things together.

This moon is romantic, social, sensitive to social rules and mores, and desirous of being liked and loved. Because their need for love is so great, they often give to get, and take great pains to look perfect. Like no other moon sign except Leo, they can create the most pleasing, alluring atmosphere that speaks of beauty, fantasy, and the best life has to offer.

Generally easygoing and good at minimizing emotional problems, Moon in Libra people can be a joy to be around. And this is their choice for the rest of their life. They may not be the most emotionally deep people, but they do understand that sharing a life with someone should be a beautiful, harmonious prospect that should bring great pleasure. To that end they are totally committed. And, let's face it, it's not such a bad choice. As a matter of fact, in many ways they may have a lot to teach the rest of the world.

Moon in Scorpio

Element: Water
Cosmic Quality: Fixed
Key Action Phrase: I scrutinize.
Key Need Phrase: I need passion, soulfulness, and someone
  I can trust.

Often emotionally enigmatic, the Moon in Scorpio person is the deepest, most complex personality in the zodiac. Scorpio is the sign of death, sex, and transformation, and they all come to bear under the umbrella of this moon sign. The Moon in Scorpio person is most intense, but also most inscrutable. Obsessive, often volatile emotions are usually stuffed underneath the surface or repressed altogether, emerging as moods, depression, blue periods, or out-of-sorts feelings requiring solitude. This is a highly secretive moon that does not share its inner world readily—if at all. At the same time, this might be the most emotionally intelligent and deeply perceptive moon. Instinctively it sees beneath the surface everything that other people miss. It also analyzes, scrutinizes, and perceives the hidden complexities of other people. Highly intuitive, it also senses their darkness and their depths. Moon in Scorpio people psychically know things, and what they know is usually the truth.

Control is a key issue for this moon sign that can easily feel out of control when anything strongly arouses its emotions. Therefore, a cool, unflappable facade is cultivated from a very early age, which serves as a self-preservation factor that puts them emotionally out of reach. The typical Moon in Scorpio personality cannot bear to show pain. They can also never cry, since to lose their bone-deep control is like dying.

Some Moon in Scorpio people so repress their emotions that they don't know what they're feeling, although they are remarkably acute in sensing the feelings of others. This is particularly true of the men of this moon sign. Moon in Scorpio men tend to be control freaks who are extremely cut off and repressed. Moon in Scorpio women tend to be extremely compassionate to others in pain, but poor at self-care and -nurturance. Neither the men nor the women are easy to know, and both have deep-seated trust issues that can cause them to hold back and put up walls, regardless of how superficially friendly they may appear.

This highly complex, contradictory sign is also deeply passionate and erotic. However, falling in love poses just as many problems as it brings pleasure. This all-or-nothing moon sign has deep abandonment fears, as well as terrors around intimacy, since that requires letting down one's guard. There are also anger and jealousy issues and a tendency to cut off completely at the slightest sign of rejection. Therefore, falling in love for Moon in Scorpio people is like descending into hell with occasional vacations to an island paradise. First of all, in order to fall in love, you need to be surprised from behind. Secondly, once you have fallen, because of fear, some of the choices you make can be deeply undermining.

However, when the Moon in Scorpio person manages to transform and grow emotionally so that they are able to get beyond their fears, they can be the most loving and devoted of the moon signs. Their extraordinary emotional intelligence works for them, instead of against them, and their heart flowers open to full-fledged commitment. Deep down, this moon sign needs love more than any other moon sign. That is why loving becomes such a life-and-death prospect.

When they love through their spirit instead of needing to control and possess through their ego, they ascend one big level on the ladder of evolution. The spiritual and healing potential here is limitless when they choose not to be controlled by their own darkness. Sometimes it takes deep pain to break them out of the control mode that fractures their feelings. After all, this is the sign of death, rebirth, and transformation, so meaningful growth experience must be intense. However, when that challenge is taken on and the leap of faith begins, the love that can blossom can be both profound and lasting. Nevertheless, before that leap can begin, they must decide that the divine mystery of love is worth the risk of pain.

Moon in Sagittarius

Element: Fire
Cosmic Quality: Mutable
Key Action Phrase: I travel.
Key Need Phrase: I need to laugh, and feel free and fully alive.

Moon in Sagittarius people usually are optimists, full of humor and overflowing with *joie de vivre*. Adventurous, freedom-loving, and always journeying in new directions, they love life and only look at the big picture. Restless, curious, and full of anticipation for what may be around the corner, they need to keep moving, exploring, and experiencing life on many levels. Whether philosophical, intellectual, or more interested in the great outdoors, they are at their best when covering new ground. With a natural zest for living and learning, they love to travel and take on new people, countries, languages, and philosophies. Moon in Sagittarius people will try anything once, and instinctively know how to make the best of a bad situation. Seeking to live life to the fullest, they hate to feel fettered by any situation, and as soon as something gets boring, want to move on.

Whether they have a philosophical-spiritual-ecological world view or a self-indulgent appetite for the forbidden, this type of moon must follow its inclinations. Whatever they do—whether a philosopher, a humorist, or a full-time libertine—they do it to the max. John Belushi and Krishnamurti shared this moon sign, as does EST founder Werner

Erhard. On the female side, Oprah Winfrey has this moon sign, as does Yoko Ono. Each has traveled in different ways and in different directions, but all followed their chosen path to the extreme.

Usually inspirational and enthusiastic, they are often characterized by lofty aspirations and flights of fantasy that sometimes never get grounded in reality. The soaring experience is what they like best, and whether they are in love or living for some ideal, they never want to come down. The Moon in Sagittarius type finds the confines of the earth too dark and depressing.

Honest, independent, and people-oriented, Moon in Sagittarius types are free spirits who move fluidly through their feelings. With great ease, they let go of the negative and move on to the positive in record time. However, because their feelings are so mutable and changeable, they often don't dive very deeply beneath the surface of any situation, encounter, or relationship. Therefore, the Moon in Sagittarius person can be something of a butterfly who moves from flower to flower. They can also turn emotions into abstractions that have philosophical weight and seemingly eternal value but that misses the mark personally and empathetically. In general, they need a lot of thinking and breathing space and can be more detached than emotional, depending on personal plans and how consumed they are by them in the moment.

When bad times do besiege the Moon in Sagittarius person, they don't stay down for long. They will think things out and try to find some silver lining. Before long, they can be seen bouncing back and are once again soaring above the clouds. The typical Moon in Sagittarius cannot tolerate negativity and prolonged depression, whether it's in themselves or someone else. Therefore, they'll do their best to turn a dark situation around and gain something positive from it.

Impulsive, with a tendency to live in the moment, they can fall in love in about fifteen minutes and out of love in about four. It's no surprise that Casanova was a Moon in Sagittarius man. Generally, this is a freedom-oriented sign, and one slow to commit. This sign does best with someone who is more of a great friend than a passionate lover and who shares their values, interests, and avid pursuits. Generous, outgoing, and wanting to befriend the world, they can bring a lot of light to a lot of people and in the process provide themselves with the sort of higher-minded satisfactions that their heart desires. Free spirits who live with the big picture in mind, their goals can often be more transpersonal than romantic. Even when in love, they can't be fenced in. Their perfect choice is someone as independent, freedom-loving, philosophical, and adventurous as they are. Also, often allergic to mundane responsibilities, they can't have someone waiting in the wings to make them feel guilty for doing what they most want to do.

However the Moon in Sagittarius person chooses to travel—physically, spiritually, philosophically—no one can try to clip their wings and stay around for long. This sign needs a soul mate, not a cell mate, and all choices originate from that perspective.

Moon in Capricorn

Element: Earth
Cosmic Quality: Cardinal
Key Action Phrase: I materialize.
Key Need Phrase: I need material and emotional security.

Like the Moon in Scorpio, this is a very difficult moon for emotional self-expression. The moon is in its detriment in this sign, which means that the moon, the deep inner planet of feelings, has problems being heard, respected, and acknowledged. This means that the inner world is not valued. Feelings are not valued, and empathy and compassion are not valued. What is valued is the outer material world, and self-approval is derived from this realm. Therefore, control, power, money, material security, status, and stature within the societal structure is all-important and is the determining value of their self-worth.

It should therefore not be surprising that Adolf Hitler had this moon sign as did Adolf Eichmann and Napoleon. The Moon in

Capricorn person can be cold, completely cut off, and very ambitious. Here, the drive for power can be so overwhelming that it completely stifles the soul. Feelings take a backseat to responsibilities that pave the way to financial security and, ideally, affluence. This is the classic workaholic moon sign that is competitive, insecure, and driven to compensate through achieving money, status, and power.

Money and power are extremely important to this moon sign and a strong motivating force in everything they do. Moon in Capricorn people have deep-seated fears of rejection and poverty. Therefore, they can never trust that there will be enough money, approval, or power to allow them to relax that cool, controlled facade.

These people are pragmatic, responsible, and usually have a natural, shrewd business acumen. And since they have such a need to be financially independent, they will usually do whatever it takes to accomplish this goal, including making personal and romantic sacrifices. Women married to Moon in Capricorn men often feel like widows. Men married to Moon in Capricorn women often feel they have to beg or compete for attention with the career. The typical Moon in Capricorn person will sacrifice any amount of personal time to their quest for success. They will also sacrifice love. They feel that they are doing the responsible thing in putting their relationship on the back burner to pursue bigger goals. They are right and just and good and serious and all the things they feel they should be.

In the process, they are protecting themselves from failure or personal rejection. Hiding behind their self-created castles of money and material goods, they are able to ward off the deep-seated demons of anxiety, fear, and helplessness that are always lurking somewhere in the depths of the consciousness. They also feel great pride in being not only envied for their material achievements, but in seeming beyond vulnerability. Therefore, Moon in Capricorn types will often submerge their frailer human emotions and assume a stiff upper lip to save themselves from their own fear. Over time they will become so good at putting a lid on the feelings that might betray them that they will be seen as cold.

The typical Moon in Capricorn sublimates deeper feelings. Their denial of emotions fuels them in the avid, ruthless drive for wealth and power. They feel that they always must be busy, and the more they are consumed with constant enterprising activity in the outside world, the less they feel the gnawing emptiness on the inside. Although they have the capability for depth, they choose to live in the shallow end of the emotional pool. This is their foolish choice—and it *is* a choice.

There is another way for this person to take in the world. They do not have to limit themselves to left-brain activity. However, they do have to make the choice to grow and give some attention to the inner world. There are Moon in Capricorn people who grow into themselves, giving spiritual attention to their inner life. Through prayer, contemplation, and meditation, they are able to develop a sense of compassion for others as well as for themselves. (A wealth of meaning can spring up from that that will sustain them during those hard times when life is most challenging.)

Like Moon in Scorpio people, evolved Moon in Capricorn people are not easy to live with, but they can offer great inner riches, wisdom, meaning, and understanding. These moon sign people are gifts unto themselves, free of the emotional dependencies of the outer world and forever growing deeper and more powerful in their own right, on their own terms. Theirs is a life defined not by power *over*, but power *within*. It serves them well. For the first time in their lives, these people who were once so contrived, controlling, and distrustful are now free enough to be compassionate and loving.

Moon in Aquarius

Element: Air
Cosmic Quality: Fixed
Key Action Phrase: I observe.
Key Need Phrase: I need a best friend who allows me my freedom.

The Moon in Aquarius is the most detached moon of the twelve signs. Independent, freedom-loving, and something of a rebel these people want to live life on their own terms.

Emotionally restless and intellectually free-spirited, the Moon in Aquarius type is often ahead of their time. They dance only to their own beat and are best off when immersed in their own internal music. Many controversial, progressive philosophers and thinkers have had this moon sign, including the father of Existentialism, Jean-Paul Sartre; the father of LSD consciousness, Timothy Leary; and the great anthropologist Margaret Mead. Lenin, the father of the Russian Revolution and of the fall of the Russian aristocracy, also had this moon sign. Although this moon sign is often seen in rebels and reformers, it is interesting to note that it is also unusually prevalent with psychopathic serial killers such as Charles Manson, David Berkowitz (Son of Sam), and others. That is because the Moon in Aquarius is noted for profound detachment and emotional disconnection. In the chart of someone who already has serious psychological problems, the disconnection can result in dehumanization. Disowned emotions become an overriding theme, and the person becomes a law unto themselves, existing in the shadow of a self.

However, all Moon in Aquarius people are detached to some degree. Usually superficially friendly, they are cerebral, not emotional, and are comfortable in a world of ideas where contact with people is light, social, and fleeting. Often more interested in ideas than in deep connections, the Moon in Aquarius usually gravitates toward the unusual. Valuing their own freedom and individuality above all else, they are also attracted to other interesting individuals whose wild ideas, statements, and attitudes define them. Moon in Aquarius people can have very challenging, rebellious attitudes and can frequently be seen daring any sort of constraint that defies them. Whether it be positive or negative, at some point or other they tend to be taken by extremes. Taken in a positive direction, this tendency can produce a powerful political figure who is motivated to change society for the better, such as Woodrow Wilson. However, the Moon in Aquarius is also associated with more than its share of powerful political dictators—men like Lenin and Fidel Castro—who coldly believe that the end completely justifies the means.

Cool and sometimes downright cold, these people are usually not suited to conventional relationships. Platonic connections suit them well. Likewise, their ideal lover is someone who is first and foremost friend and playmate, as opposed to a passionate soul love. Like all air signs, they are most attracted to exciting conversationalists. Easily bored by anyone or anything too "normal," they are often attracted by someone who seems to offer a lot of surface or intellectual excitement. Usually cut off from deeper feelings, they neither understand nor appreciate the feelings of others. The Moon in Aquarius style is to keep everything light, friendly, funny, and sociable without delving into any intense personal or emotional territory. Too much emotional intensity can feel very overwhelming and suffocating to this sign.

This moon sign's great strength is that it can be intellectually brilliant and emotionally objective. Because they are astute with coping with other people's problems, they can be great counselors. As a great friend, they don't bear grudges or hold on to bad moments. Their choice is to move on and find meaning in life that can make experience worthwhile. In love, they don't get caught up in the contagious hysteria of an altercation, but deal with it with calm, insight, and understanding. Using their head, not just their heart, they can bring brand-new perspectives to a relationship that can make it more expansive. With the right person, this moon sign can be an innovative partner who never lets things get boring, but instead promises new experiences that could change the course of the future.

Moon in Pisces

Element: Water
Cosmic Quality: Mutable
Key Action Phrase: I fantasize.
Key Need Phrase: I need a soul mate who is like a dream come true.

The inner world of the Moon in Pisces person is an emotional cauldron characterized by a variety of moods, feelings, empathies, fantasies, and secret longings. At times the moods make these people a mystery unto themselves. At other times they are all-knowing, all-seeing vessels of pure intuition. Then there are the times when they don't even know *what* they are feeling, or when a sense of apathy overtakes them and their first thought may be escape.

This is a sign that runs the gamut from great creative artists such as Cézanne, Michelangelo, and Leonardo da Vinci to alcoholic and drug-addicted personalities such as Elvis Presley. In between are to be found psychics, healers, psychologists, and occultists, such as Aleister Crowley. Pisces is a mysterious, psychic, intuitive sign that is changeable (mutable), fluid, and closely connected to the unconscious. Some Moon in Pisces people unpredictably run cold and are completely cut off from a compassionate perspective on life and people. Some sublimate their emotional longings through spiritual studies, while others live at the mercy of their own fantasies and illusions. In general, this sign is a psychic sponge, unconsciously picking up on the psychic and emotional dimensions of other people.

Moon in Pisces people can be highly intuitive, healing, and loving. This type of person can also be highly fantasy-oriented and become so involved with their inner life that they end up living in a disengaged dream world. Whatever the case, they usually have a boundless imagination. Moon in Pisces types conceive of both the best and the worst of what can lie around the corner in life, which can produce both far-reaching vision and free-floating fear. This sensibility is one that needs to be channeled and directed, for although it has great creative and healing possibility, such diffuse consciousness can also lead to aimless daydreaming and overall dissipation of energies.

Moon in Pisces people are subjectively emotional. They are also very romantic, and their vision of romance is often a vivid spectacle. Sensitive and psychically attuned to the people and situations around them, they can often pick up on other people's vibrations. In this way, they tune into their lover and leave the world behind. They share of themselves from a place deep inside them. When touched in that place, they are prepared to sacrifice a great deal to make the dream perfect.

What the Moon in Pisces yearns for is a soul mate. What they want most is to merge beyond ego boundaries to enter a perfect world that is like a poem. This need for color and for intense experience can also lead them to escape everyday life. All sorts of escapist tendencies are common in this sign, from drug and alcohol addiction to romantic addiction and deep denial.

The Moon in Pisces person is always searching for something elusive, whether that be big or small, significant or the smallest, fleeting fantasy. Creative and often spiritual, they can usually find many constructive ways to express this soulful urge. However, often a sense of deep longing still exists somewhere deep inside that they can't seem to satisfy. As a matter of fact, many Moon in Pisces people are in love with longing. Some try to fill this hole with sex or alcohol. However, the most successful souls choose to grow through spirituality.

Highly emotional and sometimes moody, this supersensitive moon sign often experiences fluctuations of feeling that can make them feel as flat one day as they are euphoric the next. Impressionable and easily influenced when their emotions are appealed to, Moon in Pisces types can be led in a lot of different directions. When caught up in the glow of the moment, they radiate the wondrous joy of life. However, when cut off in their own alcove of melancholy, they can be cold, withdrawn, and extremely distant. Dreamy, changeable, and given to emotional vacillation, Moon in Pisces people can be enigmatic. The best rule for dealing with these people is that if you don't like the personality they happen to be announcing with their eyes, just wait a day.

A confluence of emotions, feelings, and impressions run through them in any given time period. Often, they are not even in touch with the import of all that inner activity, and are just as confused as they are confusing. They can be tender, caring, and compassionate, and as sympathetic and empathetic a person as you will ever find. However, at other times they can be cold, detached, removed, even angry and completely caught up in a world of their own. Often, so much is going on inside them that their mind is like a psychic stew.

At its best, this moon sign is spiritual and soulful. Their longing is to live beyond the earth in a beatific existence illuminated by God and love. Each Moon in Pisces person yearns for a little piece of heaven that they can pull out of their pocket at will. And this sort of joy, that is not only lasting but timeless, they search for in love. When in love, they will love to the fullest. And when making love, they will leave the world and their waking consciousness behind—just as much and as long as they can.

The Four Lunar Elements

The four lunar elements influence how we express our feelings. They determine if we are fiery and passionate, cool and detached, pragmatic, or emotional. These elements color our emotional approach to the world and have a great deal to say about the range of our emotional expression. Because of this, they are significant indicators of how we are likely to behave in a relationship and how we express love. The four lunar elements are fire, air, earth, and water.

Moon in Fire

The fire sign moon (Aries, Leo, Sagittarius) is the most impulsive. Restless, impatient, and highly impressionable, these people often fall in love at first sight but don't have the best staying power. Fire sign moons feed off excitement and gravitate toward others who move at the same pace. The fire sign moon likes to feel like they are falling in love for the first time, even if it is the fortieth. They are emotionally quickened by a sense of glamour, adventure, great personality, and towering presence. They like to watch themselves from afar being swept away by sensational experience. A sense of drama captures their complete attention, and often it is the drama itself with which they fall in love.

Since all fire signs have an ego orientation, the fire moon wants to be with someone they feel enhances their self-esteem. Because they care very much about what people think, they want someone they can feel proud of, and can instantaneously run cold should their chosen one engage in embarrassing behavior. Fire sign moons are great romantics who are in love with the idea of great love. Because they can so easily depersonalize the person with whom they are involved in favor of their fantasies, their behavior can be very immature and self-centered. Easily bored by the mundane, they can completely lose interest when things fall into predictable patterns that they find confining.

People with their moons in fire are freedom-loving, thrill-seeking, and brimming with the need to live life to the fullest. Pleasure-oriented and living life in the moment, they are also a lot of fun to play with, especially if everything happens to be going their way. Passionate, filled with ardor, and often amusing and childlike, they have a positive, optimistic view of life that is spontaneous, contagious, and often a pleasure to be around.

Moon in Air

The air sign moon (Gemini, Libra, Aquarius) is emotionally detached, cerebral, and uses the mind to process feelings. The air sign moon can remove itself from an emotional situation with remarkable ease. They slide through experience on their thoughts, and as quickly as their thoughts can change, so can their emotions. Air sign moons are highly convivial and seek mental stimulation over emotional passion. An onslaught of passion alone, without exciting communication, puts out their flame.

Air sign moons can feel drowned by someone's emotions. Easily suffocated, they need their space. They also need to be mentally turned on—by intelligence, humor, and thought-provoking topics. Friendly, sociable, outgoing, and gregarious, air signs like a lot of people on a purely impersonal level but have little or no need for emotionally intense forays. Usually enjoying a wide range of friends and acquaintances, they roam from person to person, living in the moment and making the most of each social experience. Air signs enjoy talking about feelings and analyzing emotions more than feeling them. Detached, objective, and often tolerant of other people's foibles since they are aware of their own, they are able to look at emotional experience from a removed and insightful perspective.

Air sign moons are adaptable, versatile, flexible, and usually restless. Easily bored, they seek new ideas, interesting people, and fascinating pursuits. However, sometimes afraid of deeper feelings, they get contained by endless rounds of conversations and thoughts that can deteriorate into the trivial. Air sign moons can be chatterers who get caught up in myriad meaningless details about superficial subjects. They therefore often live life from the surface rather than seek more profound experiences. Coming from this place, they can get caught up in ideas of what they would like to do without ever getting to the next plan of action.

Air sign moons are often emotionally ambivalent about a lot of things, and terribly disengaged at times that they should be involved. Living in their head, bombarded by ideas, their great challenge is to develop emotional compassion and feel with their heart. Those air sign moons who do develop a unique intelligence are characterized by a deep understanding and wisdom that can distinguish them as someone very special in this world.

Moon in Earth

The earth sign moon (Taurus, Virgo, Capricorn) is pragmatic, security-conscious, and materially oriented. Money is the emotional mainstay of the earth sign moon, who sees it as the basis and meaning of life. The earth sign moon can never have enough money and always worries about dying in poverty. Earth sign moons are grounded in tangible things. Their needs are a solid bank account, a new car, a condo for investment purposes, trustworthy stocks, bonds, and mutual funds, and a retirement plan that paves the way for security and comfort.

Stability, reliability, and dependability are extremely important to earth sign moons. In life they need to know where they are going, not why they are here. Work, responsibility, order, and organization are their ticket to the only kind of life they want: materially secure, financially stable, and full of investment benefits. Earth sign moons are highly conventional, emotionally superficial, and base their well-being on their bank account.

In romantic matters they are loyal, steadfast, and faithful, but emotionally myopic and not easily able to see beneath the surface. Simple and uncomplicated, earth sign moons don't understand emotional complexities; nor do they understand emotional positions that are different from theirs. Prone to tunnel vision, they stick to the surface, making sure that their material needs are met and that their partnership is stable, secure, dependable, and enduring.

Earth sign moons can get too caught up in the material realm and have difficulty going to a deeper emotional level. Sometimes they view emotional situations from such a pragmatic stance that more emotional sun and moon signs can be offended. In general, business comes before pleasure, and subtle emotional considerations can often be lost.

Moon in Water

The water sign moon (Cancer, Scorpio, Pisces) is emotional, sensitive, intuitive, and sometimes psychic. They filter all experience through their feelings and are very emotionally retentive. The water sign moon is the most emotionally deep, and feels experiences long after they are over. Water moon signs are often sponges, picking up on the emotional climate around them and tuning in to other people's feelings with remarkable sensitivity.

Water moon signs are ruled by their feelings and often by their moods. They are often introverted, complicated, fantasy-oriented, and absorbed by their inner world. They can also be empathetic, compassionate, and deeply sympathetic to the feelings of others. They prefer close, intimate relationships in which they feel secure enough to share their soul. Because they tend to have problems finding these deep, meaningful contacts, they often suffer from an inexpressible inner loneliness. Water moon sign people hold their feelings inside until they meet the right person. Because it is often very difficult for them to open up, it can be impossible to know what they are really feeling. They also tend to be secretive and irrationally fearful about really revealing themselves. Because they have such a hidden inner life, they often seem very different on the surface than their true inner persona. This split can be the cause of deep depression and an alienation that follows them through their entire life.

Of all the moon signs, the water moon has the hardest time of it and can get lost in an inner battleground of moods and consuming emotions. They need a partner to whom they can profoundly connect in order to open up that inner world that defines the deepest part of them.

15. THE RISING SIGNS AND ESSENTIAL CHOICES

———◆———

Another significant factor influencing our choices is our rising sign, also called our ascendant. Our rising sign is the sign that was coming up on the horizon at the moment of our birth. If we were born at sunrise, our rising, or ascendant, sign is the same as our sun sign, since our sun sign was rising at that time.

While the sun sign is our essential character and ego structure and the moon sign is our feeling nature, the rising sign is our outer personality and represents how we present ourselves to the outer world, what we choose to take in from the outer world, and how we perceive that the outer world perceives us. Since relationships are about how we get beyond ourselves to relate to another, the rising sign is obviously significant in the give and take of love.

The rising sign tells us if a person is shy or outgoing, secretive or lighthearted and outwardly humorous. It also shows if a person is very serious, depression-prone, or psychic, creative, highly communicative, or dreamy. The rising sign also indicates what we tend to look like physically and whether we have a weak or robust constitution. Certain rising signs have boundless energy and great recuperative powers, while others are frail, low on energy, and need a lot more sleep.

The rising sign shows what we tend to expect from life and relationships, as well as how we go about engaging in life and relationships. If we are using our rising sign properly, it should be a high-powered lens superimposing our highest expectations of ourselves on the surrounding world. Therefore, the rising sign connects our inner world to the outer world we must adapt to and live in. People who have a very afflicted ascendant (hard, heavy-duty planets sitting on it or hitting it by angle) have a hard time adapting, and consequently have relationship problems that they need to work on by analyzing those blocks and personality strictures. On the other hand, people with a very easy and outgoing ascendant can be very popular, but in truth be introverts who don't like to be around people yet know how to show that face to the world. Such could be the case with someone successful in sales who becomes a silent couch potato the minute he or she walks in the front door.

Since the rising sign changes approximately every two hours, we need tables to look it up. The rising sign tables in Appendix B at the end of this book give an approximation of which sign was most likely rising at the time you were born. First, find the day closest to the day you were born, then look up your time of birth, subtracting an hour for Daylight Savings Time, World War One, or World War Two, if necessary. Finally, look up your rising sign in the following pages and read!

Aries Rising

Element: Fire

Ardent, enthusiastic, and energetic, the Aries Rising type are born leaders who are bound to have their way. Ruled by Mars, the planet of motivation, Aries Rising is always moving forward to fulfill some goal. Passionate and prepared to go the distance to get anything they want, they are supreme extroverts who are not shy about taking it all. Independent, assertive, and born to take charge, Aries Rising people have courage to spare. They burn with life and ambition, and have no patience for meek, cowardly souls who hang back in fear. Often ahead of their time and pioneers in their field, they have strong goals from an early age and are defined by the need to impress their panache on the world at large. As athletes, executives, politicians, or company presidents, they rule with confidence and sometimes arrogance, but always with an endless drive that assures them of winning.

Wanting to be impressive to the world, they may marry for money or status. Impulsive, impatient, and often ahead of themselves, this rising sign is one for love at first sight and for having affairs should they get bored. In romance, Aries Rising seeks emotional and sexual excitement and doesn't want to hear about a partner having a headache. Daring, dauntless, and devoid of empathy when their desires are interfered with, this is one sign determined to get what it wants when it wants it, regardless. At high risk for divorce, they move on quickly and never stay mired in the past. In their mind, mistakes are best forgotten.

Taurus Rising

Element: Earth

Stable, stubborn, and motivated by material security, Taurus Rising is solid as a rock. Even if the rest of the chart has indications of instability, this rising sign provides a grounding that can keep the person on *terra firma* for life. Since Taurus is ruled by Venus, Taurus Rising people are often physically attractive, creative, gracious, great hosts and hostesses, and love their creature comforts. Their home is their palace and provides emotional solace in down times of distress and anxiety. Calm and persevering but also obstinate and inflexible, this sign sticks to its plan and cannot be persuaded otherwise. Taurus Rising can be unreasonable, prejudiced, and judgmental. That is their challenging fatal flaw. Living life by instinct, not objective analysis, they are often at the mercy of their feelings at the time.

Practical, materially oriented, and often obsessed with money, this rising sign is conventional and concerned with security at all costs. Needing to feel financially autonomous, they know how to put first things first, making sure that their money is in the best hands for growth.

This is a simple, uncomplicated rising sign that gravitates toward everyday basics and issues of survival. Since Taurus Rising people dislike living alone, marriage is a must and partnership a priority. Home, family, and children are extremely important to this sign, who would rather spend an evening at home puttering around than go out to a fancy party. This ascendant is one sign that can be happy with old-fashioned pleasures and a sense of peace.

Gemini Rising

Element: Air

Sociable, charming, chatty, and curious, Gemini Rising is the communicative ascendant. (The Gemini Rising person is a repository for ideas that often don't go any farther than the latest party.) Spontaneously, words tumble out of their mouth, and it is best to not take them too seriously. This is one rising sign that easily says one thing and does another. And with a mind that moves like quicksilver, they seldom even remember what they say.

Quick-witted, glib, superficially smart, with a great sense of humor, these people can charm their way out of a concentration camp. However, they often don't have the staying power to make a relationship last. The Gemini Rising person is restless and always ready to move on. They also enjoy diversity. Liking a lot of different people a little of the time, they usually don't stay put for long—unless they meet up with someone just as restless as they are.

Mentally agile, they often squander their energies on shallow pursuits such as partying, chatting, and scattering their attention among subjects that interest them only in passing. Glib, personable, and always prepared for a party, when immature, they tend to use their personality for the most superficial reasons. The Gemini Rising person is after fun in the moment and then they're on the run—to the next thing, person, subject, or relationship that will only last so long. It takes a long time for people with this rising sign to grow up and get serious. Should that happen at some point, they have the potential for great intellectual achievement, as is the case with the brilliant writer Sir Arthur Conan Doyle, the originator of Sherlock Holmes.

All charm and no soul may adequately describe the impression that this sort of person often leaves behind them. Like a great party, they can only be fun for so long and then the entertainment value attenuates. Until they know themselves and stop running from themselves, they can never really know another person, and thus tend to make very bad relationship choices. The Gemini Rising person chooses someone based on their idea of them. Should that idea change, as it usually does in time, they no longer have any use for that person. They run cold, run away, and run to a new person who represents a fresher idea. During the course of this workout, there is no sense of compassion or responsibility toward the human being who has been dumped. To the Gemini Rising mind, all people are dispensable once they get boring. And once they get boring, they become history fast. Needless to say, this is one rising sign that can be married many times, and often is. The sad part is that with each new partner, nothing ever seems to be learned. There is only the sense that there's still a lot of living to do.

Cancer Rising

Element: Water

Cancer Rising people are the best cooks. Sensitive and sensual in every sense of the word, they have an instinctive sense of taste and a creative way with food that is both original and arresting. Home, and the entire domestic sphere, is extremely important to this ascendant sign, who looks to the living situation as a source of solace. Intuitive, instinctive, subjective, and emotional, the Cancer Rising person often looks at the world as how they would like it, not necessarily as how it is.

Often moody, emotionally changeable, and given to occasional murky periods where they are best left by themselves, this sign often recharges its batteries by cooking, gardening, redecorating, and even cleaning. Sensitive to the conditions of their environment, Cancer Rising people need to see beauty and order when they look about—or the disorder quietly unnerves them and diminishes their sense of creativity.

Cancer Rising people often nurture and like to be nurtured. Family ties are strong, especially to parents. Children and a family are usually a must, and even in the face of strong career commitments, make up a very important part of life. These people tend to be loyal, devoted, and have a deeply protective quality that extends from family to friends. Generally kind, caring, sensitive, and solicitous, they instinctively understand the delicate nuance of feelings, and react to others' pain with compassion, prepared to do whatever they can to make a bad experience better. Highly intuitive and sometimes psychic, they often sense situations without being told beforehand. Cancer Rising people can be like psychic sponges. For that reason, it is important for them to establish strong self-protective boundaries and to learn how to say no.

Because these people seek close, intimate contacts, they are usually in relationships, even if the relationships bring suffering and sacrifice. In the early years, out of need, they may go from one bad relationship to another, never learning how to first have a relationship with themselves. In the later years, if they have learned how to be alone and like it, they have much more potential for having a healthy relationship based on giving and nurturing rather than living a needy life that is about giving up and giving in.

Leo Rising

Element: Fire

Like their ruler, the Sun, Leo Rising people usually shine. It's in their smile which can light up a room. It's also in their attitude, which always shows itself to the world as positive, regardless of what happens to be going on on the inside. This is the most positive, enthusiastic ascendant sign. Leo Rising people love life and all the good things that life has to offer. Outgoing, ambitious, confident, and clear about what they want and how to get it, they usually come out on top in whatever they do. Aiming high and giving a goal everything they've got, they win with regularity. However, they usually don't lord it over lesser souls who are stragglers, struggling with their own confusion.

Leo Rising people believe in the power of potential and in using it to make their own golden opportunities. As the most optimistic ascendant sign of the zodiac, they thrive around like-minded people, and turn a deaf ear to negative individuals who whine or run a woe-is-me party.

Of all of the rising signs, the Leo ascendant has the strongest physical vitality. Not only blessed with abundant recuperative powers, Leo Rising people have the gift of healing others through connecting to the Higher Source within. At its highest, this ascendant sign is a Light Bearer and a vehicle for Spirit. As such, it can heal other people's sick spirits and bring about a brand-new outlook to those lost, self-despairing, and forlorn.

However, as it is also a highly pleasure-loving ascendant, Leo Rising people can also dissipate their energies through excess play. Often flamboyant and completely taken in by the glamour of the world, they can also get seduced by the trappings of the rich and famous, and completely forfeit their spirit to what seems to be the "good life." Having a great deal of pride and sometimes a great deal of ego, this rising sign can get caught up in allowing material objects, jobs, and illustrious lovers to define their identity and worth. Should all these things come crashing down, life can seem worthless, and they must do some deep soul-searching to get on the right track.

Leo Rising people might be the most romantic. They love to be in love, and each time they fall in love, want it to be larger than life. Emotional, fantasy-oriented, and sentimental about romance, they can be prone to illusion since they are looking at the shining scenario and not the whole picture. If the Leo Rising type keeps chasing this rainbow, they will end up with a long string of lost loves that never seem to work for too long. At this point, they have some serious growing up to do, and must come to distinguish between infatuation and full, deep feeling from the heart. When the Leo Rising person chooses to come from the heart instead of the ego, they have magic—the magic to be a powerful, connecting force to someone else's heart. And it is here that the mystery of love begins.

Virgo Rising

Element: Earth

Somewhat shy, insecure, and definitely unassuming, the Virgo Rising person might be the most capable of the zodiac. Hardworking, organized, with all their ducks in a row, this is the dream employee. The Virgo Rising person was born to figure out how to fix things and how to do things better. They are a godsend for all those fire signs who lose patience with frustrating little problems. Even if they don't feel it under the surface, the Virgo Rising person appears calm. Likewise they impart this sense of calm to all the crazies gathering around them, shrieking and wringing their hands. Virgo Rising people are so competent that every day they should win an award. Instead, because their egos are not very big, they almost back into a room and minimize their own impeccable contributions. Virgo Rising is a perfectionist who never comes up to their own standards. In their realm of thinking, no one is perfect and so what's the big deal. At the same time, they strain to make everything as orderly, perfect, well organized, and up-and-running as it possibly can be. And they usually achieve it.

Virgo Rising people are serious and have a very profound need to serve. They make wonderful nurses, organizers, legal counselors, drug and alcohol counselors, editors, and consciousness-raising writers. They suffer when they give too much attention to petty details and fail to see the import of the big picture. The weakness of this ascendant sign is that they can get caught in the cracks and fail to move forward. While they can excel when it comes to taking care of others, they often fail when it comes to themselves.

This is a rising sign that carries around a great deal of fear that it projects on the surrounding world. This fear is often experienced as worry, fear of rejection, fear of being exposed as not perfect, fear of people, fear of what people might say, and fear that what they want most will never materialize. It might be said that there is no rising sign that is as hard on themselves as Virgo Rising. Likewise, they can also be highly critical and hard on others. In the long run it all boils down to the fact that their prism on life leads to a personal vision that is too small to accommodate true creativity—the courage to constructivly use imagination to make life larger.

The Virgo Rising person craves love and approval, and is prepared to go the distance to earn that. Intimate relationships are usually very important to them, although they may go out of their way not to let that show. They may also sabotage relationships through giving excessive attention to the job or the tasks at hand. This is the ascendant sign of the taskmaster. And so sometimes this sign allows the small, insignificant tasks of life to interfere with, even to diminish, the emotional side of their life. Having a strong sense of duty and responsibility, these rising sign people have to learn how to not overdo it. Love, marriage, and, often, family are important to them. However, in the initial stages of a relationship they have a hard time establishing a balance between what they would like to do and what they feel obliged to do.

Often very health-conscious, they know the importance of learning about health practices that will improve the quality of their life. However, they also need to focus on emotional practices, habits, and choices that will improve their life and add to the richness of their significant relationship. This ascendant sign can get so caught up in the petty details of life that it pulls everything else down. Their choice needs to be beauty, joy, heartfelt moments, and the sort of soulful talk that makes life worthwhile. In the end, their life will be as large as their imagination. And every Virgo Rising person who can summon that imagination often enough to create a consciousness that both sustains and elevates them is finally being true to themselves and their life. This is a choice. And it is an extraordinarily smart one.

Libra Rising

Element: Air

Libra Rising people take great pains to be the most pleasant people you'll encounter for miles. Unless they are in a very bad mood, they are the people pleasers. And since the ascendant has to do with only the mask we choose to show to the world, all this pleasing is not necessarily sincere.

Libra Rising people love harmony and hate confrontation, discord, or emotional turbulence of any kind. However, certain individuals, while offering the most charming social face to the world, can also create all of the above as soon as the company leaves. Nevertheless, the typical Libra Rising personality is usually gracious, charming, entertaining, and a joy to be with. Their ambition is to be likable, and they usually accomplish this end with élan.

Libra Rising people are also often articulate and diplomatic, getting their point across in the least offensive manner possible. They make highly persuasive lawyers and can also be acutely talented arbiters who see both sides of a situation but remain neutral. Because they are ruled by Venus, the planet of beauty and creativity, they are also remarkably talented at decorating, beautifying, and creating everything from clothing to environments that are a pleasure to the eye.

Often charismatic, Libra Rising people can still ingratiate themselves if they feel it will get them what they want. Great at entertaining, they can put on a grand event with an arresting sense of detail. Environment is critical to their sense of well-being, as are order and cleanliness. Sensitive to the beauty that surrounds them, Libra Rising people can create an atmosphere that is seductive, enticing, and completely conducive to having the best time.

Smart, clever, and mentally agile, Libra Rising individuals are also creative and talented in such areas of the arts as music, sculpture, art, poetry, photography, and multimedia. Their talents range widely and so often do their interests. Inventive, often ingenious, usually verbal and very socially aware, their talents can take them in many different directions, from business and law to the creative and artistic realm.

Relationships are all-important for people of this sign. As a matter of fact, many people with this ascendant sign value their partner far more than themselves. Since Libra is the sign of partnership and marriage, people with this ascendant sign almost always marry and stay married. Hating to be alone, they will stick with a bad marriage even if it is breaking their heart. Because they often have serious dependency issues, if dumped, they will find a new partner in record time. Their hardest lesson, which they seldom learn, is the power of first having a self-sustaining relationship with themselves that allows entering into partnerships as a full person, rather than one that seeks to be affirmed and filled up. The more independent a Libra ascendant person can manage to be, the better the chances of happiness in their life. Indeed, working on an independent mindset is their smartest choice.

Scorpio Rising

Element: Water

It is hard to really get to know someone with Scorpio Rising. They will let you know exactly what they want you to know—and nothing more. This is the most secretive ascendant. Scorpio is the sign of the occult, which literally means "hidden things," and, likewise, people with this ascendant always have some hidden things, especially in their past, that they are not going to talk about.

Because Scorpio is such a deep, intense sign, people with this rising sign can be moody, complicated, depressive, and often need alone time to sort out their feelings. They are usually highly intuitive and often psychic, although these gifts can also frighten them and force them to try to live a life that is purely superficial.

Although they reveal little of themselves, Scorpio Rising people are remarkably astute at seeing and sensing what is beneath the surface with others. That is why these people can make excellent counselors, psychologists, and astrologers. The Scorpio Rising person is a psychic sponge, picking up on the feelings of others and often unconsciously carrying their moods. That is why they need to be around positive people who don't drain them, because the psychic draining process can occur without their awareness.

These people seek deep, trusted, emotionally intimate connections that allow them to feel free enough to reveal themselves. Trust is a key issue to this sign that trusts few and far between and also never forgets a grudge, even if they have somehow managed to forgive it.

Scorpio Rising people are often afraid of their own intensity, doing their best to remain cool on the surface and never show the feelings that might be seething underneath. Control is a key factor in their personality. Should they lose emotional control, it takes them a long time to get it back. Usually, they exhibit control even in their emotional delivery with a low, well-modulated voice and a steady, focused look. To the Scorpio Rising mind, to lose control is to give away their power, and, being highly survival-oriented, they instinctively understand that power is something that they need to function well in this world.

Shrewd, perceptive, and often insightful, they are usually successful in both medicine and the business world due to their depth and emotional intelligence. Great at research and at getting down to the essential truth of a situation, they have penetrating minds, keen memories, and the wherewithal to stick with a challenging situation until they have conquered it.

This sign never talks its way into a relationship with someone where there is no chemistry. However, when there is chemistry, they can talk themselves into staying with a person who is emotionally unsuitable. Scorpio Rising people can be overtaken by their passionate responses. Having an all-or-nothing approach to sex, they seek to be blown off the planet. Passion is their *raison d'etre*, and it does affect their thinking process.

When these people fall in love, they never stray. Loyalty and fidelity are part of the package of intimacy, and it is intimacy they seek, not simply a one-night stand. They also need to trust that their partner is staying put. When involved, the Scorpio Rising person can be very jealous and doesn't want to worry about their partner. They want an intense union that allows of the sort of deep, soulful connectedness that fills up the inner reaches. Once they have had that, it always stays with them, even after it is over. This is one rising sign that would rather be alone than with the wrong person for security's sake. The Scorpio ascendant needs to feel alive in love. And for that, there is no substitute.

Sagittarius Rising

Element: Fire

Freedom-loving and full of humor, Sagittarius Rising people seek to minimize problems and to maximize the limitless panorama of possibility before them. Because of the sheer positivity associated with this sign, this might be the best rising sign to have. Resilient, ready for action, and always ready to move on after a major challenge, these people go about life with gusto.

With an expansive, exuberant attitude, they take on life with a smile and can be heard laughing for miles. It comes as naturally as breathing. Friendly, outgoing, and always finding opportunity wherever they land, Sagittarius Rising people know how to make the most of life and try to live according to their visions.

Restless, independent, freedom-loving, and often happiest when traveling, whether in a car, a caravan, or a plane, the Sagittarius Rising person loves to be on the move, to leave their security blankets behind while they go out exploring the world, both near and far.

This is the adventure-loving ascendant that lives to experience the new things, people, challenges, and events that can project them into a new sense of life. New experience keeps their spirits high and their perspectives open. This is a sign that likes to learn, grow, and be challenged by the adventure of living. Sagittarius Rising people believe that each day should be a little different so that life doesn't get boring. Sagittarius Rising people hate to be bored, confined, fenced in, controlled, or suffocated. This sign needs to feel free to do its own thing without worrying that someone is spying on them.

Sagittarius Rising people are often inclined to spiritual or philosophical pursuits, mountain climbing, cocktail conversation, and travel of all kinds. They are clever, quick-witted, friendly, flirtatious, and probably have had their share of affairs. This is an ascendant usually associated with more than one marriage or serious involvement. Their greatest challenge is to limit their seeking on the outside, and go within to find wisdom in their inner world. When they find a partner who reflects that quality of connection, the restlessness abates and they begin to explore life anew.

Capricorn Rising

Element: Earth

Serious, responsible, and often taking on more than their share in life, Capricorn Rising people are always prepared to do more, and never feel they've done enough. People with this ascendant are often shy, self-critical, depression-prone and deeply insecure. Afraid of rejection and prone to self-pity, they often anticipate the worst and feel justified should it come. Hard-working, disciplined, and driven by their goals, they do everything they can to do their best, but seldom enjoy the fruits of their rewards. People with Capricorn Rising can be very negative and prone to put themselves down before they ever think of building themselves up. Consequently, they often make life harder than it need be. However, they are also painstaking, prudent, and very persistent, and will pursue a chosen goal to the end, regardless of all the challenges they may meet along the way.

Conservative in their outlook and cautious in their thinking, this sign compensates for insecurity through money, achievement, and workaholic patterns that put them in a class all their own. Nevertheless, none of these usually make them happy. On a very deep level, it is love that this sign needs, and sadly enough it is so hard for them to trust it. Quiet and shy but enormously ambitious, the Capricorn Rising person is usually fueled by intense career plans that entail time-consuming situations that keep them constantly busy. Feeling they have to be productive at all times, it is hard for this rising sign to relax, kick back, and simply be serious about having a good time. Controlled by a strong sense of obligation and duty, this sign suffers under its own guilt-producing setup that probably carries on even in sleep.

Pragmatic, realistic, and ready to do more than their share, Capricorn Rising people cannot stop once they have gotten going on their chosen course. However, they instinctively understand that progress takes time and tenacity, and their patience and endurance puts them far ahead of flighty people with big plans. This tradition-bound ascendant sign has a hard time thinking for itself, and instead judges its own worth by society's values. Lacking spiritual and psychological foresight, these people often live at the mercy of shallow social values and status-conscious rules.

Capricorn Rising's drive to attain money and symbols of affluence can seriously undermine its own authentic self-value. Becoming an authentic self is a serious life challenge for these people who can so easily dehumanize themselves and destroy relationships in the drive for ever-greater wealth. This rising sign can so easily fall into the classic trap of Capricorn, believing that hard work, material objects, and lots of money can make everything all right. Meanwhile, their relationship is empty and gets emptier—and they don't get it. This is one rising sign that can make the same bad choices over and over again because they are so convinced that those are the only choices.

It takes a very long time for this rising sign to learn that material power cannot replace the power of the heart and spirit. The path that makes them feel so secure is also the path that can emotionally kill them. Like other power-oriented signs, unfortunately they will only wake up and learn their lessons through suffering. The Capricorn Rising type, however, who has managed to get beyond mere materialism to live through their own depths can be wonderful partners who takes their relationship seriously and grow with it.

Aquarius Rising

Element: Air

In their minds, Aquarius Rising people march to a different drummer. Intellectually, these people are often ahead of their time, have progressive attitudes, are somewhat rebellious in nature, and have to do things their own way, all of which often conflict with the rules of society. If the rest of the chart indicates that there are deep security needs, this ascendant can run havoc with satisfying them. It does well with superficial social contacts that come and go like the wind. However, these people often have a tendency to alienate those close to them through erratic, fractious, and trouble-producing behavior.

This is generally a freedom-loving ascendant that probably does best either working freelance or being self-employed, unless other factors in the chart seriously conflict. Aquarius Rising people need space, hate having anyone looking over their shoulder, and easily feel suffocated by too much intense people contact. Caught up in the study of unusual and interesting subjects and often fascinated by computers, they are very happy being alone, learning and exploring both inner and cyberspace. The Aquarius Rising person likes to think, analyze, learn, speculate, and, most of all, be stimulated. They are easily bored by and shun people who they feel have mundane mentalities, and are fascinated by minds that are bright and brilliant lights who seem to make the world open up. Aquarius Rising people usually have very good minds themselves. However, they can also be cold, calculating, and manipulative. They can also be emotionally rigid and lacking in compassion. Sometimes rebellious just for the sake of being rebellious, these people have to be brought down to earth hard. They do not learn their lessons easily, but tend to keep on shooting themselves in the foot, despite getting the same negative results.

These people can be brilliant, inventive, scientific, individualistic, but down the road, also unpredictable. Fixed in their ways and determined to have their own way, they can be difficult people to deal with if frustrated, crossed, or denied their willful desires. They tend to be risk-takers, iconoclasts, and resistant to being told what to do—for very long. In their minds, it is *their* world, not *the* world, and as far as they are concerned, *the* world can quickly disappear. Wherever conformity is rewarded, that is a place that this person does not want to be. Therefore, the Aquarius Rising person can easily be misunderstood in those conforming environments, such as an office, where brilliance and individuality are not rewarded, but indeed, seen as a menace to all concerned.

The love connection for an Aquarius Rising person has to be with someone also individualistic who is interesting, stimulating, and earns their respect. Having a horror of being bored, trapped, or suffocated by the wrong sort of mentality, these people feel it necessary to choose well, and a high priority is someone they adore being with and talking to. In other words, someone who is their ideal best friend makes their most successful life partner. When connected meaningfully in marriage or partnership, this is a rising sign who would never think to cheat. It took them long enough to find the perfect fantasy friend to fulfill their mental needs, and they're not foolish enough to think that there are a lot more like that out there floating around.

Pisces Rising

Element: Water

Pisces Rising people can be a kind of conundrum. Emotional, changeable, moody, and inspired, they can be cool, remote, and detached and then compassionate, sympathetic and empathetic. The Pisces Rising person can move through a lot of different emotional spaces in a short time, living out several different personas during the course of a day.

People with this most sensitive and psychic ascendant sometimes get completely caught up in the problems of others and sometimes actually become a problem themselves. Very impressionable, and wanting to escape the more unattractive details of the mundane world, they live through their vivid imagination and veer toward what is romantic, creative, and exotic. This can take them down artistic paths—or through an escapist panorama colored by drugs, alcohol, or romantic delusions.

Pisces Rising people often want larger-than-life experiences. Often creative, artistic, intuitive, and musically inclined, with both the talent and the desire to help and heal, they are often very gifted people, who, through their gifts, have many choices put before them. However, idealistic rather than realistic, they often impulsively follow their first inclinations, which are not always the best.

Sometimes Pisces Rising people vacillate and have a hard time making up their mind what it is they really want to do. Sometimes they manage to rule out all possibilities, one by one, until they set up a situation where they are prevented from moving forward. This is one of those signs, talented though it may be, that can get in its own way to such a degree that there is no progress. The danger of this ascendant sign is dissipation—both emotional and physical. All water signs can be insidiously self-destructive, and certainly Pisces is no exception. Water signs are emotional signs, and too much emotion leaning in the wrong direction can sink the ship. However, when this ascendant sign is able to behave prudently and express its energies with balance and discipline, it can accomplish much that is worthwhile, often achieving fame and fortune in the process.

The problem with having an ascendant ruled by Neptune, the planet of both transcendent love and illusion, is that one can get easily fooled by one's own emotions. Therefore, a person or experience that at one point seemed like such magic may, down the road, become not only unworthy but downright dangerous. The difficulty for this ascendant is that, in the moment, they are blinded by what appears to be the light. Needless to say, this almost always happens in the realm of romance. Neptune has its way of playing tricks with our minds. Therefore, a Pisces Rising person will swear up and down that the person who did them in over time started out as a saint, while another person who happened to be there at the inception canonly roll his or her eyes.

These people, who tend to be very giving and loving, need to be very careful if they're not going to repeat the same mistake. Maybe it would pay to bring their best friend along on the first date. At the very least, they need to look before they leap and not be so eager to fall in love that they are willing to give their reason, their life, and maybe even their bank account away. Regardless of how great something may look from the start, only the smart choice will bring a happily-ever-after ending.

CONCLUSION

———◆———

It has always amazed me when occasionally a certain type of individual at a cocktail party has the audacity to ask me, "Do you really believe in all that stuff?" I have learned that the best answer, which secretly amuses me, is "What stuff?" That gets them because, of course, they don't even know.

All this "stuff" I have put before you in this book is a mere fraction of what makes up a complete horoscope. Nevertheless, even in its slightness, it is still an indication of the many factors that go into making up people and their choices. What it all amounts to is that the horoscope is an X ray of the psyche, and the information in this book provides insight into the psyche. However, the psyche, whether it is cool and detached or emotional and passionate, still has free will in its choices. The less we operate on autopilot and the more we know ourselves, the better our choices and the happier our lives. Astrology confirms how complex we all are and helps explain those situations we may find ourselves in that just seemed to reflect the blind spot of our personality. Of course, we can't walk around determined never to make a "mistake." But we can be more aware and come to understand why we did make the choices we did. This understanding can help make the next set of choices much smarter.

Looking at astrology, from this close perspective of some very important horoscope influences that reflect our relationship patterns, we start to get a glimpse of a picture that makes sense. While so many people think that astrology begins and ends with the sun sign, it is but one influence that determines the direction of some of our choices.

The elements are the most basic—whether our sun or other important planets are in fire, air, earth, or water signs. Everything in the natural universe is made up of the elements. The elements explain our basic temperament—emotional, fiery, passionate, cool, cerebral, dreamy, practical, objective, subjective, deep, secretive, or suspicious. Just looking at the elements of the important planetary placements, we get a picture of a person and how they are going to react in a relationship.

Adding to this picture is the Cosmic Qualities of whether someone's sun sign is cardinal, mutable, or fixed. This tells us if they start things and lose interest halfway, if they are generally changeable and so fluid that they forget they're getting married and end up at a party, or if they hang in there long after something should be over and keep retreading their old path until it becomes a trench. Combine these Cosmic Qualities with the elements, and already you start to get a profile of a person that is a lot more complex than merely saying they are a Sagittarius.

Then, of course, we move into a complex analysis of the sun signs, which are indicators of our conscious ego state. The sun sign indicates what we want and how we go about getting it. It is the self we have grown up with and have come to trust as "I am." It is who we feel we are, without any intensive further analysis. For instance, I *am* a Gemini. Therefore, I am social and like to talk. I *am* a Scorpio. Therefore, I am secretive and don't like to talk. I *am* a Capricorn. Therefore I am success-oriented and like to make money. I *am* an Aquarius. Therefore I am freedom-oriented and like my space more than money.

This is modified by the moon sign, which indicates the emotional nature and deep inner self. This shows how we feel and if or how we show our feelings. It also shows what we need emotionally, and, interestingly enough, that is not always something emotional. For instance, the restless Moon in Gemini needs stimulation, fun, great conversation, and lots of social activity. It is an air sign, which has to do with thinking, not feeling. On the other hand, the watery Moon in Cancer needs just the opposite: nurturance, love, emotional security, and hugs. Intellectual conversation alone leaves them cold. Already we can see a problem between these two people should they try to get close. Not a good choice for a lasting relationship.

Finally, we have the rising sign, which shows how we project ourselves to the world and what we choose to take in. The rising sign shows our outer behavior in a relationship. Are we outgoing, or shy and withdrawn? Are we happy-go-lucky and a little irresponsible, or serious, distrustful, and slow to reveal anything personal? The rising sign modifies the sun sign and hides the moon sign. For instance, a person could have the smiling, charming, gregarious Sagittarius Rising and, out in the world, be able to sell ice to the Eskimos. However, if the sun sign is in Scorpio, that is not the person they are at home at all. And if their moon is in secretive, shut-tight Scorpio, you'll never find out who they are or what they're thinking unless they choose to make an unusual exception in the direction of disclosure.

And so all of these influences coming together not only show us a great deal about ourselves, but also about a potential partner who may seem either so attractive or so difficult in the short run. Will this choice make the long run, or is it a situation to be learned from so that the next choice is truly successful? Learning and growing is a very important part of it. That is the spiritual part that can add invaluable richness and dimension to our relationships.

Potentially, all the signs are smart. It is simply a matter of how we choose to live through them. And hopefully this book has offered some stimulating insights, bringing you out of the dark and into a different dimension that has to do with awareness, compassion, and consciousness. With that increasing consciousness in mind, make miracles—miracles of love.

Appendix A: Moon Sign Tables

January 1935		
2nd	4:23 am	Sagittarius
4th	6:41 am	Capricorn
6th	7:04 am	Aquarius
8th	7:20 am	Pisces
10th	9:08 am	Aries
12th	1:31 pm	Taurus
14th	8:45 pm	Gemini
17th	6:40 am	Cancer
19th	6:28 pm	Leo
22nd	7:19 am	Virgo
24th	7:57 pm	Libra
27th	6:42 am	Scorpio
29th	2:04 pm	Sagittarius
31st	5:43 pm	Capricorn

February 1935		
2nd	6:23 pm	Aquarius
4th	5:48 pm	Pisces
6th	5:53 pm	Aries
8th	8:26 pm	Taurus
11th	2:39 am	Gemini
13th	12:29 pm	Cancer
16th	0:37 am	Leo
18th	1:33 pm	Virgo
21st	2:03 am	Libra
23rd	1:01 pm	Scorpio
25th	9:39 pm	Sagittarius
28th	1:03 am	Capricorn

March 1935		
2nd	5:14 am	Aquarius
4th	5:12 am	Pisces
6th	4:43 am	Aries
8th	5:48 am	Taurus
10th	10:18 am	Gemini
12th	6:55 pm	Cancer
15th	6:50 am	Leo
17th	7:52 pm	Virgo
20th	8:07 am	Libra
22nd	6:44 pm	Scorpio
25th	3:23 am	Sagittarius
27th	9:46 am	Capricorn
29th	1:39 pm	Aquarius
31st	3:13 pm	Pisces

April 1935		
2nd	3:32 pm	Aries
4th	4:23 pm	Taurus
6th	7:39 pm	Gemini
9th	2:52 am	Cancer
11th	1:55 pm	Leo
14th	2:48 am	Virgo
16th	3:00 pm	Libra
19th	1:10 am	Scorpio
21st	9:05 am	Sagittarius
23rd	3:11 pm	Capricorn
25th	7:42 pm	Aquarius
27th	10:41 pm	Pisces
30th	0:26 am	Aries

May 1935		
2nd	2:11 am	Taurus
4th	5:30 am	Gemini
6th	11:56 am	Cancer
8th	9:56 pm	Leo
11th	10:27 am	Virgo
13th	10:48 pm	Libra
16th	1:52 am	Scorpio
18th	4:11 pm	Sagittarius
20th	9:21 pm	Capricorn
23rd	1:10 am	Aquarius
25th	4:14 am	Pisces
27th	6:50 am	Aries
29th	10:01 am	Taurus
31st	2:15 pm	Gemini

June 1935		
2nd	8:46 pm	Cancer
5th	6:22 am	Leo
7th	6:26 pm	Virgo
10th	6:58 am	Libra
12th	5:32 pm	Scorpio
15th	0:57 am	Sagittarius
17th	5:20 am	Capricorn
19th	7:56 am	Aquarius
21st	9:58 am	Pisces
23rd	12:25 pm	Aries
25th	3:57 pm	Taurus
27th	9:08 pm	Gemini
30th	4:29 am	Cancer

July 1935		
2nd	2:15 pm	Leo
5th	2:10 am	Virgo
7th	2:51 pm	Libra
10th	2:14 am	Scorpio
12th	10:22 am	Sagittarius
14th	2:59 pm	Capricorn
16th	4:52 pm	Aquarius
18th	5:32 pm	Pisces
20th	6:36 pm	Aries
22nd	9:24 pm	Taurus
25th	2:46 am	Gemini
27th	10:47 am	Cancer
29th	9:07 pm	Leo

August 1935		
1st	9:08 am	Virgo
3rd	9:54 pm	Libra
6th	9:53 am	Scorpio
8th	7:21 pm	Sagittarius
11th	1:08 am	Capricorn
13th	3:20 am	Aquarius
15th	3:19 am	Pisces
17th	2:56 am	Aries
19th	4:12 am	Taurus
21st	8:31 am	Gemini
23rd	4:22 pm	Cancer
26th	3:02 am	Leo
28th	3:22 pm	Virgo
31st	4:08 am	Libra

September 1935		
2nd	4:21 pm	Scorpio
5th	2:46 am	Sagittarius
7th	10:03 am	Capricorn
9th	1:19 pm	Aquarius
11th	2:12 pm	Pisces
13th	1:22 pm	Aries
15th	1:15 pm	Taurus
17th	3:12 pm	Gemini
19th	10:29 pm	Cancer
22nd	11:13 am	Leo
24th	9:20 pm	Virgo
27th	10:05 am	Libra
29th	10:07 pm	Scorpio

October 1935		
2nd	8:39 am	Sagittarius
4th	4:59 pm	Capricorn
6th	10:19 pm	Aquarius
9th	0:26 am	Pisces
11th	0:19 am	Aries
12th	11:14 pm	Taurus
11th	1:18 am	Gemini
17th	6:24 am	Cancer
19th	3:38 pm	Leo
22nd	2:45 am	Virgo
24th	4:30 pm	Libra
27th	4:14 am	Scorpio
29th	2:16 pm	Sagittarius
31st	10:31 pm	Capricorn

November 1935		
3rd	4:35 am	Aquarius
5th	8:17 am	Pisces
7th	9:52 am	Aries
9th	10:30 am	Taurus
11th	11:57 am	Gemini
13th	4:01 pm	Cancer
11th	11:50 pm	Leo
18th	11:13 am	Virgo
20th	11:12 pm	Libra
23rd	11:33 am	Scorpio
25th	9:08 pm	Sagittarius
28th	4:27 am	Capricorn
30th	9:57 am	Aquarius

December 1935		
2nd	2:01 pm	Pisces
4th	4:52 pm	Aries
6th	7:04 pm	Taurus
8th	9:38 pm	Gemini
11th	1:55 am	Cancer
13th	9:10 am	Leo
15th	7:34 pm	Virgo
18th	7:57 am	Libra
20th	8:00 pm	Scorpio
23rd	5:41 am	Sagittarius
25th	12:24 pm	Capricorn
27th	4:44 pm	Aquarius
29th	7:42 pm	Pisces
31st	10:11 pm	Aries

January 1936		
3rd	1:12 am	Taurus
5th	1:06 am	Gemini
7th	10:32 am	Cancer
9th	6:04 pm	Leo
12th	4:06 am	Virgo
14th	4:11 pm	Libra
17th	4:36 am	Scorpio
19th	3:06 pm	Sagittarius
21st	10:17 pm	Capricorn
24th	1:60 am	Aquarius
26th	3:34 am	Pisces
28th	4:37 am	Aries
30th	6:40 am	Taurus

February 1936		
1st	10:43 am	Gemini
3rd	5:02 pm	Cancer
6th	1:27 am	Leo
8th	11:51 am	Virgo
10th	11:46 pm	Libra
13th	12:23 pm	Scorpio
11th	11:14 pm	Sagittarius
18th	8:15 am	Capricorn
20th	12:40 pm	Aquarius
22nd	1:52 pm	Pisces
24th	1:36 pm	Aries
26th	1:55 pm	Taurus
28th	4:35 pm	Gemini
31st	1:08 pm	Leo

March 1936		
1st	10:27 pm	Cancer
4th	7:23 am	Leo
6th	6:20 pm	Virgo
9th	6:28 am	Libra
11th	7:05 pm	Scorpio
14th	7:03 am	Sagittarius
16th	4:48 pm	Capricorn
18th	10:11 pm	Aquarius
21st	0:18 am	Pisces
23rd	0:31 am	Aries
24th	11:38 pm	Taurus
27th	0:32 am	Gemini
29th	4:56 am	Cancer

April 1936		
3rd	0:08 am	Virgo
5th	12:32 pm	Libra
8th	1:06 am	Scorpio
10th	1:01 pm	Sagittarius
12th	11:24 pm	Capricorn
15th	6:41 am	Aquarius
17th	10:33 am	Pisces
19th	11:18 am	Aries
21st	10:39 am	Taurus
23rd	10:43 am	Gemini
25th	1:28 pm	Cancer
27th	8:06 pm	Leo
30th	6:21 am	Virgo

May 1936		
2nd	6:44 pm	Libra
5th	7:17 am	Scorpio
7th	6:11 pm	Sagittarius
10th	4:11 am	Capricorn
12th	12:44 pm	Aquarius
14th	1:10 pm	Pisces
16th	8:12 pm	Aries
18th	8:49 pm	Taurus
20th	9:14 pm	Gemini
22nd	11:21 pm	Cancer
25th	4:41 pm	Leo
27th	1:12 pm	Virgo
30th	1:39 am	Libra

June 1936		
1st	2:12 pm	Scorpio
4th	1:37 am	Sagittarius
6th	11:01 am	Capricorn
8th	6:15 pm	Aquarius
10th	11:28 pm	Pisces
13th	2:46 am	Aries
15th	4:49 am	Taurus
17th	6:32 am	Gemini
19th	9:14 am	Cancer
21st	2:11 pm	Leo
23rd	10:17 pm	Virgo
26th	9:26 am	Libra
28th	9:53 pm	Scorpio
31st	3:22 am	Capricorn

July 1936		
1st	9:24 am	Sagittarius
3rd	6:32 pm	Capricorn
6th	0:16 am	Aquarius
8th	5:10 am	Pisces
10th	8:11 am	Aries
12th	10:48 am	Taurus
14th	1:42 pm	Gemini
16th	5:31 pm	Cancer
18th	11:00 pm	Leo
21st	6:58 am	Virgo
23rd	5:33 pm	Libra
26th	5:13 am	Scorpio
28th	1:14 pm	Sagittarius
31st	10:05 pm	Pisces

August 1936		
2nd	9:21 am	Aquarius
4th	12:34 pm	Pisces
6th	2:23 pm	Aries
8th	4:15 pm	Taurus
10th	7:15 pm	Gemini
12th	11:53 pm	Cancer
15th	6:24 am	Leo
17th	2:49 pm	Virgo
20th	1:18 am	Libra
22nd	1:37 pm	Scorpio
25th	2:09 am	Sagittarius
27th	12:30 pm	Capricorn
29th	7:08 pm	Aquarius

September 1936		
2nd	10:44 pm	Aries
4th	11:01 pm	Taurus
7th	0:15 am	Gemini
9th	1:19 am	Cancer
11th	12:17 pm	Leo
13th	9:22 pm	Virgo
16th	8:16 am	Libra
18th	8:34 pm	Scorpio
21st	9:24 am	Sagittarius
23rd	8:11 pm	Capricorn
26th	4:49 am	Aquarius
28th	8:35 am	Pisces
30th	9:08 am	Aries

October 1936		
2nd	8:28 am	Taurus
4th	8:41 am	Gemini
6th	11:34 am	Cancer
8th	5:49 pm	Leo
11th	3:02 am	Virgo
13th	2:21 pm	Libra
16th	2:48 am	Scorpio
18th	3:38 pm	Sagittarius
21st	3:37 am	Capricorn
23rd	12:55 pm	Aquarius
25th	6:24 pm	Pisces
27th	8:06 pm	Aries
29th	7:35 pm	Taurus
31st	6:52 pm	Gemini

November 1936		
2nd	8:03 pm	Cancer
5th	0:37 am	Leo
7th	9:03 am	Virgo
9th	8:16 pm	Libra
12th	8:51 am	Scorpio
14th	9:35 pm	Sagittarius
17th	9:19 am	Capricorn
19th	7:08 pm	Aquarius
22nd	2:03 am	Pisces
24th	5:33 am	Aries
26th	6:28 am	Taurus
28th	6:14 am	Gemini
30th	6:44 am	Cancer

December 1936		
2nd	9:48 am	Leo
4th	4:36 pm	Virgo
7th	2:56 am	Libra
9th	3:28 pm	Scorpio
12th	4:06 am	Sagittarius
14th	3:24 pm	Capricorn
17th	0:43 am	Aquarius
19th	7:42 am	Pisces
21st	12:23 pm	Aries
23rd	3:03 pm	Taurus
25th	4:24 pm	Gemini
27th	5:37 pm	Cancer
29th	8:15 pm	Leo

January 1937		
1st	1:46 am	Virgo
3rd	10:18 am	Libra
5th	10:57 pm	Scorpio
8th	11:41 am	Sagittarius
10th	10:52 pm	Capricorn
13th	7:22 am	Aquarius
15th	1:26 pm	Pisces
17th	5:47 pm	Aries
19th	9:06 pm	Taurus
21st	11:55 pm	Gemini
24th	2:40 am	Cancer
26th	6:10 am	Leo
28th	11:34 am	Virgo
30th	7:51 pm	Libra

February 1937		
2nd	7:10 am	Scorpio
4th	7:57 pm	Sagittarius
7th	7:30 am	Capricorn
9th	3:55 pm	Aquarius
11th	9:08 pm	Pisces
14th	6:12 am	Aries
16th	2:35 am	Taurus
18th	5:24 am	Gemini
20th	9:07 am	Cancer
22nd	1:54 pm	Leo
24th	8:06 pm	Virgo
27th	4:29 am	Libra

March 1937		
1st	3:26 pm	Scorpio
4th	4:07 am	Sagittarius
6th	4:19 pm	Capricorn
9th	1:34 am	Aquarius
11th	6:46 am	Pisces
13th	8:57 am	Aries
15th	9:55 am	Taurus
17th	11:22 am	Gemini
19th	2:29 pm	Cancer
21st	7:38 pm	Leo
24th	2:45 am	Virgo
26th	11:50 am	Libra
28th	10:52 pm	Scorpio
31st	11:34 am	Sagittarius

April 1937		
3rd	0:16 am	Capricorn
5th	10:34 am	Aquarius
7th	4:54 pm	Pisces
9th	7:25 pm	Aries
11th	7:39 pm	Taurus
13th	7:35 pm	Gemini
15th	9:04 pm	Cancer
18th	1:12 am	Leo
20th	8:18 am	Virgo
22nd	5:54 pm	Libra
25th	5:22 am	Scorpio
27th	6:06 pm	Sagittarius
30th	6:56 am	Capricorn

May 1937		
2nd	6:06 pm	Aquarius
5th	1:57 am	Pisces
7th	5:44 am	Aries
9th	6:31 am	Taurus
11th	5:58 am	Gemini
13th	6:03 am	Cancer
15th	8:33 am	Leo
17th	2:23 pm	Virgo
19th	11:35 pm	Libra
22nd	11:21 am	Scorpio
25th	0:10 am	Sagittarius
27th	12:51 pm	Capricorn
30th	0:13 am	Aquarius

June 1937		
1st	8:54 am	Pisces
3rd	2:17 pm	Aries
5th	4:34 pm	Taurus
7th	4:46 pm	Gemini
9th	4:34 pm	Cancer
11th	5:49 pm	Leo
13th	10:04 pm	Virgo
16th	6:11 am	Libra
18th	5:34 pm	Scorpio
21st	6:26 am	Sagittarius
23rd	6:58 pm	Capricorn
26th	5:52 am	Aquarius
28th	2:35 pm	Pisces
30th	8:50 pm	Aries

July 1937		
3rd	0:35 am	Taurus
5th	2:17 am	Gemini
7th	2:55 am	Cancer
9th	4:03 am	Leo
11th	7:22 am	Virgo
13th	2:09 pm	Libra
16th	0:36 am	Scorpio
18th	1:21 pm	Sagittarius
21st	1:51 am	Capricorn
23rd	12:17 pm	Aquarius
25th	8:21 pm	Pisces
28th	2:15 am	Aries
30th	6:31 am	Taurus
30th	6:06 pm	Cancer

August 1937		
1st	9:30 am	Gemini
3rd	11:35 am	Cancer
5th	1:39 pm	Leo
7th	4:59 pm	Virgo
9th	10:59 pm	Libra
12th	8:41 am	Scorpio
14th	8:59 pm	Sagittarius
17th	9:36 am	Capricorn
19th	8:03 pm	Aquarius
22nd	3:27 am	Pisces
24th	8:23 am	Aries
26th	11:57 am	Taurus
28th	3:03 pm	Gemini

September 1937		
1st	9:24 pm	Leo
4th	1:56 am	Virgo
6th	7:53 am	Libra
8th	5:03 pm	Scorpio
11th	5:01 am	Sagittarius
13th	5:51 pm	Capricorn
16th	4:48 am	Aquarius
18th	12:14 pm	Pisces
20th	4:28 pm	Aries
22nd	6:49 pm	Taurus
24th	8:46 pm	Gemini
26th	11:26 pm	Cancer
29th	3:17 am	Leo

October 1937		
1st	8:31 am	Virgo
3rd	3:36 pm	Libra
6th	0:57 am	Scorpio
8th	12:47 pm	Sagittarius
11th	1:47 am	Capricorn
13th	1:35 pm	Aquarius
15th	10:02 pm	Pisces
18th	2:32 am	Aries
20th	4:09 am	Taurus
22nd	4:41 am	Gemini
24th	5:49 am	Cancer
26th	8:46 am	Leo
28th	2:05 pm	Virgo
30th	9:48 pm	Libra

November 1937		
2nd	7:51 am	Scorpio
4th	7:48 pm	Sagittarius
7th	8:51 am	Capricorn
9th	9:18 pm	Aquarius
12th	7:04 am	Pisces
14th	12:55 pm	Aries
16th	3:08 pm	Taurus
18th	3:09 pm	Gemini
20th	2:50 pm	Cancer
22nd	4:00 pm	Leo
24th	7:59 pm	Virgo
27th	3:23 am	Libra
29th	1:49 pm	Scorpio

December 1937		
2nd	2:06 am	Sagittarius
4th	3:07 pm	Capricorn
7th	3:40 am	Aquarius
9th	2:18 pm	Pisces
11th	9:53 pm	Aries
14th	1:49 am	Taurus
16th	2:42 am	Gemini
18th	2:03 am	Cancer
20th	1:50 am	Leo
22nd	4:01 am	Virgo
24th	9:58 am	Libra
26th	7:46 pm	Scorpio
29th	8:13 am	Sagittarius
31st	9:17 pm	Capricorn

January 1938		
3rd	9:29 am	Aquarius
5th	8:06 pm	Pisces
8th	4:26 am	Aries
10th	10:02 am	Taurus
12th	12:47 pm	Gemini
14th	1:20 pm	Cancer
16th	1:11 pm	Leo
18th	2:17 pm	Virgo
20th	6:32 pm	Libra
23rd	2:57 am	Scorpio
25th	2:52 pm	Sagittarius
28th	3:57 am	Capricorn
30th	3:57 pm	Aquarius

February 1938		
2nd	1:57 am	Pisces
4th	9:53 am	Aries
6th	3:56 pm	Taurus
8th	8:07 pm	Gemini
10th	10:25 pm	Cancer
12th	11:34 pm	Leo
15th	0:57 am	Virgo
17th	4:32 am	Libra
19th	11:42 am	Scorpio
21st	10:34 pm	Sagittarius
24th	11:26 am	Capricorn
26th	11:34 pm	Aquarius

March 1938		
1st	9:10 am	Pisces
3rd	4:14 pm	Aries
5th	9:29 pm	Taurus
8th	1:33 am	Gemini
10th	4:46 am	Cancer
12th	7:24 am	Leo
14th	10:07 am	Virgo
16th	2:13 pm	Libra
18th	8:56 pm	Scorpio
21st	7:03 am	Sagittarius
23rd	7:32 pm	Capricorn
26th	7:52 am	Aquarius
28th	5:48 pm	Pisces
31st	0:33 am	Aries

April 1938		
2nd	4:41 am	Taurus
4th	7:32 am	Gemini
6th	10:08 am	Cancer
8th	1:06 pm	Leo
10th	4:52 pm	Virgo
12th	10:03 pm	Libra
15th	5:24 am	Scorpio
17th	3:22 pm	Sagittarius
20th	3:33 am	Capricorn
22nd	4:09 pm	Aquarius
25th	2:51 am	Pisces
27th	10:03 am	Aries
29th	1:57 pm	Taurus

May 1938		
1st	3:43 pm	Gemini
3rd	4:50 pm	Cancer
5th	6:43 pm	Leo
7th	10:17 pm	Virgo
10th	4:07 am	Libra
12th	12:19 pm	Scorpio
14th	10:41 pm	Sagittarius
17th	10:52 am	Capricorn
19th	11:38 pm	Aquarius
22nd	11:05 am	Pisces
24th	7:32 pm	Aries
27th	0:17 am	Taurus
29th	1:51 am	Gemini
31st	1:52 am	Cancer

June 1938		
2nd	2:10 am	Leo
4th	4:14 pm	Virgo
6th	9:40 am	Libra
8th	6:03 pm	Scorpio
11th	4:58 am	Sagittarius
13th	5:22 pm	Capricorn
16th	6:07 am	Aquarius
18th	6:01 pm	Pisces
21st	5:58 am	Aries
23rd	9:44 am	Taurus
25th	12:21 pm	Gemini
27th	12:26 pm	Cancer
29th	11:48 am	Leo

July 1938		
1st	12:29 pm	Virgo
3rd	4:14 pm	Libra
5th	11:49 pm	Scorpio
8th	10:49 am	Sagittarius
10th	11:23 pm	Capricorn
13th	12:05 pm	Aquarius
15th	11:56 pm	Pisces
18th	9:50 am	Aries
20th	1:28 pm	Taurus
22nd	9:42 pm	Gemini
24th	10:55 pm	Cancer.
26th	10:27 pm	Leo
28th	10:19 pm	Virgo
31st	0:35 am	Libra

August 1938		
2nd	6:54 am	Scorpio
4th	5:05 pm	Sagittarius
7th	5:33 am	Capricorn
9th	6:14 pm	Aquarius
12th	5:43 am	Pisces
14th	3:33 pm	Aries
16th	11:27 pm	Taurus
19th	4:50 am	Gemini
21st	7:58 am	Cancer
23rd	8:27 am	Leo
25th	8:47 am	Virgo
27th	10:33 am	Libra
29th	5:53 pm	Scorpio

September 1938			October 1938			November 1938			December 1938		
1st	0:28 am	Sagittarius	3rd	8:57 am	Aquarius	2nd	5:09 am	Pisces	2nd	0:04 am	Aries
3rd	12:51 pm	Capricorn	5th	8:27 pm	Pisces	4th	2:32 pm	Aries	4th	6:57 am	Taurus
6th	1:10 am	Aquarius	8th	5:20 am	Aries	6th	8:40 pm	Taurus	6th	10:15 am	Gemini
8th	12:26 pm	Pisces	10th	11:40 am	Taurus	9th	0:03 am	Gemini	8th	11:07 am	Cancer
10th	9:41 pm	Aries	12th	4:09 pm	Gemini	11th	1:59 am	Cancer	10th	11:20 am	Leo
13th	4:54 am	Taurus	14th	7:31 pm	Cancer	13th	5:52 am	Leo	12th	12:42 pm	Virgo
15th	10:22 am	Gemini	16th	10:20 pm	Leo	15th	6:40 am	Virgo	14th	4:31 pm	Libra
17th	2:08 pm	Cancer	19th	1:10 am	Virgo	17th	11:06 am	Libra	16th	11:14 pm	Scorpio
19th	4:27 pm	Leo	21st	4:46 am	Libra	19th	5:28 pm	Scorpio	19th	8:54 am	Sagittarius
21st	6:03 pm	Virgo	23rd	10:05 am	Scorpio	22nd	1:58 am	Sagittarius	21st	7:59 pm	Capricorn
23rd	8:23 pm	Libra	25th	1:59 pm	Sagittarius	24th	12:42 pm	Capricorn	24th	7:50 am	Aquarius
26th	0:59 am	Scorpio	28th	4:42 am	Capricorn	27th	1:01 am	Aquarius	26th	8:42 pm	Pisces
28th	9:08 am	Sagittarius	30th	5:09 pm	Aquarius	29th	1:29 pm	Pisces	29th	8:10 am	Aries
30th	8:23 pm	Capricorn							31st	4:44 pm	Taurus

January 1939			February 1939			March 1939			April 1939		
2nd	9:18 pm	Gemini	1st	9:17 am	Cancer	2nd	7:28 pm	Leo	1st	4:39 am	Virgo
4th	10:19 pm	Cancer	3rd	9:05 am	Leo	4th	7:17 pm	Virgo	3rd	5:50 am	Libra
6th	9:33 pm	Leo	5th	8:06 am	Virgo	6th	7:29 pm	Libra	5th	8:26 am	Scorpio
8th	9:10 pm	Virgo	7th	8:35 am	Libra	8th	10:01 pm	Scorpio	7th	1:52 pm	Sagittarius
10th	11:12 pm	Libra	9th	12:28 pm	Scorpio	11th	4:26 am	Sagittarius	9th	10:46 pm	Capricorn
13th	4:57 am	Scorpio	11th	8:26 pm	Sagittarius	13th	2:38 pm	Capricorn	12th	10:33 am	Aquarius
15th	2:13 pm	Sagittarius	14th	7:43 am	Capricorn	16th	3:00 am	Aquarius	14th	11:04 pm	Pisces
18th	1:45 am	Capricorn	16th	8:21 pm	Aquarius	18th	3:29 pm	Pisces	17th	10:10 am	Aries
20th	2:16 pm	Aquarius	19th	8:51 am	Pisces	21st	2:38 am	Aries	19th	6:53 pm	Taurus
23rd	2:51 am	Pisces	21st	8:23 pm	Aries	23rd	11:55 am	Taurus	22nd	1:14 am	Gemini
25th	2:40 pm	Aries	24th	6:17 am	Taurus	25th	7:13 pm	Gemini	24th	5:41 am	Cancer
28th	0:30 am	Taurus	26th	1:44 pm	Gemini	28th	0:19 am	Cancer	26th	8:52 am	Leo
30th	6:45 am	Gemini	28th	6:04 pm	Cancer	30th	3:14 am	Leo	28th	11:26 am	Virgo

May 1939			June 1939			July 1939			August 1939		
2nd	5:39 pm	Scorpio	1st	7:18 am	Sagittarius	3rd	9:56 am	Aquarius	2nd	4:42 am	Pisces
4th	11:11 pm	Sagittarius	3rd	3:52 pm	Capricorn	5th	10:17 pm	Pisces	4th	5:21 pm	Aries
7th	7:57 am	Capricorn	6th	2:42 am	Aquarius	8th	10:47 am	Aries	7th	4:45 am	Taurus
9th	6:42 pm	Aquarius	8th	3:05 pm	Pisces	10th	9:25 pm	Taurus	9th	1:01 pm	Gemini
12th	7:08 am	Pisces	11th	3:10 am	Aries	13th	4:17 am	Gemini	11th	5:17 pm	Cancer
14th	6:38 pm	Aries	13th	12:37 pm	Taurus	15th	7:12 am	Cancer	13th	6:07 pm	Leo
17th	3:26 am	Taurus	15th	6:28 pm	Gemini	17th	7:30 am	Leo	15th	5:20 pm	Virgo
19th	9:02 am	Gemini	17th	9:04 pm	Cancer	19th	7:10 am	Virgo	17th	5:08 pm	Libra
21st	12:19 pm	Cancer	19th	9:57 pm	Leo	21st	8:14 am	Libra	19th	7:24 pm	Scorpio
23rd	2:33 pm	Leo	21st	10:56 pm	Virgo	23rd	12:08 pm	Scorpio	22nd	1:15 am	Sagittarius
25th	4:51 pm	Virgo	24th	1:30 am	Libra	25th	7:12 pm	Sagittarius	24th	10:36 am	Capricorn
27th	8:06 pm	Libra	26th	6:28 am	Scorpio	28th	4:52 am	Capricorn	26th	10:10 pm	Aquarius
30th	0:47 am	Scorpio	28th	1:41 pm	Sagittarius	30th	4:16 pm	Aquarius	29th	10:43 am	Pisces
			30th	10:54 pm	Capricorn	31st	11:16 pm	Aries			

September 1939			October 1939			November 1939			December 1939		
3rd	10:45 am	Taurus	3rd	1:38 am	Gemini	1st	1:39 pm	Cancer	3rd	2:22 am	Virgo
5th	8:00 pm	Gemini	5th	8:14 am	Cancer	3rd	5:50 pm	Leo	5th	5:23 am	Libra
8th	1:51 am	Cancer	7th	12:07 pm	Leo	5th	8:56 pm	Virgo	7th	8:60 am	Scorpio
10th	4:11 am	Leo	9th	1:44 pm	Virgo	7th	11:03 pm	Libra	9th	1:35 pm	Sagittarius
12th	4:09 am	Virgo	11th	2:18 pm	Libra	10th	1:15 am	Scorpio	11th	7:54 pm	Capricorn
14th	3:42 am	Libra	13th	3:22 pm	Scorpio	12th	4:46 am	Sagittarius	14th	4:47 am	Aquarius
16th	4:47 am	Scorpio	15th	6:40 pm	Sagittarius	14th	10:48 am	Capricorn	16th	4:17 pm	Pisces
16th	9:08 am	Sagittarius	18th	1:24 am	Capricorn	16th	8:04 pm	Aquarius	19th	5:02 am	Aries
20th	5:15 pm	Capricorn	20th	11:44 am	Aquarius	19th	8:02 am	Pisces	21st	4:30 pm	Taurus
23rd	4:24 am	Aquarius	23rd	0:06 am	Pisces	21st	8:35 pm	Aries	24th	0:37 am	Gemini
25th	4:59 pm	Pisces	25th	12:27 pm	Aries	24th	7:19 am	Taurus	26th	5:02 am	Cancer
28th	5:21 am	Aries	27th	11:10 pm	Taurus	26th	3:05 pm	Gemini	28th	7:05 am	Leo
30th	4:27 pm	Taurus	30th	7:28 am	Gemini	28th	8:10 pm	Cancer	30th	8:30 am	Virgo
			30th	11:34 pm	Leo						

January 1940
1st	10:47 am	Libra
3rd	2:40 pm	Scorpio
5th	8:14 pm	Sagittarius
8th	3:31 am	Capricorn
10th	12:46 pm	Aquarius
14th	0:04 am	Pisces
15th	12:56 pm	Aries
18th	1:16 am	Taurus
20th	10:27 am	Gemini
22nd	3:30 pm	Cancer
24th	5:09 pm	Leo
26th	5:14 pm	Virgo
28th	5:46 pm	Libra
30th	8:20 pm	Scorpio

February 1940
2nd	1:37 am	Sagittarius
4th	9:30 am	Capricorn
6th	7:23 pm	Aquarius
9th	7:01 am	Pisces
11th	7:49 pm	Aries
14th	8:33 am	Taurus
16th	7:08 pm	Gemini
19th	1:47 am	Cancer
21st	4:17 am	Leo
23rd	4:12 am	Virgo
25th	3:31 am	Libra
27th	4:17 am	Scorpio
29th	7:59 am	Sagittarius

March 1940
2nd	3:07 pm	Capricorn
5th	1:07 am	Aquarius
7th	1:08 pm	Pisces
10th	1:60 am	Aries
12th	2:44 pm	Taurus
15th	1:55 am	Gemini
17th	9:53 am	Cancer
19th	2:11 pm	Leo
21st	3:18 pm	Virgo
23rd	2:49 pm	Libra
25th	2:38 pm	Scorpio
27th	4:36 pm	Sagittarius
29th	10:02 pm	Capricorn

April 1940
1st	7:15 am	Aquarius
3rd	7:11 pm	Pisces
6th	8:09 am	Aries
8th	8:38 pm	Taurus
11th	7:29 am	Gemini
13th	4:01 pm	Cancer
15th	9:43 pm	Leo
18th	0:34 am	Virgo
20th	1:23 am	Libra
22nd	1:34 am	Scorpio
24th	2:50 am	Sagittarius
26th	6:54 am	Capricorn
28th	2:44 pm	Aquarius

May 1940
1st	1:55 am	Pisces
3rd	2:51 pm	Aries
6th	3:11 am	Taurus
8th	1:29 pm	Gemini
10th	9:31 pm	Cancer
13th	3:20 am	Leo
15th	7:15 am	Virgo
17th	9:39 am	Libra
19th	11:12 am	Scorpio
21st	1:03 pm	Sagittarius
23rd	4:39 pm	Capricorn
25th	11:21 pm	Aquarius
28th	9:42 am	Pisces
30th	10:18 pm	Aries

June 1940
2nd	10:41 am	Taurus
4th	8:46 pm	Gemini
7th	3:59 am	Cancer
9th	8:58 am	Leo
11th	12:38 pm	Virgo
13th	3:41 pm	Libra
15th	6:31 pm	Scorpio
17th	9:33 pm	Sagittarius
20th	1:45 am	Capricorn
22nd	8:19 am	Aquarius
24th	5:59 pm	Pisces
27th	6:14 am	Aries
29th	6:51 pm	Taurus

July 1940
2nd	5:11 am	Gemini
4th	12:05 pm	Cancer
6th	4:09 pm	Leo
8th	6:43 pm	Virgo
10th	9:07 pm	Libra
13th	0:07 am	Scorpio
15th	4:06 am	Sagittarius
17th	9:19 am	Capricorn
19th	4:24 pm	Aquarius
22nd	1:59 am	Pisces
24th	2:02 pm	Aries
27th	2:54 am	Taurus
29th	1:59 pm	Gemini
31st	9:30 pm	Cancer

August 1940
3rd	1:20 am	Leo
5th	2:50 am	Virgo
7th	3:51 am	Libra
9th	5:48 am	Scorpio
11th	9:32 am	Sagittarius
13th	3:17 pm	Capricorn
15th	11:07 pm	Aquarius
18th	9:12 am	Pisces
20th	9:14 pm	Aries
23rd	10:15 am	Taurus
25th	10:12 pm	Gemini
28th	6:49 am	Cancer
30th	11:25 am	Leo

September 1940
1st	12:54 pm	Virgo
3rd	12:55 pm	Libra
5th	1:20 pm	Scorpio
7th	3:41 pm	Sagittarius
9th	8:47 pm	Capricorn
12th	4:53 am	Aquarius
14th	3:27 pm	Pisces
17th	3:43 am	Aries
19th	4:45 pm	Taurus
22nd	5:03 am	Gemini
24th	2:54 pm	Cancer
26th	9:07 pm	Leo
28th	11:42 pm	Virgo
30th	11:47 pm	Libra

October 1940
2nd	11:12 pm	Scorpio
4th	11:53 pm	Sagittarius
7th	3:31 am	Capricorn
9th	10:48 am	Aquarius
11th	9:18 pm	Pisces
14th	9:50 am	Aries
16th	10:49 pm	Taurus
19th	10:57 am	Gemini
21st	9:17 pm	Cancer
24th	4:47 am	Leo
26th	9:06 am	Virgo
28th	10:35 am	Libra
30th	10:26 am	Scorpio

November 1940
1st	10:26 am	Sagittarius
3rd	12:29 pm	Capricorn
5th	6:08 pm	Aquarius
8th	3:49 am	Pisces
10th	4:14 pm	Aries
13th	5:12 am	Taurus
15th	4:58 pm	Gemini
18th	2:51 am	Cancer
20th	10:35 am	Leo
22nd	4:07 pm	Virgo
24th	7:22 pm	Libra
26th	8:45 pm	Scorpio
28th	9:20 pm	Sagittarius
30th	10:52 pm	Capricorn

December 1940
3rd	3:16 am	Aquarius
5th	11:41 am	Pisces
7th	11:28 pm	Aries
10th	12:26 pm	Taurus
13th	0:08 am	Gemini
15th	9:17 am	Cancer
17th	4:14 pm	Leo
19th	9:34 pm	Virgo
22nd	1:36 am	Libra
24th	4:30 am	Scorpio
26th	6:37 am	Sagittarius
28th	9:02 am	Capricorn
30th	1:15 pm	Aquarius

January 1941
1st	8:38 pm	Pisces
4th	7:38 am	Aries
6th	8:29 pm	Taurus
9th	8:25 am	Gemini
11th	5:51 pm	Cancer
13th	11:40 pm	Leo
16th	3:46 am	Virgo
18th	7:00 am	Libra
20th	10:05 am	Scorpio
22nd	1:18 pm	Sagittarius
24th	5:03 pm	Capricorn
26th	10:07 pm	Aquarius
29th	5:38 am	Pisces
31st	4:05 pm	Aries

February 1941
3rd	4:41 am	Taurus
5th	5:08 pm	Gemini
8th	2:55 am	Cancer
10th	9:05 am	Leo
12th	2:20 pm	Virgo
14th	2:08 pm	Libra
16th	3:54 pm	Scorpio
18th	6:39 pm	Sagittarius
20th	10:55 pm	Capricorn
23rd	5:03 am	Aquarius
25th	1:21 pm	Pisces
27th	11:54 pm	Aries

March 1941
2nd	12:24 pm	Taurus
5th	1:12 am	Gemini
7th	11:59 am	Cancer
9th	7:17 pm	Leo
11th	10:52 pm	Virgo
13th	11:52 pm	Libra
16th	0:03 am	Scorpio
18th	1:09 am	Sagittarius
20th	4:27 am	Capricorn
22nd	10:36 am	Aquarius
24th	7:32 pm	Pisces
27th	6:41 am	Aries
29th	7:14 pm	Taurus

April 1941
1st	8:05 am	Gemini
3rd	7:42 pm	Cancer
6th	4:23 am	Leo
8th	9:17 am	Virgo
10th	10:52 am	Libra
12th	10:32 am	Scorpio
14th	10:12 am	Sagittarius
16th	11:45 am	Capricorn
18th	4:36 pm	Aquarius
21st	1:07 am	Pisces
23rd	12:36 pm	Aries
26th	1:21 am	Taurus
28th	2:09 pm	Gemini

May 1941

1st	1:55 am	Cancer
3rd	11:29 am	Leo
5th	6:02 pm	Virgo
7th	9:10 pm	Libra
9th	9:33 pm	Scorpio
11th	8:51 pm	Sagittarius
13th	9:07 pm	Capricorn
16th	0:16 am	Aquarius
18th	7:39 am	Pisces
20th	6:36 pm	Aries
23rd	7:25 am	Taurus
25th	8:09 pm	Gemini
28th	7:34 am	Cancer
30th	5:13 pm	Leo

June 1941

2nd	0:37 am	Virgo
4th	5:14 am	Libra
6th	7:10 am	Scorpio
8th	7:23 am	Sagittarius
10th	7:36 am	Capricorn
12th	9:47 am	Aquarius
14th	3:40 pm	Pisces
17th	1:32 am	Aries
19th	2:04 pm	Taurus
22nd	2:43 am	Gemini
24th	1:48 pm	Cancer
26th	10:54 pm	Leo
29th	6:00 am	Virgo

July 1941

1st	11:13 am	Libra
3rd	2:30 pm	Scorpio
5th	4:11 pm	Sagittarius
7th	5:22 pm	Capricorn
9th	7:38 pm	Aquarius
12th	0:43 am	Pisces
14th	9:38 am	Aries
16th	9:31 pm	Taurus
19th	10:08 am	Gemini
21st	9:13 pm	Cancer
24th	5:45 am	Leo
26th	12:00 pm	Virgo
28th	4:39 pm	Libra
30th	8:08 pm	Scorpio

August 1941

1st	10:49 pm	Sagittarius
4th	1:16 am	Capricorn
6th	4:34 am	Aquarius
8th	9:55 am	Pisces
10th	6:14 pm	Aries
13th	5:33 am	Taurus
15th	6:09 pm	Gemini
18th	5:34 am	Cancer
20th	2:11 pm	Leo
22nd	7:51 pm	Virgo
24th	11:21 pm	Libra
27th	1:49 am	Scorpio
29th	4:14 am	Sagittarius
31st	7:20 am	Capricorn

September 1941

2nd	11:40 am	Aquarius
4th	5:54 pm	Pisces
7th	2:28 am	Aries
9th	1:33 pm	Taurus
12th	2:05 am	Gemini
14th	2:06 pm	Cancer
16th	11:36 pm	Leo
19th	5:26 am	Virgo
21st	8:14 am	Libra
23rd	9:23 am	Scorpio
25th	10:27 am	Sagittarius
27th	12:48 pm	Capricorn
29th	5:19 pm	Aquarius

October 1941

2nd	0:17 am	Pisces
4th	9:39 am	Aries
6th	8:51 pm	Taurus
9th	9:22 am	Gemini
11th	9:52 pm	Cancer
14th	8:25 am	Leo
16th	3:31 pm	Virgo
18th	6:51 pm	Libra
20th	7:24 pm	Scorpio
22nd	7:02 pm	Sagittarius
24th	7:43 pm	Capricorn
26th	11:02 pm	Aquarius
29th	5:54 am	Pisces
31st	3:40 pm	Aries

November 1941

3rd	3:19 am	Taurus
5th	3:52 pm	Gemini
8th	4:24 am	Cancer
10th	3:45 pm	Leo
13th	0:29 am	Virgo
15th	5:18 am	Libra
17th	6:38 am	Scorpio
19th	5:54 am	Sagittarius
21st	5:15 am	Capricorn
23rd	6:52 am	Aquarius
25th	12:16 pm	Pisces
27th	9:28 pm	Aries
30th	9:19 am	Taurus

December 1941

2nd	9:59 pm	Gemini
5th	10:20 am	Cancer
7th	9:41 pm	Leo
10th	7:08 am	Virgo
12th	1:41 pm	Libra
14th	4:47 pm	Scorpio
16th	5:08 pm	Sagittarius
18th	4:30 pm	Capricorn
20th	4:59 pm	Aquarius
22nd	8:37 pm	Pisces
25th	4:28 am	Aries
27th	5:46 pm	Taurus
30th	4:27 am	Gemini

January 1942

1st	4:40 pm	Cancer
4th	3:32 am	Leo
6th	12:19 pm	Virgo
8th	7:47 pm	Libra
11th	0:24 am	Scorpio
13th	2:30 am	Sagittarius
15th	3:07 am	Capricorn
17th	3:54 am	Aquarius
19th	6:46 am	Pisces
21st	1:14 pm	Aries
23rd	11:21 pm	Taurus
26th	11:45 am	Gemini
29th	0:04 am	Cancer
31st	10:35 am	Leo

February 1942

2nd	6:56 pm	Virgo
5th	1:18 am	Libra
7th	5:55 am	Scorpio
9th	9:06 am	Sagittarius
11th	11:18 am	Capricorn
13th	1:30 pm	Aquarius
15th	4:55 pm	Pisces
17th	10:47 pm	Aries
20th	8:01 am	Taurus
22nd	7:48 pm	Gemini
25th	8:15 am	Cancer
27th	7:05 pm	Leo

March 1942

2nd	3:06 am	Virgo
4th	8:21 am	Libra
6th	11:49 am	Scorpio
8th	2:29 pm	Sagittarius
10th	5:10 pm	Capricorn
12th	8:32 pm	Aquarius
15th	1:10 am	Pisces
17th	7:44 am	Aries
19th	4:41 pm	Taurus
22nd	4:02 am	Gemini
24th	4:32 pm	Cancer
27th	4:03 am	Leo
29th	12:33 pm	Virgo
31st	5:34 pm	Libra

April 1942

2nd	7:55 pm	Scorpio
4th	9:05 pm	Sagittarius
6th	10:43 pm	Capricorn
9th	1:58 am	Aquarius
11th	7:21 am	Pisces
13th	2:51 pm	Aries
16th	0:18 am	Taurus
18th	11:39 am	Gemini
21st	0:10 am	Cancer
23rd	12:19 pm	Leo
25th	10:01 pm	Virgo
28th	5:49 am	Libra
30th	5:58 am	Scorpio

May 1942

2nd	6:04 am	Sagittarius
4th	6:09 am	Capricorn
6th	8:01 am	Aquarius
8th	12:48 pm	Pisces
10th	8:32 pm	Aries
13th	6:38 am	Taurus
15th	6:16 pm	Gemini
18th	6:49 am	Cancer
20th	7:19 pm	Leo
23rd	6:04 am	Virgo
25th	1:15 pm	Libra
27th	4:26 pm	Scorpio
29th	4:38 pm	Sagittarius
31st	3:47 pm	Capricorn

June 1942

2nd	4:05 pm	Aquarius
4th	7:18 pm	Pisces
7th	2:14 am	Aries
9th	12:18 pm	Taurus
12th	0:12 am	Gemini
14th	12:49 pm	Cancer
17th	1:18 am	Leo
19th	12:29 pm	Virgo
21st	9:01 pm	Libra
24th	1:49 am	Scorpio
26th	3:06 am	Sagittarius
28th	2:30 am	Capricorn
30th	2:02 am	Aquarius

July 1942

2nd	3:49 am	Pisces
4th	9:16 am	Aries
6th	6:25 pm	Taurus
9th	6:12 am	Gemini
11th	6:51 pm	Cancer
14th	7:07 am	Leo
16th	6:06 pm	Virgo
19th	2:50 am	Libra
21st	8:56 am	Scorpio
23rd	11:53 am	Sagittarius
25th	12:36 pm	Capricorn
27th	12:39 pm	Aquarius
29th	1:53 pm	Pisces
31st	5:50 pm	Aries

August 1942

3rd	1:49 am	Taurus
5th	12:56 pm	Gemini
8th	1:31 am	Cancer
10th	1:37 pm	Leo
13th	0:09 am	Virgo
15th	8:29 am	Libra
17th	2:35 pm	Scorpio
19th	6:32 pm	Sagittarius
21st	8:44 pm	Capricorn
23rd	10:07 pm	Aquarius
25th	11:55 pm	Pisces
28th	3:40 am	Aries
30th	10:33 am	Taurus

September 1942

1st	8:41 pm	Gemini
4th	9:00 am	Cancer
6th	9:14 pm	Leo
9th	7:28 am	Virgo
11th	3:01 pm	Libra
13th	8:18 pm	Scorpio
15th	11:58 pm	Sagittarius
18th	2:47 am	Capricorn
20th	5:27 am	Aquarius
22nd	8:35 am	Pisces
24th	12:59 pm	Aries
26th	7:35 pm	Taurus
29th	5:06 am	Gemini

October 1942

1st	5:04 pm	Cancer
4th	5:33 am	Leo
6th	4:10 pm	Virgo
8th	11:33 pm	Libra
11th	3:45 am	Scorpio
13th	6:10 am	Sagittarius
15th	8:13 am	Capricorn
17th	11:03 am	Aquarius
19th	3:06 pm	Pisces
21st	8:36 pm	Aries
24th	3:52 am	Taurus
26th	1:20 pm	Gemini
29th	0:59 am	Cancer
31st	1:46 pm	Leo

November 1942

3rd	1:18 am	Virgo
5th	9:16 am	Libra
7th	1:22 pm	Scorpio
9th	2:45 pm	Sagittarius
11th	3:19 pm	Capricorn
13th	4:51 pm	Aquarius
15th	8:30 pm	Pisces
18th	2:32 am	Aries
20th	10:39 am	Taurus
22nd	8:35 pm	Gemini
25th	8:17 am	Cancer
27th	9:09 pm	Leo
30th	9:25 am	Virgo

December 1942

2nd	6:51 pm	Libra
5th	0:07 am	Scorpio
7th	1:32 am	Sagittarius
9th	1:08 am	Capricorn
11th	0:57 am	Aquarius
13th	2:59 am	Pisces
15th	8:09 am	Aries
17th	4:20 pm	Taurus
20th	2:47 am	Gemini
22nd	2:57 pm	Cancer
25th	3:35 am	Leo
27th	4:07 pm	Virgo
30th	2:41 am	Libra

January 1943

1st	9:32 am	Scorpio
3rd	12:28 pm	Sagittarius
5th	12:33 pm	Capricorn
7th	11:45 am	Aquarius
9th	12:09 pm	Pisces
11th	3:27 pm	Aries
13th	10:24 pm	Taurus
16th	8:42 am	Gemini
18th	8:54 pm	Cancer
21st	9:43 am	Leo
23rd	10:02 pm	Virgo
26th	8:44 am	Libra
28th	4:46 pm	Scorpio
30th	9:32 pm	Sagittarius

February 1943

1st	11.14 pm	Capricorn
3rd	11:11 pm	Aquarius
5th	11:09 pm	Pisces
8th	1:01 am	Aries
10th	6:22 am	Taurus
12th	3:29 pm	Gemini
15th	3:25 am	Cancer
17th	4:18 pm	Leo
20th	4:19 am	Virgo
22nd	2:28 pm	Libra
24th	10:24 pm	Scorpio
27th	3:58 am	Sagittarius

March 1943

1st	7:17 am	Capricorn
3rd	8:56 am	Aquarius
5th	9:56 am	Pisces
7th	11:46 am	Aries
9th	3:58 pm	Taurus
11th	11:39 pm	Gemini
14th	10:53 am	Cancer
16th	11:42 pm	Leo
19th	11:41 am	Virgo
21st	9:21 pm	Libra
24th	4:23 am	Scorpio
26th	9:22 am	Sagittarius
28th	1:04 pm	Capricorn

April 1943

1st	6:28 pm	Pisces
3rd	9:18 pm	Aries
6th	1:39 am	Taurus
8th	8:46 am	Gemini
10th	7:04 pm	Cancer
13th	7:39 am	Leo
15th	7:59 pm	Virgo
18th	5:39 am	Libra
20th	12:01 pm	Scorpio
22nd	3:55 pm	Sagittarius
24th	6:40 pm	Capricorn
26th	9:22 pm	Aquarius
29th	0:36 am	Pisces
30th	3:57 pm	Aquarius

May 1943

1st	4:40 am	Aries
3rd	9:60 am	Taurus
5th	5:18 pm	Gemini
8th	3:19 am	Cancer
10th	3:40 pm	Leo
13th	4:20 am	Virgo
15th	2:40 pm	Libra
17th	9:18 pm	Scorpio
20th	0:33 am	Sagittarius
22nd	2:01 am	Capricorn
24th	3:25 am	Aquarius
26th	6:01 am	Pisces
28th	10:20 am	Aries
30th	4:26 pm	Taurus

June 1943

2nd	0:31 am	Gemini
4th	10:48 am	Cancer
6th	11:03 pm	Leo
9th	12:01 pm	Virgo
11th	11:21 pm	Libra
14th	6:54 am	Scorpio
16th	10:32 am	Sagittarius
18th	11:29 am	Capricorn
20th	11:36 am	Aquarius
22nd	12:42 pm	Pisces
24th	3:58 pm	Aries
26tn	9:54 pm	Taurus
29th	6:30 am	Gemini

July 1943

1st	5:15 pm	Cancer
4th	5:40 am	Leo
6th	6:43 pm	Virgo
9th	6:41 am	Libra
11th	3:34 pm	Scorpio
13th	8:34 pm	Sagittarius
15th	10:05 pm	Capricorn
17th	9:46 pm	Aquarius
19th	9:32 pm	Pisces
21st	11:10 pm	Aries
24th	3:56 am	Taurus
26th	12:08 pm	Gemini
28th	11:04 pm	Cancer
31st	11:44 am	Leo

August 1943

3rd	0:44 am	Virgo
5th	12:48 pm	Libra
7th	10:39 pm	Scorpio
10th	5:04 am	Sagittarius
12th	8:05 am	Capricorn
14th	8:34 am	Aquarius
16th	8:07 am	Pisces
18th	8:36 am	Aries
20th	11:46 am	Taurus
22nd	6:38 pm	Gemini
25th	5:09 am	Cancer
27th	5:49 pm	Leo
30th	6:47 am	Virgo

September 1943

1st	6:31 pm	Libra
4th	4:19 am	Scorpio
6th	11:34 am	Sagittarius
8th	4:09 pm	Capricorn
10th	6:15 pm	Aquarius
12th	6:45 pm	Pisces
14th	7:09 pm	Aries
16th	9:15 pm	Taurus
19th	2:43 am	Gemini
21st	12:15 pm	Cancer
24th	0:33 am	Leo
26th	1:29 pm	Virgo
29th	0:56 am	Libra

October 1943

1st	10:02 am	Scorpio
3rd	5:01 pm	Sagittarius
5th	10:10 pm	Capricorn
8th	1:39 am	Aquarius
10th	3:43 am	Pisces
12th	5:12 am	Aries
14th	7:27 am	Taurus
16th	12:11 pm	Gemini
18th	8:29 pm	Cancer
21st	8:13 am	Leo
23rd	9:08 pm	Virgo
26th	8:53 am	Libra
28th	5:11 pm	Scorpio
30th	11:14 pm	Sagittarius

November 1943

2nd	3:36 am	Capricorn
4th	7:09 am	Aquarius
6th	10:15 am	Pisces
8th	1:11 pm	Aries
10th	4:33 pm	Taurus
12th	9:31 pm	Gemini
15th	5:24 am	Cancer
17th	4:28 pm	Leo
20th	5:20 am	Virgo
22nd	5:15 pm	Libra
25th	2:07 am	Scorpio
27th	7:31 am	Sagittarius
29th	10:41 am	Capricorn

December 1943

1st	1:01 pm	Aquarius
3rd	3:36 pm	Pisces
5th	7:01 pm	Aries
7th	11:30 pm	Taurus
10th	5:34 am	Gemini
12th	1:49 pm	Cancer
15th	0:36 am	Leo
17th	1:20 pm	Virgo
20th	1:54 am	Libra
22nd	11:39 am	Scorpio
24th	5:39 pm	Sagittarius
26th	8:22 pm	Capricorn
28th	9:21 pm	Aquarius
30th	10:17 pm	Pisces

January 1944
2nd	0:35 am	Aries
4th	5:02 am	Taurus
6th	11:48 am	Gemini
8th	8:49 pm	Cancer
11th	7:59 am	Leo
13th	8:39 pm	Virgo
16th	9:26 am	Libra
18th	8:24 pm	Scorpio
21st	3:49 am	Sagittarius
23rd	7:22 am	Capricorn
25th	8:07 am	Aquarius
27th	7:49 am	Pisces
29th	8:18 am	Aries
31st	11:13 am	Taurus

February 1944
2nd	5:22 pm	Gemini
5th	2:42 am	Cancer
7th	2:22 pm	Leo
10th	3:07 am	Virgo
12th	3:53 pm	Libra
15th	3:21 am	Scorpio
17th	12:08 pm	Sagittarius
19th	5:28 pm	Capricorn
21st	7:23 pm	Aquarius
23rd	7:07 pm	Pisces
25th	6:33 pm	Aries
27th	7:40 pm	Taurus

March 1944
1st	0:06 am	Gemini
3rd	8:42 am	Cancer
5th	8:20 pm	Leo
8th	9:19 am	Virgo
10th	9:55 pm	Libra
13th	9:10 am	Scorpio
15th	6:29 pm	Sagittarius
18th	1:12 am	Capricorn
20th	4:53 am	Aquarius
22nd	5:56 am	Pisces
24th	5:42 am	Aries
26th	6:04 am	Taurus
28th	9:04 am	Gemini
30th	4:04 pm	Cancer

April 1944
2nd	2:56 am	Leo
4th	3:49 pm	Virgo
7th	4:22 am	Libra
9th	3:10 pm	Scorpio
12th	0:04 am	Sagittarius
14th	6:54 am	Capricorn
16th	11:44 am	Aquarius
18th	2:26 pm	Pisces
20th	3:35 pm	Aries
22nd	4:31 pm	Taurus
24th	7:03 pm	Gemini
27th	0:49 am	Cancer
29th	10:40 am	Leo

May 1944
1st	11:05 pm	Virgo
4th	11:38 am	Libra
6th	10:18 pm	Scorpio
9th	6:26 am	Sagittarius
11th	12:32 pm	Capricorn
13th	5:08 pm	Aquarius
15th	8:34 pm	Pisces
17th	11:03 pm	Aries
20th	1:16 am	Taurus
22nd	4:30 am	Gemini
24th	10:09 am	Cancer
26th	7:07 pm	Leo
29th	6:59 am	Virgo
31st	7:37 pm	Libra

June 1944
3rd	6:29 am	Scorpio
5th	2:25 pm	Sagittarius
7th	7:41 pm	Capricorn
9th	11:12 pm	Aquarius
12th	1:50 am	Pisces
14th	4:42 am	Aries
16th	7:54 am	Taurus
18th	12:14 pm	Gemini
20th	6:32 pm	Cancer
23rd	3:27 am	Leo
25th	2:59 pm	Virgo
28th	3:39 am	Libra
30th	3:07 pm	Scorpio

July 1944
2nd	11:38 pm	Sagittarius
5th	4:40 am	Capricorn
7th	7:13 am	Aquarius
9th	8:40 am	Pisces
11th	10:22 am	Aries
13th	1:21 pm	Taurus
15th	6:14 pm	Gemini
18th	1:23 am	Cancer
20th	10:55 am	Leo
22nd	10:24 pm	Virgo
25th	11:06 am	Libra
27th	11:16 pm	Scorpio
30th	8:44 am	Sagittarius

August 1944
1st	2:37 pm	Capricorn
3rd	5:07 pm	Aquarius
5th	5:34 pm	Pisces
7th	5:45 pm	Aries
9th	7:23 pm	Taurus
11th	11:39 pm	Gemini
14th	7:07 am	Cancer
16th	5:11 pm	Leo
19th	5:03 am	Virgo
21st	5:45 pm	Libra
24th	6:11 am	Scorpio
26th	4:47 pm	Sagittarius
29th	0:12 am	Capricorn
31st	3:42 am	Aquarius

September 1944
2nd	4:13 am	Pisces
4th	3:27 am	Aries
6th	3:30 am	Taurus
8th	6:18 am	Gemini
10th	12:52 pm	Cancer
12th	10:51 pm	Leo
15th	11:01 am	Virgo
17th	11:48 pm	Libra
20th	12:11 pm	Scorpio
22nd	11:17 pm	Sagittarius
25th	7:51 am	Capricorn
27th	1:04 pm	Aquarius
29th	2:53 pm	Pisces

October 1944
1st	2:28 pm	Aries
3rd	1:49 pm	Taurus
5th	3:05 pm	Gemini
7th	7:58 pm	Cancer
10th	5:04 am	Leo
12th	5:05 pm	Virgo
15th	5:53 am	Libra
17th	6:02 pm	Scorpio
20th	4:49 am	Sagittarius
22nd	1:45 pm	Capricorn
24th	8:17 pm	Aquarius
26th	11:53 pm	Pisces
29th	0:53 am	Aries
31st	0:45 am	Taurus

November 1944
2nd	1:29 am	Gemini
4th	5:07 am	Cancer
6th	12:48 pm	Leo
8th	11:58 pm	Virgo
11th	12:42 pm	Libra
14th	0:47 am	Scorpio
16th	10:50 am	Sagittarius
18th	7:18 pm	Capricorn
21st	1:46 am	Aquarius
23rd	6:16 am	Pisces
25th	8:54 am	Aries
27th	10:22 am	Taurus
29th	11:57 am	Gemini

December 1944
1st	3:21 pm	Cancer
3rd	9:53 pm	Leo
6th	8:06 am	Virgo
8th	8:28 pm	Libra
11th	8:40 am	Scorpio
13th	6:48 pm	Sagittarius
16th	2:20 am	Capricorn
18th	7:41 am	Aquarius
20th	11:38 am	Pisces
22nd	2:42 pm	Aries
24th	5:25 pm	Taurus
26th	8:26 pm	Gemini
29th	0:43 am	Cancer
31st	7:22 am	Leo

January 1945
2nd	4:50 pm	Virgo
5th	4:43 am	Libra
7th	5:09 pm	Scorpio
10th	3:51 am	Sagittarius
12th	11:22 am	Capricorn
14th	3:53 pm	Aquarius
16th	6:26 pm	Pisces
18th	8:22 pm	Aries
20th	10:49 pm	Taurus
23rd	2:37 am	Gemini
25th	8:08 am	Cancer
27th	3:35 pm	Leo
30th	1:09 am	Virgo

February 1945
1st	12:46 pm	Libra
4th	1:20 am	Scorpio
6th	12:53 pm	Sagittarius
8th	9:27 pm	Capricorn
11th	2:09 am	Aquarius
13th	3:51 am	Pisces
15th	4:13 am	Aries
17th	5:07 am	Taurus
19th	8:05 am	Gemini
21st	1:46 pm	Cancer
23rd	10:00 pm	Leo
26th	8:15 am	Virgo
28th	7:57 pm	Libra

March 1945
3rd	8:32 am	Scorpio
5th	8:43 pm	Sagittarius
8th	6:32 am	Capricorn
10th	12:34 pm	Aquarius
12th	2:44 pm	Pisces
14th	2:30 pm	Aries
16th	1:57 pm	Taurus
18th	3:09 pm	Gemini
20th	7:35 pm	Cancer
23rd	3:34 am	Leo
25th	2:13 pm	Virgo
28th	2:15 am	Libra
30th	2:51 pm	Scorpio

April 1945
2nd	3:07 am	Sagittarius
4th	1:48 pm	Capricorn
6th	9:28 pm	Aquarius
9th	1:10 am	Pisces
11th	1:37 am	Aries
13th	0:39 am	Taurus
15th	0:31 am	Gemini
17th	3:16 am	Cancer
19th	9:56 am	Leo
21st	8:05 pm	Virgo
24th	8:16 am	Libra
26th	8:52 pm	Scorpio
29th	8:55 am	Sagittarius

May 1945

1st	7:39 pm	Capricorn
4th	4:03 am	Aquarius
6th	9:16 am	Pisces
8th	11:21 am	Aries
10th	11:24 am	Taurus
12th	11:16 am	Gemini
14th	12:57 pm	Cancer
16th	6:01 pm	Leo
19th	2:57 am	Virgo
21st	2:43 pm	Libra
24th	3:21 am	Scorpio
26th	3:09 pm	Sagittarius
29th	1:23 am	Capricorn
31st	9:32 am	Aquarius

June 1945

2nd	3:22 pm	Pisces
4th	6:48 pm	Aries
6th	8:22 pm	Taurus
8th	9:15 pm	Gemini
10th	11:03 pm	Cancer
13th	3:22 am	Leo
15th	11:12 am	Virgo
17th	10:06 pm	Libra
20th	10:35 am	Scorpio
22nd	10:27 pm	Sagittarius
25th	8:13 am	Capricorn
27th	3:34 pm	Aquarius
29th	8:51 pm	Pisces

July 1945

2nd	0:30 am	Aries
4th	3:04 am	Taurus
6th	5:21 am	Gemini
8th	8:14 am	Cancer
10th	12:48 pm	Leo
12th	8:01 pm	Virgo
15th	6:14 am	Libra
17th	6:29 pm	Scorpio
20th	6:33 am	Sagittarius
22nd	4:25 pm	Capricorn
24th	11:17 pm	Aquarius
27th	3:26 am	Pisces
29th	6:09 am	Aries
31st	8:31 am	Taurus

August 1945

2nd	11:27 am	Gemini
4th	3:26 pm	Cancer
6th	8:54 pm	Leo
9th	4:26 am	Virgo
11th	2:24 pm	Libra
14th	2:24 am	Scorpio
16th	2:54 pm	Sagittarius
19th	1:30 am	Capricorn
21st	8:26 am	Aquarius
23rd	12:02 pm	Pisces
25th	1:30 pm	Aries
27th	2:56 pm	Taurus
29th	4:50 pm	Gemini
31st	9:02 pm	Cancer

September 1945

3rd	3:22 am	Leo
5th	11:40 am	Virgo
7th	9:51 pm	Libra
10th	9:49 am	Scorpio
12th	10:37 pm	Sagittarius
15th	10:07 am	Capricorn
17th	6:15 pm	Aquarius
19th	10:17 pm	Pisces
21st	11:10 pm	Aries
23rd	10:53 pm	Taurus
25th	11:51 pm	Gemini
28th	2:40 am	Cancer
30th	8:50 am	Leo

October 1945

2nd	5:35 pm	Virgo
5th	4:19 am	Libra
7th	4:26 pm	Scorpio
10th	5:18 am	Sagittarius
12th	5:31 pm	Capricorn
15th	3:05 am	Aquarius
17th	8:27 am	Pisces
19th	10:05 am	Aries
21st	9:30 am	Taurus
23rd	8:53 am	Gemini
25th	10:15 am	Cancer
27th	2:60 pm	Leo
29th	11:12 pm	Virgo

November 1945

1st	10:08 am	Libra
3rd	10:29 pm	Scorpio
6th	11:18 am	Sagittarius
8th	11:36 pm	Capricorn
11th	9:55 am	Aquarius
13th	5:01 pm	Pisces
15th	8:21 pm	Aries
17th	8:46 pm	Taurus
19th	8:04 pm	Gemini
21st	8:15 pm	Cancer
23rd	11:11 pm	Leo
26th	6:02 am	Virgo
28th	4:20 pm	Libra

December 1945

1st	4:42 am	Scorpio
3rd	5:28 pm	Sagittarius
6th	5:22 am	Capricorn
8th	3:31 pm	Aquarius
10th	11:20 pm	Pisces
13th	4:12 am	Aries
15th	6:27 am	Taurus
17th	7:02 am	Gemini
19th	7:30 am	Cancer
21st	9:35 am	Leo
23rd	2:49 pm	Virgo
25th	11:45 pm	Libra
28th	11:43 am	Scorpio
31st	0:32 am	Sagittarius

January 1946

2nd	12:07 pm	Capricorn
4th	9:56 pm	Aquarius
7th	4:45 am	Pisces
9th	9:53 am	Aries
11th	1:23 pm	Taurus
13th	3:42 pm	Gemini
15th	5:33 pm	Cancer
17th	8:05 pm	Leo
20th	0:40 am	Virgo
22nd	8:35 am	Libra
24th	7:40 pm	Scorpio
27th	8:24 am	Sagittarius
29th	8:15 pm	Capricorn

February 1946

1st	5:20 am	Aquarius
3rd	11:28 am	Pisces
5th	3:37 pm	Aries
7th	6:46 pm	Taurus
9th	9:46 pm	Gemini
12th	1:00 am	Cancer
14th	4:51 am	Leo
16th	10:06 am	Virgo
18th	5:38 pm	Libra
21st	4:04 am	Scorpio
23rd	4:39 pm	Sagittarius
26th	4:58 am	Capricorn
28th	2:28 pm	Aquarius

March 1946

2nd	8:22 pm	Pisces
4th	11:23 pm	Aries
7th	1:08 am	Taurus
9th	3:13 am	Gemini
11th	6:31 am	Cancer
13th	11:16 am	Leo
15th	5:33 pm	Virgo
18th	1:42 am	Libra
20th	12:07 pm	Scorpio
23rd	0:31 am	Sagittarius
25th	1:15 pm	Capricorn
27th	11:50 pm	Aquarius
30th	6:20 am	Pisces

April 1946

1st	9:12 am	Aries
3rd	9:55 am	Taurus
5th	10:27 am	Gemini
7th	12:25 pm	Cancer
9th	4:40 pm	Leo
11th	11:19 pm	Virgo
14th	8:15 am	Libra
16th	7:04 pm	Scorpio
19th	7:32 am	Sagittarius
21st	8:27 pm	Capricorn
24th	7:53 am	Aquarius
26th	3:49 pm	Pisces
28th	7:42 pm	Aries
30st	8:29 pm	Taurus

May 1946

2nd	8:04 pm	Gemini
4th	8:23 pm	Cancer
6th	11:05 pm	Leo
9th	4:60 am	Virgo
11th	1:55 pm	Libra
14th	1:08 am	Scorpio
16th	1:47 pm	Sagittarius
19th	2:41 am	Capricorn
21st	2:29 pm	Aquarius
23rd	11:39 pm	Pisces
26th	5:01 am	Aries
28th	7:01 am	Taurus
30th	6:54 am	Gemini

June 1946

1st	6:31 am	Cancer
3rd	7:44 am	Leo
5th	12:02 pm	Virgo
7th	7:59 pm	Libra
10th	7:06 am	Scorpio
12th	7:52 pm	Sagittarius
15th	8:38 am	Capricorn
17th	8:14 pm	Aquarius
20th	5:40 am	Pisces
22nd	12:15 pm	Aries
24th	3:52 pm	Taurus
26th	5:06 pm	Gemini
28th	5:12 pm	Cancer
30th	5:51 pm	Leo

July 1946

2nd	8:48 pm	Virgo
5th	3:24 am	Libra
7th	1:45 pm	Scorpio
10th	2:20 am	Sagittarius
12th	3:04 pm	Capricorn
15th	2:17 am	Aquarius
17th	11:13 am	Pisces
19th	5:57 pm	Aries
21st	10:15 pm	Taurus
24th	1:19 am	Gemini
26th	2:45 am	Cancer
28th	3:59 am	Leo
30th	6:37 am	Virgo

August 1946

1st	12:11 pm	Libra
3rd	9:24 pm	Scorpio
6th	9:37 am	Sagittarius
8th	10:23 am	Capricorn
11th	9:20 am	Aquarius
13th	5:39 pm	Pisces
15th	11:39 pm	Aries
18th	3:59 am	Taurus
20th	7:23 am	Gemini
22nd	10:07 am	Cancer
24th	12:41 pm	Leo
26th	3:57 pm	Virgo
28th	9:17 pm	Libra
31st	5:52 am	Scorpio

September 1946
2nd	5:32 pm	Sagittarius
5th	6:22 am	Capricorn
7th	5:38 pm	Aquarius
10th	1:44 am	Pisces
12th	6:47 am	Aries
14th	10:03 am	Taurus
16th	12:47 pm	Gemini
18th	3:44 pm	Cancer
20th	7:15 pm	Leo
22nd	11:39 am	Virgo
25th	5:44 am	Libra
27th	2:17 pm	Scorpio
30th	1:33 am	Sagittarius

October 1946
2nd	2:29 pm	Capricorn
5th	2:27 am	Aquarius
7th	11:03 am	Pisces
9th	4:01 pm	Aries
11th	6:19 am	Taurus
13th	7:37 pm	Gemini
15th	9:23 pm	Cancer
18th	0:35 am	Leo
20th	5:38 am	Virgo
22nd	12:36 pm	Libra
24th	9:43 pm	Scorpio
27th	9:06 am	Sagittarius
29th	9:50 pm	Capricorn

November 1946
1st	10:35 am	Aquarius
3rd	8:31 pm	Pisces
6th	2:27 am	Aries
8th	4:48 am	Taurus
10th	5:08 am	Gemini
12th	5:18 am	Cancer
14th	6:55 am	Leo
16th	11:09 am	Virgo
18th	6:15 pm	Libra
21st	3:59 am	Scorpio
23rd	3:46 pm	Sagittarius
26th	4:39 am	Capricorn
28th	5:29 pm	Aquarius

December 1946
1st	4:28 am	Pisces
3rd	11:59 am	Aries
5th	3:44 pm	Taurus
7th	4:27 pm	Gemini
9th	3:51 pm	Cancer
11th	3:50 pm	Leo
13th	6:12 pm	Virgo
16th	0:08 am	Libra
18th	9:46 am	Scorpio
20th	9:49 pm	Sagittarius
23rd	10:49 am	Capricorn
25th	11:30 pm	Aquarius
28th	10:41 am	Pisces
30th	7:29 pm	Aries

January 1947
2nd	1:05 am	Taurus
4th	3:24 am	Gemini
6th	3:27 am	Cancer
8th	2:53 am	Leo
10th	3:47 am	Virgo
12th	7:59 am	Libra
14th	4:19 pm	Scorpio
17th	4:04 am	Sagittarius
19th	5:09 pm	Capricorn
22nd	5:35 am	Aquarius
24th	4:21 pm	Pisces
27th	1:10 am	Aries
29th	7:42 am	Taurus
31st	11:48 am	Gemini

February 1947
2nd	1:36 pm	Cancer
4th	2:01 pm	Leo
6th	2:45 pm	Virgo
8th	5:43 pm	Libra
11th	0:27 am	Scorpio
13th	11:17 am	Sagittarius
16th	0:10 am	Capricorn
18th	12:35 pm	Aquarius
20th	10:57 pm	Pisces
23rd	6:55 am	Aries
25th	1:05 pm	Taurus
27th	5:45 pm	Gemini

March 1947
1st	8:59 pm	Cancer
3rd	11:00 pm	Leo
6th	0:47 am	Virgo
8th	3:54 am	Libra
10th	9:55 am	Scorpio
12th	7:34 pm	Sagittarius
15th	7:59 am	Capricorn
17th	8:34 pm	Aquarius
20th	6:53 am	Pisces
22nd	2:18 pm	Aries
24th	7:27 pm	Taurus
26th	11:15 pm	Gemini
29th	2:56 am	Cancer
31st	5:23 am	Leo

April 1947
2nd	8:32 am	Virgo
4th	12:42 pm	Libra
6th	6:59 pm	Scorpio
9th	4:14 am	Sagittarius
11th	4:09 pm	Capricorn
14th	4:50 am	Aquarius
16th	3:43 pm	Pisces
18th	11:24 pm	Aries
21st	3:55 am	Taurus
23rd	6:26 am	Gemini
25th	8:22 am	Cancer
27th	10:45 am	Leo
29th	2:17 pm	Virgo

May 1947
1st	7:24 pm	Libra
4th	2:37 am	Scorpio
6th	12.12 pm	Sagittarius
8th	11:54 pm	Capricorn
11th	12:39 pm	Aquarius
14th	0:19 am	Pisces
16th	8:51 am	Aries
18th	1:46 pm	Taurus
20th	3:49 pm	Gemini
22nd	4:26 pm	Cancer
24th	5:10 pm	Leo
26th	7:52 pm	Virgo
29th	0:53 am	Libra
31st	8:45 am	Scorpio

June 1947
2nd	6:55 pm	Sagittarius
5th	6:52 am	Capricorn
7th	7:38 pm	Aquarius
10th	7:44 am	Pisces
12th	5:30 pm	Aries
14th	11:46 pm	Taurus
17th	2:20 am	Gemini
19th	2:32 am	Cancer
21st	2:07 am	Leo
23rd	3:03 am	Virgo
25th	6:55 am	Libra
27th	2:21 pm	Scorpio
30th	0:46 am	Sagittarius

July 1947
2nd	1:03 pm	Capricorn
5th	1:49 am	Aquarius
7th	2:01 pm	Pisces
10th	0:34 am	Aries
12th	8:08 am	Taurus
14th	12:12 pm	Gemini
16th	1:13 pm	Cancer
18th	12:35 pm	Leo
20th	12:24 pm	Virgo
22nd	2:19 pm	Libra
24th	8:44 pm	Scorpio
27th	6:42 am	Sagittarius
29th	7:02 pm	Capricorn
31st	2:03 am	Pisces

August 1947
1st	7:49 am	Aquarius
3rd	7:48 pm	Pisces
6th	6:18 am	Aries
8th	2:40 pm	Taurus
10th	8:16 pm	Gemini
12th	10:49 pm	Cancer
14th	11:06 pm	Leo
16th	10:50 pm	Virgo
19th	0:05 am	Libra
21st	4:48 am	Scorpio
23rd	1:39 pm	Sagittarius
26th	1:31 am	Capricorn
28th	2:16 pm	Aquarius

September 1947
2nd	12:01 pm	Aries
4th	8:09 pm	Taurus
7th	2:19 am	Gemini
9th	6:11 am	Cancer
11th	8:02 am	Leo
13th	8:53 am	Virgo
15th	10:21 am	Libra
17th	2:17 pm	Scorpio
19th	9:51 pm	Sagittarius
22nd	8:60 am	Capricorn
24th	9:36 pm	Aquarius
27th	9:22 am	Pisces
29th	6:56 am	Aries

October 1947
2nd	2:15 am	Taurus
4th	7:42 am	Gemini
6th	11:46 am	Cancer
8th	2:41 pm	Leo
10th	4:58 pm	Virgo
12th	7:33 pm	Libra
14th	11:48 pm	Scorpio
17th	6:57 am	Sagittarius
19th	5:17 pm	Capricorn
22nd	5:39 am	Aquarius
24th	5:44 pm	Pisces
27th	3:30 am	Aries
29th	10:13 am	Taurus
31st	2:34 pm	Gemini

November 1947
2nd	5:32 pm	Cancer
4th	8:04 pm	Leo
6th	10:55 pm	Virgo
9th	2:44 am	Libra
11th	8:07 am	Scorpio
13th	3:38 pm	Sagittarius
16th	1:39 am	Capricorn
18th	1:47 pm	Aquarius
21st	2:17 am	Pisces
23rd	12:50 pm	Aries
25th	8:04 pm	Taurus
27th	11:55 pm	Gemini
30th	1:31 am	Cancer

December 1947
2nd	2:32 am	Leo
4th	4:26 am	Virgo
6th	8:17 am	Libra
8th	2:27 pm	Scorpio
10th	10:50 pm	Sagittarius
13th	9:17 am	Capricorn
15th	9:17 pm	Aquarius
18th	9:59 am	Pisces
20th	9:35 pm	Aries
23rd	6:07 am	Taurus
25th	10:42 am	Gemini
27th	12:00 pm	Cancer
29th	11:43 am	Leo
31st	11:52 am	Virgo

January 1948		
2nd	2:15 pm	Libra
4th	7:53 pm	Scorpio
7th	4:42 am	Sagittarius
9th	3:43 pm	Capricorn
12th	3:55 am	Aquarius
14th	4:35 am	Pisces
17th	4:42 am	Aries
19th	2:38 pm	Taurus
21st	8:50 pm	Gemini
23rd	11:22 pm	Cancer
25th	10:59 pm	Leo
27th	9:58 pm	Virgo
29th	10:31 pm	Libra

February 1948		
1st	2:29 am	Scorpio
3rd	10:30 am	Sagittarius
5th	9:30 pm	Capricorn
8th	9:59 am	Aquarius
10th	10:37 pm	Pisces
13th	10:36 am	Aries
15th	9:07 pm	Taurus
18th	4:53 am	Gemini
20th	9:04 am	Cancer
22nd	10:03 am	Leo
24th	9:23 am	Virgo
26th	9:10 am	Libra
28th	11:30 am	Scorpio
31st	11:37 am	Capricorn

March 1948		
1st	5:45 pm	Sagittarius
4th	3:52 am	Capricorn
6th	4:14 pm	Aquarius
9th	4:51 am	Pisces
11th	4:31 pm	Aries
14th	2:39 am	Taurus
16th	10:41 am	Gemini
18th	4:11 pm	Cancer
20th	6:56 pm	Leo
22nd	7:42 pm	Virgo
24th	8:02 pm	Libra
26th	9:50 pm	Scorpio
29th	2:48 am	Sagittarius

April 1948		
2nd	11:18 pm	Aquarius
5th	11:54 am	Pisces
7th	11:27 pm	Aries
10th	8:55 am	Taurus
12th	4:17 pm	Gemini
14th	9:39 pm	Cancer
17th	1:14 am	Leo
19th	3:29 am	Virgo
21st	5:17 am	Libra
23rd	7:53 am	Scorpio
25th	12:36 pm	Sagittarius
27th	8:23 pm	Capricorn
30th	7:17 am	Aquarius

May 1948		
2nd	7:44 pm	Pisces
5th	7:25 am	Aries
7th	4:44 pm	Taurus
9th	11:19 pm	Gemini
12th	3:35 am	Cancer
14th	6:37 am	Leo
16th	9:14 am	Virgo
18th	12:08 pm	Libra
20th	3:58 pm	Scorpio
22nd	9:23 pm	Sagittarius
25th	5:10 am	Capricorn
27th	3:33 pm	Aquarius
30th	3:46 am	Pisces

June 1948		
1st	3:53 pm	Aries
4th	1:42 am	Taurus
6th	8:01 am	Gemini
8th	11:24 am	Cancer
10th	1:11 pm	Leo
12th	2:49 pm	Virgo
14th	5:35 pm	Libra
16th	10:03 pm	Scorpio
19th	4:29 am	Sagittarius
21st	12:53 pm	Capricorn
23rd	11:15 pm	Aquarius
26th	11:24 am	Pisces
28th	11:56 pm	Aries

July 1948		
1st	10:35 am	Taurus
3rd	5:43 pm	Gemini
5th	9:04 pm	Cancer
7th	9:51 pm	Leo
9th	10:04 pm	Virgo
11th	11:30 pm	Libra
14th	3:30 am	Scorpio
16th	10:14 am	Sagittarius
18th	7:15 pm	Capricorn
21st	6:04 am	Aquarius
23rd	6:13 pm	Pisces
26th	6:55 am	Aries
28th	6:31 pm	Taurus
31st	2:59 am	Gemini

August 1948		
2nd	7:15 am	Cancer
4th	8:11 am	Leo
6th	7:33 am	Virgo
8th	7:33 am	Libra
10th	10:01 am	Scorpio
12th	3:53 pm	Sagittarius
15th	0:51 am	Capricorn
17th	12:03 pm	Aquarius
20th	0:22 am	Pisces
22nd	1:04 pm	Aries
25th	1:03 am	Taurus
27th	10:34 am	Gemini
29th	4:29 pm	Cancer
31st	6:38 pm	Leo

September 1948		
2nd	6:20 pm	Virgo
4th	5:38 pm	Libra
6th	6:38 pm	Scorpio
8th	10:52 pm	Sgittarius
11th	6:59 am	Capricorn
13th	5:59 pm	Aquarius
16th	6:26 am	Pisces
18th	7:02 pm	Aries
21st	6:44 am	Taurus
23rd	4:58 pm	Gemini
25th	11:47 pm	Cancer
28th	3:33 am	Leo
30th	4:40 am	Virgo

October 1948		
2nd	4:32 am	Libra
4th	5:02 am	Scorpio
6th	7:60 am	Sagittarius
8th	2:37 pm	Capricorn
11th	0:42 am	Aquarius
13th	1:04 pm	Pisces
16th	1:36 am	Aries
18th	12:52 pm	Taurus
20th	10:14 pm	Gemini
23rd	5:18 am	Cancer
25th	10:07 am	Leo
27th	12:51 pm	Virgo
29th	2:16 pm	Libra
31st	3:34 pm	Scorpio

November 1948		
2nd	6:15 pm	Sagittarius
4th	11:42 pm	Capricorn
7th	8:46 am	Aquarius
9th	8:34 pm	Pisces
12th	9:12 am	Aries
14th	8:22 pm	Taurus
17th	4:59 am	Gemini
19th	11:08 am	Cancer
21st	3:31 pm	Leo
23rd	6:47 pm	Virgo
25th	9:33 pm	Libra
28th	0:19 am	Scorpio
30th	3:55 am	Sagittarius

December 1948		
2nd	9:22 am	Capricorn
4th	5:37 pm	Aquarius
7th	4:48 am	Pisces
9th	5:30 pm	Aries
12th	5:07 am	Taurus
14th	1:40 pm	Gemini
16th	6:59 pm	Cancer
18th	10:02 pm	Leo
21st	0:19 am	Virgo
23rd	2:60 am	Libra
25th	6:40 am	Scorpio
27th	11:31 am	Sagittarius
29th	5:49 pm	Capricorn

January 1949		
1st	2:10 am	Aquarius
3rd	1:02 pm	Pisces
6th	1:41 am	Aries
8th	2:01 pm	Taurus
10th	11:32 pm	Gemini
11th	4:54 am	Cancer
15th	7:07 am	Leo
17th	7:54 am	Virgo
19th	9:07 am	Libra
21st	12:03 pm	Scorpio
23rd	5:11 pm	Sagittarius
26th	0:23 am	Capricorn
28th	9:30 am	Aquarius
30th	8:27 pm	Pisces

February 1949		
2nd	9:06 am	Aries
4th	9:57 pm	Taurus
7th	8:35 am	Gemini
9th	3:17 pm	Cancer
11th	5:58 pm	Leo
13th	6:05 pm	Virgo
15th	5:46 pm	Libra
17th	6:57 pm	Scorpio
19th	10:51 pm	Sagittarius
22nd	5:53 am	Capricorn
24th	3:27 pm	Aquarius
27th	2:55 am	Pisces

March 1949		
1st	3:36 pm	Aries
4th	4:32 am	Taurus
6th	4:01 pm	Gemini
9th	0:21 am	Cancer
11th	4:30 am	Leo
13th	5:23 am	Virgo
15th	4:41 am	Libra
17th	4:28 am	Scorpio
19th	6:36 am	Sagittarius
21st	12:09 pm	Capricorn
23rd	9:11 pm	Aquarius
26th	8:50 am	Pisces
28th	9:42 pm	Aries
31st	10:27 am	Taurus

April 1949		
2nd	10:02 pm	Gemini
5th	7:07 am	Cancer
7th	12:55 pm	Leo
9th	3:28 pm	Virgo
11th	3:47 pm	Libra
13th	3:29 pm	Scorpio
15th	4:28 pm	Sagittarius
17th	8:19 pm	Capricorn
20th	4:02 am	Aquarius
22nd	3:10 pm	Pisces
25th	3:60 am	Aries
27th	4:39 pm	Taurus
30th	3:45 am	Gemini

May 1949

2nd	12:40 pm	Cancer
4th	7:07 pm	Leo
6th	11:10 pm	Virgo
9th	1:07 am	Libra
11th	1:54 am	Scorpio
13th	2:59 am	Sagittarius
15th	6:02 am	Capricorn
17th	12:24 pm	Aquarius
19th	10:27 pm	Pisces
22nd	11:02 am	Aries
24th	11:42 pm	Taurus
27th	10:22 am	Gemini
29th	6:35 pm	Cancer

June 1949

1st	0:35 am	Leo
3rd	4:51 am	Virgo
5th	7:55 am	Libra
7th	10:12 am	Scorpio
9th	12:25 pm	Sagittarius
11th	3:43 pm	Capricorn
13th	9:28 pm	Aquarius
16th	6:42 am	Pisces
18th	6:46 pm	Aries
21st	7:28 am	Taurus
23rd	6:16 pm	Gemini
26th	1:60 am	Cancer
28th	6:58 am	Leo
30th	10:25 am	Virgo

July 1949

2nd	1:21 pm	Libra
4th	4:22 pm	Scorpio
6th	7:45 pm	Sagittarius
9th	0:02 am	Capricorn
11th	6:12 am	Aquarius
13th	3:04 pm	Pisces
16th	2:42 am	Aries
18th	3:34 pm	Taurus
21st	2:55 am	Gemini
23rd	10:46 am	Cancer
25th	3:16 pm	Leo
27th	5:35 pm	Virgo
29th	7:19 pm	Libra
31st	9:45 pm	Scorpio

August 1949

3rd	1:26 am	Sagittarius
5th	6:37 am	Capricorn
7th	1:37 pm	Aquarius
9th	10:47 pm	Pisces
12th	10:20 am	Aries
14th	11:17 pm	Taurus
17th	11:19 am	Gemini
19th	8:11 pm	Cancer
22nd	1:07 am	Leo
24th	2:55 am	Virgo
26th	3:24 am	Libra
28th	4:21 am	Scorpio
30th	7:03 am	Sagittarius

September 1949

1st	12:08 pm	Capricorn
3rd	7:39 pm	Aquarius
6th	5:27 am	Pisces
8th	5:13 pm	Aries
11th	6:11 am	Taurus
13th	6:44 pm	Gemini
16th	4:43 am	Cancer
18th	10:59 am	Leo
20th	1:30 pm	Virgo
22nd	1:41 pm	Libra
24th	1:23 pm	Scorpio
26th	2:25 pm	Sagittarius
28th	6:10 pm	Capricorn

October 1949

1st	1:14 am	Aquarius
3rd	11:21 am	Pisces
5th	11:28 pm	Aries
8th	12:25 pm	Taurus
11th	1:02 am	Gemini
13th	11:47 am	Cancer
15th	7:32 pm	Leo
17th	11:43 pm	Virgo
20th	0:48 am	Libra
22nd	0:19 am	Scorpio
24th	0:08 am	Sagittarius
26th	2:13 am	Capricorn
28th	7:56 am	Aquarius
30th	5:25 pm	Pisces

November 1949

2nd	5:36 am	Aries
4th	6:35 pm	Taurus
7th	6:53 am	Gemini
9th	5:33 pm	Cancer
12th	1:58 am	Leo
14th	7:38 am	Virgo
16th	10:32 am	Libra
18th	11:18 am	Scorpio
20th	11:18 am	Sagittarius
22nd	12:26 pm	Capricorn
24th	4:30 pm	Aquarius
27th	0:37 am	Pisces
29th	12:21 pm	Aries

December 1949

2nd	1:23 am	Taurus
4th	1:27 pm	Gemini
6th	11:31 pm	Cancer
9th	7:25 am	Leo
11th	1:27 pm	Virgo
13th	5:42 pm	Libra
15th	8:12 pm	Scorpio
17th	9:33 pm	Sagittarius
19th	11:02 pm	Capricorn
22nd	2:28 am	Aquarius
24th	9:26 am	Pisces
26th	8:08 pm	Aries
29th	8:58 am	Taurus
31st	9:13 pm	Gemini

January 1950

3rd	6:53 am	Cancer
5th	1:55 pm	Leo
7th	7:05 pm	Virgo
9th	11:08 pm	Libra
12th	2:28 am	Scorpio
14th	5:17 am	Sagittarius
16th	8:09 am	Capricorn
18th	12:12 pm	Aquarius
20th	6:46 pm	Pisces
23rd	4:41 am	Aries
25th	5:09 pm	Taurus
28th	5:42 am	Gemini
30th	3:47 pm	Cancer

February 1950

1st	10:34 pm	Leo
4th	2:36 am	Virgo
6th	5:20 am	Libra
8th	7:52 am	Scorpio
10th	10:53 am	Sagittarius
12th	2:47 pm	Capricorn
14th	7:60 am	Aquarius
17th	3:14 am	Pisces
19th	1:04 pm	Aries
22nd	1:13 am	Taurus
24th	2:02 pm	Gemini
27th	1:02 am	Cancer

March 1950

1st	8:27 am	Leo
3rd	12:22 pm	Virgo
5th	2:00 pm	Libra
7th	2:57 pm	Scorpio
9th	4:41 pm	Sagittarius
11th	8:09 pm	Capricorn
14th	1:53 am	Aquarius
16th	10:02 am	Pisces
18th	8:21 pm	Aries
21st	8:33 am	Taurus
23rd	9:28 pm	Gemini
26th	9:13 am	Cancer
28th	6:02 pm	Leo
30th	11:01 pm	Virgo

April 1950

2nd	0:42 am	Libra
4th	0:37 am	Scorpio
6th	0:38 am	Sagittarius
8th	2:32 am	Capricorn
10th	7:28 am	Aquarius
12th	3:41 pm	Pisces
15th	2:32 am	Aries
17th	3:01 pm	Taurus
20th	3:54 am	Gemini
22nd	4:01 pm	Cancer
25th	1:55 am	Leo
27th	8:25 am	Virgo
29th	11:21 am	Libra

May 1950

1st	11:36 am	Scorpio
3rd	10:54 am	Sagittarius
5th	11:14 am	Capricorn
7th	2:28 pm	Aquarius
9th	9:37 pm	Pisces
12th	8:21 am	Aries
14th	8:59 pm	Taurus
17th	9:51 am	Gemini
19th	9:49 pm	Cancer
22nd	8:03 am	Leo
24th	3:46 pm	Virgo
26th	8:24 pm	Libra
28th	9:60 pm	Scorpio
30th	9:44 pm	Sagittarius

June 1950

1st	9:29 pm	Capricorn
3rd	11:19 pm	Aquarius
6th	5:02 am	Pisces
8th	2:48 pm	Aries
11th	3:13 am	Taurus
13th	4:04 pm	Gemini
16th	3:42 am	Cancer
18th	1:34 pm	Leo
20th	9:29 pm	Virgo
23rd	3:07 am	Libra
25th	6:15 am	Scorpio
27th	7:24 am	Sagittarius
29th	7:50 am	Capricorn

July 1950

1st	9:25 am	Aquarius
3rd	1:58 pm	Pisces
5th	10:26 pm	Aries
8th	10:16 am	Taurus
10th	11:01 pm	Gemini
13th	10:30 am	Cancer
15th	7:51 pm	Leo
18th	3:04 am	Virgo
20th	8:32 am	Libra
22nd	12:24 pm	Scorpio
24th	2:53 pm	Sagittarius
26th	4:39 pm	Capricorn
28th	6:57 pm	Aquarius
30th	11:19 pm	Pisces

August 1950

2nd	7:06 am	Aries
4th	6:08 pm	Taurus
7th	6:43 am	Gemini
9th	6:25 pm	Cancer
12th	3:34 am	Leo
14th	10:00 am	Virgo
16th	2:28 pm	Libra
18th	5:49 pm	Scorpio
20th	8:35 pm	Sagittarius
22nd	11:23 pm	Capricorn
25th	2:53 am	Aquarius
27th	8:05 am	Pisces
29th	3:48 pm	Aries

September 1950
1st	2:18 am	Taurus
3rd	2:45 pm	Gemini
6th	2:52 am	Cancer
8th	12:29 pm	Leo
10th	6:52 pm	Virgo
12th	10:27 pm	Libra
15th	0:26 am	Scorpio
17th	2:12 am	Sagittarius
19th	4:50 am	Capricorn
21st	9:02 am	Aquarius
23rd	3:11 pm	Pisces
25th	11:31 pm	Aries
28th	10:09 am	Taurus
30th	10:27 pm	Gemini

October 1950
3rd	10:57 am	Cancer
5th	9:39 pm	Leo
8th	4:50 am	Virgo
10th	8:25 am	Libra
12th	9:30 am	Scorpio
14th	9:47 am	Sagittarius
16th	10:60 am	Capricorn
18th	2:31 pm	Aquarius
20th	8:55 pm	Pisces
23rd	5:60 am	Aries
25th	5:04 pm	Taurus
28th	5:22 am	Gemini
30th	6:03 pm	Cancer

November 1950
2nd	5:35 am	Leo
4th	2:16 pm	Virgo
6th	7:07 pm	Libra
8th	8:27 pm	Scorpio
10th	7:52 pm	Sagittarius
12th	7:29 pm	Capricorn
14th	9:17 pm	Aquarius
17th	2:40 am	Pisces
19th	11:43 am	Aries
21st	11:08 pm	Taurus
24th	11:38 am	Gemini
27th	0:12 am	Cancer
29th	11:59 am	Leo

December 1950
1st	9:51 pm	Virgo
4th	4:26 am	Libra
6th	7:15 am	Scorpio
8th	7:16 am	Sagittarius
10th	6:20 am	Capricorn
12th	6:40 am	Aquarius
14th	10:18 am	Pisces
16th	6:04 pm	Aries
19th	5:12 am	Taurus
21st	5:49 pm	Gemini
24th	6:17 am	Cancer
26th	5:43 pm	Leo
29th	3:39 am	Virgo
31st	11:16 am	Libra

January 1951
2nd	3:53 pm	Scorpio
4th	5:35 pm	Sagittarius
6th	5:32 pm	Capricorn
8th	5:39 pm	Aquarius
10th	7:60 pm	Pisces
13th	2:09 am	Aries
15th	12:15 pm	Taurus
18th	0:36 am	Gemini
20th	1:06 pm	Cancer
23rd	0:13 am	Leo
25th	9:24 am	Virgo
27th	4:44 pm	Libra
29th	10:02 pm	Scorpio

February 1951
1st	1:17 am	Sagittarius
3rd	2:53 am	Capricorn
5th	4:06 am	Aquarius
7th	6:33 am	Pisces
9th	11:48 am	Aries
11th	8:37 pm	Taurus
14th	8:19 am	Gemini
16th	8:51 pm	Cancer
19th	7:60 am	Leo
21st	4:41 pm	Virgo
23rd	11:01 pm	Libra
26th	3:32 am	Scorpio
28th	6:50 am	Sagittarius

March 1951
2nd	9:30 am	Capricorn
4th	12:13 pm	Aquarius
6th	3:49 pm	Pisces
8th	9:19 pm	Aries
11th	5:35 am	Taurus
13th	4:38 pm	Gemini
16th	5:06 am	Cancer
18th	4:43 pm	Leo
21st	1:40 am	Virgo
23rd	7:19 am	Libra
25th	10:35 am	Scorpio
27th	12:42 pm	Sagittarius
29th	2:53 pm	Capricorn
31st	6:05 pm	Aquarius

April 1951
2nd	10:46 pm	Pisces
5th	5:18 am	Aries
7th	1:55 pm	Taurus
10th	0:42 am	Gemini
12th	1:05 pm	Cancer
15th	1:18 am	Leo
17th	11:03 am	Virgo
19th	5:10 pm	Libra
21st	7:54 pm	Scorpio
23rd	8:41 pm	Sagittarius
25th	9:22 pm	Capricorn
27th	11:33 pm	Aquarius
30th	4:15 am	Pisces

May 1951
2nd	11:29 am	Aries
4th	8:47 pm	Taurus
7th	7:51 am	Gemini
9th	8:13 pm	Cancer
12th	8:48 am	Leo
14th	7:42 pm	Virgo
17th	3:04 am	Libra
19th	6:21 am	Scorpio
21st	6:43 am	Sagittarius
23rd	6:10 am	Capricorn
25th	6:47 am	Aquarius
27th	10:12 am	Pisces
29th	4:57 pm	Aries

June 1951
1st	2:35 am	Taurus
3rd	2:04 pm	Gemini
6th	2:32 am	Cancer
8th	3:10 pm	Leo
11th	2:44 am	Virgo
13th	11:25 am	Libra
15th	4:11 pm	Scorpio
17th	5:23 pm	Sagittarius
19th	4:39 pm	Capricorn
21st	4:09 pm	Aquarius
23rd	5:54 pm	Pisces
25th	11:15 pm	Aries
28th	8:21 am	Taurus
30th	7:53 pm	Gemini

July 1951
3rd	8:28 am	Cancer
5th	8:59 pm	Leo
8th	8:32 am	Virgo
10th	6:01 pm	Libra
13th	0:17 am	Scorpio
15th	3:00 am	Sagittarius
17th	3:13 am	Capricorn
19th	2:44 am	Aquarius
21st	3:31 am	Pisces
23rd	7:28 am	Aries
25th	3:12 pm	Taurus
28th	2:09 am	Gemini
30th	2:43 pm	Cancer

August 1951
2nd	3:07 am	Leo
4th	2:16 pm	Virgo
6th	11:35 pm	Libra
9th	6:21 am	Scorpio
11th	10:26 am	Sagittarius
13th	12:15 pm	Capricorn
15th	12:53 pm	Aquarius
17th	1:55 pm	Pisces
19th	5:02 pm	Aries
21st	11:27 pm	Taurus
24th	9:30 am	Gemini
26th	9:44 pm	Cancer
29th	10:08 am	Leo
31st	8:50 pm	Virgo

September 1951
3rd	5:31 am	Libra
5th	11:47 am	Scorpio
7th	4:10 pm	Sagittarius
9th	7:05 pm	Capricorn
11th	9:12 pm	Aquarius
13th	11:21 pm	Pisces
16th	2:48 am	Aries
18th	8:45 am	Taurus
20th	5:49 pm	Gemini
23rd	5:35 am	Cancer
25th	6:07 pm	Leo
28th	5:05 am	Virgo
30th	1:05 pm	Libra

October 1951
2nd	6:21 pm	Scorpio
4th	9:47 pm	Sagittarius
7th	0:30 am	Capricorn
9th	3:20 am	Aquarius
11th	6:48 am	Pisces
13th	11:21 am	Aries
15th	5:39 pm	Taurus
18th	2:22 am	Gemini
20th	1:45 pm	Cancer
23rd	2:25 am	Leo
25th	1:58 pm	Virgo
27th	10:24 pm	Libra
30th	3:08 am	Scorpio

November 1951
1st	5:19 am	Sagittarius
3rd	6:41 am	Capricorn
5th	8:46 am	Aquarius
7th	12:26 pm	Pisces
9th	5:54 pm	Aries
12th	1:08 am	Taurus
14th	10:17 am	Gemini
16th	9:28 pm	Cancer
19th	10:11 am	Leo
21st	10:34 pm	Virgo
24th	8:04 am	Libra
26th	1:27 pm	Scorpio
28th	3:17 pm	Sagittarius
30th	3:23 pm	Capricorn

December 1951
2nd	3:48 pm	Aquarius
4th	6:12 pm	Pisces
6th	11:19 pm	Aries
9th	7:07 am	Taurus
11th	4:56 pm	Gemini
14th	4:23 am	Cancer
16th	5:05 pm	Leo
19th	5:50 am	Virgo
21st	4:36 pm	Libra
23rd	11:39 pm	Scorpio
26th	2:26 am	Sagittarius
28th	2:24 am	Capricorn
30th	1:37 am	Aquarius

January 1952

1st	2:13 am	Pisces
3rd	5:47 am	Aries
5th	12:49 pm	Taurus
7th	10:44 pm	Gemini
10th	10:56 am	Cancer
12th	11:19 pm	Leo
15th	11:59 am	Virgo
17th	11:19 pm	Libra
20th	7:59 am	Scorpio
22nd	12:16 pm	Sagittarius
24th	1:56 pm	Capricorn
26th	1:07 pm	Aquarius
28th	12:50 pm	Pisces
30th	2:39 am	Aries

February 1952

1st	7:55 pm	Taurus
4th	4:59 am	Gemini
6th	4:46 pm	Cancer
9th	5:37 am	Leo
11th	6:02 pm	Virgo
14th	4:58 am	Libra
16th	1:42 pm	Scorpio
18th	7:41 pm	Sagittarius
20th	10:49 pm	Capricorn
22nd	11:49 pm	Aquarius
25th	0:02 am	Pisces
27th	1:15 am	Aries
29th	5:05 am	Taurus

March 1952

2nd	12:42 pm	Gemini
4th	11:40 pm	Cancer
7th	12:31 pm	Leo
10th	0:53 am	Virgo
12th	11:15 am	Libra
14th	7:20 pm	Scorpio
17th	1:15 am	Sagittarius
19th	5:18 am	Capricorn
21st	7:54 am	Aquarius
23rd	9:40 am	Pisces
25th	11:37 am	Aries
27th	3:10 pm	Taurus
29th	9:37 pm	Gemini

April 1952

1st	7:42 am	Cancer
3rd	8:10 pm	Leo
6th	8:40 am	Virgo
8th	6:55 pm	Libra
11th	2:14 am	Scorpio
13th	7:07 am	Sagittarius
15th	10:42 am	Capricorn
17th	1:44 pm	Aquarius
19th	4:41 pm	Pisces
21st	7:58 pm	Aries
24th	0:16 am	Taurus
26th	6:44 am	Gemini
28th	4:10 pm	Cancer

May 1952

1st	4:14 am	Leo
3rd	4:56 pm	Virgo
6th	3:38 am	Libra
8th	10:45 am	Scorpio
10th	2:49 pm	Sagittarius
12th	5:10 pm	Capricorn
14th	7:15 pm	Aquarius
16th	10:07 pm	Pisces
19th	2:09 am	Aries
21st	7:32 am	Taurus
23rd	2:41 pm	Gemini
26th	0:06 am	Cancer
28th	12:01 pm	Leo
31st	0:58 am	Virgo

June 1952

2nd	12:21 pm	Libra
4th	8:17 pm	Scorpio
7th	0:22 am	Sagittarius
9th	1:47 am	Capricorn
11th	2:29 am	Aquarius
13th	4:04 am	Pisces
15th	7:34 am	Aries
17th	1:14 pm	Taurus
19th	9:05 pm	Gemini
22nd	7:07 am	Cancer
24th	7:05 pm	Leo
27th	8:05 am	Virgo
29th	8:16 pm	Libra

July 1952

2nd	5:20 am	Scorpio
4th	10:21 am	Sagittarius
6th	12:00 pm	Capricorn
8th	11:55 am	Aquarius
10th	12:04 pm	Pisces
12th	2:03 pm	Aries
14th	6:50 pm	Taurus
17th	2:40 am	Gemini
19th	1:08 pm	Cancer
22nd	1:21 am	Leo
24th	2:24 pm	Virgo
27th	2:52 am	Libra
29th	12:58 pm	Scorpio
31st	7:33 pm	Sagittarius

August 1952

2nd	10:25 pm	Capricorn
4th	10:40 pm	Aquarius
6th	10:06 pm	Pisces
8th	10:35 pm	Aries
11th	1:47 am	Taurus
13th	8:42 am	Gemini
15th	6:55 pm	Cancer
18th	7:21 am	Leo
20th	8:25 pm	Virgo
23rd	8:40 am	Libra
25th	7:09 pm	Scorpio
28th	2:51 am	Sagittarius
30th	7:19 am	Capricorn

September 1952

5th	9:01 am	Aries
7th	10:53 am	Taurus
9th	4:10 pm	Gemini
12th	1:25 am	Cancer
14th	1:40 pm	Leo
17th	2:42 am	Virgo
19th	2:40 pm	Libra
22nd	0:45 am	Scorpio
24th	8:31 am	Sagittarius
26th	2:01 pm	Capricorn
28th	5:21 pm	Aquarius
30th	6:51 pm	Pisces

October 1952

2nd	7:54 pm	Aries
4th	9:06 pm	Taurus
7th	1:15 am	Gemini
9th	9:20 am	Cancer
11th	8:50 pm	Leo
14th	9:49 am	Virgo
16th	9:44 pm	Libra
19th	7:07 am	Scorpio
21st	2:10 pm	Sagittarius
23rd	7:27 pm	Capricorn
25th	11:27 pm	Aquarius
28th	2:22 am	Pisces
30th	4:54 am	Aries

November 1952

1st	6:50 am	Taurus
3rd	11:07 am	Gemini
5th	6:15 pm	Cancer
8th	4:58 am	Leo
10th	5:47 pm	Virgo
13th	5:54 am	Libra
15th	3:15 pm	Scorpio
17th	9:32 pm	Sagittarius
20th	1:39 am	Capricorn
22nd	4:51 am	Aquarius
24th	7:55 am	Pisces
26th	11:10 am	Aries
28th	2:56 pm	Taurus
30th	7:55 pm	Gemini

December 1952

3rd	3:10 am	Cancer
5th	1:24 pm	Leo
8th	1:58 am	Virgo
10th	2:32 pm	Libra
13th	0:39 am	Scorpio
15th	6:55 am	Sagittarius
17th	10:15 am	Capricorn
19th	12:02 pm	Aquarius
21st	1:48 pm	Pisces
23rd	4:33 pm	Aries
25th	8:48 pm	Taurus
28th	2:50 am	Gemini
30th	10:57 am	Cancer

January 1953

1st	9:18 pm	Leo
4th	9:42 am	Virgo
6th	10:55 pm	Libra
9th	9:59 am	Scorpio
11th	5:09 pm	Sagittarius
13th	8:55 pm	Capricorn
15th	9:57 pm	Aquarius
17th	10:08 pm	Pisces
19th	11:11 pm	Aries
22nd	2:25 am	Taurus
24th	8:26 am	Gemini
26th	5:10 pm	Cancer
29th	4:08 am	Leo
31st	4:56 pm	Virgo

February 1953

3rd	5:51 am	Libra
5th	5:18 pm	Scorpio
8th	2:18 am	Sagittarius
10th	7:27 am	Capricorn
12th	9:12 am	Aquarius
14th	8:58 am	Pisces
16th	8:54 am	Aries
18th	9:56 am	Taurus
20th	2:33 pm	Gemini
22nd	10:49 pm	Cancer
25th	10:09 am	Leo
27th	10:53 pm	Virgo

March 1953

2nd	11:41 am	Libra
4th	11:32 pm	Scorpio
7th	9:16 am	Sagittarius
9th	4:07 pm	Capricorn
11th	7:55 pm	Aquarius
13th	8:16 pm	Pisces
15th	7:40 pm	Aries
17th	7:48 pm	Taurus
19th	10:37 pm	Gemini
22nd	5:33 am	Cancer
24th	4:18 pm	Leo
27th	5:06 am	Virgo
29th	5:51 pm	Libra

April 1953

1st	5:19 am	Scorpio
3rd	2:57 pm	Sagittarius
5th	10:29 pm	Capricorn
8th	3:26 am	Aquarius
10th	5:48 am	Pisces
12th	6:19 am	Aries
14th	6:35 am	Taurus
16th	8:33 am	Gemini
18th	2:00 pm	Cancer
20th	11:29 pm	Leo
23rd	11:54 am	Virgo
26th	0:42 am	Libra
28th	11:50 am	Scorpio
30th	8:52 pm	Sagittarius

May 1953		
3rd	3:55 am	Capricorn
5th	9:11 am	Aquarius
7th	12:45 pm	Pisces
9th	2:48 pm	Aries
11th	4:14 pm	Taurus
13th	6:51 pm	Gemini
15th	11:17 pm	Cancer
18th	7:51 am	Leo
20th	7:33 am	Virgo
23rd	8:16 am	Libra
25th	7:31 am	Scorpio
28th	4:07 am	Sagittarius
30th	10:16 am	Capricorn

June 1953		
1st	2:44 pm	Aquarius
3rd	6:12 pm	Pisces
5th	9:05 pm	Aries
7th	11:41 pm	Taurus
10th	5:05 am	Gemini
12th	8:23 am	Cancer
14th	4:31 pm	Leo
17th	3:38 am	Virgo
19th	4:17 pm	Libra
22nd	3:56 am	Scorpio
24th	12:44 pm	Sagittarius
26th	6:27 pm	Capricorn
28th	9:53 pm	Aquarius

July 1953		
1st	0:10 am	Pisces
3rd	2:25 am	Aries
5th	5:26 am	Taurus
7th	9:46 am	Gemini
9th	3:59 pm	Cancer
12th	0:29 am	Leo
14th	11:31 am	Virgo
17th	0:04 am	Libra
19th	12:14 pm	Scorpio
21st	9:57 pm	Sagittarius
24th	4:04 am	Capricorn
26th	7:01 am	Aquarius
28th	8:07 am	Pisces
30th	8:59 am	Aries

August 1953		
1st	11:02 am	Taurus
3rd	3:16 pm	Gemini
5th	10:03 pm	Cancer
8th	7:20 am	Leo
10th	6:36 pm	Virgo
13th	7:09 am	Libra
15th	7:43 pm	Scorpio
18th	6:27 am	Sagittarius
20th	1:47 pm	Capricorn
22nd	5:25 pm	Aquarius
24th	6:10 pm	Pisces
26th	5:47 pm	Aries
28th	6:14 pm	Taurus
30th	9:10 pm	Gemini

September 1953		
2nd	3:33 am	Cancer
4th	1:09 pm	Leo
7th	0:48 am	Virgo
9th	1:28 pm	Libra
12th	2:06 am	Scorpio
14th	1:30 pm	Sagittarius
16th	10:20 pm	Capricorn
19th	3:28 am	Aquarius
21st	5:04 am	Pisces
23rd	4:31 am	Aries
25th	3:47 am	Taurus
27th	5:05 am	Gemini
29th	10:01 am	Cancer

October 1953		
1st	6:57 pm	Leo
4th	6:42 am	Virgo
6th	7:28 pm	Libra
9th	7:56 am	Scorpio
11th	7:19 pm	Sagittarius
14th	4:49 am	Capricorn
16th	11:29 am	Aquarius
18th	2:51 pm	Pisces
20th	3:24 pm	Aries
22nd	2:48 pm	Taurus
24th	3:09 pm	Gemini
26th	6:27 pm	Cancer
29th	1:56 am	Leo
31st	1:06 pm	Virgo

November 1953		
3rd	1:51 am	Libra
5th	2:10 pm	Scorpio
8th	1:07 am	Sagittarius
10th	10:16 am	Capricorn
12th	5:29 pm	Aquarius
14th	10:16 pm	Pisces
17th	0:34 am	Aries
19th	1:14 am	Taurus
21st	1:56 am	Gemini
23rd	4:34 am	Cancer
25th	10:45 am	Leo
27th	8:43 pm	Virgo
30th	9:06 am	Libra

December 1953		
2nd	9:30 pm	Scorpio
5th	8:06 am	Sagittarius
7th	4:30 pm	Capricorn
9th	10:59 pm	Aquarius
12th	3:44 am	Pisces
14th	7:05 am	Aries
16th	9:22 am	Taurus
18th	11:30 am	Gemini
20th	2:44 pm	Cancer
22nd	8:25 pm	Leo
25th	5:26 am	Virgo
27th	5:11 pm	Libra
30th	5:41 am	Scorpio

January 1954		
1st	4:37 pm	Sagittarius
4th	0:45 am	Capricorn
6th	6:07 am	Aquarius
8th	9:42 am	Pisces
10th	12:28 pm	Aries
12th	3:12 pm	Taurus
14th	6:51 pm	Gemini
16th	11:02 pm	Cancer
19th	5:27 am	Leo
21st	2:16 pm	Virgo
24th	1:31 am	Libra
26th	2:01 pm	Scorpio
29th	1:40 am	Sagittarius
31st	10:21 am	Capricorn

February 1954		
2nd	3:34 pm	Aquarius
4th	6:02 pm	Pisces
6th	7:15 pm	Aries
8th	8:49 pm	Taurus
10th	11:55 pm	Gemini
13th	5:13 am	Cancer
15th	12:59 pm	Leo
17th	10:02 pm	Virgo
20th	9:17 am	Libra
22nd	9:44 pm	Scorpio
25th	9:57 am	Sagittarius
27th	7:54 pm	Capricorn

March 1954		
2nd	2:05 am	Aquarius
4th	4:29 am	Pisces
6th	4:40 am	Aries
8th	4:35 am	Taurus
10th	6:11 am	Gemini
12th	10:42 am	Cancer
14th	6:20 pm	Leo
17th	4:22 am	Virgo
19th	3:59 pm	Libra
22nd	4:27 am	Scorpio
24th	4:55 pm	Sagittarius
27th	3:52 am	Capricorn
29th	11:32 am	Aquarius
31st	3:12 pm	Pisces

April 1954		
2nd	3:37 pm	Aries
4th	2:44 pm	Taurus
6th	2:45 pm	Gemini
8th	5:33 pm	Cancer
11th	0:06 am	Leo
13th	10:06 am	Virgo
15th	9:59 pm	Libra
18th	10:34 am	Scorpio
20th	10:56 pm	Sagittarius
23rd	10:09 am	Capricorn
25th	6:50 pm	Aquarius
28th	0:22 am	Pisces
30th	2:08 am	Aries

May 1954		
2nd	1:44 am	Taurus
4th	1:08 am	Gemini
6th	2:33 am	Cancer
8th	7:34 am	Leo
10th	4:27 pm	Virgo
13th	4:04 am	Libra
15th	4:43 pm	Scorpio
18th	4:54 am	Sagittarius
20th	3:48 pm	Capricorn
23rd	0:48 am	Aquarius
25th	7:06 am	Pisces
27th	10:28 am	Aries
29th	11:35 am	Taurus
31st	11:44 am	Gemini

June 1954		
2nd	12:51 pm	Cancer
4th	4:40 pm	Leo
7th	0:08 am	Virgo
9th	11:01 am	Libra
11th	11:30 pm	Scorpio
14th	11:37 am	Sagittarius
16th	10:04 pm	Capricorn
19th	6:25 am	Aquarius
21st	12:35 pm	Pisces
23rd	4:42 pm	Aries
25th	7:09 pm	Taurus
27th	8:44 pm	Gemini
29th	10:38 pm	Cancer

July 1954		
2nd	2:19 am	Leo
4th	9:01 am	Virgo
6th	6:57 pm	Libra
9th	7:04 am	Scorpio
11th	7:19 pm	Sagittarius
14th	5:38 am	Capricorn
16th	1:16 pm	Aquarius
18th	6:53 pm	Pisces
20th	10:09 pm	Aries
23rd	0:54 am	Taurus
25th	3:32 am	Gemini
27th	6:45 am	Cancer
29th	11:15 am	Leo
31st	5:54 pm	Virgo

August 1954		
3rd	3:17 am	Libra
5th	3:04 pm	Scorpio
8th	3:31 am	Sagittarius
10th	2:16 pm	Capricorn
12th	9:53 pm	Aquarius
15th	2:17 am	Pisces
17th	4:39 am	Aries
19th	6:29 am	Taurus
21st	8:50 am	Gemini
23rd	12:54 pm	Cancer
25th	6:26 pm	Leo
28th	1:46 am	Virgo
30th	11:16 am	Libra

September 1954		October 1954		November 1954		December 1954	
1st	10:50 pm Scorpio	1st	6:43 pm Sagittarius	3rd	0:23 am Aquarius	2nd	2:35 pm Pisces
4th	11:32 am Sagittarius	4th	7:02 am Capricorn	5th	7:30 am Pisces	4th	7:33 pm Aries
6th	11:09 pm Capricorn	6th	4:41 pm Aquarius	7th	10:37 am Aries	6th	9:22 pm Taurus
9th	7:26 am Aquarius	8th	10:16 pm Pisces	9th	10:47 am Taurus	8th	9:16 pm Gemini
11th	11:51 am Pisces	10th	11:58 pm Aries	11th	9:53 am Gemini	10th	9:06 pm Cancer
13th	1:21 pm Aries	12th	11:33 pm Taurus	13th	10:05 am Cancer	12th	10:49 pm Leo
15th	1:47 pm Taurus	14th	11:10 pm Gemini	15th	1:09 pm Leo	15th	3:57 am Virgo
17th	2:59 pm Gemini	17th	0:50 am Cancer	17th	7:55 pm Virgo	17th	12:56 pm Libra
19th	6:17 pm Cancer	19th	5:44 am Leo	20th	6:03 am Libra	20th	0:43 am Scorpio
22nd	0:06 am Leo	21st	1:48 pm Virgo	22nd	6:14 pm Scorpio	22nd	1:34 pm Sagittarius
24th	8:14 am Virgo	24th	0:12 am Libra	25th	7:01 am Sagittarius	25th	1:40 am Capricorn
26th	6:14 pm Libra	26th	12:12 pm Scorpio	27th	7:24 pm Capricorn	27th	11:58 am Aquarius
29th	5:55 am Scorpio	29th	1:01 am Sagittarius	30th	6:18 am Aquarius	29th	8:08 pm Pisces
		31st	1:35 pm Capricorn				

January 1955		February 1955		March 1955		April 1955	
1st	1:55 am Aries	1st	2:03 pm Gemini	2nd	10:41 pm Cancer	1st	8:23 am Leo
3rd	5:23 am Taurus	3rd	4:37 pm Cancer	5th	2:51 am Leo	3rd	2:33 pm Virgo
5th	7:03 am Gemini	5th	7:30 pm Leo	7th	8:12 am Virgo	5th	10:35 pm Libra
7th	8:02 am Cancer	7th	11:42 pm Virgo	9th	3:24 pm Libra	8th	8:41 am Scorpio
9th	9:45 am Leo	10th	6:37 am Libra	12th	1:05 am Scorpio	10th	8:44 pm Sagittarius
11th	1:48 pm Virgo	12th	4:41 pm Scorpio	14th	1:14 pm Sagittarius	13th	9:40 am Capricorn
13th	9:17 pm Libra	15th	5:06 am Sagittarius	17th	1:50 am Capricorn	15th	9:20 pm Aquarius
16th	8:15 am Scorpio	17th	5:32 pm Capricorn	19th	12:41 pm Aquarius	18th	5:24 am Pisces
18th	9:01 pm Sagittarius	20th	3:30 am Aquarius	21st	7:41 pm Pisces	20th	9:25 am Aries
21st	9:06 am Capricorn	22nd	10:04 am Pisces	23rd	11:08 pm Aries	22nd	10:27 am Taurus
23rd	6:55 pm Aquarius	24th	2:04 pm Aries	26th	0:31 am Taurus	24th	10:25 am Gemini
26th	2:11 am Pisces	26th	4:46 pm Taurus	28th	1:42 am Gemini	26th	11:12 am Cancer
28th	7:19 am Aries	28th	7:26 pm Gemini	30th	4:07 am Cancer	28th	2:12 pm Leo
30th	11:05 am Taurus					30th	7:59 pm Virgo

May 1955		June 1955		July 1955		August 1955	
3rd	4:28 am Libra	1st	8:55 pm Scorpio	1st	3:36 pm Sagittarius	2nd	10:51 pm Aquarius
5th	3:06 pm Scorpio	4th	9:25 am Sagittarius	4th	4:30 am Capricorn	5th	8:02 am Pisces
8th	3:19 am Sagittarius	6th	10:21 pm Capricorn	6th	4:17 pm Aquarius	7th	2:59 pm Aries
10th	4:19 pm Capricorn	9th	10:28 am Aquarius	9th	2:09 am Pisces	9th	8:04 pm Taurus
13th	4:28 am Aquarius	11th	8:31 pm Pisces	11th	9:31 am Aries	11th	11:34 pm Gemini
15th	1:48 pm Pisces	14th	3:21 am Aries	13th	2:17 pm Taurus	14th	1:53 am Cancer
17th	7:18 pm Aries	16th	6:47 am Taurus	15th	4:42 pm Gemini	16th	3:36 am Leo
19th	9:10 pm Taurus	18th	7:36 am Gemini	17th	5:31 pm Cancer	18th	6:02 am Virgo
21st	8:57 pm Gemini	20th	7:18 am Cancer	19th	6:07 pm Leo	20th	10:40 am Libra
23rd	8:34 pm Cancer	22nd	7:41 am Leo	21st	8:09 pm Virgo	22nd	6:42 pm Scorpio
25th	9:55 pm Leo	24th	10:32 am Virgo	24th	1:18 am Libra	25th	6:05 am Sagittarius
28th	2:17 am Virgo	26th	5:01 pm Libra	26th	10:23 am Scorpio	27th	6:56 pm Capricorn
30th	10:12 am Libra	29th	3:06 am Scorpio	28th	10:25 pm Sagittarius	30th	6:33 am Aquarius
				31st	11:18 am Capricorn		

September 1955		October 1955		November 1955		December 1955	
1st	3:20 pm Pisces	1st	5:45 am Aries	1st	7:23 pm Gemini	1st	5:49 am Cancer
3rd	9:24 pm Aries	3rd	8:51 am Taurus	3rd	8:13 pm Cancer	3rd	6:11 am Leo
6th	1:38 am Taurus	5th	10:50 am Gemini	5th	10:20 pm Leo	5th	8:55 am Virgo
8th	4:50 am Gemini	7th	1:25 pm Cancer	8th	2.38 am Virgo	7th	2:53 pm Libra
10th	8:03 am Cancer	9th	4:44 pm Leo	10th	9:19 am Libra	9th	12:00 pm Scorpio
12th	11:05 am Leo	11th	9:13 pm Virgo	12th	6:15 pm Scorpio	12th	11:36 am Sagittarius
14th	2:37 pm Virgo	14th	3:16 am Libra	15th	5:19 am Sagittarius	15th	0:24 am Capricorn
16th	7:40 pm Libra	16th	11:29 am Scorpio	17th	6:02 pm Capricorn	17th	1:20 pm Aquarius
19th	3:22 am Scorpio	18th	10:09 pm Sagittarius	20th	6:58 am Aquarius	20th	1:02 pm Pisces
21st	2:15 pm Sagittarius	21st	10:54 am Capricorn	22nd	6:08 pm Pisces	22nd	10:01 am Aries
24th	3:02 am Capricorn	23rd	11:34 pm Aquarius	25th	1:47 am Aries	24th	3:28 pm Taurus
26th	3:05 pm Aquarius	26th	9:33 am Pisces	27th	5:24 am Taurus	26th	5:31 pm Gemini
29th	0:13 am Pisces	28th	3:43 pm Aries	29th	6:11 am Gemini	28th	5:17 pm Cancer
		30th	6:28 pm Taurus			30th	4:39 pm Leo

January 1956		
1st	5:35 pm	Virgo
3rd	9:46 pm	Libra
6th	6:03 am	Scorpio
8th	5:35 pm	Sagittarius
11th	6:33 am	Capricorn
13th	7:18 am	Aquarius
16th	6:47 am	Pisces
18th	4:15 pm	Aries
20th	11:11 pm	Taurus
23rd	3:05 am	Gemini
25th	4:19 am	Cancer
27th	4:07 am	Leo
29th	4:21 am	Virgo
31st	7:01 am	Libra

February 1956		
2nd	1:38 pm	Scorpio
5th	0:12 am	Sagittarius
7th	1:07 pm	Capricorn
10th	1:51 am	Aquarius
12th	12:49 pm	Pisces
14th	9:49 pm	Aries
17th	4:47 am	Taurus
19th	9:48 am	Gemini
21st	12:48 pm	Cancer
23rd	2:10 pm	Leo
25th	3:07 pm	Virgo
27th	5:25 pm	Libra
29th	10:45 pm	Scorpio

March 1956		
3rd	8:13 am	Sagittarius
5th	8:33 pm	Capricorn
8th	9:16 am	Aquarius
10th	8:08 pm	Pisces
13th	4:25 am	Aries
15th	10:30 am	Taurus
17th	3:10 pm	Gemini
19th	6:47 pm	Cancer
21st	9:32 pm	Leo
23rd	11:53 pm	Virgo
26th	3:02 am	Libra
28th	8:23 am	Scorpio
30th	4:50 pm	Sagittarius

April 1956		
2nd	4:38 am	Capricorn
4th	5:23 pm	Aquarius
7th	4:33 am	Pisces
9th	12:42 pm	Aries
11th	6:00 pm	Taurus
13th	9:30 pm	Gemini
16th	0:14 am	Cancer
18th	3:00 am	Leo
20th	6:18 am	Virgo
22nd	10:39 am	Libra
24th	4:48 pm	Scorpio
27th	1:26 am	Sagittarius
29th	12:46 pm	Capricorn

May 1956		
2nd	1:29 am	Aquarius
4th	1:11 pm	Pisces
6th	10:05 pm	Aries
9th	3:22 am	Taurus
11th	5:59 am	Gemini
13th	7:20 am	Cancer
15th	8:53 am	Leo
17th	11:43 am	Virgo
19th	4:27 pm	Libra
21st	11:27 pm	Scorpio
24th	8:49 am	Sagittarius
26th	8:12 pm	Capricorn
29th	8:53 am	Aquarius
31st	9:09 pm	Pisces

June 1956		
3rd	7:01 am	Aries
5th	1:16 pm	Taurus
7th	4:06 pm	Gemini
9th	4:41 pm	Cancer
11th	4:47 pm	Leo
13th	6:07 pm	Virgo
15th	10:00 pm	Libra
18th	5:05 am	Scorpio
20th	2:59 pm	Sagittarius
23rd	2:44 am	Capricorn
25th	3:26 pm	Aquarius
28th	3:54 am	Pisces
30th	2:39 pm	Aries

July 1956		
2nd	10:25 pm	Taurus
5th	2:24 am	Gemini
7th	3:20 am	Cancer
9th	2:43 am	Leo
11th	2:36 am	Virgo
13th	4:58 am	Libra
15th	11:02 am	Scorpio
17th	8:40 pm	Sagittarius
20th	8:42 am	Capricorn
22nd	9:28 pm	Aquarius
25th	9:50 am	Pisces
27th	8:53 pm	Aries
30th	5:37 am	Taurus

August 1956		
1st	11:12 am	Gemini
3rd	1:29 pm	Cancer
5th	1:27 pm	Leo
7th	12:53 pm	Virgo
9th	1:57 pm	Libra
11th	6:25 pm	Scorpio
14th	3:01 am	Sagittarius
16th	2:49 pm	Capricorn
19th	3:38 am	Aquarius
21st	3:45 pm	Pisces
24th	2:30 am	Aries
26th	11:21 am	Taurus
28th	5:57 pm	Gemini
30th	9:51 pm	Cancer

September 1956		
1st	11:14 pm	Leo
3rd	11:22 pm	Virgo
6th	0:05 am	Libra
8th	3:30 am	Scorpio
10th	10:51 am	Sagittarius
12th	9:46 pm	Capricorn
15th	10:27 am	Aquarius
17th	10:35 pm	Pisces
20th	8:46 am	Aries
22nd	5:00 pm	Taurus
24th	11:26 pm	Gemini
27th	3:50 am	Cancer
29th	6:48 am	Leo

October 1956		
1st	8:25 am	Virgo
3rd	10:06 am	Libra
5th	1:25 pm	Scorpio
7th	7:51 pm	Sagittarius
10th	5:51 am	Capricorn
12th	6:10 pm	Aquarius
15th	6:23 am	Pisces
17th	4:33 pm	Aries
20th	0:07 am	Taurus
22nd	5:28 am	Gemini
24th	9:22 am	Cancer
26th	12:27 pm	Leo
28th	3:11 pm	Virgo
30th	6:12 pm	Libra

November 1956		
1st	10:27 pm	Scorpio
4th	5:00 am	Sagittarius
6th	2:30 pm	Capricorn
9th	2:22 am	Aquarius
11th	2:51 pm	Pisces
14th	1:36 am	Aries
16th	9:09 am	Taurus
18th	1:43 pm	Gemini
20th	4:16 pm	Cancer
22nd	6:11 pm	Leo
24th	8:34 pm	Virgo
27th	0:11 am	Libra
29th	5:37 am	Scorpio

December 1956		
1st	1:03 pm	Sagittarius
3rd	10:38 pm	Capricorn
6th	10:19 am	Aquarius
8th	10:59 pm	Pisces
11th	10:34 am	Aries
13th	7:13 pm	Taurus
16th	0:07 am	Gemini
18th	1:52 am	Cancer
20th	2:12 am	Leo
22nd	2:58 am	Virgo
24th	5:43 am	Libra
26th	11:12 am	Scorpio
28th	7:22 pm	Sagittarius
31st	5:40 am	Capricorn

January 1957		
2nd	5:26 pm	Aquarius
5th	6:06 am	Pisces
7th	6:21 pm	Aries
10th	4:24 am	Taurus
12th	10:39 am	Gemini
14th	1:01 pm	Cancer
16th	12:50 pm	Leo
18th	12:08 pm	Virgo
20th	1:02 pm	Libra
22nd	5:07 pm	Scorpio
25th	0:54 am	Sagittarius
27th	11:34 am	Capricorn
29th	11:42 pm	Aquarius

February 1957		
1st	12:21 pm	Pisces
4th	0:44 am	Aries
6th	11:34 am	Taurus
8th	7:32 pm	Gemini
10th	11:40 pm	Cancer
13th	0:19 am	Leo
14th	11:18 pm	Virgo
16th	10:51 pm	Libra
19th	1:07 am	Scorpio
21st	7:28 am	Sagittarius
23rd	5:29 pm	Capricorn
26th	5:42 am	Aquarius
28th	6:25 pm	Pisces

March 1957		
3rd	6:30 am	Aries
5th	5:19 pm	Taurus
8th	2:02 am	Gemini
10th	7:42 am	Cancer
12th	10:08 am	Leo
14th	10:19 am	Virgo
16th	10:03 am	Libra
18th	11:20 am	Scorpio
20th	3:59 pm	Sagittarius
23rd	0:35 am	Capricorn
25th	12:18 pm	Aquarius
28th	0:58 am	Pisces
30th	12:52 pm	Aries

April 1957		
1st	11:10 pm	Taurus
4th	7:28 am	Gemini
6th	1:35 pm	Cancer
8th	5:21 pm	Leo
10th	7:12 pm	Virgo
12th	8:09 pm	Libra
14th	9:46 pm	Scorpio
17th	1:45 am	Sagittarius
19th	9:13 am	Capricorn
21st	7:55 pm	Aquarius
24th	8:22 am	Pisces
26th	8:20 pm	Aries
29th	6:15 am	Taurus

May 1957
1st	1:43 pm	Gemini
3rd	7:06 pm	Cancer
5th	10:55 pm	Leo
8th	1:36 am	Virgo
10th	5:57 am	Libra
12th	6:50 am	Scorpio
14th	11:17 am	Sagittarius
16th	6:17 pm	Capricorn
19th	4:14 am	Aquarius
21st	4:22 pm	Pisces
24th	4:32 am	Aries
26th	2:39 pm	Taurus
28th	9:45 pm	Gemini
31st	2:04 am	Cancer

June 1957
2nd	4:45 am	Leo
4th	6:59 am	Virgo
6th	9:47 am	Libra
8th	1:43 pm	Scorpio
10th	7:11 pm	Sagittarius
13th	2:58 am	Capricorn
15th	12:27 pm	Aquarius
18th	0:16 am	Pisces
20th	12:45 pm	Aries
22nd	11:39 pm	Taurus
25th	7:02 am	Gemini
27th	10:56 am	Cancer
29th	12:50 pm	Leo

July 1957
1st	1:25 pm	Virgo
3rd	5:18 pm	Libra
5th	7:12 pm	Scorpio
8th	1:22 am	Sagittarius
10th	9:57 am	Capricorn
12th	7:45 pm	Aquarius
15th	7.54 am	Pisces
17th	8:15 pm	Aries
20th	7:54 am	Taurus
22nd	4:29 pm	Gemini
24th	9:02 pm	Cancer
26th	10:15 pm	Leo
28th	9:59 pm	Virgo
30th	10:21 pm	Libra

August 1957
2nd	1:02 am	Scorpio
4th	6:51 am	Sagittarius
6th	5:25 pm	Capricorn
9th	2:01 am	Aquarius
11th	2:05 pm	Pisces
14th	2:46 am	Aries
16th	2:59 pm	Taurus
19th	0:51 am	Gemini
21st	6:45 am	Cancer
23rd	8:47 am	Leo
25th	8:27 am	Virgo
27th	7:46 am	Libra
29th	8:51 am	Scorpio
31st	1:12 pm	Sagittarius

September 1957
2nd	9:07 pm	Capricorn
5th	7:51 am	Aquarius
7th	8:04 pm	Pisces
10th	8:45 am	Aries
12th	8:57 pm	Taurus
15th	7:25 am	Gemini
17th	2:45 pm	Cancer
19th	6:28 pm	Leo
21st	7:11 pm	Virgo
23rd	6:35 pm	Libra
25th	6:44 pm	Scorpio
27th	9:50 pm	Sagittarius
30th	4:03 am	Capricorn

October 1957
2nd	2:07 pm	Aquarius
5th	2:18 am	Pisces
7th	2:56 pm	Aries
10th	2:47 am	Taurus
12th	12:58 pm	Gemini
14th	8:55 pm	Cancer
17th	1:59 am	Leo
19th	4:25 am	Virgo
21st	5:04 am	Libra
23rd	5:55 am	Scorpio
25th	7:58 am	Sagittarius
27th	12:48 pm	Capricorn
29th	9:55 pm	Aquarius

November 1957
1st	9:20 am	Pisces
3rd	10:01 pm	Aries
6th	9:56 am	Taurus
8th	7:07 pm	Gemini
11th	2:25 am	Cancer
13th	7:34 am	Leo
15th	11:05 am	Virgo
17th	1:25 pm	Libra
19th	5:20 pm	Scorpio
21st	5:55 pm	Sagittarius
23rd	10:33 pm	Capricorn
26th	6:22 am	Aquarius
28th	5:20 pm	Pisces

December 1957
1st	5:57 am	Aries
3rd	5:47 pm	Taurus
6th	2:58 am	Gemini
8th	9:13 am	Cancer
10th	1:22 pm	Leo
12th	4.28 pm	Virgo
14th	7:25 pm	Libra
16th	10:56 pm	Scorpio
19th	2:55 am	Sagittarius
21st	7:52 am	Capricorn
23rd	3:23 pm	Aquarius
26th	1:44 am	Pisces
28th	2:14 pm	Aries
31st	2:37 am	Taurus

January 1958
2nd	12:18 pm	Gemini
4th	6:19 pm	Cancer
6th	9:21 pm	Leo
8th	10:59 pm	Virgo
11th	0:52 am	Libra
13th	4:04 am	Scorpio
15th	8:53 am	Sagittarius
17th	5:16 pm	Capricorn
19th	11:24 pm	Aquarius
22nd	9:45 am	Pisces
24th	10:04 pm	Aries
27th	10:55 am	Taurus
29th	9:47 pm	Gemini

February 1958
1st	4:58 am	Cancer
3rd	7:55 am	Leo
5th	8:12 am	Virgo
7th	8:28 am	Libra
9th	10:08 am	Scorpio
11th	2:16 pm	Sagittarius
13th	8:57 pm	Capricorn
16th	5:55 am	Aquarius
18th	4:42 pm	Pisces
21st	5:05 am	Aries
23rd	6:05 pm	Taurus
26th	5:50 am	Gemini
28th	2:12 pm	Cancer

March 1958
2nd	6:24 pm	Leo
4th	7:14 pm	Virgo
6th	6:57 pm	Libra
8th	6:58 pm	Scorpio
10th	8:59 pm	Sagittarius
13th	2:58 am	Capricorn
15th	11:51 am	Aquarius
17th	10:42 pm	Pisces
20th	11:17 am	Aries
23rd	0:16 am	Taurus
25th	12:17 pm	Gemini
27th	9:52 pm	Cancer
30th	3:44 am	Leo

April 1958
1st	5:59 am	Virgo
3rd	5:54 am	Libra
5th	5:19 am	Scorpio
7th	6:11 am	Sagittarius
9th	10:07 am	Capricorn
11th	5:45 pm	Aquarius
14th	4:40 am	Pisces
16th	5:25 pm	Aries
19th	6:15 am	Taurus
21st	6:01 pm	Gemini
24th	5:44 am	Cancer
26th	10:59 am	Leo
28th	2:57 pm	Virgo
30th	4:05 pm	Libra

May 1958
2nd	4:14 pm	Scorpio
4th	4:46 pm	Sagittarius
6th	7:24 pm	Capricorn
9th	1:51 am	Aquarius
11th	11:50 am	Pisces
15th	11:58 pm	Aries
16th	12:48 pm	Taurus
19th	0:15 am	Gemini
21st	9:19 am	Cancer
23rd	4:11 pm	Leo
25th	8:58 pm	Virgo
27th	11:55 pm	Libra
30th	1:34 am	Scorpio

June 1958
1st	2:55 am	Sagittarius
3rd	5:26 am	Capricorn
5th	10:40 am	Aquarius
7th	7:27 pm	Pisces
10th	7:22 am	Aries
12th	8:12 pm	Taurus
15th	7:28 am	Gemini
17th	3:50 pm	Cancer
19th	10:03 pm	Leo
22nd	2:21 am	Virgo
24th	5:41 am	Libra
26th	8:30 am	Scorpio
28th	11:12 am	Sagittarius
30th	2:55 pm	Capricorn

July 1958
2nd	7:47 pm	Aquarius
5th	5:59 am	Pisces
7th	5:20 pm	Aries
10th	4:08 am	Taurus
12th	5:45 pm	Gemini
15th	0:14 am	Cancer
17th	5:28 am	Leo
19th	8:41 am	Virgo
21st	11:12 am	Libra
23rd	1:58 pm	Scorpio
25th	5:26 pm	Sagittarius
27th	9:55 pm	Capricorn
30th	3:54 am	Aquarius

August 1958
1st	12:14 pm	Pisces
3rd	11:14 pm	Aries
6th	12:04 pm	Taurus
9th	0:16 am	Gemini
11th	9:19 am	Cancer
13th	2:39 pm	Leo
15th	5:05 pm	Virgo
17th	6:16 pm	Libra
19th	7:50 pm	Scorpio
21st	10:48 pm	Sagittarius
24th	3:40 am	Capricorn
26th	10:50 am	Aquarius
28th	7:27 pm	Pisces
31st	6:36 am	Aries

September 1958

2nd	7:25 pm	Taurus
5th	8:04 am	Gemini
7th	6:19 pm	Cancer
10th	0:41 am	Leo
12th	3:19 pm	Virgo
14th	3:45 am	Libra
16th	3:51 am	Scorpio
18th	5:19 am	Sagittarius
20th	9:17 am	Capricorn
22nd	4:06 pm	Aquarius
25th	1:34 am	Pisces
27th	1:08 pm	Aries
30th	1:58 am	Taurus

October 1958

2nd	2:48 pm	Gemini
5th	1:50 am	Cancer
7th	9:46 am	Leo
9th	1:46 pm	Virgo
11th	2:42 pm	Libra
13th	2:13 pm	Scorpio
15th	2:13 pm	Sagittarius
17th	4:28 pm	Capricorn
19th	10:07 pm	Aquarius
22nd	7:22 am	Pisces
24th	7:12 pm	Aries
27th	8:07 am	Taurus
29th	8:49 pm	Gemini

November 1958

1st	8:06 am	Cancer
3rd	4:59 pm	Leo
5th	10:44 pm	Virgo
8th	1:16 am	Libra
10th	1:30 am	Scorpio
12th	1:04 am	Sagittarius
14th	1:57 am	Capricorn
16th	5:59 am	Aquarius
18th	2:02 pm	Pisces
21st	1:29 am	Aries
23rd	2:31 pm	Taurus
26th	2:59 am	Gemini
28th	1:48 pm	Cancer
30th	10:39 pm	Leo

December 1958

3rd	5:15 am	Virgo
5th	9:27 am	Libra
7th	11:26 am	Scorpio
9th	12:02 pm	Sagittarius
11th	12:51 pm	Capricorn
13th	3:45 pm	Aquarius
15th	10:16 pm	Pisces
18th	8:50 am	Aries
20th	9:39 pm	Taurus
23rd	10:07 am	Gemini
25th	8:31 pm	Cancer
28th	4:32 am	Leo
30th	10:38 am	Virgo

January 1959

1st	3:19 pm	Libra
3rd	6:41 pm	Scorpio
5th	8:57 pm	Sagittarius
7th	10:52 pm	Capricorn
10th	1:54 am	Aquarius
12th	7:46 am	Pisces
14th	5:13 am	Aries
17th	5:34 am	Taurus
19th	6:15 pm	Gemini
22nd	4:45 am	Cancer
24th	12:12 pm	Leo
26th	5:12 pm	Virgo
28th	8:55 pm	Libra
31st	0:07 am	Scorpio

February 1959

2nd	3:13 am	Sagittarius
4th	6:31 am	Capricorn
6th	10:44 am	Aquarius
8th	4:55 pm	Pisces
11th	1:56 am	Aries
13th	1:48 pm	Taurus
16th	2:40 am	Gemini
18th	1:48 pm	Cancer
20th	9:38 pm	Leo
23rd	2:07 am	Virgo
25th	4:29 am	Libra
27th	6:16 am	Scorpio

March 1959

1st	8:36 am	Sagittarius
3rd	12:09 pm	Capricorn
5th	5:19 pm	Aquarius
8th	0:26 am	Pisces
10th	9:57 am	Aries
12th	9:37 pm	Taurus
15th	10:31 am	Gemini
17th	10:27 pm	Cancer
20th	7:19 am	Leo
22nd	12:25 pm	Virgo
24th	2:25 pm	Libra
26th	2:55 pm	Scorpio
28th	3:35 pm	Sagittarius
30th	5:53 pm	Capricorn

April 1959

1st	10:43 pm	Aquarius
4th	6:25 am	Pisces
6th	4:35 am	Aries
9th	4:31 am	Taurus
11th	5:25 pm	Gemini
14th	5:46 am	Cancer
16th	3:51 pm	Leo
18th	10:27 pm	Virgo
21st	1:20 am	Libra
23rd	1:35 am	Scorpio
25th	1:01 am	Sagittarius
27th	1:36 am	Capricorn
29th	5:01 am	Aquarius

May 1959

1st	12:04 pm	Pisces
3rd	10:19 pm	Aries
6th	10:39 am	Taurus
8th	11:34 pm	Gemini
11th	11:55 am	Cancer
13th	10:39 pm	Leo
16th	6:34 am	Virgo
18th	11:02 am	Libra
20th	12:21 pm	Scorpio
22nd	11:52 am	Sagittarius
24th	11:29 am	Capricorn
26th	1:17 pm	Aquarius
28th	6:47 pm	Pisces
31st	4:21 am	Aries

June 1959

2nd	4:38 pm	Taurus
5th	5:35 am	Gemini
7th	5:43 pm	Cancer
10th	4:16 am	Leo
12th	12:45 pm	Virgo
14th	6:38 pm	Libra
16th	9:37 pm	Scorpio
18th	10:14 pm	Sagittarius
20th	10:02 pm	Capricorn
22nd	11:02 pm	Aquarius
25th	3:12 am	Pisces
27th	11:34 am	Aries
29th	11:12 pm	Taurus

July 1959

2nd	12:04 pm	Gemini
5th	0:04 am	Cancer
7th	10:05 am	Leo
9th	6:13 pm	Virgo
12th	0:26 am	Libra
14th	4:31 am	Scorpio
16th	6:39 am	Sagittarius
18th	7:42 am	Capricorn
20th	9:09 am	Aquarius
22nd	12:46 pm	Pisces
24th	7:57 pm	Aries
27th	6:44 am	Taurus
29th	7:23 pm	Gemini

August 1959

1st	7:21 am	Cancer
3rd	5:06 pm	Leo
6th	0:29 am	Virgo
8th	5:55 am	Libra
10th	9:58 am	Scorpio
12th	12:57 pm	Sagittarius
14th	3:19 pm	Capricorn
16th	5:55 pm	Aquarius
18th	10:00 pm	Pisces
21st	4:54 am	Aries
23rd	3:01 pm	Taurus
26th	3:18 am	Gemini
28th	3:30 pm	Cancer
31st	1:33 am	Leo

September 1959

2nd	8:27 am	Virgo
4th	12:54 pm	Libra
6th	3:53 pm	Scorpio
8th	6:20 pm	Sagittarius
10th	9:05 pm	Capricorn
13th	0:44 am	Aquarius
15th	5:56 am	Pisces
17th	1:19 pm	Aries
19th	11:11 pm	Taurus
22nd	11:16 am	Gemini
24th	11:50 pm	Cancer
27th	10:32 am	Leo
29th	6:01 pm	Virgo

October 1959

1st	10:07 pm	Libra
3rd	11:13 pm	Scorpio
6th	0:54 am	Sagittarius
8th	2:39 am	Capricorn
10th	6:14 am	Aquarius
12th	12:09 pm	Pisces
14th	8:21 pm	Aries
17th	6:40 am	Taurus
19th	6:39 pm	Gemini
22nd	7:21 am	Cancer
24th	7:02 pm	Leo
27th	3:46 am	Virgo
29th	8:37 am	Libra
31st	10:11 am	Scorpio

November 1959

2nd	10:03 am	Sagittarius
4th	10:10 am	Capricorn
6th	12:19 pm	Aquarius
8th	5:39 pm	Pisces
11th	2:10 am	Aries
13th	1:06 pm	Taurus
16th	1:15 am	Gemini
18th	1:55 pm	Cancer
21st	2:02 am	Leo
23rd	12:03 pm	Virgo
25th	6:37 pm	Libra
27th	9:20 pm	Scorpio
29th	9:11 pm	Sagittarius

December 1959

1st	8:14 pm	Capricorn
3rd	8:38 pm	Aquarius
6th	0:16 am	Pisces
8th	8:04 am	Aries
10th	6:57 pm	Taurus
13th	7:25 am	Gemini
15th	8:00 pm	Cancer
18th	7:56 am	Leo
20th	6:27 pm	Virgo
23rd	2:27 am	Libra
25th	6:57 am	Scorpio
27th	8:13 am	Sagittarius
29th	7:39 am	Capricorn
31st	7:20 am	Aquarius

January 1960		
2nd	9:26 am	Pisces
4th	3:28 pm	Aries
7th	1:24 am	Taurus
9th	1:46 pm	Gemini
12th	2:24 am	Cancer
14th	1:59 pm	Leo
17th	0:04 am	Virgo
19th	8:10 am	Libra
21st	1:55 pm	Scorpio
23rd	4:50 pm	Sagittarius
25th	5:58 pm	Capricorn
27th	6:21 pm	Aquarius
29th	7:59 pm	Pisces

February 1960		
1st	0:41 am	Aries
3rd	9:21 am	Taurus
5th	9:01 pm	Gemini
8th	9:36 am	Cancer
10th	9:09 pm	Leo
13th	6:33 am	Virgo
15th	1:53 pm	Libra
17th	7:23 pm	Scorpio
19th	11:12 pm	Sagittarius
22nd	1:40 am	Capricorn
24th	3:34 am	Aquarius
26th	6:06 am	Pisces
28th	10:42 am	Aries

March 1960		
1st	6:22 pm	Taurus
4th	5:09 am	Gemini
6th	5:36 am	Cancer
9th	5:23 am	Leo
11th	2:45 pm	Virgo
13th	9:19 pm	Libra
16th	1:37 am	Scorpio
18th	4:39 am	Sagittarius
20th	7:16 am	Capricorn
22nd	10:12 am	Aquarius
24th	2:05 pm	Pisces
26th	7:31 pm	Aries
29th	3:15 am	Taurus
31st	1:34 pm	Gemini

April 1960		
3rd	1:47 am	Cancer
5th	1:59 pm	Leo
8th	0:04 am	Virgo
10th	6:34 am	Libra
12th	9:59 am	Scorpio
14th	11:38 am	Sagittarius
16th	1:04 pm	Capricorn
18th	3:34 pm	Aquarius
20th	7:57 pm	Pisces
23rd	2:23 am	Aries
25th	10:53 am	Taurus
27th	9:16 pm	Gemini
30th	9:24 am	Cancer

May 1960		
2nd	9:59 pm	Leo
5th	8:55 am	Virgo
7th	4:26 pm	Libra
9th	8:05 pm	Scorpio
11th	8:55 pm	Sagittarius
13th	8:53 pm	Capricorn
15th	9:54 pm	Aquarius
18th	1:26 am	Pisces
20th	7:59 am	Aries
22nd	5:02 pm	Taurus
25th	3:55 am	Gemini
27th	4:07 pm	Cancer
30th	4:50 am	Leo

June 1960		
1st	4:35 pm	Virgo
4th	1:30 am	Libra
6th	6:16 am	Scorpio
8th	7:29 am	Sagittarius
10th	6:50 am	Capricorn
12th	6:28 am	Aquarius
14th	8:24 am	Pisces
16th	1:48 pm	Aries
18th	10:35 pm	Taurus
21st	9:48 am	Gemini
23rd	10:11 pm	Cancer
26th	10:50 am	Leo
28th	10:52 pm	Virgo

July 1960		
1st	8:41 am	Libra
3rd	3:02 pm	Scorpio
5th	5:37 pm	Sagittarius
7th	5:52 pm	Capricorn
9th	4:45 pm	Aquarius
11th	5:24 pm	Pisces
13th	9:10 pm	Aries
16th	4:51 am	Taurus
18th	3:43 pm	Gemini
21st	4:09 am	Cancer
23rd	4:46 pm	Leo
26th	4:30 am	Virgo
28th	2:30 pm	Libra
30th	9:53 pm	Scorpio

August 1960		
2nd	2:02 am	Sagittarius
4th	3:24 am	Capricorn
6th	3:21 am	Aquarius
8th	3:43 am	Pisces
10th	6:25 am	Aries
12th	12:41 pm	Taurus
14th	10:30 pm	Gemini
17th	10:43 am	Cancer
19th	11:18 pm	Leo
22nd	10:39 am	Virgo
24th	8:08 pm	Libra
27th	3:22 am	Scorpio
29th	8:16 am	Sagittarius
31st	11:06 am	Capricorn

September 1960		
2nd	12:34 pm	Aquarius
4th	1:53 pm	Pisces
6th	4:29 pm	Aries
8th	9:46 pm	Taurus
11th	6:33 am	Gemini
13th	6.12 pm	Cancer
16th	6:45 am	Leo
18th	6:05 pm	Virgo
21st	2:57 am	Libra
23rd	9:16 am	Scorpio
25th	1:41 pm	Sagittarius
27th	4:53 pm	Capricorn
29th	7:32 pm	Aquarius

October 1960		
1st	10:13 pm	Pisces
4th	1:47 am	Aries
6th	7:11 am	Taurus
8th	3:19 pm	Gemini
11th	2:19 am	Cancer
13th	2:54 pm	Leo
16th	2:39 am	Virgo
18th	11:27 am	Libra
20th	5:03 pm	Scorpio
22nd	8:15 pm	Sagittarius
24th	10:28 pm	Capricorn
27th	0:58 am	Aquarius
29th	4:27 am	Pisces
31st	9:13 am	Aries

November 1960		
2nd	3:28 pm	Taurus
4th	11:43 pm	Gemini
7th	10:27 am	Cancer
9th	10:59 pm	Leo
12th	11:20 am	Virgo
14th	9:05 pm	Libra
17th	2:51 am	Scorpio
19th	5:15 am	Sagittarius
21st	6:03 am	Capricorn
23rd	7:07 am	Aquarius
25th	9:53 am	Pisces
27th	2:54 pm	Aries
29th	10:01 pm	Taurus

December 1960		
2nd	7:02 am	Gemini
4th	5:53 pm	Cancer
7th	6:20 am	Leo
9th	7:12 pm	Virgo
12th	6:05 am	Libra
14th	1:07 pm	Scorpio
16th	4:02 pm	Sagittarius
18th	4:15 pm	Capricorn
20th	3:52 pm	Aquarius
22nd	4:52 pm	Pisces
24th	8:37 pm	Aries
27th	3:34 am	Taurus
29th	1:04 pm	Gemini

January 1961		
1st	0:22 am	Cancer
3rd	12:55 pm	Leo
6th	1:47 am	Virgo
8th	1:26 pm	Libra
10th	10:06 pm	Scorpio
13th	2:38 am	Sagittarius
15th	3:39 am	Capricorn
17th	2:56 am	Aquarius
19th	2:33 am	Pisces
21st	4:31 am	Aries
23rd	9:57 am	Taurus
25th	6:54 pm	Gemini
28th	6:25 am	Cancer
30th	7:06 pm	Leo

February 1961		
2nd	7:48 am	Virgo
4th	7:25 pm	Libra
7th	4:48 am	Scorpio
9th	10:56 am	Sagittarius
11th	1:46 pm	Capricorn
13th	2:13 pm	Aquarius
15th	1:55 pm	Pisces
17th	2:45 pm	Aries
19th	6:26 pm	Taurus
22nd	1:54 am	Gemini
24th	12:52 pm	Cancer
27th	1:35 am	Leo

March 1961		
1st	2:11 pm	Virgo
4th	1:21 am	Libra
6th	10:21 am	Scorpio
8th	5:01 pm	Sagittarius
10th	9:18 pm	Capricorn
12th	11:30 pm	Aquarius
15th	0:26 am	Pisces
17th	1:34 am	Aries
19th	4:28 am	Taurus
21st	10:38 am	Gemini
23rd	8:24 pm	Cancer
26th	8:49 am	Leo
28th	9:31 pm	Virgo
31st	8:19 am	Libra

April 1961		
2nd	4:35 pm	Scorpio
4th	10:35 pm	Sagittarius
7th	2:52 am	Capricorn
9th	6:02 am	Aquarius
11th	8:32 am	Pisces
13th	10:57 am	Aries
15th	2:20 pm	Taurus
17th	7:58 pm	Gemini
20th	4:53 am	Cancer
22nd	4:45 pm	Leo
25th	5:30 am	Virgo
27th	4:33 pm	Libra
30th	0:29 am	Scorpio

May 1961
2nd	5:24 am	Sagittarius
4th	8:40 am	Capricorn
6th	11:25 am	Aquarius
8th	2:24 pm	Pisces
10th	5:57 pm	Aries
12th	10:25 pm	Taurus
15th	4:36 am	Gemini
17th	1:21 pm	Cancer
20th	0:45 am	Leo
22nd	1:38 pm	Virgo
25th	1:17 am	Libra
27th	9:30 am	Scorpio
29th	2:08 pm	Sagittarius
31st	4:20 pm	Capricorn

June 1961
2nd	5:47 pm	Aquarius
4th	7:52 pm	Pisces
6th	11:25 pm	Aries
9th	4:39 am	Taurus
11th	11:44 am	Gemini
13th	8:51 pm	Cancer
16th	8:17 am	Leo
18th	9:11 pm	Virgo
21st	9:29 am	Libra
23rd	6:47 pm	Scorpio
26th	0:05 am	Sagittarius
28th	1:50 am	Capricorn
30th	2:18 am	Aquarius

July 1961
2nd	2:55 am	Pisces
4th	5:16 am	Aries
6th	10:06 am	Taurus
8th	5:31 pm	Gemini
11th	3:15 am	Cancer
13th	2:58 pm	Leo
16th	3:54 am	Virgo
18th	4:35 pm	Libra
21st	3:01 am	Scorpio
23rd	9:35 am	Sagittarius
25th	12:24 pm	Capricorn
27th	12:40 pm	Aquarius
29th	12:15 pm	Pisces
31st	1:01 pm	Aries

August 1961
2nd	4:25 pm	Taurus
4th	11:06 pm	Gemini
7th	8:59 am	Cancer
9th	9:01 pm	Leo
12th	10:01 am	Virgo
14th	10:43 pm	Libra
17th	9:41 am	Scorpio
19th	5:40 pm	Sagittarius
21st	10:05 pm	Capricorn
23rd	11:24 pm	Aquarius
25th	11:02 pm	Pisces
27th	10:49 pm	Aries
30th	0:37 am	Taurus

September 1961
1st	5:56 am	Gemini
3rd	3:04 pm	Cancer
6th	3:01 am	Leo
8th	4:05 pm	Virgo
11th	4:32 am	Libra
13th	3:21 pm	Scorpio
11th	11:54 pm	Sagittarius
18th	5:38 am	Capricorn
20th	8:40 am	Aquarius
22nd	9:34 am	Pisces
24th	9:41 am	Aries
26th	10:46 am	Taurus
28th	2:36 pm	Gemini
30th	10:19 pm	Cancer

October 1961
3rd	9:44 am	Leo
5th	10:45 pm	Virgo
8th	11:01 am	Libra
10th	9:19 pm	Scorpio
13th	5:19 am	Sagittarius
15th	11:21 am	Capricorn
17th	5:34 pm	Aquarius
19th	6:08 pm	Pisces
21st	7:34 pm	Aries
23rd	9:07 pm	Taurus
26th	0:23 am	Gemini
28th	7:06 am	Cancer
30th	5:32 pm	Leo

November 1961
2nd	6:16 am	Virgo
4th	6:40 pm	Libra
7th	4:37 am	Scorpio
9th	11:47 am	Sagittarius
11th	4:58 pm	Capricorn
13th	8:59 pm	Aquarius
16th	0:19 am	Pisces
18th	3:10 am	Aries
20th	6:03 am	Taurus
22nd	10:01 am	Gemini
24th	4:24 pm	Cancer
27th	2:01 am	Leo
29th	2:24 pm	Virgo

December 1961
2nd	3:06 am	Libra
4th	1:24 pm	Scorpio
6th	8:21 pm	Sagittarius
9th	0:31 am	Capricorn
11th	3:12 am	Aquarius
13th	5:42 am	Pisces
15th	8:45 am	Aries
17th	12:40 pm	Taurus
19th	5:49 pm	Gemini
22nd	0:49 am	Cancer
24th	10:28 am	Leo
26th	10:29 pm	Virgo
29th	11:24 am	Libra
31st	10:40 pm	Scorpio

January 1962
3rd	6:19 am	Sagittarius
5th	10:19 am	Capricorn
7th	11:58 am	Aquarius
9th	12:55 pm	Pisces
11th	2:37 pm	Aries
13th	6:05 pm	Taurus
15th	11:42 pm	Gemini
18th	7:42 am	Cancer
20th	5:52 pm	Leo
23rd	5:54 am	Virgo
25th	6:51 pm	Libra
28th	6:50 am	Scorpio
30th	3:54 pm	Sagittarius

February 1962
1st	9:07 pm	Capricorn
3rd	10:56 pm	Aquarius
5th	10:52 pm	Pisces
7th	10:51 pm	Aries
10th	0:36 am	Taurus
12th	5:22 am	Gemini
14th	1:24 pm	Cancer
17th	0:04 am	Leo
19th	12:28 pm	Virgo
22nd	1:21 am	Libra
24th	1:34 pm	Scorpio
26th	11:45 pm	Sagittarius

March 1962
1st	6:33 am	Capricorn
3rd	9:47 am	Aquarius
5th	10:14 am	Pisces
7th	9:34 am	Aries
9th	9:45 am	Taurus
11th	12:41 pm	Gemini
13th	7:50 pm	Cancer
16th	5:58 am	Leo
18th	6:?5 pm	Virgo
21st	7:28 am	Libra
23rd	7:28 pm	Scorpio
26th	5:48 am	Sagittarius
28th	1:41 pm	Capricorn
30th	6:41 pm	Aquarius

April 1962
1st	8:42 pm	Pisces
3rd	8:40 pm	Aries
5th	8:27 pm	Taurus
7th	10:02 pm	Gemini
10th	3:14 am	Cancer
12th	12:39 pm	Leo
15th	0:57 am	Virgo
17th	1:54 pm	Libra
20th	1:37 am	Scorpio
22nd	11:26 am	Sagittarius
24th	7:19 pm	Capricorn
27th	1:08 am	Aquarius
29th	4:39 am	Pisces

May 1962
1st	6:12 am	Aries
3rd	6:50 am	Taurus
5th	8:21 am	Gemini
7th	12:34 pm	Cancer
9th	8:39 pm	Leo
12th	8:12 am	Virgo
14th	9:04 pm	Libra
17th	8:42 am	Scorpio
19th	6:01 pm	Sagittarius
22nd	1:08 am	Capricorn
24th	6:30 am	Aquarius
26th	10:28 am	Pisces
28th	1:15 pm	Aries
30th	3:17 pm	Taurus

June 1962
1st	5:43 pm	Gemini
3rd	9:50 pm	Cancer
6th	5:26 am	Leo
8th	4:14 pm	Virgo
11th	4:51 am	Libra
13th	4:43 pm	Scorpio
16th	2:03 am	Sagittarius
18th	8:28 am	Capricorn
20th	12:47 pm	Aquarius
22nd	3:59 pm	Pisces
24th	6:44 pm	Aries
26th	9:35 pm	Taurus
29th	1:10 am	Gemini

July 1962
1st	6:23 am	Cancer
3rd	2:00 pm	Leo
6th	0:22 am	Virgo
8th	12:48 pm	Libra
11th	1:05 am	Scorpio
13th	10:55 am	Sagittarius
15th	5:28 pm	Capricorn
17th	9:07 pm	Aquarius
19th	11:00 pm	Pisces
22nd	0:35 am	Aries
24th	2:50 am	Taurus
26th	7:00 am	Gemini
28th	1:05 pm	Cancer
30th	9:24 pm	Leo

August 1962
2nd	7:50 am	Virgo
4th	8:18 pm	Libra
7th	8:54 am	Scorpio
9th	7:46 pm	Sagittarius
12th	3:14 am	Capricorn
14th	7:05 am	Aquarius
16th	8:16 am	Pisces
18th	8:27 am	Aries
20th	9:24 am	Taurus
22nd	12:33 pm	Gemini
24th	6:38 pm	Cancer
27th	3:32 am	Leo
29th	2:38 pm	Virgo

September 1962

1st	3:02 am	Libra
3rd	3:46 pm	Scorpio
6th	3:25 am	Sagittarius
8th	12:15 pm	Capricorn
10th	5:21 pm	Aquarius
12th	6:59 pm	Pisces
14th	6:33 pm	Aries
16th	6:04 pm	Taurus
18th	7:32 pm	Gemini
21st	0:26 am	Cancer
23rd	9:11 am	Leo
25th	8:32 am	Virgo
28th	9:09 am	Libra
30th	9:49 am	Scorpio

October 1962

3rd	9:38 am	Sagittarius
5th	7:32 pm	Capricorn
8th	2:19 am	Aquarius
10th	5:25 am	Pisces
12th	5:38 am	Aries
14th	4:45 am	Taurus
16th	4:54 am	Gemini
18th	8:10 am	Cancer
20th	3:35 pm	Leo
23rd	2:31 am	Virgo
25th	3:13 pm	Libra
28th	3:48 am	Scorpio
30th	5:18 pm	Sagittarius

November 1962

2nd	1:17 am	Capricorn
4th	8:58 am	Aquarius
6th	1:47 pm	Pisces
8th	3:42 pm	Aries
10th	3:44 pm	Taurus
12th	3:47 pm	Gemini
14th	5:52 pm	Cancer
16th	11:40 pm	Leo
19th	9:36 am	Virgo
21st	9:58 pm	Libra
24th	10:30 am	Scorpio
26th	9:41 pm	Sagittarius
29th	6:58 am	Capricorn
31st	1:19 am	Pisces

December 1962

1st	2:23 pm	Aquarius
3rd	7:52 pm	Pisces
5th	11:16 pm	Aries
8th	0:59 am	Taurus
10th	2:07 am	Gemini
12th	4:24 am	Cancer
14th	9:24 am	Leo
16th	6:02 pm	Virgo
19th	5:41 am	Libra
21st	6:16 pm	Scorpio
24th	5:29 am	Sagittarius
26th	2:14 pm	Capricorn
28th	8:41 pm	Aquarius

January 1963

2nd	4:47 am	Aries
4th	7:34 am	Taurus
6th	10:16 am	Gemini
8th	1:44 pm	Cancer
10th	7:03 pm	Leo
13th	3:08 am	Virgo
15th	2:06 pm	Libra
18th	2:33 am	Scorpio
20th	2:16 pm	Sagittarius
22nd	11:23 pm	Capricorn
25th	5:11 am	Aquarius
27th	8:33 am	Pisces
29th	10:43 am	Aries
31st	12:56 pm	Taurus

February 1963

2nd	4:06 pm	Gemini
4th	8:42 pm	Cancer
7th	3:08 am	Leo
9th	11:39 am	Virgo
11th	10:19 pm	Libra
14th	10:37 am	Scorpio
16th	10:54 pm	Sagittarius
19th	8:54 am	Capricorn
21st	3:18 pm	Aquarius
23rd	6:13 pm	Pisces
25th	7:04 pm	Aries
27th	7:40 pm	Taurus

March 1963

1st	9:40 pm	Gemini
4th	2:09 am	Cancer
6th	9:18 am	Leo
8th	6:35 pm	Virgo
11th	5:36 am	Libra
13th	5:52 pm	Scorpio
16th	6:26 am	Sagittarius
18th	5:31 pm	Capricorn
21st	1:19 am	Aquarius
23rd	4:60 am	Pisces
25th	5:35 am	Aries
27th	4:58 am	Taurus
29th	5:16 am	Gemini
31st	8:18 am	Cancer

April 1963

2nd	2:49 pm	Leo
5th	0:22 am	Virgo
7th	11:51 am	Libra
10th	0:14 am	Scorpio
12th	12:48 pm	Sagittarius
15th	0:27 am	Capricorn
17th	9:30 am	Aquarius
19th	2:48 pm	Pisces
21st	4:25 pm	Aries
23rd	3:50 pm	Taurus
25th	3:09 pm	Gemini
27th	4:32 pm	Cancer
29th	9:26 pm	Leo

May 1963

2nd	6:16 am	Virgo
4th	5:43 pm	Libra
7th	6:16 am	Scorpio
9th	6:43 pm	Sagittarius
12th	6:13 am	Capricorn
14th	3:48 pm	Aquarius
16th	10:52 pm	Pisces
19th	1:46 am	Aries
21st	2:21 am	Taurus
23rd	1:55 am	Gemini
25th	2:31 am	Cancer
27th	6:03 am	Leo
29th	1:27 pm	Virgo

June 1963

1st	0:10 am	Libra
3rd	12:38 pm	Scorpio
6th	1:02 am	Sagittarius
8th	12:05 pm	Capricorn
10th	9:22 pm	Aquarius
13th	4:20 am	Pisces
15th	8:44 am	Aries
17th	10:53 am	Taurus
19th	11:45 am	Gemini
21st	12:51 pm	Cancer
23rd	3:50 pm	Leo
25th	9:58 pm	Virgo
28th	7:43 am	Libra
30th	7:48 pm	Scorpio

July 1963

3rd	8:10 am	Sagittarius
5th	7:02 pm	Capricorn
8th	3:35 am	Aquarius
10th	9:51 am	Pisces
12th	2:15 pm	Aries
14th	5:15 pm	Taurus
16th	7:28 pm	Gemini
18th	9:47 pm	Cancer
21st	1:16 am	Leo
23rd	7:11 am	Virgo
25th	4:06 pm	Libra
28th	3:58 am	Scorpio
30th	4:06 pm	Sagittarius

August 1963

2nd	3:11 am	Capricorn
4th	11:22 am	Aquarius
6th	4:44 pm	Pisces
8th	8:07 pm	Aries
10th	10:39 pm	Taurus
13th	1:17 am	Gemini
15th	4:41 am	Cancer
17th	9:20 am	Leo
19th	3:44 pm	Virgo
22nd	0:27 am	Libra
24th	11:41 am	Scorpio
27th	0:14 am	Sagittarius
29th	11:53 am	Capricorn
31st	8:35 pm	Aquarius

September 1963

3rd	1:37 am	Pisces
5th	3:52 am	Aries
7th	5:04 am	Taurus
9th	6:49 am	Gemini
11th	10:12 am	Cancer
13th	3:33 pm	Leo
15th	10:49 pm	Virgo
18th	8:03 am	Libra
20th	7:12 pm	Scorpio
23rd	7:51 am	Sagittarius
25th	8:15 pm	Capricorn
28th	5:58 am	Aquarius
30th	11:40 am	Pisces

October 1963

2nd	1:44 pm	Aries
4th	1:50 pm	Taurus
6th	2:01 pm	Gemini
8th	4:04 pm	Cancer
10th	8:55 pm	Leo
13th	4:36 am	Virgo
15th	2:27 pm	Libra
18th	1:53 am	Scorpio
20th	2:33 pm	Sagittarius
23rd	3:20 am	Capricorn
25th	2:15 pm	Aquarius
27th	9:55 pm	Pisces
30th	9:59 am	Aries

November 1963

1st	0:42 am	Taurus
2nd	11:49 pm	Gemini
5th	12:08 am	Cancer
7th	3:26 am	Leo
9th	10:17 am	Virgo
11th	8:09 pm	Libra
14th	7:57 am	Scorpio
16th	8:41 pm	Sagittarius
19th	9:22 am	Capricorn
21st	8:50 pm	Aquarius
24th	5:28 am	Pisces
26th	10:19 am	Aries
28th	11:46 am	Taurus
30th	11:15 am	Gemini

December 1963

2nd	10:48 am	Cancer
4th	12:26 pm	Leo
6th	5:30 pm	Virgo
9th	2:23 am	Libra
11th	2:05 pm	Scorpio
14th	2:52 am	Sagittarius
16th	3:20 pm	Capricorn
19th	2:28 am	Aquarius
21st	11:25 am	Pisces
23rd	5:57 pm	Aries
25th	6:55 pm	Taurus
27th	9:57 pm	Gemini
29th	10:08 pm	Cancer
31st	11:09 pm	Leo

January 1964
3rd	2:49 am	Virgo
5th	10:14 am	Libra
7th	9:04 pm	Scorpio
16th	9:47 am	Sagittarius
12th	10:12 pm	Capricorn
15th	8:44 am	Aquarius
17th	5:01 pm	Pisces
19th	11:10 pm	Aries
22nd	3:23 am	Taurus
24th	6:03 am	Gemini
26th	7:52 am	Cancer
28th	9:47 am	Leo
30th	1:13 pm	Virgo

February 1964
1st	7:28 pm	Libra
4th	5:14 am	Scorpio
6th	5:34 pm	Sagittarius
9th	6:07 am	Capricorn
11th	4:35 pm	Aquarius
14th	0:07 am	Pisces
16th	5:08 am	Aries
18th	8:44 am	Taurus
20th	11:48 am	Gemini
22nd	2:50 pm	Cancer
24th	6:12 pm	Leo
26th	10:30 pm	Virgo
29th	4:49 am	Libra

March 1964
2nd	1:57 pm	Scorpio
5th	1:46 am	Sagittarius
7th	2:32 pm	Capricorn
10th	1:33 am	Aquarius
12th	9:00 am	Pisces
14th	1:11 pm	Aries
16th	3:30 pm	Taurus
18th	5:27 pm	Gemini
20th	8:13 pm	Cancer
23rd	0:16 am	Leo
25th	5:43 am	Virgo
27th	12:50 pm	Libra
29th	10:04 pm	Scorpio

April 1964
1st	9:42 am	Sagittarius
3rd	10:37 pm	Capricorn
6th	10:19 am	Aquarius
8th	6:42 pm	Pisces
10th	11:07 pm	Aries
13th	0:36 am	Taurus
15th	1:05 am	Gemini
17th	2:23 am	Cancer
19th	5:42 am	Leo
21st	11:20 am	Virgo
23rd	7:09 pm	Libra
26th	5:03 am	Scorpio
28th	4:47 pm	Sagittarius

May 1964
1st	5:42 am	Capricorn
3rd	6:04 pm	Aquarius
6th	3:40 am	Pisces
8th	9:11 am	Aries
10th	11:05 am	Taurus
12th	11:01 am	Gemini
14th	10:56 am	Cancer
16th	12:36 pm	Leo
18th	5:06 pm	Virgo
21st	0:40 am	Libra
23rd	11:01 am	Scorpio
25th	11:04 pm	Sagittarius
28th	12:00 pm	Capricorn
31st	0:32 am	Aquarius

June 1964
2nd	10:57 am	Pisces
4th	5:50 pm	Aries
6th	9:18 pm	Taurus
8th	9:49 pm	Gemini
10th	9:17 pm	Cancer
12th	9:37 pm	Leo
15th	0:27 am	Virgo
17th	6:57 am	Libra
19th	4:52 pm	Scorpio
22nd	5:05 am	Sagittarius
24th	6:01 pm	Capricorn
27th	6:20 am	Aquarius
29th	4:54 pm	Pisces

July 1964
2nd	0:52 am	Aries
4th	5:40 am	Taurus
6th	7:41 am	Gemini
8th	7:57 am	Cancer
10th	8:04 am	Leo
12th	9:49 am	Virgo
14th	2:47 pm	Libra
16th	11:33 pm	Scorpio
19th	11:30 am	Sagittarius
22nd	0:28 am	Capricorn
24th	12:28 pm	Aquarius
26th	10:36 pm	Pisces
29th	6:23 am	Aries
31st	11:57 am	Taurus

August 1964
2nd	3:27 pm	Gemini
4th	5:13 pm	Cancer
6th	6:12 pm	Leo
8th	7:52 pm	Virgo
10th	11:53 pm	Libra
13th	7:36 am	Scorpio
15th	6:45 pm	Sagittarius
18th	7:38 am	Capricorn
20th	7:37 pm	Aquarius
23rd	5:11 am	Pisces
25th	12:13 pm	Aries
27th	5:22 pm	Taurus
29th	9:17 pm	Gemini

September 1964
1st	0:15 am	Cancer
3rd	2:38 am	Leo
5th	5:15 am	Virgo
7th	9:24 am	Libra
9th	4:24 pm	Scorpio
12th	2:49 am	Sagittarius
14th	3:29 pm	Capricorn
17th	3:45 am	Aquarius
19th	1:18 pm	Pisces
21st	7:42 pm	Aries
23rd	11:46 pm	Taurus
26th	2:46 am	Gemini
28th	5:40 am	Cancer
30th	8:54 am	Leo

October 1964
2nd	12:45 pm	Virgo
4th	5:47 pm	Libra
7th	0:59 am	Scorpio
9th	11:06 am	Sagittarius
11th	11:34 pm	Capricorn
14th	12:13 pm	Aquarius
16th	10:32 pm	Pisces
19th	5:02 am	Aries
21st	8:22 am	Taurus
23rd	10:04 am	Gemini
25th	11:39 am	Cancer
27th	2:17 pm	Leo
29th	6:27 pm	Virgo

November 1964
1st	0:24 am	Libra
3rd	8:28 am	Scorpio
5th	6:46 pm	Sagittarius
8th	7:08 am	Capricorn
10th	8:09 pm	Aquarius
13th	7:26 am	Pisces
15th	3:05 pm	Aries
17th	6:55 pm	Taurus
19th	7:58 pm	Gemini
21st	8:04 pm	Cancer
23rd	9:00 pm	Leo
26th	0:02 am	Virgo
28th	5:57 am	Libra
30th	2:34 pm	Scorpio

December 1964
3rd	1:24 am	Sagittarius
5th	1:55 pm	Capricorn
8th	2:58 am	Aquarius
10th	2:57 pm	Pisces
13th	0:13 am	Aries
15th	5:29 am	Taurus
17th	7:18 am	Gemini
19th	7:02 am	Cancer
21st	6:34 am	Leo
23rd	7:46 am	Virgo
25th	12:10 pm	Libra
27th	8:12 pm	Scorpio
30th	7:22 am	Sagittarius

January 1965
1st	8:06 pm	Capricorn
4th	9:03 am	Aquarius
6th	9:05 pm	Pisces
9th	7:05 am	Aries
11th	2:05 pm	Taurus
13th	5:44 pm	Gemini
15th	6:32 pm	Cancer
17th	5:58 pm	Leo
19th	5:58 pm	Virgo
21st	8:31 pm	Libra
24th	3:03 am	Scorpio
26th	1:34 pm	Sagittarius
29th	2:21 am	Capricorn
31st	3:16 pm	Aquarius

February 1965
3rd	2:55 am	Pisces
5th	12:41 pm	Aries
7th	8:22 pm	Taurus
10th	1:36 am	Gemini
12th	4:12 am	Cancer
14th	4:53 am	Leo
16th	5:08 am	Virgo
18th	6:50 am	Libra
20th	11:51 am	Scorpio
22nd	8:58 pm	Sagittarius
25th	9:16 am	Capricorn
27th	10:13 pm	Aquarius

March 1965
2nd	9:34 am	Pisces
4th	6:43 pm	Aries
7th	1:50 am	Taurus
9th	7:12 am	Gemini
11th	11:01 am	Cancer
13th	1:22 pm	Leo
15th	2:57 pm	Virgo
17th	5.07 pm	Libra
19th	9:34 pm	Scorpio
22nd	5:39 am	Sagittarius
24th	5:09 pm	Capricorn
27th	5:56 am	Aquarius
29th	5:28 pm	Pisces

April 1965
1st	2:17 am	Aries
3rd	8:25 am	Taurus
5th	12:53 pm	Gemini
7th	4:22 pm	Cancer
9th	7:24 pm	Leo
11th	10:15 pm	Virgo
14th	1:39 am	Libra
16th	6:45 am	Scorpio
18th	2:35 pm	Sagittarius
21st	1:25 am	Capricorn
23rd	2:03 pm	Aquarius
26th	2:00 am	Pisces
28th	11:06 am	Aries
30th	4:59 pm	Taurus

May 1965

2nd	8:25 pm	Gemini
4th	10:38 pm	Cancer
7th	0:49 am	Leo
9th	3:48 am	Virgo
11th	8:05 am	Libra
13th	2:12 pm	Scorpio
15th	10:32 pm	Sagittarius
18th	9:21 am	Capricorn
20th	9:50 pm	Aquarius
23rd	10:12 am	Pisces
25th	8:16 pm	Aries
28th	2:47 am	Taurus
30th	5:56 am	Gemini

June 1965

1st	7:04 am	Cancer
3rd	7:48 am	Leo
5th	9:36 am	Virgo
7th	1:33 pm	Libra
9th	8:05 pm	Scorpio
12th	5:12 am	Sagittarius
14th	4:21 pm	Capricorn
17th	4:52 am	Aquarius
19th	5:28 pm	Pisces
22nd	4:27 am	Aries
24th	12:11 pm	Taurus
26th	4:13 pm	Gemini
28th	5:17 pm	Cancer
30th	4:50 pm	Leo

July 1965

2nd	5:14 pm	Virgo
4th	7:45 pm	Libra
7th	1:40 am	Scorpio
9th	10:56 am	Sagittarius
11th	10:30 pm	Capricorn
14th	11:07 am	Aquarius
16th	11:44 pm	Pisces
19th	11:09 am	Aries
21st	8:11 pm	Taurus
24th	1:47 am	Gemini
26th	3:52 am	Cancer
28th	3:37 am	Leo
30th	2:57 am	Virgo

August 1965

1st	3:57 am	Libra
3rd	8:26 am	Scorpio
5th	4:53 pm	Sagittarius
8th	4:23 am	Capricorn
10th	5:08 pm	Aquarius
13th	5:37 am	Pisces
15th	4:55 pm	Aries
18th	2:27 am	Taurus
20th	9:17 am	Gemini
22nd	1:00 pm	Cancer
24th	1:59 pm	Leo
26th	1:38 pm	Virgo
28th	1:57 pm	Libra
30th	4:50 pm	Scorpio

September 1965

1st	11:60 pm	Sagittarius
4th	10:54 am	Capricorn
6th	11:54 pm	Aquarius
9th	11:35 am	Pisces
11th	10:50 pm	Aries
14th	7:54 am	Taurus
16th	3:03 pm	Gemini
18th	8:00 pm	Cancer
20th	10:35 pm	Leo
22nd	11:31 pm	Virgo
25th	0:17 am	Libra
27th	2:50 am	Scorpio
29th	8:47 am	Sagittarius

October 1965

1st	6:31 pm	Capricorn
4th	6:49 am	Aquarius
6th	7:12 pm	Pisces
9th	5:51 am	Aries
11th	2:15 pm	Taurus
13th	8:39 pm	Gemini
16th	1:26 am	Cancer
18th	4:50 am	Leo
20th	7:14 am	Virgo
22nd	9:24 am	Libra
24th	12:37 pm	Scorpio
26th	6:14 pm	Sagittarius
29th	3:09 am	Capricorn
31st	2:51 pm	Aquarius

November 1965

3rd	3:23 am	Pisces
5th	2:19 pm	Aries
7th	10:30 pm	Taurus
10th	3:52 am	Gemini
12th	7:28 am	Cancer
14th	10:14 am	Leo
16th	12:55 pm	Virgo
18th	4:11 pm	Libra
20th	8:39 pm	Scorpio
23rd	2:59 am	Sagittarius
25th	11:49 am	Capricorn
27th	11:06 pm	Aquarius
30th	11:40 am	Pisces

December 1965

2nd	11:23 pm	Aries
5th	8:07 am	Taurus
7th	1:24 pm	Gemini
9th	3:55 pm	Cancer
11th	5:08 pm	Leo
13th	6:37 pm	Virgo
15th	9:34 pm	Libra
18th	2:42 am	Scorpio
20th	10:04 am	Sagittarius
22nd	7:29 pm	Capricorn
25th	6:46 am	Aquarius
27th	7:18 pm	Pisces
30th	7:38 am	Aries

January 1966

1st	5:42 pm	Taurus
4th	0:07 am	Gemini
6th	2:39 am	Cancer
8th	2:50 am	Leo
10th	2:37 am	Virgo
12th	3:57 am	Libra
14th	8:13 am	Scorpio
16th	3:42 pm	Sagittarius
19th	1:45 am	Capricorn
21st	1:27 pm	Aquarius
24th	1:59 am	Pisces
26th	2:32 pm	Aries
29th	1:41 am	Taurus
31st	9:38 am	Gemini

February 1966

2nd	1:35 pm	Cancer
4th	2:11 pm	Leo
6th	1:13 pm	Virgo
8th	12:56 pm	Libra
10th	3:20 pm	Scorpio
12th	9:35 pm	Sagittarius
15th	7:27 am	Capricorn
17th	7:26 pm	Aquarius
20th	8:05 am	Pisces
22nd	8:29 pm	Aries
25th	7:51 am	Taurus
27th	4:59 pm	Gemini

March 1966

1st	10:48 pm	Cancer
4th	0:56 am	Leo
6th	0:36 am	Virgo
7th	11:49 pm	Libra
10th	0:48 am	Scorpio
12th	5:22 am	Sagittarius
14th	1:50 pm	Capricorn
17th	1:35 am	Aquarius
19th	2:18 pm	Pisces
22nd	2:33 am	Aries
24th	1:29 pm	Taurus
26th	10:41 pm	Gemini
29th	5:21 am	Cancer
31st	9:08 am	Leo

April 1966

2nd	10:29 am	Virgo
4th	10:41 am	Libra
6th	11:35 am	Scorpio
8th	2:59 pm	Sagittarius
10th	10:03 pm	Capricorn
13th	8:44 am	Aquarius
15th	9:12 pm	Pisces
18th	9:25 am	Aries
20th	7:57 pm	Taurus
23rd	4:24 am	Gemini
25th	10:45 am	Cancer
27th	3:06 pm	Leo
29th	5:47 pm	Virgo

May 1966

1st	7:31 pm	Libra
3rd	9:24 pm	Scorpio
6th	0:53 am	Sagittarius
8th	7:17 am	Capricorn
10th	4:54 pm	Aquarius
13th	4:55 am	Pisces
15th	5:13 pm	Aries
18th	3:45 am	Taurus
20th	11:35 am	Gemini
22nd	4:57 pm	Cancer
24th	8:35 pm	Leo
26th	11:21 pm	Virgo
29th	1:59 am	Libra
31st	5:12 am	Scorpio

June 1966

2nd	9:41 am	Sagittarius
4th	4:13 pm	Capricorn
7th	1:23 am	Aquarius
9th	12:58 pm	Pisces
12th	1:26 am	Aries
14th	12:26 pm	Taurus
16th	8:23 pm	Gemini
19th	1:03 am	Cancer
21st	3:27 am	Leo
23rd	5:08 am	Virgo
25th	7:24 am	Libra
27th	11:06 am	Scorpio
29th	4:33 pm	Sagittarius

July 1966

1st	11:51 pm	Capricorn
4th	9:16 am	Aquarius
6th	8:40 pm	Pisces
9th	9:15 am	Aries
11th	9:01 pm	Taurus
14th	5:46 am	Gemini
16th	10:38 am	Cancer
18th	12:24 pm	Leo
20th	12:47 pm	Virgo
22nd	1:41 pm	Libra
24th	4:35 pm	Scorpio
26th	10:06 pm	Sagittarius
29th	6:06 am	Capricorn
31st	4:03 pm	Aquarius

August 1966

3rd	3:35 am	Pisces
5th	4:14 pm	Aries
8th	4:36 am	Taurus
10th	2:33 pm	Gemini
12th	8:38 pm	Cancer
14th	10:49 pm	Leo
16th	10:35 pm	Virgo
18th	10:05 pm	Libra
20th	11:23 pm	Scorpio
23rd	3:53 am	Sagittarius
25th	11:40 am	Capricorn
27th	9:56 pm	Aquarius
30th	9:48 am	Pisces

September 1966

1st	10:27 pm	Aries
4th	10:57 am	Taurus
6th	9:50 pm	Gemini
9th	5:23 am	Cancer
11th	8:57 am	Leo
13th	9:24 am	Virgo
15th	8:36 am	Libra
17th	8:38 am	Scorpio
19th	11:27 am	Sagittarius
21st	5:56 pm	Capricorn
24th	3:48 am	Aquarius
26th	3:48 pm	Pisces
29th	4:29 am	Aries

October 1966

1st	4:45 pm	Taurus
4th	3:42 am	Gemini
6th	12:08 pm	Cancer
8th	5:21 pm	Leo
10th	7:25 pm	Virgo
12th	7:30 pm	Libra
14th	7:24 pm	Scorpio
16th	9:01 pm	Sagittarius
19th	1:58 am	Capricorn
21st	10:46 am	Aquarius
23rd	10:21 pm	Pisces
26th	11:02 am	Aries
28th	11:04 pm	Taurus
31st	9:25 am	Gemini

November 1966

2nd	5:40 pm	Cancer
4th	11:35 pm	Leo
7th	3:08 am	Virgo
9th	4:54 am	Libra
11th	5:56 am	Scorpio
13th	7:41 am	Sagittarius
15th	11:43 am	Capricorn
17th	7:08 pm	Aquarius
20th	5:55 am	Pisces
22nd	6:32 pm	Aries
25th	6:35 am	Taurus
27th	4:28 pm	Gemini
29th	11:49 pm	Cancer

December 1966

2nd	4:59 am	Leo
4th	8:46 am	Virgo
6th	11:42 am	Libra
8th	2:18 pm	Scorpio
10th	5:15 pm	Sagittarius
12th	9:34 pm	Capricorn
15th	4:23 am	Aquarius
17th	2:22 pm	Pisces
20th	2:40 am	Aries
22nd	3:06 pm	Taurus
25th	1:14 am	Gemini
27th	7:55 am	Cancer
29th	11:55 am	Leo
31st	2:33 pm	Virgo

January 1967

2nd	5:04 pm	Libra
4th	8:17 pm	Scorpio
7th	0:28 am	Sagittarius
9th	5:55 am	Capricorn
11th	1:10 pm	Aquarius
13th	10:46 pm	Pisces
16th	10:49 am	Aries
18th	11:40 pm	Taurus
21st	10:34 am	Gemini
23rd	5:48 pm	Cancer
25th	9:20 pm	Leo
27th	10:37 pm	Virgo
29th	11:34 pm	Libra

February 1967

1st	1:45 am	Scorpio
3rd	5:58 am	Sagittarius
5th	12:14 pm	Capricorn
7th	8:19 pm	Aquarius
10th	6:21 am	Pisces
12th	6:19 pm	Aries
15th	7:18 am	Taurus
17th	7:13 pm	Gemini
20th	3:46 am	Cancer
22nd	8:01 am	Leo
24th	9:03 am	Virgo
26th	8:47 am	Libra
28th	9:14 am	Scorpio

March 1967

2nd	11:58 am	Sagittarius
4th	5:38 pm	Capricorn
7th	2:04 am	Aquarius
9th	12:44 pm	Pisces
12th	0:53 am	Aries
14th	1:54 pm	Taurus
17th	2:18 am	Gemini
19th	12:06 pm	Cancer
21st	6:01 pm	Leo
23rd	8:06 pm	Virgo
25th	7:49 pm	Libra
27th	7:13 pm	Scorpio
29th	8:11 pm	Sagittarius

April 1967

1st	0:11 am	Capricorn
3rd	7:52 am	Aquarius
5th	6:30 pm	Pisces
8th	6:56 am	Aries
10th	7:54 pm	Taurus
13th	8:12 am	Gemini
15th	6:33 pm	Cancer
18th	1:53 am	Leo
20th	5:39 am	Virgo
22nd	6:39 am	Libra
24th	6:20 am	Scorpio
26th	6:31 am	Sagittarius
28th	8:59 am	Capricorn
30th	3:02 pm	Aquarius

May 1967

3rd	0:48 am	Pisces
5th	1:10 pm	Aries
8th	2:09 am	Taurus
10th	2:05 pm	Gemini
13th	0:09 am	Cancer
15th	7:46 am	Leo
17th	12:48 pm	Virgo
19th	3:27 pm	Libra
21st	4:29 pm	Scorpio
23rd	5:08 pm	Sagittarius
25th	7:01 pm	Capricorn
27th	11:46 pm	Aquarius
30th	8:22 am	Pisces

June 1967

1st	8:08 pm	Aries
4th	9:03 am	Taurus
6th	8:49 pm	Gemini
9th	6:14 am	Cancer
11th	1:16 pm	Leo
13th	6:21 pm	Virgo
15th	9:57 pm	Libra
18th	0:25 am	Scorpio
20th	2:20 am	Sagittarius
22nd	4:48 am	Capricorn
24th	9:15 am	Aquarius
26th	4:53 pm	Pisces
29th	3:54 am	Aries

July 1967

1st	4:42 pm	Taurus
4th	4:36 am	Gemini
6th	1:42 pm	Cancer
8th	7:56 pm	Leo
11th	0:07 am	Virgo
13th	3:19 am	Libra
15th	6:17 am	Scorpio
17th	9:23 am	Sagittarius
19th	12:50 pm	Capricorn
21st	6:01 pm	Aquarius
24th	1:28 am	Pisces
26th	12:02 pm	Aries
29th	0:41 am	Taurus
31st	12:56 pm	Gemini

August 1967

2nd	10:30 pm	Cancer
5th	4:23 am	Leo
7th	7:34 am	Virgo
9th	9:34 am	Libra
11th	11:45 am	Scorpio
13th	2:54 pm	Sagittarius
15th	7:19 pm	Capricorn
18th	1:17 am	Aquarius
20th	9:20 am	Pisces
22nd	7:48 pm	Aries
25th	8:21 am	Taurus
27th	9:07 pm	Gemini
30th	7:30 am	Cancer

September 1967

1st	2:02 pm	Leo
3rd	5:04 pm	Virgo
5th	6:02 pm	Libra
7th	6:45 pm	Scorpio
9th	8:41 pm	Sagittarius
12th	0:43 am	Capricorn
14th	7:10 am	Aquarius
16th	3:55 pm	Pisces
19th	2:46 am	Aries
21st	3:19 pm	Taurus
24th	4:19 am	Gemini
26th	3:42 pm	Cancer
28th	11:42 pm	Leo

October 1967

1st	3:37 am	Virgo
3rd	4:34 am	Libra
5th	4:15 am	Scorpio
7th	4:34 am	Sagittarius
9th	7:08 am	Capricorn
11th	12:49 pm	Aquarius
13th	9:39 pm	Pisces
16th	8:58 am	Aries
18th	9:40 pm	Taurus
21st	10:36 am	Gemini
23rd	10:27 pm	Cancer
26th	7:36 am	Leo
28th	1:14 pm	Virgo
30th	3:27 pm	Libra

November 1967

1st	3:26 pm	Scorpio
3rd	2:54 pm	Sagittarius
5th	3:50 pm	Capricorn
7th	7:49 pm	Aquarius
10th	3:45 am	Pisces
12th	3:01 pm	Aries
15th	3:52 am	Taurus
17th	4:39 pm	Gemini
20th	4:11 am	Cancer
22nd	1:43 pm	Leo
24th	8:44 pm	Virgo
27th	0:48 am	Libra
29th	2:13 am	Scorpio

December 1967

1st	2:11 am	Sagittarius
3rd	2:27 am	Capricorn
5th	5:03 am	Aquarius
7th	11:26 am	Pisces
9th	9:45 pm	Aries
12th	10:32 am	Taurus
14th	11:18 pm	Gemini
17th	10:20 am	Cancer
19th	7:19 pm	Leo
22nd	2:20 am	Virgo
24th	7:24 am	Libra
26th	10:34 am	Scorpio
28th	12:08 pm	Sagittarius
30th	1:14 pm	Capricorn

January 1968			February 1968			March 1968			April 1968		
1st	3:29 pm	Aquarius	2nd	2:44 pm	Aries	3rd	10:29 am	Taurus	2nd	6:41 am	Gemini
3rd	8:40 pm	Pisces	5th	2:16 am	Taurus	5th	11:17 pm	Gemini	4th	7:12 pm	Cancer
6th	5:50 am	Aries	7th	3:08 pm	Gemini	8th	11:18 am	Cancer	7th	5:25 am	Leo
8th	6:05 pm	Taurus	10th	2:33 am	Cancer	10th	8:26 pm	Leo	9th	12:00 pm	Virgo
11th	6:54 am	Gemini	12th	10:47 am	Leo	13th	1:51 am	Virgo	11th	2:58 pm	Libra
13th	5:51 pm	Cancer	14th	4:01 pm	Virgo	15th	4:23 am	Libra	13th	3:32 pm	Scorpio
16th	2:09 am	Leo	16th	7:22 pm	Libra	17th	5:34 am	Scorpio	15th	3:26 pm	Sagittarius
18th	8:10 am	Virgo	18th	10:00 pm	Scorpio	19th	6:57 am	Sagittarius	17th	4:28 pm	Capricorn
20th	12:46 pm	Libra	21st	0:49 am	Sagittarius	21st	9:39 am	Capricorn	19th	7:50 pm	Aquarius
22nd	4:27 pm	Scorpio	23rd	4:13 am	Capricorn	23rd	2:20 pm	Aquarius	22nd	2:47 am	Pisces
24th	7:25 pm	Sagittarius	25th	8:40 am	Aquarius	25th	9:16 pm	Pisces	24th	12:34 pm	Aries
26th	9:57 pm	Capricorn	27th	2:46 pm	Pisces	28th	6:34 am	Aries	27th	0:22 am	Taurus
29th	1:08 am	Aquarius	29th	11:16 pm	Aries	30th	5:55 pm	Taurus	29th	1:10 pm	Gemini
31st	6:21 am	Pisces									

May 1968			June 1968			July 1968			August 1968		
2nd	1:50 am	Cancer	3rd	3:50 am	Virgo	2nd	4:06 pm	Libra	1st	2:10 am	Scorpio
4th	12:50 pm	Leo	5th	9:44 am	Libra	4th	8:18 pm	Scorpio	3rd	5:09 am	Sagittarius
6th	8:57 pm	Virgo	7th	12:25 pm	Scorpio	6th	10:04 pm	Sagittarius	5th	6:57 am	Capricorn
9th	1:20 am	Libra	9th	12:40 pm	Sagittarius	8th	10:24 pm	Capricorn	7th	8:39 am	Aquarius
11th	2:29 am	Scorpio	11th	12:09 pm	Capricorn	10th	11:04 pm	Aquarius	9th	11:50 am	Pisces
13th	1:54 am	Sagittarius	13th	12:53 pm	Aquarius	13th	2:05 am	Pisces	11th	5:57 pm	Aries
15th	1:33 am	Capricorn	15th	4:49 pm	Pisces	15th	8:57 am	Aries	14th	3:37 am	Taurus
17th	3:27 am	Aquarius	18th	0:51 am	Aries	17th	7:33 pm	Taurus	16th	3:52 pm	Gemini
19th	8:59 am	Pisces	20th	12:27 pm	Taurus	20th	8:13 am	Gemini	19th	4:13 am	Cancer
21st	6:18 am	Aries	23rd	1:23 am	Gemini	22nd	8:31 pm	Cancer	21st	2:36 pm	Leo
24th	6:17 am	Taurus	25th	1:41 pm	Cancer	25th	6:53 am	Leo	23rd	10:19 pm	Virgo
26th	7:12 pm	Gemini	28th	0:31 am	Leo	27th	3:07 pm	Virgo	26th	3:43 am	Libra
29th	7:41 am	Cancer	30th	9:22 am	Virgo	29th	9:31 pm	Libra	28th	7:37 am	Scorpio
31st	6:52 pm	Leo							30th	10:40 am	Sagittarius

September 1968			October 1968			November 1968			December 1968		
1st	1:22 pm	Capricorn	3rd	3:22 am	Pisces	1st	4:53 pm	Aries	1st	9:00 am	Taurus
3rd	4:30 pm	Aquarius	5th	10:37 am	Aries	4th	3:02 am	Taurus	3rd	9:05 pm	Gemini
5th	8:29 pm	Pisces	7th	8:07 pm	Taurus	6th	2:48 pm	Gemini	6th	9:42 am	Cancer
8th	2:51 am	Aries	10th	7:44 am	Gemini	9th	3:26 am	Cancer	8th	10:02 pm	Leo
10th	12-08 pm	Taurus	12th	8:24 pm	Cancer	11th	3:43 pm	Leo	11th	8:54 am	Virgo
12th	11.54 pm	Gemini	15th	8:05 am	Leo	14th	1:53 am	Virgo	13th	5:04 pm	Libra
15th	12:27 pm	Cancer	17th	4:54 pm	Virgo	16th	8:21 am	Libra	15th	9:30 pm	Scorpio
17th	11:25 pm	Leo	19th	10:04 pm	Libra	18th	11:01 am	Scorpio	17th	10:27 pm	Sagittarius
20th	7:11 am	Virgo	22nd	0:06 am	Scorpio	20th	11:03 am	Sagittarius	19th	9:33 pm	Capricorn
22nd	11:57 am	Libra	24th	0:32 am	Sagittarius	22nd	10.24 am	Capricorn	21st	9:03 pm	Aquarius
24th	2:37 pm	Scorpio	26th	1:15 am	Capricorn	24th	11:08 am	Aquarius	23rd	11:02 pm	Pisces
26th	4:31 pm	Sagittarius	28th	3:45 am	Aquarius	26th	2:58 pm	Pisces	26th	5:08 am	Aries
28th	6:46 pm	Capricorn	30th	8:58 am	Pisces	28th	10:27 pm	Aries	28th	3:01 am	Taurus
30th	10:11 pm	Aquarius							31st	3:12 am	Gemini

January 1969			February 1969			March 1969			April 1969		
2nd	3:52 pm	Cancer	1st	10:28 am	Leo	3rd	4:06 am	Virgo	1st	8:02 pm	Libra
5th	3:53 am	Leo	3rd	8:41 pm	Virgo	5th	11:32 am	Libra	4th	0:24 am	Scorpio
7th	2:39 pm	Virgo	6th	4:59 am	Libra	7th	4:55 pm	Scorpio	6th	2:59 am	Sagittarius
9th	11:32 pm	Libra	8th	11:16 am	Scorpio	9th	8:48 pm	Sagittarius	8th	5:05 am	Capricorn
12th	5:29 am	Scorpio	10th	3:20 pm	Sagittarius	11th	11:41 pm	Capricorn	10th	7:49 am	Aquarius
14th	8:15 am	Sagittarius	12th	5:27 pm	Capricorn	14th	2:10 am	Aquarius	12th	11:44 am	Pisces
16th	8:38 am	Capricorn	14th	6:32 pm	Aquarius	16th	5:07 am	Pisces	14th	5:15 pm	Aries
18th	8:20 am	Aquarius	16th	8:05 pm	Pisces	18th	9:32 am	Aries	17th	0:44 am	Taurus
20th	9:27 am	Pisces	18th	11:49 pm	Aries	20th	4:24 pm	Taurus	19th	10:31 am	Gemini
22nd	1:50 pm	Aries	21st	7:06 am	Taurus	23rd	2:13 am	Gemini	21st	10:17 pm	Cancer
24th	10:16 pm	Taurus	23rd	5:44 pm	Gemini	25th	2:18 pm	Cancer	24th	10:50 am	Leo
27th	9:56 am	Gemini	26th	6:12 am	Cancer	28th	2:36 am	Leo	26th	9:56 pm	Virgo
29th	10:37 pm	Cancer	28th	6:12 pm	Leo	30th	12:51 pm	Virgo	29th	5:42 am	Libra

May 1969

1st	9:46 am	Scorpio
3rd	11:18 am	Sagittarius
5th	11:60 am	Capricorn
7th	1:32 pm	Aquarius
9th	5:08 pm	Pisces
11th	11:09 pm	Aries
14th	7:30 am	Taurus
16th	5:43 pm	Gemini
19th	5:31 am	Cancer
21st	6:12 pm	Leo
24th	6:04 am	Virgo
26th	3:02 pm	Libra
28th	8:03 pm	Scorpio
30th	9:29 pm	Sagittarius

June 1969

1st	9:08 pm	Capricorn
3rd	9:07 pm	Aquarius
5th	11:16 pm	Pisces
8th	4:41 am	Aries
10th	1:10 pm	Taurus
12th	11:48 pm	Gemini
15th	11:54 am	Cancer
18th	0:34 am	Leo
20th	12:51 pm	Virgo
22nd	11:03 pm	Libra
25th	5:27 am	Scorpio
27th	7:55 am	Sagittarius
29th	7:44 am	Capricorn

July 1969

1st	6:53 am	Aquarius
3rd	7:33 am	Pisces
5th	11:23 am	Aries
7th	6:58 pm	Taurus
10th	5:33 am	Gemini
12th	5:48 pm	Cancer
15th	6:29 am	Leo
17th	6:41 pm	Virgo
20th	5:16 am	Libra
22nd	12:58 pm	Scorpio
24th	5:05 pm	Sagittarius
26th	6:06 pm	Capricorn
28th	5:35 pm	Aquarius
30th	5:34 pm	Pisces

August 1969

1st	7:58 pm	Aries
4th	2:05 am	Taurus
6th	11:53 am	Gemini
8th	11:58 pm	Cancer
11th	12:38 pm	Leo
14th	0:33 am	Virgo
16th	10:48 am	Libra
18th	6:52 pm	Scorpio
21st	0:12 am	Sagittarius
23rd	2:47 am	Capricorn
25th	3:36 am	Aquarius
27th	4:04 am	Pisces
29th	6:01 am	Aries
31st	10:55 am	Taurus

September 1969

2nd	7:26 am	Gemini
5th	6:57 am	Cancer
7th	7:35 pm	Leo
10th	7:18 am	Virgo
12th	4:50 pm	Libra
15th	0:25 am	Scorpio
17th	5:40 am	Sagittarius
19th	9:12 am	Capricorn
21st	11:30 am	Aquarius
23rd	1:23 pm	Pisces
25th	3:57 pm	Aries
27th	8:30 pm	Taurus
30th	4:08 am	Gemini

October 1969

2nd	2:55 pm	Cancer
5th	3:24 am	Leo
7th	3:19 pm	Virgo
10th	0:48 am	Libra
12th	7:16 am	Scorpio
14th	11:32 am	Sagittarius
16th	2:35 pm	Capricorn
18th	5:22 pm	Aquarius
20th	8:26 pm	Pisces
23rd	0:18 am	Aries
25th	5:34 am	Taurus
27th	1:03 pm	Gemini
29th	11:13 pm	Cancer

November 1969

1st	11:35 am	Leo
3rd	12:00 pm	Virgo
6th	9:54 am	Libra
8th	4:13 pm	Scorpio
10th	7:28 pm	Sagittarius
12th	9:09 pm	Capricorn
14th	10:53 pm	Aquarius
17th	1:53 am	Pisces
19th	6:34 am	Aries
21st	12:54 pm	Taurus
23rd	9:00 pm	Gemini
26th	7:12 am	Cancer
28th	7:23 pm	Leo

December 1969

1st	8:11 am	Virgo
3rd	7:13 pm	Libra
6th	2:28 am	Scorpio
8th	5:40 am	Sagittarius
10th	6:21 am	Capricorn
12th	6:30 am	Aquarius
14th	8:00 am	Pisces
16th	12:01 pm	Aries
18th	6:38 pm	Taurus
21st	3:29 am	Gemini
23rd	2:11 pm	Cancer
26th	2:22 am	Leo
28th	3:19 pm	Virgo
31st	3:16 am	Libra

January 1970

2nd	11:56 am	Scorpio
4th	4:28 pm	Sagittarius
6th	5:27 pm	Capricorn
8th	4:49 pm	Aquarius
10th	4:42 pm	Pisces
12th	6:52 pm	Aries
15th	0:22 am	Taurus
17th	9:11 am	Gemini
19th	4:15 pm	Cancer
22nd	8:41 am	Leo
24th	9:32 pm	Virgo
27th	9:40 am	Libra
29th	7:32 pm	Scorpio

February 1970

1st	1:48 am	Sagittarius
3rd	4:19 am	Capricorn
5th	4:18 am	Aquarius
7th	3:39 am	Pisces
9th	4:21 am	Aries
11th	8:05 am	Taurus
13th	3:34 pm	Gemini
16th	2:19 am	Cancer
18th	2:56 pm	Leo
21st	3:43 am	Virgo
23rd	3:28 pm	Libra
26th	1:22 am	Scorpio
28th	8:35 am	Sagittarius

March 1970

2nd	12:50 pm	Capricorn
4th	2:32 pm	Aquarius
6th	2:49 pm	Pisces
8th	3:20 pm	Aries
10th	5:48 pm	Taurus
12th	11:38 pm	Gemini
15th	9:23 am	Cancer
17th	9:40 pm	Leo
20th	10:29 am	Virgo
22nd	9:57 pm	Libra
25th	7:08 am	Scorpio
27th	2:05 pm	Sagittarius
29th	6:59 pm	Capricorn
31st	10:08 pm	Aquarius

April 1970

3rd	0:02 am	Pisces
5th	1:33 am	Aries
7th	4:04 am	Taurus
9th	9:07 am	Gemini
11th	5:37 pm	Cancer
14th	5:16 am	Leo
16th	6:08 pm	Virgo
19th	5:33 am	Libra
21st	2:13 pm	Scorpio
23rd	8:15 pm	Sagittarius
26th	0:27 am	Capricorn
28th	3:43 am	Aquarius
30th	6:38 am	Pisces

May 1970

2nd	9:34 am	Aries
4th	1:08 pm	Taurus
6th	6:21 pm	Gemini
9th	2:20 am	Cancer
11th	1:25 pm	Leo
14th	2:11 am	Virgo
16th	2:00 pm	Libra
18th	10:49 pm	Scorpio
21st	4:10 am	Sagittarius
23rd	7:13 am	Capricorn
25th	9:28 am	Aquarius
27th	12:02 pm	Pisces
29th	3:29 pm	Aries
31st	8:05 pm	Taurus

June 1970

3rd	2:11 am	Gemini
5th	10:30 am	Cancer
7th	9:19 pm	Leo
10th	10:02 am	Virgo
12th	10:28 pm	Libra
15th	7:58 am	Scorpio
17th	1:55 pm	Sagittarius
19th	4:03 pm	Capricorn
21st	5:02 pm	Aquarius
23rd	6:10 pm	Pisces
25th	8:55 pm	Aries
28th	1:37 am	Taurus
30th	8:28 am	Gemini

July 1970

2nd	5:25 pm	Cancer
5th	4:27 am	Leo
7th	5:11 pm	Virgo
10th	6:01 am	Libra
12th	4:36 pm	Scorpio
14th	11:24 pm	Sagittarius
17th	2:19 am	Capricorn
19th	2:45 am	Aquarius
21st	2:39 am	Pisces
23rd	3:46 am	Aries
25th	7:24 am	Taurus
27th	1:58 pm	Gemini
29th	11:15 pm	Cancer

August 1970

1st	10:48 am	Leo
3rd	11:36 pm	Virgo
6th	12:30 pm	Libra
8th	11:56 pm	Scorpio
11th	8:02 am	Sagittarius
13th	12:19 pm	Capricorn
15th	1:28 pm	Aquarius
17th	1:02 pm	Pisces
19th	12:54 pm	Aries
21st	2:51 pm	Taurus
23rd	8:07 pm	Gemini
26th	5:00 am	Cancer
28th	4:40 pm	Leo
31st	5:58 am	Virgo

September 1970			October 1970			November 1970			December 1970		
2nd	6:25 pm	Libra	2nd	11:34 am	Scorpio	1st	2:24 am	Sagittarius	2nd	6:43 pm	Aquarius
5th	5:53 am	Scorpio	4th	8:51 pm	Sagittarius	3rd	8:31 am	Capricorn	4th	9:56 pm	Pisces
7th	2:54 pm	Sagittarius	7th	3:09 am	Capricorn	5th	1:08 pm	Aquarius	7th	1:03 am	Aries
9th	8:46 pm	Capricorn	9th	7:23 am	Aquarius	7th	4:31 pm	Pisces	9th	4:26 am	Taurus
11th	11:33 pm	Aquarius	11th	9:28 am	Pisces	9th	6:51 pm	Aries	11th	8:36 am	Gemini
13th	11:57 pm	Pisces	13th	10:12 am	Aries	11th	8:50 pm	Taurus	13th	2:36 pm	Cancer
15th	11:35 pm	Aries	15th	11:02 am	Taurus	13th	11:48 pm	Gemini	15th	11:21 pm	Leo
18th	0:20 am	Taurus	17th	1:48 pm	Gemini	16th	5:26 am	Cancer	18th	11:06 am	Virgo
20th	4:06 am	Gemini	19th	8:02 pm	Cancer	18th	2:39 pm	Leo	21st	0:02 am	Libra
22nd	11:46 am	Cancer	22nd	6:15 am	Leo	21st	2:51 am	Virgo	23rd	11:22 am	Scorpio
24th	10:54 pm	Leo	24th	6:57 pm	Virgo	23rd	3:38 pm	Libra	25th	7:23 pm	Sagittarius
27th	11:54 am	Virgo	27th	7:35 am	Libra	26th	2:23 am	Scorpio	28th	0:02 am	Capricorn
30th	0:34 am	Libra	29th	6:12 pm	Scorpio	28th	9:58 am	Sagittarius	30th	2:24 am	Aquarius
						30th	3:04 pm	Capricorn			

January 1971			February 1971			March 1971			April 1971		
1st	4:08 am	Pisces	1st	3:54 pm	Taurus	3rd	3:05 am	Gemini	1st	4:56 pm	Cancer
3rd	6:29 am	Aries	3rd	8:38 pm	Gemini	5th	9:52 am	Cancer	4th	2:07 am	Leo
5th	10:04 am	Taurus	6th	4:10 am	Cancer	7th	7:48 pm	Leo	6th	2:19 pm	Virgo
7th	3:11 pm	Gemini	8th	2:10 pm	Leo	10th	8:13 am	Virgo	9th	3:18 am	Libra
9th	10:11 pm	Cancer	11th	1:59 am	Virgo	12th	9:07 pm	Libra	11th	3:28 pm	Scorpio
12th	7:27 am	Leo	13th	2:51 pm	Libra	15th	9:30 am	Scorpio	14th	2:04 am	Sagittarius
14th	6:58 pm	Virgo	16th	3:20 am	Scorpio	17th	8:23 pm	Sagittarius	16th	10:35 am	Capricorn
17th	7:51 am	Libra	18th	1:40 pm	Sagittarius	20th	4:34 am	Capricorn	18th	4:44 pm	Aquarius
19th	8:01 pm	Scorpio	20th	8:33 pm	Capricorn	22nd	9:24 am	Aquarius	20th	8:06 pm	Pisces
22nd	5:10 am	Sagittarius	22nd	11:43 pm	Aquarius	24th	11:04 am	Pisces	22nd	9:09 pm	Aries
24th	10:27 am	Capricorn	25th	0:05 am	Pisces	26th	10:45 am	Aries	24th	9:07 pm	Taurus
26th	12:15 pm	Aquarius	26th	11:30 pm	Aries	28th	10:19 am	Taurus	26th	10:01 pm	Gemini
28th	1:02 pm	Pisces	28th	11:55 pm	Taurus	30th	11:50 am	Gemini	29th	1:45 am	Cancer
30th	1:39 pm	Aries									

May 1971			June 1971			July 1971			August 1971		
1st	9:40 am	Leo	2nd	5:27 pm	Libra	2nd	1:43 pm	Scorpio	1st	8:45 am	Sagittarius
3rd	9:05 pm	Virgo	5th	5:35 am	Scorpio	4th	11:60 pm	Sagittarius	3rd	4:28 pm	Capricorn
6th	9:59 am	Libra	7th	3:26 pm	Sagittarius	7th	7:01 am	Capricorn	5th	8:45 am	Aquarius
8th	10:05 pm	Scorpio	9th	10:45 pm	Capricorn	9th	11:25 am	Aquarius	7th	10:35 pm	Pisces
11th	8:07 am	Sagittarius	12th	4:03 am	Aquarius	11th	2:15 pm	Pisces	9th	11:27 pm	Aries
13th	4:09 pm	Capricorn	14th	8:02 am	Pisces	13th	4:35 pm	Aries	12th	0:57 am	Taurus
15th	10:20 pm	Aquarius	16th	11:06 am	Aries	15th	7:13 pm	Taurus	14th	4:15 am	Gemini
18th	2:40 am	Pisces	18th	1:40 pm	Taurus	17th	10:49 pm	Gemini	16th	9:54 am	Cancer
20th	5:11 am	Aries	20th	4:27 am	Gemini	20th	3:50 am	Cancer	18th	6:02 pm	Leo
22nd	6:32 am	Taurus	22nd	8:34 pm	Cancer	22nd	11:21 am	Leo	21st	4:22 am	Virgo
24th	8:05 am	Gemini	25th	3:15 am	Leo	24th	9:12 pm	Virgo	23rd	4:24 pm	Libra
26th	1 1:33 am	Cancer	27th	1:10 pm	Virgo	27th	9:13 am	Libra	26th	5:09 am	Scorpio
28th	6:20 pm	Leo	30th	1:23 am	Libra	29th	9:49 pm	Scorpio	28th	4:54 pm	Sagittarius
31st	4:51 am	Virgo							31st	1:52 am	Capricorn

September 1971			October 1971			November 1971			December 1971		
2nd	6:59 am	Aquarius	1st	7:33 pm	Pisces	2nd	5:56 am	Taurus	1st	4:26 pm	Gemini
4th	8:48 am	Pisces	3rd	7:39 pm	Aries	4th	5:31 am	Gemini	3rd	5:55 pm	Cancer
6th	8:44 am	Aries	5th	6:44 pm	Taurus	6th	7:20 am	Cancer	5th	10:18 pm	Leo
8th	8:41 am	Taurus	7th	6:56 pm	Gemini	8th	1:02 pm	Leo	8th	6:44 am	Virgo
10th	10:31 am	Gemini	9th	10:12 pm	Cancer	10th	10:45 pm	Virgo	10th	6:21 pm	Libra
12th	3:26 pm	Cancer	12th	5:34 am	Leo	13th	11:05 am	Libra	13th	7:00 am	Scorpio
14th	11:39 pm	Leo	14th	4:18 pm	Virgo	15th	11:50 pm	Scorpio	15th	6:35 pm	Sagittarius
17th	10:52 am	Virgo	17th	4:48 am	Libra	18th	11:28 am	Sagittarius	18th	4:05 am	Capricorn
19th	10:49 pm	Libra	19th	5:31 pm	Scorpio	20th	9:36 pm	Capricorn	20th	11:30 am	Aquarius
22nd	11:34 am	Scorpio	22nd	5:32 am	Sagittarius	23rd	5:50 am	Aquarius	22nd	5:09 pm	Pisces
24th	11:44 pm	Sagittarius	24th	4:03 pm	Capricorn	25th	11:44 am	Pisces	24th	9:08 pm	Aries
27th	9:49 am	Capricorn	27th	0:11 am	Aquarius	27th	2:50 pm	Aries	26th	11:45 pm	Taurus
29th	4:34 pm	Aquarius	29th	4:53 am	Pisces	29th	4:06 pm	Taurus	29th	1:38 am	Gemini
			31st	6:24 am	Aries				31st	4:03 am	Cancer

January 1972
2nd	8:26 am	Leo
4th	3:54 pm	Virgo
7th	2:34 am	Libra
9th	3:03 pm	Scorpio
12th	2:55 am	Sagittarius
14th	12:51 pm	Capricorn
16th	7:01 pm	Aquarius
18th	11:27 pm	Pisces
21st	2:36 am	Aries
23rd	5:18 am	Taurus
25th	8:16 am	Gemini
27th	12:05 pm	Cancer
29th	5:25 pm	Leo

February 1972
1st	0:56 am	Virgo
3rd	11:09 am	Libra
5th	11:18 pm	Scorpio
8th	11:33 am	Sagittarius
10th	9:48 pm	Capricorn
13th	4:33 am	Aquarius
15th	8:07 am	Pisces
17th	9:51 am	Aries
19th	11:14 am	Taurus
21st	1:39 pm	Gemini
23rd	5:56 pm	Cancer
26th	0:17 am	Leo
28th	9:43 am	Virgo

March 1972
1st	7:03 pm	Libra
4th	7:02 am	Scorpio
6th	7:36 pm	Sagittarius
9th	6:46 am	Capricorn
11th	2:37 pm	Aquarius
13th	6:36 pm	Pisces
15th	7:35 pm	Aries
17th	7:29 pm	Taurus
19th	8:15 pm	Gemini
21st	11:27 pm	Cancer
24th	5:50 am	Leo
26th	2:51 pm	Virgo
29th	1:44 am	Libra
31st	1:51 pm	Scorpio

April 1972
3rd	2:29 am	Sagittarius
5th	2:18 pm	Capricorn
7th	11:37 pm	Aquarius
10th	4:54 am	Pisces
12th	6:30 am	Aries
14th	5:55 am	Taurus
16th	5:20 am	Gemini
18th	6:50 am	Cancer
20th	11:53 am	Leo
22nd	8:26 pm	Virgo
25th	7:36 am	Libra
27th	7:58 pm	Scorpio
30th	8:32 am	Sagittarius

May 1972
2nd	8:29 pm	Capricorn
5th	6:32 am	Aquarius
7th	1:23 pm	Pisces
9th	4:31 pm	Aries
11th	4:46 pm	Taurus
13th	5:59 pm	Gemini
15th	4:21 pm	Cancer
17th	7:42 pm	Leo
20th	2:59 am	Virgo
22nd	1:40 pm	Libra
25th	2:01 am	Scorpio
27th	2:34 pm	Sagittarius
30th	2:13 am	Capricorn

June 1972
1st	12:13 pm	Aquarius
3rd	7:31 pm	Pisces
6th	0:29 am	Aries
8th	2:14 am	Taurus
10th	2:26 am	Gemini
12th	2:48 am	Cancer
14th	5:15 am	Leo
16th	11:09 am	Virgo
18th	8:40 pm	Libra
21st	8:44 am	Scorpio
23rd	9:15 pm	Sagittarius
26th	8:35 am	Capricorn
28th	6:01 pm	Aquarius

July 1972
1st	1:19 am	Pisces
3rd	6:21 am	Aries
5th	9:24 am	Taurus
7th	11:06 am	Gemini
9th	12:53 pm	Cancer
11th	5:11 pm	Leo
13th	8:19 pm	Virgo
16th	4:55 am	Libra
18th	4:16 pm	Scorpio
21st	4:46 am	Sagittarius
23rd	4:08 pm	Capricorn
26th	1:08 am	Aquarius
28th	7:28 am	Pisces
30th	11:31 am	Aries

August 1972
1st	2:59 pm	Taurus
3rd	5:56 pm	Gemini
5th	8:21 pm	Cancer
7th	11:58 pm	Leo
10th	5:27 am	Virgo
12th	1:52 pm	Libra
15th	0:20 am	Scorpio
17th	12:48 pm	Sagittarius
20th	0:59 am	Capricorn
22nd	9:58 am	Aquarius
24th	3:26 pm	Pisces
26th	6:40 pm	Aries
28th	8:45 pm	Taurus
30th	10:58 pm	Gemini

September 1972
2nd	2:14 am	Cancer
4th	6:57 am	Leo
6th	1:19 pm	Virgo
8th	9:39 pm	Libra
11th	8:19 am	Scorpio
15th	8:44 pm	Sagittarius
16th	9:05 am	Capricorn
18th	7:02 pm	Aquarius
21st	1:09 am	Pisces
23rd	3:44 am	Aries
25th	4:28 am	Taurus
27th	5:17 am	Gemini
29th	7:42 am	Cancer

October 1972
1st	12:30 pm	Leo
3rd	7:54 pm	Virgo
6th	4:38 am	Libra
8th	3:31 pm	Scorpio
11th	3:54 am	Sagittarius
13th	4:44 pm	Capricorn
16th	5:49 am	Aquarius
18th	11:07 am	Pisces
20th	2:18 pm	Aries
22nd	2:36 pm	Taurus
24th	2:06 pm	Gemini
26th	2:49 pm	Cancer
28th	6:17 pm	Leo
31st	1:01 am	Virgo

November 1972
2nd	10:29 am	Libra
4th	9:48 pm	Scorpio
7th	10:19 am	Sagittarius
9th	11:11 pm	Capricorn
12th	11:00 am	Aquarius
14th	7:54 pm	Pisces
17th	0:45 am	Aries
19th	1:52 am	Taurus
21st	1:06 am	Gemini
23rd	0:55 am	Cancer
25th	2:14 am	Leo
27th	7:29 am	Virgo
29th	4:19 pm	Libra

December 1972
2nd	5:44 am	Scorpio
4th	4:24 pm	Sagittarius
7th	5:06 am	Capricorn
9th	4:55 pm	Aquarius
12th	2:52 am	Pisces
14th	8:55 am	Aries
16th	11:54 am	Taurus
18th	12:65 pm	Gemini
20th	11:59 am	Cancer
22nd	12:40 pm	Leo
24th	4:08 pm	Virgo
26th	11:22 pm	Libra
29th	10:15 am	Scorpio
31st	10:31 pm	Sagittarius

January 1973
3rd	11:29 am	Capricorn
5th	10:48 pm	Aquarius
8th	8:01 am	Pisces
10th	2:55 pm	Aries
12th	7:23 pm	Taurus
14th	9:41 pm	Gemini
16th	10:59 pm	Cancer
18th	11:40 pm	Leo
21st	2:26 am	Virgo
23rd	8:21 am	Libra
25th	5:55 pm	Scorpio
28th	6:10 am	Sagittarius
30th	6:52 pm	Capricorn

February 1973
2nd	5:52 am	Aquarius
4th	2:19 pm	Pisces
6th	8:28 pm	Aries
9th	0:53 am	Taurus
11th	4:10 am	Gemini
13th	6:45 am	Cancer
15th	9:14 am	Leo
17th	12:35 pm	Virgo
19th	6:02 pm	Libra
22nd	2:37 am	Scorpio
24th	2:14 pm	Sagittarius
27th	1:03 am	Capricorn

March 1973
1st	2:18 pm	Aquarius
3rd	10:30 pm	Pisces
6th	5:35 am	Aries
8th	6:31 am	Taurus
10th	9:52 am	Gemini
12th	12:31 pm	Cancer
14th	4:09 pm	Leo
16th	8:44 pm	Virgo
19th	2:30 am	Libra
21st	11:19 am	Scorpio
23rd	10:26 pm	Sagittarius
26th	11:15 am	Capricorn
28th	11:15 am	Aquarius
31st	7:30 am	Pisces

April 1973
2nd	12:43 pm	Aries
4th	2:56 pm	Taurus
6th	4:12 pm	Gemini
8th	6:06 pm	Cancer
10th	9:53 pm	Leo
13th	2:47 am	Virgo
15th	9:55 am	Libra
17th	6:55 pm	Scorpio
20th	6:04 am	Sagittarius
22nd	6:30 pm	Capricorn
25th	7:19 am	Aquarius
27th	5:06 pm	Pisces
29th	10:52 pm	Aries

May 1973

2nd	1:01 am	Taurus
4th	1:15 am	Gemini
6th	1:15 am	Cancer
8th	3:39 am	Leo
10th	8:16 am	Virgo
12th	3:54 pm	Libra
15th	1:11 am	Scorpio
17th	12:44 pm	Sagittarius
20th	1:30 am	Capricorn
22nd	2:16 pm	Aquarius
25th	1:06 am	Pisces
27th	8:09 am	Aries
29th	11:24 am	Taurus
31st	11:31 am	Gemini

June 1973

2nd	11:23 am	Cancer
4th	11:53 am	Leo
6th	2:57 pm	Virgo
8th	9:19 pm	Libra
11th	6:54 am	Scorpio
15th	6:45 pm	Sagittarius
16th	7:37 am	Capricorn
18th	8:19 pm	Aquarius
21st	7:26 am	Pisces
23rd	3:45 pm	Aries
25th	8:55 pm	Taurus
27th	10:17 pm	Gemini
29th	10:09 pm	Cancer

July 1973

1st	9:57 pm	Leo
3rd	11:32 pm	Virgo
6th	4:27 am	Libra
8th	1:10 pm	Scorpio
11th	0:49 am	Sagittarius
13th	1:47 pm	Capricorn
16th	2:15 am	Aquarius
18th	1:06 pm	Pisces
20th	9:44 pm	Aries
23rd	3:39 am	Taurus
25th	6:57 am	Gemini
27th	8:11 am	Cancer
29th	8:32 am	Leo
31st	9:40 am	Virgo

August 1973

2nd	1:19 pm	Libra
4th	8:39 pm	Scorpio
7th	7:59 am	Sagittarius
9th	8:31 pm	Capricorn
12th	8:51 am	Aquarius
14th	7:13 pm	Pisces
17th	3:17 am	Aries
19th	9:13 am	Taurus
21st	1:26 pm	Gemini
23rd	4:08 pm	Cancer
25th	5:31 pm	Leo
27th	7:36 pm	Virgo
29th	10:54 pm	Libra

September 1973

1st	5:22 am	Scorpio
3rd	3:28 pm	Sagittarius
6th	4:02 am	Capricorn
8th	4:28 pm	Aquarius
11th	2:39 am	Pisces
13th	9:53 am	Aries
15th	2:59 pm	Taurus
17th	6:49 pm	Gemini
19th	10:02 pm	Cancer
22nd	0:58 am	Leo
24th	4:01 am	Virgo
26th	8:03 am	Libra
28th	2:25 pm	Scorpio
30th	11:48 pm	Sagittarius

October 1973

3rd	12:04 pm	Capricorn
6th	0:30 am	Aquarius
8th	11:19 am	Pisces
10th	6:26 pm	Aries
12th	10:36 pm	Taurus
15th	1:09 am	Gemini
17th	3:29 am	Cancer
19th	6:26 am	Leo
21st	10:21 am	Virgo
23rd	3:32 pm	Libra
25th	10:31 pm	Scorpio
28th	8:02 am	Sagittarius
30th	7:59 pm	Capricorn

November 1973

2nd	8:59 am	Aquarius
4th	8:26 pm	Pisces
7th	4:18 am	Aries
9th	8:22 am	Taurus
11th	9:59 am	Gemini
13th	10:48 am	Cancer
15th	12:23 pm	Leo
17th	3:45 pm	Virgo
19th	9:17 pm	Libra
22nd	5:09 am	Scorpio
24th	3:15 pm	Sagittarius
27th	3:15 am	Capricorn
29th	4:18 pm	Aquarius

December 1973

2nd	4:32 am	Pisces
4th	1:46 pm	Aries
6th	7:06 pm	Taurus
8th	8:57 pm	Gemini
10th	8:53 pm	Cancer
12th	8:47 pm	Leo
14th	10:23 pm	Virgo
17th	2:55 am	Libra
19th	10:48 am	Scorpio
21st	9:22 pm	Sagittarius
24th	9:43 am	Capricorn
26th	10:45 pm	Aquarius
29th	11:08 am	Pisces
31st	9:33 pm	Aries

January 1974

3rd	4:35 am	Taurus
5th	7:57 am	Gemini
7th	8:26 am	Cancer
9th	7:44 am	Leo
11th	7:47 am	Virgo
13th	10:28 am	Libra
15th	4:59 pm	Scorpio
18th	3:14 am	Sagittarius
20th	3:48 pm	Capricorn
23rd	4:49 am	Aquarius
25th	4:59 pm	Pisces
28th	3:31 am	Aries
30th	11:37 am	Taurus

February 1974

1st	4:51 pm	Gemini
3rd	7:04 pm	Cancer
5th	7:11 pm	Leo
7th	6:53 pm	Virgo
9th	8:14 pm	Libra
12th	0:59 am	Scorpio
14th	10:05 am	Sagittarius
16th	10:16 pm	Capricorn
19th	11:20 am	Aquarius
21st	11:15 pm	Pisces
24th	9:11 am	Aries
26th	5:10 pm	Taurus
28th	11:10 pm	Gemini

March 1974

3rd	2:50 am	Cancer
5th	4:49 am	Leo
7th	5:35 am	Virgo
9th	6:56 am	Libra
11th	10:46 am	Scorpio
13th	6:24 pm	Sagittarius
16th	5:42 am	Capricorn
18th	6:37 pm	Aquarius
21st	6:30 am	Pisces
23rd	3:59 pm	Aries
25th	11:09 pm	Taurus
28th	4:32 am	Gemini
30th	8:38 am	Cancer

April 1974

1st	11:40 am	Leo
3rd	1:57 pm	Virgo
5th	4:25 pm	Libra
7th	8:28 pm	Scorpio
10th	3:30 am	Sagittarius
12th	1:60 pm	Capricorn
15th	2:34 am	Aquarius
17th	2:41 pm	Pisces
20th	0:20 am	Aries
22nd	6:50 am	Taurus
24th	11:08 am	Gemini
26th	2:17 pm	Cancer
28th	5:04 pm	Leo
30th	7:50 pm	Virgo

May 1974

2nd	11:39 pm	Libra
5th	4:45 am	Scorpio
7th	12:09 pm	Sagittarius
9th	10:16 pm	Capricorn
12th	10:36 am	Aquarius
14th	11:04 pm	Pisces
17th	9:15 am	Aries
19th	4:07 pm	Taurus
21st	7:52 pm	Gemini
23rd	9:45 pm	Cancer
25th	11:12 pm	Leo
28th	1:26 am	Virgo
30th	5:17 am	Libra

June 1974

1st	11:13 am	Scorpio
3rd	7:24 pm	Sagittarius
6th	5:50 am	Capricorn
8th	6:04 pm	Aquarius
11th	6:43 am	Pisces
13th	5:50 pm	Aries
16th	1:45 am	Taurus
18th	5:55 am	Gemini
20th	7:19 am	Cancer
22nd	7:30 am	Leo
24th	8:15 am	Virgo
26th	11:02 am	Libra
28th	4:43 pm	Scorpio

July 1974

1st	1:22 am	Sagittarius
3rd	12:22 pm	Capricorn
6th	0:41 am	Aquarius
8th	1:25 pm	Pisces
11th	1:10 am	Aries
13th	10:17 am	Taurus
15th	3:50 pm	Gemini
17th	5:53 pm	Cancer
19th	5:43 pm	Leo
21st	5:12 pm	Virgo
23rd	6:23 pm	Libra
25th	10:47 pm	Scorpio
28th	7:03 am	Sagittarius
30th	6:12 pm	Capricorn

August 1974

2nd	6:47 am	Aquarius
4th	7:26 pm	Pisces
7th	7:14 am	Aries
9th	5:10 pm	Taurus
12th	0:16 am	Gemini
14th	3:47 am	Cancer
16th	4:26 am	Leo
18th	3:45 am	Virgo
20th	3:48 am	Libra
22nd	6:43 am	Scorpio
24th	1:40 pm	Sagittarius
27th	0:16 am	Capricorn
29th	12:53 pm	Aquarius

September 1974

1st	1:30 am	Pisces
3rd	12:56 pm	Aries
5th	10:51 pm	Taurus
8th	6:34 am	Gemini
10th	11:37 am	Cancer
12th	1:52 pm	Leo
14th	2:13 pm	Virgo
16th	2:22 pm	Libra
18th	4:20 pm	Scorpio
20th	9:48 pm	Sagittarius
23rd	7:26 am	Capricorn
25th	7:39 am	Aquarius
28th	8:13 am	Pisces
30th	7:25 pm	Aries

October 1974

3rd	4:38 am	Taurus
5th	11:59 am	Gemini
7th	5:28 pm	Cancer
9th	9:02 pm	Leo
11th	10:57 pm	Virgo
14th	0:12 am	Libra
16th	2:27 am	Scorpio
18th	7:21 am	Sagittarius
20th	3:50 pm	Capricorn
23rd	3:22 am	Aquarius
25th	3:57 pm	Pisces
28th	3:12 am	Aries
30th	11:57 am	Taurus

November 1974

1st	6:22 pm	Gemini
3rd	11:01 pm	Cancer
6th	2:30 am	Leo
8th	5:19 am	Virgo
10th	8:01 am	Libra
12th	11:28 am	Scorpio
14th	4:44 pm	Sagittarius
17th	0:45 am	Capricorn
19th	11:43 am	Aquarius
22nd	0:14 am	Pisces
24th	11:57 am	Aries
26th	9:04 pm	Taurus
29th	2:57 am	Gemini

December 1974

1st	6:21 am	Cancer
3rd	8:32 am	Leo
5th	10:42 am	Virgo
7th	1:45 pm	Libra
9th	6:16 pm	Scorpio
12th	0:35 am	Sagittarius
14th	9:09 am	Capricorn
16th	7:52 pm	Aquarius
19th	8:14 am	Pisces
21st	8:36 pm	Aries
24th	6:42 am	Taurus
26th	1:12 pm	Gemini
28th	4:13 pm	Cancer
30th	5:05 pm	Leo

January 1975

1st	5:35 pm	Virgo
3rd	7:25 pm	Libra
5th	11:39 pm	Scorpio
8th	6:43 am	Sagittarius
10th	4:01 pm	Capricorn
13th	3:04 am	Aquarius
15th	3:26 pm	Pisces
18th	4:04 am	Aries
20th	3:17 pm	Taurus
22nd	11:23 pm	Gemini
25th	3:20 am	Cancer
27th	3:50 am	Leo
29th	3:16 am	Virgo
31st	3:17 am	Libra

February 1975

2nd	5:58 am	Scorpio
4th	12:16 pm	Sagittarius
6th	9:44 pm	Capricorn
9th	9:18 am	Aquarius
11th	9:47 pm	Pisces
14th	10:22 am	Aries
16th	10:09 pm	Taurus
19th	7:31 am	Gemini
21st	1:14 pm	Cancer
23rd	3:09 pm	Leo
25th	2:36 pm	Virgo
27th	1:43 pm	Libra

March 1975

1st	2:40 pm	Scorpio
3rd	7:10 pm	Sagittarius
6th	3:41 am	Capricorn
8th	3:11 pm	Aquarius
11th	3:49 am	Pisces
13th	4:18 pm	Aries
16th	3:53 am	Taurus
18th	1:40 pm	Gemini
20th	8:47 pm	Cancer
23rd	0:31 am	Leo
25th	1:21 am	Virgo
27th	0:53 am	Libra
29th	1:10 am	Scorpio
31st	4:13 am	Sagittarius

April 1975

2nd	11:13 am	Capricorn
4th	9:45 pm	Aquarius
7th	10:16 am	Pisces
9th	10:44 pm	Aries
12th	9:51 am	Taurus
14th	7:13 pm	Gemini
17th	2:27 am	Cancer
19th	7:11 am	Leo
21st	9:40 am	Virgo
23rd	10:41 am	Libra
25th	11:43 am	Scorpio
27th	2:25 pm	Sagittarius
29th	8:12 pm	Capricorn

May 1975

2nd	5:36 am	Aquarius
4th	5:35 pm	Pisces
7th	6:01 am	Aries
9th	5:00 pm	Taurus
12th	1:43 am	Gemini
14th	8:05 am	Cancer
16th	12:35 pm	Leo
18th	3:44 pm	Virgo
20th	6:04 pm	Libra
22nd	8:26 pm	Scorpio
24th	11:31 pm	Sagittarius
27th	5:35 am	Capricorn
29th	2:14 pm	Aquarius

June 1975

1st	1:33 am	Pisces
3rd	2:01 pm	Aries
6th	1:19 am	Taurus
8th	3:17 am	Gemini
10th	6:43 pm	Cancer
12th	9:10 pm	Leo
14th	11:40 pm	Virgo
16th	2:59 am	Libra
19th	7:37 am	Scorpio
21st	1:59 am	Sagittarius
23rd	10:34 pm	Capricorn
25th	9:35 pm	Aquarius
28th	10:03 am	Pisces
30th	7:12 pm	Aries

July 1975

3rd	9:51 am	Taurus
5th	6:55 pm	Gemini
8th	0:22 am	Cancer
10th	2:49 am	Leo
12th	3:56 am	Virgo
14th	5:24 am	Libra
16th	8:26 am	Scorpio
18th	1:33 pm	Sagittarius
20th	8:46 pm	Capricorn
23rd	5:58 am	Aquarius
25th	4:50 pm	Pisces
28th	5:27 am	Aries
30th	5:53 pm	Taurus

August 1975

2nd	3:50 am	Gemini
4th	10:11 am	Cancer
6th	12:40 pm	Leo
8th	12:53 pm	Virgo
10th	12:54 pm	Libra
12th	2:34 pm	Scorpio
14th	7:02 pm	Sagittarius
17th	2:26 am	Capricorn
19th	12:11 pm	Aquarius
21st	11:32 pm	Pisces
24th	12:02 pm	Aries
27th	0:44 am	Taurus
29th	11:49 am	Gemini
31st	7:33 pm	Cancer

September 1975

2nd	11:08 pm	Leo
4th	11:30 pm	Virgo
6th	10:58 pm	Libra
8th	10:47 pm	Scorpio
11th	1:41 am	Sagittarius
13th	8:15 am	Capricorn
15th	5:53 pm	Aquarius
18th	5:52 am	Pisces
20th	6:08 pm	Aries
23rd	6:43 am	Taurus
25th	6:12 pm	Gemini
28th	3:05 am	Cancer
30th	8:16 am	Leo

October 1975

2nd	10:00 am	Virgo
4th	9:41 am	Libra
6th	9:13 am	Scorpio
8th	10:42 am	Sagittarius
10th	3:35 pm	Capricorn
13th	0:10 am	Aquarius
15th	11:42 am	Pisces
18th	0:20 am	Aries
20th	12:42 pm	Taurus
22nd	11:52 pm	Gemini
25th	8:54 am	Cancer
27th	3:16 pm	Leo
29th	6:44 pm	Virgo
31st	7:55 pm	Libra

November 1975

2nd	8:10 pm	Scorpio
4th	9:13 pm	Sagittarius
7th	0:47 am	Capricorn
9th	8:06 am	Aquarius
11th	6:45 pm	Pisces
14th	7:17 am	Aries
16th	7:37 pm	Taurus
19th	6:12 am	Gemini
21st	2:33 pm	Cancer
23rd	8:47 pm	Leo
26th	1:05 am	Virgo
28th	3:47 am	Libra
30th	5:38 am	Scorpio

December 1975

2nd	7:37 am	Sagittarius
4th	11:04 am	Capricorn
6th	5:18 pm	Aquarius
9th	2:55 am	Pisces
11th	3:09 pm	Aries
14th	3:40 am	Taurus
16th	2:10 pm	Gemini
18th	9:49 pm	Cancer
21st	2:53 am	Leo
23rd	6:27 am	Virgo
25th	9:27 am	Libra
27th	12:29 pm	Scorpio
29th	3:55 pm	Sagittarius
31st	8:19 pm	Capricorn

January 1976		
3rd	2:55 am	Aquarius
5th	11:40 am	Pisces
7th	1122, pm	Aries
10th	12:09 pm	Taurus
12th	11:21 pm	Gemini
15th	6:57 am	Cancer
17th	11:13 am	Leo
19th	1:25 pm	Virgo
21st	1:12 pm	Libra
23rd	5:50 pm	Scorpio
25th	9:52 pm	Sagittarius
28th	3:25 am	Capricorn
30th	10:38 am	Aquarius

February 1976		
1st	7:50 pm	Pisces
4th	7:20 am	Aries
6th	8:14 pm	Taurus
9th	8:13 am	Gemini
11th	4:55 pm	Cancer
13th	9:31 pm	Leo
15th	10:50 pm	Virgo
17th	11:15 pm	Libra
20th	0:15 am	Scorpio
22nd	3:20 am	Sagittarius
24th	8:58 am	Capricorn
26th	4:50 pm	Aquarius
29th	2:44 am	Pisces

March 1976		
2nd	2:24 pm	Aries
5th	3:19 am	Taurus
7th	3:55 pm	Gemini
10th	1:58 am	Cancer
12th	7:52 am	Leo
14th	9:56 am	Virgo
16th	9:45 am	Libra
18th	9:22 am	Scorpio
20th	10:39 am	Sagittarius
22nd	2:54 pm	Capricorn
24th	10:20 pm	Aquarius
27th	8:35 am	Pisces
29th	8:35 pm	Aries

April 1976		
1st	9:34 am	Taurus
3rd	10:15 pm	Gemini
6th	9:04 am	Cancer
8th	4:33 pm	Leo
10th	8:15 pm	Virgo
12th	8:54 pm	Libra
14th	8:16 pm	Scorpio
16th	8:18 pm	Sagittarius
18th	10:45 pm	Capricorn
21st	4:51 am	Aquarius
23rd	2:31 pm	Pisces
26th	2:36 am	Aries
28th	3:36 pm	Taurus

May 1976		
1st	4:02 am	Gemini
3rd	2:51 pm	Cancer
5th	11:08 pm	Leo
8th	4:18 am	Virgo
10th	6:37 am	Libra
12th	7:03 am	Scorpio
14th	7:06 am	Sagittarius
16th	8:37 am	Capricorn
18th	1:10 pm	Aquarius
20th	9:30 pm	Pisces
23rd	9:09 am	Aries
25th	10:08 pm	Taurus
28th	10:19 am	Gemini
30th	8:37 pm	Cancer

June 1976		
2nd	4:35 am	Leo
4th	10:17 am	Virgo
6th	1:56 pm	Libra
8th	3:57 pm	Scorpio
10th	5:07 pm	Sagittarius
12th	6:47 pm	Capricorn
14th	10:32 pm	Aquarius
17th	5:49 am	Pisces
19th	4:35 pm	Aries
22nd	5:22 am	Taurus
24th	5:35 pm	Gemini
27th	3:27 am	Cancer
29th	10:36 am	Leo

July 1976		
1st	3:44 pm	Virgo
3rd	7:33 pm	Libra
5th	10:32 pm	Scorpio
8th	1:06 am	Sagittarius
10th	3:50 am	Capricorn
12th	7:57 am	Aquarius
14th	2:41 pm	Pisces
17th	0:40 am	Aries
19th	1:11 pm	Taurus
22nd	1:40 am	Gemini
24th	11:35 am	Cancer
26th	6:16 pm	Leo
28th	10:22 pm	Virgo
31st	1:13 am	Libra

August 1976		
2nd	3:56 am	Scorpio
4th	7:04 am	Sagittarius
6th	10:56 am	Capricorn
8th	3:59 pm	Aquarius
10th	11:00 pm	Pisces
13th	8:52 am	Aries
15th	9:06 pm	Taurus
18th	9:52 am	Gemini
20th	8:31 pm	Cancer
23rd	3:28 am	Leo
25th	7:01 am	Virgo
27th	8:42 am	Libra
29th	10:06 am	Scorpio
31st	12:32 pm	Sagittarius

September 1976		
2nd	4:32 pm	Capricorn
4th	10:20 pm	Aquarius
7th	6:14 am	Pisces
9th	4:20 pm	Aries
12th	4:31 am	Taurus
14th	5:51 pm	Gemini
17th	5:03 am	Cancer
19th	1:06 pm	Leo
21st	5:13 pm	Virgo
23rd	6:27 pm	Libra
25th	6:34 pm	Scorpio
27th	7:24 pm	Sagittarius
29th	10:15 pm	Capricorn

October 1976		
2nd	3:51 am	Aquarius
4th	12:12 pm	Pisces
6th	10:51 pm	Aries
9th	11:12 am	Taurus
12th	0:14 am	Gemini
14th	12:21 pm	Cancer
16th	9:49 pm	Leo
19th	3:23 am	Virgo
21st	5:24 am	Libra
23rd	5:17 am	Scorpio.
25th	4:52 am	Sagittarius
27th	5:50 am	Capricorn
29th	10:11 am	Aquarius
31st	5:56 pm	Pisces

November 1976		
3rd	4:47 am	Aries
5th	5:23 pm	Taurus
8th	6:20 am	Gemini
10th	6:27 pm	Cancer
13th	4:34 am	Leo
15th	11:40 am	Virgo
17th	3:30 pm	Libra
19th	4:29 pm	Scorpio
21st	4:06 pm	Sagittarius
23rd	4:09 pm	Capricorn
25th	6:36 pm	Aquarius
28th	0:50 am	Pisces
30th	11:06 am	Aries

December 1976		
2nd	11:42 pm	Taurus
5th	12:36 pm	Gemini
8th	12:21 am	Cancer
10th	10:09 am	Leo
12th	5:53 pm	Virgo
14th	11:13 pm	Libra
17th	2:02 am	Scorpio
19th	2:54 am	Sagittarius
21st	3:14 am	Capricorn
23rd	4:53 am	Aquarius
25th	9:43 am	Pisces
27th	6:37 pm	Aries
30th	6:45 am	Taurus

January 1977		
1st	7:43 pm	Gemini
4th	7:10 am	Cancer
6th	4:19 pm	Leo
8th	11:24 pm	Virgo
11th	4:47 am	Libra
13th	8:43 am	Scorpio
15th	11:18 am	Sagittarius
17th	1:04 pm	Capricorn
19th	3:17 pm	Aquarius
21st	7:35 pm	Pisces
24th	3:24 am	Aries
26th	2:43 pm	Taurus
29th	3:38 am	Gemini
31st	3:18 pm	Cancer

February 1977		
3rd	0:13 am	Leo
5th	6:17 am	Virgo
7th	10:36 am	Libra
9th	2:04 pm	Scorpio
11th	5:12 pm	Sagittarius
13th	8:15 pm	Capricorn
15th	11:46 pm	Aquarius
18th	4:49 am	Pisces
20th	12:28 pm	Aries
22nd	11:06 pm	Taurus
25th	11:51 am	Gemini
28th	0:04 am	Cancer

March 1977		
2nd	9:22 am	Leo
4th	3:16 pm	Virgo
6th	6:35 pm	Libra
8th	8:39 pm	Scorpio
10th	10:43 pm	Sagittarius
13th	1:42 am	Capricorn
15th	6:03 am	Aquarius
17th	12:09 pm	Pisces
19th	8:25 pm	Aries
22nd	7:08 am	Taurus
24th	7:40 pm	Gemini
27th	8:15 am	Cancer
29th	6:38 pm	Leo

April 1977		
1st	1:25 am	Virgo
3rd	4:39 am	Libra
5th	5:41 am	Scorpio
7th	6:12 am	Sagittarius
9th	7:45 am	Capricorn
11th	11:28 am	Aquarius
13th	5:52 pm	Pisces
16th	2:54 am	Aries
18th	2:04 pm	Taurus
21st	2:38 am	Gemini
23rd	3:24 pm	Cancer
26th	2:43 am	Leo
28th	10:48 am	Virgo
30th	3:09 pm	Libra

May 1977

2nd	4:22 pm	Scorpio
4th	4:01 pm	Sagittarius
6th	3:59 pm	Capricorn
8th	6:05 pm	Aquarius
10th	11:29 pm	Pisces
13th	8:33 am	Aries
15th	8:05 pm	Taurus
18th	8:50 am	Gemini
20th	9:35 pm	Cancer
23rd	9:10 am	Leo
25th	6:27 pm	Virgo
28th	0:29 am	Libra
30th	2:55 am	Scorpio

June 1977

1st	2:54 am	Sagittarius
3rd	2:09 am	Capricorn
5th	2:47 am	Aquarius
7th	6:42 am	Pisces
9th	2:40 pm	Aries
12th	1:57 am	Taurus
14th	2:51 pm	Gemini
17th	3:28 am	Cancer
19th	2:50 pm	Leo
22nd	0:28 am	Virgo
24th	7:30 am	Libra
26th	11:36 am	Scorpio
28th	12:58 pm	Sagittarius
30th	12:48 pm	Capricorn

July 1977

2nd	1:01 pm	Aquarius
4th	3:38 pm	Pisces
6th	10:06 pm	Aries
9th	8:37 am	Taurus
11th	9:15 pm	Gemini
14th	9:48 am	Cancer
16th	8:51 pm	Leo
19th	5:56 am	Virgo
21st	1:06 pm	Libra
23rd	6:10 pm	Scorpio
25th	9:03 pm	Sagittarius
27th	10:13 pm	Capricorn
29th	11:04 pm	Aquarius

August 1977

1st	1:26 am	Pisces
3rd	6:59 am	Aries
5th	4:21 pm	Taurus
8th	4:30 am	Gemini
10th	5:03 pm	Cancer
13th	3:55 am	Leo
15th	12:24 pm	Virgo
17th	6:48 pm	Libra
19th	11:36 pm	Scorpio
22nd	3:03 am	Sagittarius
24th	5:29 am	Capricorn
26th	7:41 am	Aquarius
28th	10:50 am	Pisces
30th	4:15 pm	Aries

September 1977

2nd	0:51 am	Taurus
4th	12:28 pm	Gemini
7th	1:02 am	Cancer
9th	12:10 pm	Leo
11th	8:33 pm	Virgo
14th	2:07 am	Libra
16th	5:45 am	Scorpio
18th	8:29 am	Sagittarius
20th	11:05 am	Capricorn
22nd	2:14 pm	Aquarius
24th	6:32 pm	Pisces
27th	0:41 am	Aries
29th	9.24 am	Taurus

October 1977

1st	8:34 pm	Gemini
4th	9:09 am	Cancer
6th	8:57 pm	Leo
9th	5:55 am	Virgo
11th	11:25 am	Libra
13th	2:09 pm	Scorpio
15th	3:28 pm	Sagittarius
17th	4:53 pm	Capricorn
19th	7:38 pm	Aquarius
22nd	0:25 am	Pisces
24th	7:37 am	Aries
26th	4:54 pm	Taurus
29th	4:07 am	Gemini
31st	4:41 pm	Cancer

November 1977

3rd	5:01 am	Leo
5th	3:12 pm	Virgo
7th	9:50 pm	Libra
10th	0:42 am	Scorpio
12th	1:04 am	Sagittarius
14th	0:52 am	Capricorn
16th	2:02 am	Aquarius
18th	6:02 am	Pisces
20th	1:17 pm	Aries
22nd	11:09 pm	Taurus
25th	10:49 am	Gemini
27th	11:20 pm	Cancer
30th	11:51 am	Leo

December 1977

2nd	11:03 pm	Virgo
5th	7:13 am	Libra
7th	11:27 am	Scorpio
9th	12:18 pm	Sagittarius
11th	11:28 am	Capricorn
13th	11:06 am	Aquarius
15th	1:16 pm	Pisces
17th	7:16 pm	Aries
20th	4:57 am	Taurus
22nd	4:53 pm	Gemini
25th	5:29 am	Cancer
27th	5:51 pm	Leo
30th	5:11 am	Virgo

January 1978

1st	2:27 pm	Libra
3rd	8:32 pm	Scorpio
5th	11:02 pm	Sagittarius
7th	10:54 pm	Capricorn
9th	10:06 pm	Aquarius
11th	10:52 pm	Pisces
14th	3:09 am	Aries
16th	11:37 am	Taurus
18th	11:08 pm	Gemini
21st	11:51 am	Cancer
24th	0:04 am	Leo
26th	10:54 am	Virgo
28th	8:07 pm	Libra
31st	3:02 am	Scorpio

February 1978

2nd	7:11 am	Sagittarius
4th	8:48 am	Capricorn
6th	9:06 am	Aquarius
8th	9:52 am	Pisces
10th	1:03 pm	Aries
12th	7:54 pm	Taurus
15th	6:27 am	Gemini
17th	6:56 pm	Cancer
20th	7:09 am	Leo
22nd	5:39 pm	Virgo
25th	2:03 am	Libra
27th	8:27 am	Scorpio

March 1978

1st	1:00 pm	Sagittarius
3rd	3:57 pm	Capricorn
5th	5:51 pm	Aquarius
7th	7:47 pm	Pisces
9th	11:10 pm	Aries
12th	5:21 am	Taurus
14th	2:52 pm	Gemini
17th	2:50 am	Cancer
19th	3:11 pm	Leo
22nd	1:50 am	Virgo
24th	9:40 am	Libra
26th	3:00 pm	Scorpio
28th	6:38 pm	Sagittarius
30th	9:25 pm	Capricorn

April 1978

2nd	0:05 am	Aquarius
4th	3:21 am	Pisces
6th	7:55 am	Aries
8th	2:25 pm	Taurus
10th	11:29 pm	Gemini
13th	11:01 am	Cancer
15th	11:32 pm	Leo
18th	10:41 am	Virgo
20th	6:51 pm	Libra
22nd	11:41 pm	Scorpio
25th	2:01 am	Sagittarius
27th	3:30 am	Capricorn
29th	1:31 am	Aquarius

May 1978

1st	9:05 am	Pisces
3rd	2:29 am	Aries
5th	9:53 pm	Taurus
8th	7:22 am	Gemini
10th	6:44 pm	Cancer
13th	7:16 am	Leo
15th	7:14 pm	Virgo
18th	4:22 am	Libra
20th	9:35 am	Scorpio
22nd	11:28 am	Sagittarius
24th	11:43 am	Capricorn
26th	12:15 pm	Aquarius
28th	2:42 pm	Pisces
30th	7:56 pm	Aries

June 1978

2nd	5:52 am	Taurus
4th	1:56 pm	Gemini
7th	1:31 am	Cancer
9th	2:08 pm	Leo
12th	2:54 am	Virgo
14th	12:51 pm	Libra
16th	7:24 pm	Scorpio
18th	9:50 pm	Sagittarius
20th	9:52 pm	Capricorn
22nd	9:11 pm	Aquarius
24th	9:59 pm	Pisces
27th	1:56 am	Aries
29th	9:26 am	Taurus

July 1978

1st	7:40 pm	Gemini
4th	7:35 am	Cancer
6th	8:13 pm	Leo
9th	8:42 am	Virgo
11th	7:46 pm	Libra
14th	3:43 am	Scorpio
16th	7:44 am	Sagittarius
18th	8:30 am	Capricorn
20th	7:44 am	Aquarius
22nd	7:31 am	Pisces
24th	9:52 am	Aries
26th	3:56 pm	Taurus
29th	1:33 am	Gemini
31st	1:30 pm	Cancer

August 1978

3rd	2:11 am	Leo
5th	2:28 pm	Virgo
8th	1:28 am	Libra
10th	10:07 am	Scorpio
12th	3:38 pm	Sagittarius
14th	5:59 pm	Capricorn
16th	6:14 pm	Aquarius
18th	6:07 pm	Pisces
20th	7:32 pm	Aries
23rd	0:06 am	Taurus
25th	8:36 am	Gemini
27th	7:59 pm	Cancer
30th	8:39 am	Leo

September 1978

1st	8:47 pm	Virgo
4th	7:14 am	Libra
6th	3:36 pm	Scorpio
8th	9:58 pm	Sagittarius
11th	1:19 am	Capricorn
13th	3:08 am	Aquarius
15th	4:10 am	Pisces
17th	5:52 am	Aries
19th	9:47 am	Taurus
21st	4:50 pm	Gemini
24th	1:33 am	Cancer
26th	4:01 pm	Leo
29th	4:10 am	Virgo

October 1978

1st	2:14 pm	Libra
3rd	9:47 pm	Scorpio
6th	3:06 am	Sagittarius
8th	6:51 am	Capricorn
10th	9:42 am	Aquarius
12th	12:13 pm	Pisces
14th	3:06 pm	Aries
16th	7:23 am	Taurus
19th	2:05 am	Gemini
21st	11:55 am	Cancer
24th	0:04 am	Leo
26th	12:29 pm	Virgo
28th	10:51 pm	Libra
31st	5:49 am	Scorpio

November 1978

2nd	10:02 am	Sagittarius
4th	12:40 pm	Capricorn
6th	3:04 pm	Aquarius
8th	6:07 pm	Pisces
16th	10:12 pm	Aries
13th	3:36 am	Taurus
15th	10:48 am	Gemini
17th	8:16 pm	Cancer
20th	8:10 am	Leo
22nd	8:56 pm	Virgo
25th	8:03 am	Libra
27th	3:33 pm	Scorpio
29th	7:20 pm	Sagittarius

December 1978

1st	8:44 pm	Capricorn
3rd	9:36 pm	Aquarius
5th	11:36 pm	Pisces
8th	3:41 am	Aries
10th	9:53 am	Taurus
12th	5:57 pm	Gemini
15th	3:51 am	Cancer
17th	3:38 pm	Leo
20th	4:32 am	Virgo
22nd	4:35 pm	Libra
25th	1:30 am	Scorpio
27th	6:03 am	Sagittarius
29th	7:13 am	Capricorn
31st	6:55 am	Aquarius

January 1979

2nd	7:12 am	Pisces
4th	9:47 am	Aries
6th	3:23 pm	Taurus
8th	11:43 pm	Gemini
11th	10:16 am	Cancer
15th	10:17 pm	Leo
16th	11:10 am	Virgo
18th	11:40 pm	Libra
21st	9:45 am	Scorpio
23rd	4:02 pm	Sagittarius
25th	6:23 pm	Capricorn
27th	6:11 pm	Aquarius
29th	5:27 pm	Pisces
31st	6:15 pm	Aries

February 1979

2nd	10:05 pm	Taurus
5th	5:37 am	Gemini
7th	4:08 pm	Cancer
10th	4:28 am	Leo
12th	5:18 pm	Virgo
15th	5:35 am	Libra
17th	4:09 pm	Scorpio
19th	11:51 pm	Sagittarius
22nd	3:58 am	Capricorn
24th	5:10 am	Aquarius
26th	4:53 am	Pisces
28th	4:57 am	Aries

March 1979

2nd	7:14 am	Taurus
4th	1:04 pm	Gemini
6th	10:36 pm	Cancer
9th	10:49 am	Leo
11th	11:44 pm	Virgo
14th	11:40 am	Libra
16th	9:50 pm	Scorpio
19th	5:36 am	Sagittarius
21st	10:53 am	Capricorn
23rd	1:50 pm	Aquarius
25th	3:04 pm	Pisces
27th	3:49 pm	Aries
29th	5:40 pm	Taurus
31st	10:09 pm	Gemini

April 1979

3rd	6:27 am	Cancer
5th	5:59 pm	Leo
8th	6:52 am	Virgo
10th	6:45 pm	Libra
13th	4:15 am	Scorpio
15th	11:16 am	Sagittarius
17th	4:22 pm	Capricorn
19th	8:01 pm	Aquarius
21st	10:41 pm	Pisces
24th	0:52 am	Aries
26th	3:30 am	Taurus
28th	7:53 am	Gemini
30th	3:16 pm	Cancer

May 1979

3rd	1:57 am	Leo
5th	2:41 pm	Virgo
8th	2:48 am	Libra
10th	12:07 pm	Scorpio
12th	6:23 pm	Sagittarius
14th	10:27 pm	Capricorn
17th	1:26 am	Aquarius
19th	4:19 am	Pisces
21st	7:31 am	Aries
23rd	11:22 am	Taurus
25th	4:31 pm	Gemini
27th	11:51 pm	Cancer
30th	10:11 am	Leo

June 1979

1st	10:41 pm	Virgo
4th	11:08 am	Libra
6th	9:03 pm	Scorpio
9th	3:14 am	Sagittarius
11th	6:23 am	Capricorn
13th	8:08 am	Aquarius
15th	9:59 am	Pisces
17th	12:56 pm	Aries
19th	5:21 pm	Taurus
21st	11:24 pm	Gemini
24th	7:27 am	Cancer
26th	5:50 pm	Leo
29th	6:15 am	Virgo

July 1979

1st	7:06 pm	Libra
4th	5:53 am	Scorpio
6th	12:50 pm	Sagittarius
8th	4:04 pm	Capricorn
10th	4:59 pm	Aquarius
12th	5:26 pm	Pisces
14th	7:00 pm	Aries
16th	10:45 pm	Taurus
19th	5:03 am	Gemini
21st	1:44 pm	Cancer
24th	0:32 am	Leo
26th	1:02 pm	Virgo
29th	2:05 am	Libra
31st	1:42 pm	Scorpio

August 1979

2nd	10:03 pm	Sagittarius
5th	2:21 am	Capricorn
7th	3:27 am	Aquarius
9th	3:06 am	Pisces
11th	3:12 am	Aries
13th	5:26 am	Taurus
15th	10:47 am	Gemini
17th	7:21 pm	Cancer
20th	6:32 am	Leo
22nd	7:13 pm	Virgo
25th	8:13 am	Libra
27th	8:11 pm	Scorpio
30th	5:36 am	Sagittarius

September 1979

1st	11:28 am	Capricorn
3rd	1:55 pm	Aquarius
5th	2:02 pm	Pisces
7th	1:31 pm	Aries
9th	2:17 pm	Taurus
11th	5:59 pm	Gemini
14th	1:27 am	Cancer
16th	12:28 pm	Leo
19th	1:15 am	Virgo
21st	2:10 pm	Libra
24th	1:55 am	Scorpio
26th	11:33 am	Sagittarius
28th	6:36 pm	Capricorn
30th	10:48 pm	Aquarius

October 1979

3rd	0:23 am	Pisces
5th	0:27 am	Aries
7th	0:45 am	Taurus
9th	3:09 am	Gemini
11th	9:14 am	Cancer
13th	7:13 pm	Leo
16th	7:51 am	Virgo
18th	8:44 pm	Libra
21st	8:00 am	Scorpio
23rd	5:07 pm	Sagittarius
26th	0:11 am	Capricorn
28th	5:15 am	Aquarius
30th	8:26 am	Pisces

November 1979

1st	10:08 am	Aries
3rd	11:16 am	Taurus
5th	1:30 pm	Gemini
7th	6:27 pm	Cancer
10th	3:16 am	Leo
12th	3:21 pm	Virgo
15th	4:15 am	Libra
17th	3:26 pm	Scorpio
19th	11:56 pm	Sagittarius
22nd	6:00 am	Capricorn
24th	10:35 am	Aquarius
26th	2:16 pm	Pisces
28th	5:16 pm	Aries
30th	7:54 pm	Taurus

December 1979

2nd	11:02 pm	Gemini
5th	4:03 am	Cancer
7th	12:13 pm	Leo
9th	11:32 pm	Virgo
12th	12:27 pm	Libra
15th	0:08 am	Scorpio
17th	8:32 am	Sagittarius
19th	1:51 pm	Capricorn
21st	5:12 pm	Aquarius
23rd	7:50 pm	Pisces
25th	10:40 pm	Aries
28th	2:08 am	Taurus
30th	6:34 am	Gemini

January 1980

1st	12:33 pm	Cancer
3rd	8:49 pm	Leo
6th	7:50 am	Virgo
8th	8:37 pm	Libra
11th	8:50 am	Scorpio
13th	6:12 pm	Sagittarius
15th	11:51 pm	Capricorn
18th	2:25 am	Aquarius
20th	3:33 am	Pisces
22nd	4:54 am	Aries
24th	7:36 am	Taurus
26th	12:14 pm	Gemini
28th	7:05 pm	Cancer
31st	4:11 am	Leo

February 1980

2nd	3:23 pm	Virgo
5th	4:04 am	Libra
7th	4:43 pm	Scorpio
10th	3:15 am	Sagittarius
12th	10:06 am	Capricorn
14th	1:14 pm	Aquarius
16th	1:52 pm	Pisces
18th	1:45 pm	Aries
20th	2:39 pm	Taurus
22nd	6:03 pm	Gemini
25th	0:36 am	Cancer
27th	10:14 am	Leo
29th	9:54 pm	Virgo

March 1980

3rd	10:40 am	Libra
5th	11:24 pm	Scorpio
8th	10:35 am	Sagittarius
10th	6:59 pm	Capricorn
12th	11:46 pm	Aquarius
15th	1:10 am	Pisces
17th	0:41 am	Aries
19th	0:13 am	Taurus
21st	1:49 am	Gemini
23rd	7:00 am	Cancer
25th	4:02 pm	Leo
28th	3:53 am	Virgo
30th	4:49 pm	Libra

April 1980

2nd	5:21 am	Scorpio
4th	4:34 pm	Sagittarius
7th	1:41 am	Capricorn
9th	7:56 am	Aquarius
11th	11:03 am	Pisces
13th	11:39 am	Aries
15th	11:12 am	Taurus
17th	11:47 am	Gemini
19th	3:18 pm	Cancer
21st	10:54 pm	Leo
24th	10:14 am	Virgo
26th	11:11 pm	Libra
29th	11:34 am	Scorpio

May 1980

1st	10:23 pm	Sagittarius
4th	7:13 am	Capricorn
6th	2:01 pm	Aquarius
8th	6:31 pm	Pisces
10th	8:44 pm	Aries
12th	9:25 pm	Taurus
14th	10:09 pm	Gemini
17th	0:53 am	Cancer
19th	7:19 am	Leo
21st	5:35 pm	Virgo
24th	6:12 am	Libra
26th	6:37 pm	Scorpio
29th	5:04 am	Sagittarius
31st	1:13 pm	Capricorn

June 1980

2nd	7:28 pm	Aquarius
5th	0:10 am	Pisces
7th	3:23 am	Aries
9th	5:30 am	Taurus
11th	7:25 am	Gemini
13th	10:35 am	Cancer
15th	4:26 pm	Leo
18th	1:49 am	Virgo
20th	1:56 pm	Libra
23rd	2:27 am	Scorpio
25th	12:58 pm	Sagittarius
27th	8:45 pm	Capricorn
30th	2:03 am	Aquarius

July 1980

2nd	5:48 am	Pisces
4th	8:48 am	Aries
6th	11:32 am	Taurus
8th	2:36 pm	Gemini
10th	6:48 pm	Cancer
13th	1:04 am	Leo
15th	10:15 am	Virgo
17th	9:55 pm	Libra
20th	10:32 am	Scorpio
22nd	9:40 pm	Sagittarius
25th	5:42 am	Capricorn
27th	10:32 am	Aquarius
29th	1:10 pm	Pisces
31st	2:55 pm	Aries

August 1980

2nd	4:58 pm	Taurus
4th	8:12 pm	Gemini
7th	1:14 am	Cancer
9th	8:28 am	Leo
11th	5:58 pm	Virgo
14th	5:33 am	Libra
16th	6:14 pm	Scorpio
19th	6:04 am	Sagittarius
21st	3:06 pm	Capricorn
23rd	8:30 pm	Aquarius
25th	10:42 pm	Pisces
27th	11:12 pm	Aries
29th	11:42 pm	Taurus

September 1980

1st	1:53 am	Gemini
3rd	6:44 am	Cancer
5th	2:26 pm	Leo
8th	0:32 am	Virgo
10th	12:24 pm	Libra
13th	1:07 am	Scorpio
15th	1:26 pm	Sagittarius
17th	11:45 pm	Capricorn
20th	6:26 am	Aquarius
22nd	9:22 am	Pisces
24th	9:36 am	Aries
26th	8:55 am	Taurus
28th	9:25 am	Gemini
30th	12:51 pm	Cancer

October 1980

2nd	7:59 pm	Leo
5th	6:20 am	Virgo
7th	6:31 pm	Libra
10th	7:15 am	Scorpio
12th	7:38 pm	Sagittarius
15th	6:34 am	Capricorn
17th	2:49 pm	Aquarius
19th	7:28 pm	Pisces
21st	8:40 pm	Aries
23rd	7:55 pm	Taurus
25th	7:19 pm	Gemini
27th	9:02 pm	Cancer
30th	2:40 am	Leo

November 1980

1st	12:21 pm	Virgo
4th	0:30 am	Libra
6th	1:18 pm	Scorpio
9th	1:25 am	Sagittarius
11th	12:13 pm	Capricorn
13th	9:08 pm	Aquarius
16th	3:18 am	Pisces
18th	6:18 am	Aries
20th	6:48 am	Taurus
22nd	6:29 am	Gemini
24th	7:23 am	Cancer
26th	11:28 am	Leo
28th	7:40 pm	Virgo
31st	3:34 am	Scorpio

December 1980

1st	7:14 am	Libra
3rd	7:59 pm	Scorpio
6th	7:55 am	Sagittarius
8th	6:09 pm	Capricorn
11th	2:34 am	Aquarius
13th	8:50 am	Pisces
15th	1:18 pm	Aries
17th	3:33 pm	Taurus
19th	4:40 pm	Gemini
21st	6:05 pm	Cancer
23rd	9:35 pm	Leo
26th	4:35 am	Virgo
28th	3:06 pm	Libra

January 1981

2nd	3:38 pm	Sagittarius
5th	1:39 am	Capricorn
7th	9:09 am	Aquarius
9th	2:39 pm	Pisces
11th	6:42 pm	Aries
13th	9:45 pm	Taurus
16th	0:17 am	Gemini
18th	3:09 am	Cancer
20th	7:24 am	Leo
22nd	2:06 pm	Virgo
24th	11:44 pm	Libra
27th	11.48 am	Scorpio
30th	0:10 am	Sagittarius

February 1981

1st	10:31 am	Capricorn
3rd	5:51 pm	Aquarius
5th	10:20 pm	Pisces
8th	1:02 am	Aries
10th	3:12 am	Taurus
12th	5:53 am	Gemini
14th	9:46 am	Cancer
16th	3:14 pm	Leo
18th	10:34 pm	Virgo
21st	8:14 am	Libra
23rd	7:55 pm	Scorpio
26th	8:26 am	Sagittarius
28th	7:43 pm	Capricorn

March 1981

3rd	3:47 am	Aquarius
5th	8:07 am	Pisces
7th	9:45 am	Aries
9th	10:23 am	Taurus
11th	11:46 am	Gemini
13th	3:10 pm	Cancer
15th	9:05 pm	Leo
18th	5:22 am	Virgo
20th	3:33 pm	Libra
23rd	3:15 am	Scorpio
25th	3:51 pm	Sagittarius
28th	3:51 am	Capricorn
30th	1:09 pm	Aquarius

April 1981

1st	6:37 pm	Pisces
3rd	8:22 pm	Aries
5th	8:03 pm	Taurus
7th	7:50 pm	Gemini
9th	9:35 pm	Cancer
12th	2:39 am	Leo
14th	10:59 am	Virgo
16th	9:38 pm	Libra
19th	9:40 am	Scorpio
21st	10:15 pm	Sagittarius
24th	10:30 am	Capricorn
26th	8:56 pm	Aquarius
29th	3:54 am	Pisces

May 1981

1st	6:53 am	Aries
3rd	6:58 am	Taurus
5th	6:03 am	Gemini
7th	6:22 am	Cancer
9th	9:46 am	Leo
11th	4:59 pm	Virgo
14th	3:25 am	Libra
16th	3:39 pm	Scorpio
19th	4:14 am	Sagittarius
21st	4:19 pm	Capricorn
24th	2:59 am	Aquarius
26th	11:01 am	Pisces
28th	3:39 pm	Aries
30th	5:06 pm	Taurus

June 1981

1st	4:49 pm	Gemini
3rd	4:43 pm	Cancer
5th	6:47 pm	Leo
8th	0:26 am	Virgo
10th	9:59 am	Libra
12th	9:55 pm	Scorpio
15th	10:32 am	Sagittarius
17th	10:21 pm	Capricorn
20th	8:34 am	Aquarius
22nd	4:42 pm	Pisces
24th	10:18 pm	Aries
27th	1:16 am	Taurus
29th	2:22 am	Gemini

July 1981

1st	2:59 am	Cancer
3rd	4:51 am	Leo
5th	9:32 am	Virgo
7th	5:45 pm	Libra
10th	5:02 am	Scorpio
12th	5:35 pm	Sagittarius
15th	5:18 am	Capricorn
17th	2:50 pm	Aquarius
19th	10:25 pm	Pisces
22nd	3:44 am	Aries
24th	7:18 am	Taurus
26th	9:42 am	Gemini
28th	11:43 am	Cancer
30th	2:25 pm	Leo

August 1981

1st	6:58 pm	Virgo
4th	2:26 am	Libra
6th	1:01 pm	Scorpio
9th	1:23 am	Sagittarius
11th	1:17 pm	Capricorn
13th	10:56 pm	Aquarius
16th	5:32 am	Pisces
18th	9:48 am	Aries
20th	12:45 pm	Taurus
22nd	3:20 pm	Gemini
24th	6:18 pm	Cancer
26th	10:12 pm	Leo
29th	3:35 am	Virgo
31st	11:07 am	Libra

September 1981

2nd	9:13 pm	Scorpio
5th	9:24 am	Sagittarius
7th	9:48 pm	Capricorn
10th	7:54 am	Aquarius
12th	2:29 pm	Pisces
14th	5:53 pm	Aries
16th	7:30 pm	Taurus
18th	9:01 pm	Gemini
20th	11:40 pm	Cancer
23rd	4:11 am	Leo
25th	10:32 am	Virgo
27th	6:43 pm	Libra
30th	4:56 am	Scorpio

October 1981

2nd	5:01 pm	Sagittarius
5th	5:47 am	Capricorn
7th	4:57 pm	Aquarius
10th	0:32 am	Pisces
12th	3:59 am	Aries
14th	4:43 am	Taurus
16th	4:43 am	Gemini
18th	5:55 am	Cancer
20th	9:39 am	Leo
22nd	4:07 pm	Virgo
25th	0:56 am	Libra
27th	11:40 am	Scorpio
29th	11:50 pm	Sagittarius

November 1981

1st	12:46 pm	Capricorn
4th	0:50 am	Aquarius
6th	9:46 am	Pisces
8th	2:33 pm	Aries
10th	3:41 pm	Taurus
12th	3:00 pm	Gemini
14th	2:40 pm	Cancer
16th	4:36 pm	Leo
18th	9:55 pm	Virgo
21st	6:34 am	Libra
23rd	5:38 pm	Scorpio
26th	6:01 am	Sagittarius
28th	6:52 pm	Capricorn

December 1981

1st	7:07 am	Aquarius
3rd	5:13 pm	Pisces
5th	11:49 pm	Aries
8th	2:29 am	Taurus
10th	2:29 am	Gemini
12th	1:42 am	Cancer
14th	2:09 am	Leo
16th	5:41 am	Virgo
18th	1:03 pm	Libra
20th	11:38 pm	Scorpio
23rd	12:11 pm	Sagittarius
26th	0:58 am	Capricorn
28th	12:51 pm	Aquarius
30th	11:01 pm	Pisces

January 1982

2nd	6:29 am	Aries
4th	10:57 am	Taurus
6th	12:46 pm	Gemini
8th	1:01 pm	Cancer
10th	1:24 pm	Leo
12th	3:42 pm	Virgo
14th	9:19 pm	Libra
17th	6:48 am	Scorpio
19th	6:50 pm	Sagittarius
22nd	7:49 am	Capricorn
24th	7.22 pm	Aquarius
27th	4:47 am	Pisces
29th	11:55 am	Aries
31st	5:02 pm	Taurus

February 1982

2nd	8:19 pm	Gemini
4th	10:17 pm	Cancer
6th	11:50 pm	Leo
9th	2:16 am	Virgo
11th	7:05 am	Libra
13th	3:20 pm	Scorpio
16th	2:44 am	Sagittarius
18th	3:34 pm	Capricorn
21st	3:11 am	Aquarius
23rd	12:04 pm	Pisces
25th	6:14 pm	Aries
27th	10:32 pm	Taurus

March 1982

2nd	1:49 am	Gemini
4th	4:49 am	Cancer
6th	7:51 am	Leo
8th	11:29 am	Virgo
10th	4:37 pm	Libra
13th	0:17 am	Scorpio
15th	11:05 am	Sagittarius
17th	11:46 pm	Capricorn
20th	11:48 am	Aquarius
22nd	8:57 pm	Pisces
25th	2:35 am	Aries
27th	5:38 am	Taurus
29th	7:44 am	Gemini
31st	10:10 am	Cancer

April 1982

2nd	1:39 pm	Leo
4th	6:20 pm	Virgo
7th	0:26 am	Libra
9th	8:37 am	Scorpio
11th	7:08 pm	Sagittarius
14th	7:42 am	Capricorn
16th	8:16 pm	Aquarius
19th	6:15 am	Pisces
21st	12:17 pm	Aries
23rd	2:55 pm	Taurus
25th	3:48 pm	Gemini
27th	4:44 pm	Cancer
29th	7:10 pm	Leo

May 1982

1st	11:44 pm	Virgo
4th	6:34 am	Libra
6th	3:26 pm	Scorpio
9th	2:18 am	Sagittarius
11th	2:51 pm	Capricorn
14th	3:44 am	Aquarius
16th	2:42 pm	Pisces
18th	10:03 pm	Aries
21st	1:20 am	Taurus
23rd	1:54 am	Gemini
25th	1:38 am	Cancer
27th	2:28 am	Leo
29th	5:46 am	Virgo
31st	12:06 pm	Libra

June 1982

2nd	9:12 pm	Scorpio
5th	8:33 am	Sagittarius
7th	9:11 pm	Capricorn
10th	10:06 am	Aquarius
12th	9:43 pm	Pisces
15th	6:16 am	Aries
17th	11:01 am	Taurus
19th	12:31 pm	Gemini
21st	12:13 pm	Cancer
23rd	11:50 am	Leo
25th	1:41 pm	Virgo
27th	6:34 pm	Libra
30th	3:03 am	Scorpio

July 1982

2nd	2:27 pm	Sagittarius
5th	3:15 am	Capricorn
7th	4:01 pm	Aquarius
10th	3:33 am	Pisces
12th	12:45 pm	Aries
14th	6:56 pm	Taurus
16th	10:03 pm	Gemini
18th	10:46 pm	Cancer
20th	10:36 pm	Leo
22nd	11:21 pm	Virgo
25th	2:47 am	Libra
27th	10:04 am	Scorpio
29th	8:49 pm	Sagittarius

August 1982

1st	9:36 am	Capricorn
3rd	10:17 pm	Aquarius
6th	9:21 am	Pisces
8th	6:20 pm	Aries
11th	1:00 am	Taurus
13th	5:21 am	Gemini
15th	7:39 am	Cancer
17th	8:42 am	Leo
19th	9:44 am	Virgo
21st	12:27 pm	Libra
23rd	6:25 pm	Scorpio
26th	4:13 am	Sagittarius
28th	4:41 pm	Capricorn
31st	5:22 am	Aquarius

September 1982

2nd	4:07 pm	Pisces
5th	0:24 am	Aries
7th	6:26 am	Taurus
9th	10:57 am	Gemini
11th	2:18 pm	Cancer
13th	4:46 pm	Leo
15th	6:50 pm	Virgo
17th	10:05 pm	Libra
20th	3:36 am	Scorpio
22nd	12:35 pm	Sagittarius
25th	0:32 am	Capricorn
27th	1:19 pm	Aquarius
30th	0:19 am	Pisces

October 1982

2nd	8:02 am	Aries
4th	1:07 pm	Taurus
6th	4:38 pm	Gemini
8th	7:40 pm	Cancer
10th	10:45 pm	Leo
13th	2:10 am	Virgo
15th	6:26 am	Libra
17th	12:26 pm	Scorpio
19th	9:05 pm	Sagittarius
22nd	8:41 am	Capricorn
24th	9:36 pm	Aquarius
27th	9:08 pm	Pisces
29th	5:21 pm	Aries
31st	10:03 pm	Taurus

November 1982

3rd	0:23 am	Gemini
5th	1:58 am	Cancer
7th	4:12 am	Leo
9th	7:43 am	Virgo
11th	12:48 pm	Libra
13th	7:44 pm	Scorpio
16th	4:55 am	Sagittarius
18th	4:23 pm	Capricorn
21st	5:21 am	Aquarius
23rd	5:41 pm	Pisces
26th	3:04 am	Aries
28th	8:28 am	Taurus
30th	10:34 am	Gemini

December 1982

2nd	10:58 am	Cancer
4th	11:29 am	Leo
6th	1:37 pm	Virgo
8th	6:14 pm	Libra
11th	1:35 am	Scorpio
13th	11:30 am	Sagittarius
15th	11:16 pm	Capricorn
18th	12:13 pm	Aquarius
21st	0:56 am	Pisces
23rd	11:30 am	Aries
25th	6:33 pm	Taurus
27th	9:48 pm	Gemini
29th	10:12 pm	Cancer
31st	9:33 pm	Leo

January 1983

2nd	9:51 pm	Virgo
5th	0:45 am	Libra
7th	7:20 am	Scorpio
9th	5:16 pm	Sagittarius
12th	5:27 am	Capricorn
14th	6:26 pm	Aquarius
17th	7:01 am	Pisces
19th	6:05 pm	Aries
22nd	2:34 am	Taurus
24th	7:36 am	Gemini
26th	9:24 am	Cancer
28th	9:09 am	Leo
30th	8:58 am	Virgo

February 1983

1st	9:53 am	Libra
3rd	2:37 pm	Scorpio
5th	11:29 pm	Sagittarius
8th	11:35 am	Capricorn
11th	0:41 am	Aquarius
13th	12:50 pm	Pisces
15th	11:46 pm	Aries
18th	8:28 am	Taurus
20th	2:48 pm	Gemini
22nd	6:29 pm	Cancer
24th	7:46 pm	Leo
26th	7:49 pm	Virgo
28th	8:31 pm	Libra

March 1983

2nd	11:51 pm	Scorpio
5th	7:18 am	Sagittarius
7th	6:30 pm	Capricorn
10th	7:29 am	Aquarius
12th	7:44 pm	Pisces
15th	5:58 am	Aries
17th	2:02 pm	Taurus
19th	8:18 pm	Gemini
22nd	0:53 am	Cancer
24th	3:43 am	Leo
26th	5:19 am	Virgo
28th	6:50 am	Libra
30th	10:02 am	Scorpio

April 1983

1st	4:24 pm	Sagittarius
4th	2:30 am	Capricorn
6th	3:06 pm	Aquarius
9th	3:29 am	Pisces
11th	1:32 pm	Aries
13th	8:56 pm	Taurus
16th	2:12 am	Gemini
18th	6:12 am	Cancer
20th	9:25 am	Leo
22nd	12:11 pm	Virgo
24th	3:04 pm	Libra
26th	7:07 pm	Scorpio
29th	1:29 am	Sagittarius

May 1983

1st	11:04 am	Capricorn
3rd	11:09 pm	Aquarius
6th	11:41 am	Pisces
8th	10:14 pm	Aries
11th	5:33 am	Taurus
13th	9:59 am	Gemini
15th	12:45 pm	Cancer
17th	3:00 pm	Leo
19th	5:37 pm	Virgo
21st	9:12 pm	Libra
24th	2:18 am	Scorpio
26th	9:30 am	Sagittarius
28th	7:09 pm	Capricorn
31st	7:01 am	Aquarius

June 1983

2nd	7:42 pm	Pisces
5th	6:55 am	Aries
7th	2:59 pm	Taurus
9th	7:34 pm	Gemini
11th	9:30 pm	Cancer
13th	10:21 pm	Leo
15th	11:37 pm	Virgo
18th	2:38 am	Libra
20th	8:02 am	Scorpio
22nd	3:57 pm	Sagittarius
25th	2:09 am	Capricorn
27th	2:07 pm	Aquarius
30th	2:51 am	Pisces

July 1983

2nd	2:44 pm	Aries
5th	0:05 am	Taurus
7th	5:37 am	Gemini
9th	7:47 am	Cancer
11th	7:53 am	Leo
13th	7:45 am	Virgo
15th	9:15 am	Libra
17th	1:43 pm	Scorpio
19th	9:32 pm	Sagittarius
22nd	8:12 am	Capricorn
24th	8:26 pm	Aquarius
27th	9:10 am	Pisces
29th	9:21 pm	Aries

August 1983

1st	7:33 am	Taurus
3rd	2:38 pm	Gemini
5th	6:06 pm	Cancer
7th	6:35 pm	Leo
9th	5:50 pm	Virgo
11th	5:55 pm	Libra
13th	8:46 pm	Scorpio
16th	3:36 am	Sagittarius
18th	2:01 pm	Capricorn
21st	2:26 am	Aquarius
23rd	3:09 pm	Pisces
26th	3:07 am	Aries
28th	1:35 pm	Taurus
30th	9:47 pm	Gemini

September 1983

2nd	2:51 am	Cancer
4th	4:45 am	Leo
6th	4:36 am	Virgo
8th	4:16 am	Libra
10th	5:54 am	Scorpio
12th	11:14 am	Sagittarius
14th	8:35 pm	Capricorn
17th	8:45 am	Aquarius
19th	9:29 pm	Pisces
22nd	9:09 am	Aries
24th	7:11 pm	Taurus
27th	3:23 am	Gemini
29th	9:21 am	Cancer

October 1983

1st	12:52 pm	Leo
3rd	2:14 pm	Virgo
5th	2:44 pm	Libra
7th	4:11 pm	Scorpio
9th	8:24 pm	Sagittarius
12th	4:33 am	Capricorn
14th	4:03 pm	Aquarius
17th	4:40 am	Pisces
19th	4:16 pm	Aries
22nd	1:46 am	Taurus.
24th	9:07 am	Gemini
26th	2:45 pm	Cancer
28th	6:49 pm	Leo
30th	9:32 pm	Virgo

November 1983

1st	11:32 pm	Libra
4th	1:55 am	Scorpio
6th	6:14 am	Sagittarius
8th	1:37 pm	Capricorn
11th	0:12 am	Aquarius
13th	12:41 pm	Pisces
16th	0:37 am	Aries
18th	10:04 am	Taurus
20th	4:42 pm	Gemini
22nd	9:09 pm	Cancer
25th	0:19 am	Leo
27th	3:03 am	Virgo
29th	5:57 am	Libra

December 1983

1st	9:44 am	Scorpio
3rd	2:50 pm	Sagittarius
5th	10:30 pm	Capricorn
8th	8:44 am	Aquarius
10th	8:54 pm	Pisces
13th	9:15 am	Aries
15th	7:31 pm	Taurus
18th	2:23 am	Gemini
20th	6:00 am	Cancer
22nd	7:43 am	Leo
24th	9:03 am	Virgo
26th	11:22 am	Libra
28th	3:29 pm	Scorpio
30th	9:44 pm	Sagittarius

January 1984		
2nd	6:11 am	Capricorn
4th	4:32 pm	Aquarius
7th	4:35 am	Pisces
9th	5:15 pm	Aries
12th	4:34 am	Taurus
14th	12:35 pm	Gemini
16th	4:45 pm	Cancer
18th	5:48 pm	Leo
20th	5:37 pm	Virgo
22nd	6:11 pm	Libra
24th	9:07 pm	Scorpio
27th	3:14 am	Sagittarius
29th	12:15 pm	Capricorn
31st	11.10 pm	Aquarius

February 1984		
3rd	11:23 am	Pisces
6th	0:04 am	Aries
8th	12:03 pm	Taurus
10th	9:37 pm	Gemini
13th	3:19 am	Cancer
15th	5:07 am	Leo
17th	4:32 am	Virgo
19th	3:42 am	Libra
21st	4:48 am	Scorpio
23rd	9:28 am	Sagittarius
25th	5:52 am	Capricorn
28th	5:03 am	Aquarius

March 1984		
1st	5:30 pm	Pisces
4th	6:07 am	Aries
6th	6:08 pm	Taurus
9th	4:28 am	Gemini
11th	11:43 am	Cancer
13th	3:17 pm	Leo
15th	3:44 pm	Virgo
17th	2:54 pm	Libra
19th	2:54 pm	Scorpio
21st	5:46 pm	Sagittarius
24th	0:36 am	Capricorn
26th	11:10 am	Aquarius
28th	11:36 pm	Pisces
31st	12:12 pm	Aries

April 1984		
2nd	11:54 pm	Taurus
5th	10:01 am	Gemini
7th	5:56 pm	Cancer
9th	11:01 pm	Leo
12th	1:10 am	Virgo
14th	1:30 am	Libra
16th	1:42 am	Scorpio
18th	3:46 am	Sagittarius
20th	9:16 am	Capricorn
22nd	6:30 pm	Aquarius
25th	6:26 am	Pisces
27th	7:00 pm	Aries
30th	6:27 am	Taurus

May 1984		
2nd	3:59 pm	Gemini
4th	11:25 pm	Cancer
7th	4:41 am	Leo
9th	7:58 am	Virgo
11th	9:52 am	Libra
13th	11:24 am	Scorpio
15th	1:54 pm	Sagittarius
17th	6:46 pm	Capricorn
20th	2:57 am	Aquarius
22nd	2:10 pm	Pisces
25th	2:38 am	Aries
27th	2:10 pm	Taurus
29th	11:21 pm	Gemini

June 1984		
1st	5:50 am	Cancer
3rd	10:16 am	Leo
5th	1:25 pm	Virgo
7th	4:02 pm	Libra
9th	6:48 pm	Scorpio
11th	10:26 pm	Sagittarius
14th	3:51 am	Capricorn
16th	11:45 am	Aquarius
18th	10:19 pm	Pisces
21st	10:49 am	Aries
23rd	10:37 pm	Taurus
26th	7:59 am	Gemini
28th	2:04 pm	Cancer
30th	5:27 pm	Leo

July 1984		
2nd	7:26 pm	Virgo
4th	9:26 pm	Libra
7th	0:28 am	Scorpio
9th	5:04 am	Sagittarius
11th	11:25 am	Capricorn
13th	7:43 pm	Aquarius
16th	6:12 am	Pisces
18th	6:26 pm	Aries
21st	6:51 am	Taurus
23rd	5:06 pm	Gemini
25th	11:44 pm	Cancer
28th	2:39 am	Leo
30th	3:28 am	Virgo

August 1984		
1st	4:04 am	Libra
3rd	6:07 am	Scorpio
5th	10:33 am	Sagittarius
7th	5:27 pm	Capricorn
10th	2:26 am	Aquarius
12th	1:14 pm	Pisces
15th	1:27 am	Aries
17th	2:11 pm	Taurus
20th	1:30 am	Gemini
22nd	9:14 am	Cancer
24th	12:55 pm	Leo
26th	1:31 pm	Virgo
28th	12:59 pm	Libra
30th	1:27 pm	Scorpio

September 1984		
1st	4:34 pm	Sagittarius
3rd	10:55 pm	Capricorn
6th	8:13 am	Aquarius
8th	7:25 pm	Pisces
11th	7:46 am	Aries
13th	8:32 pm	Taurus
16th	8:22 am	Gemini
18th	5:32 pm	Cancer
20th	10:47 pm	Leo
23rd	0:19 am	Virgo
24th	11:41 pm	Libra
26th	11:04 pm	Scorpio
29th	0:31 am	Sagittarius

October 1984		
1st	5:31 am	Capricorn
3rd	2:07 pm	Aquarius
6th	1:18 am	Pisces
8th	1:50 pm	Aries
11th	2:27 am	Taurus
13th	2:12 pm	Gemini
15th	12:00 pm	Cancer
18th	6:38 am	Leo
20th	9:52 am	Virgo
22nd	10:31 am	Libra
24th	10:11 am	Scorpio
26th	10:49 am	Sagittarius
28th	2:11 pm	Capricorn
30th	9:16 pm	Aquarius

November 1984		
2nd	7:52 am	Pisces
4th	8:21 pm	Aries
7th	8:52 am	Taurus
9th	8:09 pm	Gemini
12th	5:28 am	Cancer
14th	12:30 pm	Leo
16th	5:04 pm	Virgo
18th	7:28 pm	Libra
20th	8:31 pm	Scorpio
22nd	9:35 pm	Sagittarius
25th	0:19 am	Capricorn
27th	6:12 am	Aquarius
29th	3:38 pm	Pisces

December 1984		
2nd	3:43 am	Aries
4th	4:20 pm	Taurus
7th	3:23 am	Gemini
9th	11:53 am	Cancer
11th	6:06 pm	Leo
13th	10:35 pm	Virgo
16th	1:52 am	Libra
18th	4:27 am	Scorpio
20th	7:00 am	Sagittarius
22nd	10:24 am	Capricorn
24th	3:52 pm	Aquarius
27th	0:20 am	Pisces
29th	11:52 am	Aries

January 1985		
1st	0:36 am	Taurus
3rd	11:57 am	Gemini
5th	8:16 pm	Cancer
8th	1:28 am	Leo
10th	4:40 am	Virgo
12th	7:14 am	Libra
14th	10:09 am	Scorpio
16th	1:50 pm	Sagittarius
18th	6:31 pm	Capricorn
21st	0:39 am	Aquarius
23rd	9:06 am	Pisces
25th	8:06 pm	Aries
28th	8:53 am	Taurus
30th	9:00 pm	Gemini

February 1985		
2nd	5:56 am	Cancer
4th	10:58 am	Leo
6th	1:08 pm	Virgo
8th	2:13 pm	Libra
10th	3:52 pm	Scorpio
12th	7:12 pm	Sagittarius
15th	0:27 am	Capricorn
17th	7:39 am	Aquarius
19th	4:40 pm	Pisces
22nd	3:45 am	Aries
24th	4:28 pm	Taurus
27th	5:09 am	Gemini

March 1985		
1st	3:19 pm	Cancer
3rd	9:27 pm	Leo
5th	11:44 pm	Virgo
7th	11:49 pm	Libra
9th	11:47 pm	Scorpio
12th	1:31 am	Sagittarius
14th	5:58 am	Capricorn
16th	1:14 pm	Aquarius
18th	10:50 pm	Pisces
21st	10:21 am	Aries
23rd	11:07 pm	Taurus
26th	12:01 pm	Gemini
28th	11:13 pm	Cancer
31st	6:47 am	Leo

April 1985		
2nd	10:21 am	Virgo
4th	10:53 am	Libra
6th	10:13 am	Scorpio
8th	10:22 am	Sagittarius
10th	1:03 pm	Capricorn
12th	7:06 pm	Aquarius
15th	4:32 am	Pisces
17th	4:19 pm	Aries
20th	5:11 am	Taurus
22nd	5:59 pm	Gemini
25th	5:23 am	Cancer
27th	2:06 pm	Leo
29th	7:21 pm	Virgo

May 1985
1st	9:21 pm	Libra
3rd	9:17 pm	Scorpio
5th	8:58 pm	Sagittarius
7th	10:13 pm	Capricorn
10th	2:41 am	Aquarius
12th	10:50 am	Pisces
14th	10:26 pm	Aries
17th	11:23 am	Taurus
19th	12:00 pm	Gemini
22nd	11:01 am	Cancer
24th	7:50 pm	Leo
27th	2:04 am	Virgo
29th	5:37 am	Libra
31st	7:05 am	Scorpio

June 1985
2nd	7:34 am	Sagittarius
4th	8:37 am	Capricorn
6th	11:58 am	Aquarius
8th	6:51 pm	Pisces
11th	5:26 am	Aries
13th	6:12 pm	Taurus
16th	6:43 am	Gemini
18th	5:19 pm	Cancer
21st	1:31 am	Leo
23rd	7:29 am	Virgo
25th	11:44 am	Libra
27th	2:34 pm	Scorpio
29th	4:29 pm	Sagittarius

July 1985
1st	6:23 pm	Capricorn
3rd	9:38 pm	Aquarius
6th	3:44 am	Pisces
8th	1:24 pm	Aries
11th	1:44 am	Taurus
13th	2:21 pm	Gemini
16th	0:53 am	Cancer
18th	8:22 am	Leo
20th	1:26 pm	Virgo
22nd	5:09 pm	Libra
24th	8:16 pm	Scorpio
26th	11:12 pm	Sagittarius
29th	2:21 am	Capricorn
31st	6:28 am	Aquarius

August 1985
2nd	12:37 pm	Pisces
4th	9:44 pm	Aries
7th	9:42 am	Taurus
9th	10:31 pm	Gemini
12th	9:24 am	Cancer
14th	4:53 pm	Leo
16th	9:14 pm	Virgo
18th	11:43 pm	Libra
21st	1:51 am	Scorpio
23rd	4:37 am	Sagittarius
25th	8:26 am	Capricorn
27th	1:33 pm	Aquarius
29th	8:25 pm	Pisces

September 1985
1st	5:43 am	Aries
3rd	5:28 pm	Taurus
6th	6:26 am	Gemini
8th	6:07 pm	Cancer
11th	2:25 am	Leo
13th	6:49 am	Virgo
15th	8:33 am	Libra
17th	9:17 am	Scorpio
19th	10:43 am	Sagittarius
21st	1:52 pm	Capricorn
23rd	7:13 pm	Aquarius
26th	2:51 am	Pisces
28th	12:44 pm	Aries

October 1985
1st	0:34 am	Taurus
3rd	1:35 pm	Gemini
6th	1:58 am	Cancer
8th	11:28 am	Leo
10th	5:05 pm	Virgo
12th	7:10 pm	Libra
14th	7:12 pm	Scorpio
16th	7:07 pm	Sagittarius
18th	8:37 pm	Capricorn
21st	0:55 am	Aquarius
23rd	8:31 am	Pisces
25th	6:48 pm	Aries
28th	6:50 am	Taurus
30th	7:58 pm	Gemini

November 1985
2nd	8:29 am	Cancer
4th	7:01 pm	Leo
7th	2:17 am	Virgo
9th	5:48 am	Libra
11th	6:30 am	Scorpio
13th	5:54 am	Sagittarius
15th	5:57 am	Capricorn
17th	8:32 am	Aquarius
19th	2:48 pm	Pisces
22nd	0:44 am	Aries
24th	1:08 pm	Taurus
27th	2:07 am	Gemini
29th	2:20 pm	Cancer

December 1985
2nd	0:59 am	Leo
4th	9:09 am	Virgo
6th	2:28 pm	Libra
8th	4:54 pm	Scorpio
10th	5:12 pm	Sagittarius
12th	5:02 pm	Capricorn
14th	6:20 pm	Aquarius
16th	10:52 pm	Pisces
19th	7:42 am	Aries
21st	7:42 pm	Taurus
24th	8:44 am	Gemini
26th	8:42 pm	Cancer
29th	6:42 am	Leo
31st	2:40 pm	Virgo

January 1986
2nd	8:43 pm	Libra
5th	0:44 am	Scorpio
7th	2:47 am	Sagittarius
9th	3:43 am	Capricorn
11th	5:05 am	Aquarius
13th	8:45 am	Pisces
15th	4:09 pm	Aries
18th	3:16 am	Taurus
20th	4:12 pm	Gemini
23rd	4:14 am	Cancer
25th	1:45 pm	Leo
27th	8:51 pm	Virgo
30th	2:09 am	Libra

February 1986
1st	6:18 am	Scorpio
3rd	9:31 am	Sagittarius
5th	12:02 pm	Capricorn
7th	2:38 pm	Aquarius
9th	6:36 pm	Pisces
12th	1:22 am	Aries
14th	11:42 am	Taurus
17th	0:18 am	Gemini
19th	12:38 pm	Cancer
21st	10:25 pm	Leo
24th	4:58 am	Virgo
26th	9:07 am	Libra
28th	12:06 pm	Scorpio

March 1986
2nd	2:53 pm	Sagittarius
4th	5:57 pm	Capricorn
6th	9:43 pm	Aquarius
9th	2:30 am	Pisces
11th	10:07 am	Aries
13th	8:06 pm	Taurus
16th	8:24 am	Gemini
18th	9:05 pm	Cancer
21st	7:35 am	Leo
23rd	2:36 pm	Virgo
25th	6:22 pm	Libra
27th	8:06 pm	Scorpio
29th	9:22 pm	Sagittarius
31st	11:26 pm	Capricorn

April 1986
3rd	3:13 am	Aquarius
5th	9:06 am	Pisces
7th	5:14 pm	Aries
10th	3:37 am	Taurus
12th	3:52 pm	Gemini
15th	4:42 am	Cancer
17th	4:06 pm	Leo
20th	0:25 am	Virgo
22nd	4:48 am	Libra
24th	6:15 am	Scorpio
26th	6:18 am	Sagittarius
28th	6:45 am	Capricorn
30th	9:11 am	Aquarius

May 1986
2nd	2:35 pm	Pisces
4th	11:01 pm	Aries
7th	10:00 am	Taurus
9th	10:25 pm	Gemini
12th	11:17 am	Cancer
14th	11:14 pm	Leo
17th	8:41 am	Virgo
19th	2:36 pm	Libra
21st	4:59 pm	Scorpio
23rd	4:55 pm	Sagittarius
25th	4:15 pm	Capricorn
27th	5:05 pm	Aquarius
29th	8:58 pm	Pisces

June 1986
1st	4:46 am	Aries
3rd	3:48 pm	Taurus
6th	4:26 am	Gemini
8th	5:14 pm	Cancer
11th	5:09 am	Leo
13th	3:14 pm	Virgo
15th	10:37 pm	Libra
18th	2:34 am	Scorpio
20th	3:34 am	Sagittarius
22nd	3:00 am	Capricorn
24th	2:53 am	Aquarius
26th	5:18 am	Pisces
28th	11:41 am	Aries
30th	9:55 pm	Taurus

July 1986
3rd	10:33 am	Gemini
5th	11:20 pm	Cancer
8th	10:52 am	Leo
10th	8:47 pm	Virgo
13th	4:37 am	Libra
15th	9:53 am	Scorpio
17th	12:30 pm	Sagittarius
19th	1:08 pm	Capricorn
21st	1:20 pm	Aquarius
23rd	3:03 pm	Pisces
25th	8:06 pm	Aries
28th	5:14 am	Taurus
30th	5:20 pm	Gemini

August 1986
2nd	6:03 am	Cancer
4th	5:24 pm	Leo
7th	2:44 am	Virgo
9th	10:02 am	Libra
11th	3:34 pm	Scorpio
13th	7:14 pm	Sagittarius
15th	9:21 pm	Capricorn
17th	10:44 pm	Aquarius
20th	0:52 am	Pisces
22nd	5:30 am	Aries
24th	1:40 pm	Taurus
27th	1:01 am	Gemini
29th	1:58 pm	Cancer

September 1986			October 1986			November 1986			December 1986		
1st	1:07 am	Leo	3rd	1:03 am	Libra	1st	2:16 pm	Scorpio	1st	2:07 am	Sagittarius
3rd	10:02 am	Virgo	5th	4:34 am	Scorpio	3rd	5:18 pm	Sagittarius	3rd	1:29 am	Capricorn
5th	4:32 pm	Libra	7th	6:48 am	Sagittarius	5th	3:51 pm	Capricorn	5th	1:24 am	Aquarius
7th	9:11 pm	Scorpio	9th	8:54 am	Capricorn	7th	5:31 pm	Aquarius	7th	3:52 pm	Pisces
10th	0:41 am	Sagittarius	11th	11:47 am	Aquarius	9th	9:30 pm	Pisces	9th	9:55 am	Aries
12th	3:27 am	Capricorn	13th	4:05 pm	Pisces	12th	4:16 am	Aries	11th	7:12 pm	Taurus
14th	6:07 am	Aquarius	15th	10:14 pm	Aries	14th	1:26 pm	Taurus	14th	6:42 am	Gemini
16th	9:29 am	Pisces	18th	6:37 am	Taurus	17th	0:26 am	Gemini	16th	7:09 pm	Cancer
18th	2:36 pm	Aries	20th	5:15 pm	Gemini	19th	12:46 pm	Cancer	19th	7:43 am	Leo
20th	10:25 pm	Taurus	23rd	5:36 am	Cancer	22nd	1:24 am	Leo	21st	7:28 pm	Virgo
23rd	9:15 am	Gemini	25th	6:00 pm	Leo	24th	12:41 pm	Virgo	24th	4:50 am	Libra
25th	9:44 pm	Cancer	28th	4:18 am	Virgo	26th	8:57 pm	Libra	26th	11:00 am	Scorpio
28th	9:36 am	Leo	30th	11:00 am	Libra	29th	1:13 am	Scorpio	28th	1:14 pm	Sagittarius
30th	6:55 pm	Virgo							30th	12:53 pm	Capricorn

January 1987			February 1987			March 1987			April 1987		
1st	11:58 am	Aquarius	2nd	2:12 am	Aries	1st	12:41 pm	Aries	2nd	12:20 pm	Gemini
3rd	12:43 pm	Pisces	4th	8:30 am	Taurus	3rd	6:16 pm	Taurus	4th	11:34 pm	Cancer
5th	4:57 pm	Aries	6th	7:26 pm	Gemini	6th	3:28 am	Gemini	7th	12:02 pm	Leo
8th	1:16 am	Taurus	9th	7:56 am	Cancer	8th	3:25 am	Cancer	9th	11:29 pm	Virgo
10th	12:42 pm	Gemini	11th	8:22 pm	Leo	11th	3:55 am	Leo	12th	8:02 am	Libra
13th	1:19 am	Cancer	14th	7:25 am	Virgo	13th	2:53 pm	Virgo	14th	1:39 pm	Scorpio
15th	1:43 pm	Leo	16th	4:45 pm	Libra	15th	11:36 pm	Libra	16th	5:01 pm	Sagittarius
18th	1:14 am	Virgo	19th	0:05 am	Scorpio	18th	5:56 am	Scorpio	18th	7:22 pm	Capricorn
20th	11:05 am	Libra	21st	5:08 am	Sagittarius	20th	10:30 am	Sagittarius	20th	9:45 pm	Aquarius
22nd	6:28 pm	Scorpio	23rd	7:55 am	Capricorn	22nd	1:47 pm	Capricorn	23rd	1:03 am	Pisces
24th	10:55 pm	Sagittarius	25th	9:08 am	Aquarius	24th	4:18 pm	Aquarius	25th	5:42 am	Aries
26th	11:42 pm	Capricorn	27th	10:09 am	Pisces	26th	6:47 pm	Pisces	27th	12:08 pm	Taurus
28th	11:17 pm	Aquarius				28th	10:13 pm	Aries	29th	8:45 pm	Gemini
30th	11:26 pm	Pisces				31st	3:49 am	Taurus			

May 1987			June 1987			July 1987			August 1987		
2nd	7:41 am	Cancer	1st	3:27 am	Leo	3rd	9:50 am	Libra	2nd	1:08 am	Scorpio
4th	8:07 pm	Leo	3rd	3:54 pm	Virgo	5th	5:58 pm	Scorpio	4th	6:42 am	Sagittarius
7th	8:05 am	Virgo	6th	2:22 am	Libra	7th	10:03 pm	Sagittarius	6th	8:47 am	Capricorn
9th	5:26 pm	Libra	8th	9:01 am	Scorpio	9th	10:42 pm	Capricorn	8th	8:36 am	Aquarius
11th	11:09 pm	Scorpio	10th	11:49 am	Sagittarius	11th	9:50 pm	Aquarius	10th	8:04 am	Pisces
14th	1:42 am	Sagittarius	12th	12:04 pm	Capricorn	13th	9:38 pm	Pisces	12th	9:14 am	Aries
16th	2:38 am	Capricorn	14th	11:49 am	Aquarius	16th	0:02 am	Aries	14th	1:44 pm	Taurus
18th	3:45 am	Aquarius	16th	1:00 pm	Pisces	18th	6:09 am	Taurus	16th	10:01 pm	Gemini
20th	6:27 am	Pisces	18th	5:02 pm	Aries	20th	3:36 pm	Gemini	19th	9:21 am	Cancer
22nd	11:27 am	Aries	21st	0:10 am	Taurus	23rd	3:14 am	Cancer	21st	9:58 pm	Leo
24th	6:41 pm	Taurus	23rd	9:58 am	Gemini	25th	3:50 pm	Leo	24th	10:23 am	Virgo
27th	3:56 am	Gemini	25th	9:22 pm	Cancer	28th	4:25 am	Virgo	26th	9:35 pm	Libra
29th	1:01 pm	Cancer	28th	9:52 am	Leo	30th	3:56 pm	Libra	29th	6:47 am	Scorpio
			30th	10:33 pm	Virgo				31st	1:20 pm	Sagittarius

September 1987			October 1987			November 1987			December 1987		
2nd	5:00 pm	Capricorn	2nd	1:50 am	Aquarius	2nd	1:41 pm	Aries	2nd	1:06 am	Taurus
4th	6:19 pm	Aquarius	4th	3:39 am	Pisces	4th	6:04 pm	Taurus	4th	8:16 am	Gemini
6th	6:37 pm	Pisces	6th	5:36 am	Aries	7th	0:15 am	Gemini	6th	5:22 pm	Cancer
8th	7:36 pm	Aries	8th	8:50 am	Taurus	9th	9:12 am	Cancer	9th	4:40 am	Leo
10th	10:57 pm	Taurus	10th	3:07 pm	Gemini	11th	8:45 pm	Leo	11th	5:29 pm	Virgo
13th	5:59 am	Gemini	13th	0:30 am	Cancer	14th	9:28 am	Virgo	14th	5:36 am	Libra
15th	4:25 pm	Cancer	15th	12:34 pm	Leo	16th	8:46 pm	Libra	16th	2:35 pm	Scorpio
18th	4:50 am	Leo	18th	1:06 am	Virgo	19th	4:43 am	Scorpio	18th	7:29 pm	Sagittarius
20th	5:13 pm	Virgo	20th	11:47 am	Libra	21st	9:13 am	Sagittarius	20th	9:06 pm	Capricorn
23rd	3:57 am	Libra	22nd	7:39 pm	Scorpio	23rd	11:31 am	Capricorn	22nd	9:21 pm	Aquarius
25th	12:28 pm	Scorpio	25th	0:57 am	Sagittarius	25th	1:13 pm	Aquarius	24th	10:12 pm	Pisces
27th	6:48 pm	Sagittarius	27th	4:32 am	Capricorn	27th	3:43 pm	Pisces	27th	1:07 am	Aries
29th	11:08 pm	Capricorn	29th	7:27 am	Aquarius	29th	7:38 pm	Aries	29th	6:40 am	Taurus
			31st	10:20 am	Pisces				31st	2:32 pm	Gemini

January 1988

3rd	0:18 am	Cancer
5th	11:49 am	Leo
8th	0:35 am	Virgo
10th	1:13 pm	Libra
12th	11:39 pm	Scorpio
15th	5:53 am	Sagittarius
17th	8:10 am	Capricorn
19th	8:02 am	Aquarius
21st	7:31 am	Pisces
23rd	8:37 am	Aries
25th	12:43 pm	Taurus
27th	8:06 pm	Gemini
30th	6:14 am	Cancer

February 1988

1st	6:08 pm	Leo
4th	6:54 am	Virgo
6th	7:35 pm	Libra
9th	6:38 am	Scorpio
11th	2:30 pm	Sagittarius
13th	6:32 pm	Capricorn
15th	7:23 pm	Aquarius
17th	6:44 pm	Pisces
19th	6:38 pm	Aries
21st	8:54 pm	Taurus
24th	2:45 am	Gemini
26th	12:16 pm	Cancer
29th	0:12 am	Leo

March 1988

2nd	1:07 pm	Virgo
5th	1:33 am	Libra
7th	12:25 pm	Scorpio
9th	8:58 pm	Sagittarius
12th	2:29 am	Capricorn
14th	5:06 am	Aquarius
16th	5:42 am	Pisces
18th	5:47 am	Aries
20th	7:09 am	Taurus
22nd	11:27 am	Gemini
24th	7:30 pm	Cancer
27th	6:55 am	Leo
29th	7:50 pm	Virgo

April 1988

1st	8:04 am	Libra
3rd	6:25 pm	Scorpio
6th	2:29 am	Sagittarius
8th	8:17 am	Capricorn
10th	12:08 pm	Aquarius
12th	2.23 pm	Pisces
14th	3:47 pm	Aries
16th	5:33 pm	Taurus
18th	9:12 pm	Gemini
21st	4:08 am	Cancer
23rd	2:38 pm	Leo
26th	3:17 am	Virgo
2oth	3:36 pm	Libra

May 1988

1st	1:39 am	Scorpio
3rd	8:50 am	Sagittarius
5th	1:53 pm	Capricorn
7th	5:36 am	Aquarius
9th	8:40 pm	Pisces
11th	11:24 pm	Aries
14th	2:23 am	Taurus
16th	6:35 am	Gemini
18th	1:10 pm	Cancer
20th	10:53 pm	Leo
23rd	11:13 am	Virgo
25th	11:50 pm	Libra
28th	10:02 am	Scorpio
30th	4:54 pm	Sagittarius

June 1988

1st	8:59 pm	Capricorn
3rd	11:35 pm	Aquarius
6th	2:02 am	Pisces
8th	5:06 am	Aries
10th	9:05 am	Taurus
12th	2:18 pm	Gemini
14th	9:22 pm	Cancer
17th	7:00 am	Leo
19th	7:04 pm	Virgo
22nd	7:56 am	Libra
24th	6:56 pm	Scorpio
27th	2:15 am	Sagittarius
29th	5:57 am	Capricorn

July 1988

1st	7:31 am	Aquarius
3rd	8:36 am	Pisces
5th	10:42 am	Aries
7th	2:31 pm	Taurus
9th	8:18 pm	Gemini
12th	4:12 am	Cancer
14th	2:15 pm	Leo
17th	2:18 am	Virgo
19th	3:20 pm	Libra
22nd	3:11 am	Scorpio
24th	11:36 am	Sagittarius
26th	4:02 pm	Capricorn
28th	5:22 pm	Aquarius
30th	5:24 pm	Pisces

August 1988

1st	5:57 pm	Aries
3rd	8:28 pm	Taurus
6th	1:45 am	Gemini
8th	9:56 am	Cancer
10th	8:29 pm	Leo
13th	8:48 am	Virgo
15th	9:52 pm	Libra
18th	10:08 am	Scorpio
20th	7:52 pm	Sagittarius
23rd	1:47 am	Capricorn
25th	4:02 am	Aquarius
27th	4:01 am	Pisces
29th	3:31 am	Aries
31st	4:25 am	Taurus

September 1988

2nd	8:17 am	Gemini
4th	3:41 pm	Cancer
7th	2:16 am	Leo
9th	2:49 pm	Virgo
12th	3:51 am	Libra
14th	4:05 pm	Scorpio
17th	2:25 am	Sagittarius
19th	9:40 am	Capricorn
21st	1:38 pm	Aquarius
23rd	2:47 pm	Pisces
25th	2:30 pm	Aries
27th	2:32 pm	Taurus
29th	4:47 pm	Gemini

October 1988

1st	10:39 pm	Cancer
4th	8:33 am	Leo
6th	9:01 pm	Virgo
9th	10:03 am	Libra
11th	9:57 pm	Scorpio
14th	7:57 am	Sagittarius
16th	3:42 pm	Capricorn
18th	9:03 pm	Aquarius
20th	11:58 pm	Pisces
23rd	0:58 am	Aries
25th	1:22 am	Taurus
27th	2:56 am	Gemini
29th	7:33 am	Cancer
31st	4:08 pm	Leo

November 1988

3rd	4:02 am	Virgo
5th	5:03 pm	Libra
8th	4:44 am	Scorpio
10th	2:03 pm	Sagittarius
12th	9:11 pm	Capricorn
15th	2:35 am	Aquarius
17th	6:32 am	Pisces
19th	9:11 am	Aries
21st	11:02 am	Taurus
23rd	1:15 pm	Gemini
25th	5:24 pm	Cancer
28th	0:52 am	Leo
30th	12:02 pm	Virgo

December 1988

3rd	0:57 am	Libra
5th	12:47 pm	Scorpio
7th	9:53 pm	Sagittarius
10th	4:05 am	Capricorn
12th	8:25 am	Aquarius
14th	11:52 am	Pisces
16th	3:03 pm	Aries
18th	6:12 pm	Taurus
20th	9:44 pm	Gemini
23rd	2:36 am	Cancer
25th	10:01 am	Leo
27th	8:28 pm	Virgo
30th	9:09 am	Libra

January 1989

1st	9:33 pm	Scorpio
4th	7:07 am	Sagittarius
6th	1:09 pm	Capricorn
8th	4:29 pm	Aquarius
10th	6:31 pm	Pisces
12th	8:37 pm	Aries
14th	11:38 pm	Taurus
17th	3:59 am	Gemini
19th	10:01 am	Cancer
21st	6:05 pm	Leo
24th	4:34 am	Virgo
26th	5:02 pm	Libra
29th	5:46 am	Scorpio
31st	4:24 pm	Sagittarius

February 1989

2nd	11:28 pm	Capricorn
5th	2:48 am	Aquarius
7th	3:52 am	Pisces
9th	4:19 am	Aries
11th	5:48 am	Taurus
13th	9:28 am	Gemini
15th	3:45 pm	Cancer
18th	0:33 am	Leo
20th	11:37 am	Virgo
23rd	0:06 am	Libra
25th	12:56 pm	Scorpio
28th	0:29 am	Sagittarius

March 1989

2nd	8:53 am	Capricorn
4th	1:31 pm	Aquarius
6th	2:56 pm	Pisces
8th	2:36 pm	Aries
10th	2:29 pm	Taurus
12th	4:22 pm	Gemini
14th	9:29 pm	Cancer
17th	6:17 am	Leo
19th	5:42 pm	Virgo
22nd	6:24 am	Libra
24th	7:11 pm	Scorpio
27th	6:52 am	Sagittarius
29th	4:22 pm	Capricorn
31st	10:45 pm	Aquarius

April 1989

3rd	1:36 am	Pisces
5th	1:50 am	Aries
7th	1:07 am	Taurus
9th	1:32 am	Gemini
11th	5:02 am	Cancer
13th	12:35 pm	Leo
15th	11:40 pm	Virgo
18th	12:33 pm	Libra
21st	1:14 am	Scorpio
23rd	12:38 pm	Sagittarius
25th	10:16 pm	Capricorn
28th	5:31 am	Aquarius
30th	10:00 am	Pisces

May 1989		
2nd	11:49 am	Aries
4th	11:55 am	Taurus
6th	12:08 pm	Gemini
8th	2:27 pm	Cancer
10th	8:27 pm	Leo
13th	6:33 am	Virgo
15th	7:09 pm	Libra
18th	7:47 am	Scorpio
20th	6:51 pm	Sagittarius
23rd	3:54 am	Capricorn
25th	10:59 am	Aquarius
27th	4:10 pm	Pisces
29th	7:25 pm	Aries
31st	8:50 pm	Taurus

June 1989		
2nd	10:04 pm	Gemini
5th	0:19 am	Cancer
7th	5:33 am	Leo
9th	2:35 pm	Virgo
12th	2:32 am	Libra
14th	3:11 pm	Scorpio
17th	2:12 am	Sagittarius
19th	10:39 am	Capricorn
21st	4:56 pm	Aquarius
23rd	9:37 pm	Pisces
26th	1:08 am	Aries
28th	3:47 am	Taurus
30th	6:10 am	Gemini

July 1989		
2nd	9:23 am	Cancer
4th	2:43 pm	Leo
6th	11:06 pm	Virgo
9th	10:32 am	Libra
11th	11:10 pm	Scorpio
14th	10:28 am	Sagittarius
16th	6:59 pm	Capricorn
19th	0:36 am	Aquarius
21st	4:07 am	Pisces
23rd	6:42 am	Aries
25th	9:13 am	Taurus
27th	12:19 pm	Gemini
29th	4:35 pm	Cancer
31st	10:43 pm	Leo

August 1989		
3rd	7:22 am	Virgo
5th	6:30 pm	Libra
8th	7:04 am	Scorpio
10th	7:00 pm	Sagittarius
13th	4:13 am	Capricorn
15th	9:54 am	Aquarius
17th	12:43 pm	Pisces
19th	1:59 pm	Aries
21st	3:14 pm	Taurus
23rd	5:43 pm	Gemini
25th	10:15 pm	Cancer
28th	5:16 am	Leo
30th	2:33 pm	Virgo

September 1989		
2nd	1:49 am	Libra
4th	2:24 pm	Scorpio
7th	2:50 am	Sagittarius
9th	1:08 pm	Capricorn
11th	7:59 pm	Aquarius
13th	11:06 pm	Pisces
15th	11:38 pm	Aries
17th	11:23 pm	Taurus
20th	0:17 am	Gemini
22nd	3:53 am	Cancer
24th	10:48 am	Leo
26th	8:35 pm	Virgo
29th	8:17 am	Libra

October 1989		
1st	8:54 pm	Scorpio
4th	9:29 am	Sagittarius
6th	8:43 pm	Capricorn
9th	5:02 am	Aquarius
11th	9:32 am	Pisces
13th	10:38 am	Aries
15th	9:53 am	Taurus
17th	9:23 am	Gemini
19th	11:15 am	Cancer
21st	4:52 pm	Leo
24th	2:16 am	Virgo
26th	2:12 pm	Libra
29th	2:56 am	Scorpio
31st	3:23 pm	Sagittarius

November 1989		
3rd	2:47 am	Capricorn
5th	12:06 pm	Aquarius
7th	6:21 pm	Pisces
9th	9:06 pm	Aries
11th	9:08 pm	Taurus
13th	8:19 pm	Gemini
15th	8:54 pm	Cancer
18th	0:46 am	Leo
20th	8:58 am	Virgo
22nd	8:27 pm	Libra
25th	9:12 am	Scorpio
27th	9:30 pm	Sagittarius
30th	8:25 am	Capricorn

December 1989		
2nd	5:40 pm	Aquarius
5th	0:48 am	Pisces
7th	5:09 am	Aries
9th	6:56 am	Taurus
11th	7:15 am	Gemini
13th	7:53 am	Cancer
15th	10:47 am	Leo
17th	5:24 pm	Virgo
20th	3:47 am	Libra
22nd	4:18 pm	Scorpio
25th	4:35 am	Sagittarius
27th	3:08 pm	Capricorn
29th	11:38 pm	Aquarius

January 1990		
1st	6:09 am	Pisces
3rd	10:54 am	Aries
5th	2:03 pm	Taurus
7th	4:01 pm	Gemini
9th	5:54 pm	Cancer
11th	9:04 pm	Leo
14th	2:50 am	Virgo
16th	12:21 pm	Libra
19th	0:16 am	Scorpio
21st	12:41 pm	Sagittarius
23rd	11:27 pm	Capricorn
26th	7:22 am	Aquarius
28th	12:48 pm	Pisces
30th	4:32 pm	Aries

February 1990		
1st	7:28 pm	Taurus
3rd	10:13 pm	Gemini
6th	1:28 am	Cancer
8th	5:55 am	Leo
10th	12:17 pm	Virgo
12th	9:10 pm	Libra
15th	8:35 am	Scorpio
17th	9:05 pm	Sagittarius
20th	8:25 am	Capricorn
22nd	4:48 pm	Aquarius
24th	9:48 pm	Pisces
27th	0:16 am	Aries

March 1990		
1st	1:44 am	Taurus
3rd	3:39 am	Gemini
5th	7:06 am	Cancer
7th	12:28 pm	Leo
9th	7:49 pm	Virgo
12th	5:11 am	Libra
14th	4:27 pm	Scorpio
17th	4:56 am	Sagittarius
19th	4:59 pm	Capricorn
22nd	2:28 am	Aquarius
24th	8:03 am	Pisces
26th	10:11 am	Aries
28th	10:27 am	Taurus
30th	10:46 am	Gemini

April 1990		
1st	12:55 pm	Cancer
3rd	5:53 pm	Leo
6th	1:43 am	Virgo
8th	11:46 am	Libra
10th	11:18 pm	Scorpio
13th	11:49 am	Sagittarius
16th	0:16 am	Capricorn
18th	10:48 am	Aquarius
20th	5:53 pm	Pisces
22nd	8:56 pm	Aries
24th	9:01 pm	Taurus
26th	8:13 pm	Gemini
28th	8:42 pm	Cancer

May 1990		
1st	0:09 am	Leo
3rd	7:21 am	Virgo
5th	5:30 pm	Libra
8th	5:24 am	Scorpio
10th	5:56 pm	Sagittarius
13th	6:21 am	Capricorn
15th	5:28 pm	Aquarius
18th	1:53 am	Pisces
20th	6:28 am	Aries
22nd	7:40 am	Taurus
24th	7:01 am	Gemini
26th	6:38 am	Cancer
28th	8:35 am	Leo
30th	2:13 pm	Virgo

June 1990		
1st	11:31 pm	Libra
4th	11:24 am	Scorpio
6th	12:00 pm	Sagittarius
9th	12:11 pm	Capricorn
11th	11:09 pm	Aquarius
14th	7:57 am	Pisces
16th	1:51 pm	Aries
18th	4:40 pm	Taurus
20th	5:14 pm	Gemini
22nd	5:12 pm	Cancer
24th	6:29 pm	Leo
26th	10:43 pm	Virgo
29th	6:51 am	Libra

July 1990		
1st	6:02 pm	Scorpio
4th	6:35 am	Sagittarius
6th	6:39 pm	Capricorn
9th	5:05 am	Aquarius
11th	1:28 pm	Pisces
13th	7:35 pm	Aries
15th	11:29 pm	Taurus
18th	1:32 am	Gemini
20th	2:46 am	Cancer
22nd	4:33 am	Leo
24th	8:23 am	Virgo
26th	3:24 pm	Libra
29th	1:40 am	Scorpio
31st	1:59 pm	Sagittarius

August 1990		
3rd	2:08 am	Capricorn
5th	12:16 pm	Aquarius
7th	7:54 pm	Pisces
10th	1:15 am	Aries
12th	4:56 am	Taurus
14th	7:43 am	Gemini
16th	10:14 am	Cancer
18th	1:15 pm	Leo
20th	5:37 pm	Virgo
23rd	0:19 am	Libra
25th	9:50 am	Scorpio
27th	9:59 pm	Sagittarius
30th	10:21 am	Capricorn

September 1990		October 1990		November 1990		December 1990	
1st 8:49 pm	Aquarius	1st 1:37 pm	Pisces	2nd 5:30 am	Taurus	1st 4:21 pm	Gemini
4th 4:03 am	Pisces	3rd 5:38 pm	Aries	4th 5:07 am	Gemini	3rd 3:30 pm	Cancer
6th 8:21 am	Aries	5th 7:05 pm	Taurus	6th 5:10 am	Cancer	5th 4:05 pm	Leo
8th 10:56 am	Taurus	7th 7:48 pm	Gemini	8th 7:28 am	Leo	7th 7:42 pm	Virgo
10th 1:07 pm	Gemini	9th 9:31 pm	Cancer	10th 12:52 pm	Virgo	10th 3:02 am	Libra
12th 5:56 pm	Cancer	12th 1:17 am	Leo	12th 9:10 pm	Libra	12th 1:29 pm	Scorpio
14th 7:55 pm	Leo	14th 7:24 am	Virgo	15th 7:42 am	Scorpio	15th 1:43 am	Sagittarius
17th 1:20 am	Virgo	16th 3:50 pm	Libra	17th 7:40 pm	Sagittarius	17th 2:35 pm	Capricorn
19th 8:58 am	Libra	19th 1:25 am	Scorpio	20th 8:53 am	Capricorn	20th 2:59 am	Aquarius
21st 6:09 pm	Scorpio	21st 1:13 pm	Sagittarius	22nd 9:08 pm	Aquarius	22nd 1:45 pm	Pisces
24th 5:54 am	Sagittarius	24th 2:04 am	Capricorn	25th 7:27 am	Pisces	24th 9:43 pm	Aries
26th 6:37 pm	Capricorn	26th 2:11 pm	Aquarius	27th 2:00 pm	Aries	27th 2:07 am	Taurus
29th 5:51 am	Aquarius	28th 11:23 pm	Pisces	29th 4:33 pm	Taurus	29th 2:24 am	Gemini
		31st 4:11 am	Aries	31st 3:04 am	Cancer		

January 1991		February 1991		March 1991		April 1991	
2nd 2:57 am	Leo	2nd 8:05 pm	Libra	2nd 6:06 am	Libra	3rd 8:02 am	Sagittarius
4th 5:01 am	Virgo	5th 4:03 am	Scorpio	4th 1:13 pm	Scorpio	5th 8:21 pm	Capricorn
6th 10:39 am	Libra	7th 3:24 pm	Sagittarius	6th 11:34 pm	Sagittarius	8th 8:57 am	Aquarius
8th 8:01 pm	Scorpio	10th 4:14 am	Capricorn	9th 12:13 pm	Capricorn	10th 7:14 pm	Pisces
11th 8:07 am	Sagittarius	12th 4:13 pm	Aquarius	12th 0:29 am	Aquarius	13th 1:48 am	Aries
13th 8:59 pm	Capricorn	15th 1:58 am	Pisces	14th 10:05 am	Pisces	15th 5:03 am	Taurus
16th 9:02 am	Aquarius	17th 9:09 am	Aries	16th 4:34 pm	Aries	17th 6:42 am	Gemini
18th 7:22 pm	Pisces	19th 2:23 pm	Taurus	18th 8:39 pm	Taurus	19th 8:18 am	Cancer
21st 3:27 am	Aries	21st 6:09 pm	Gemini	20th 11:36 pm	Gemini	21st 11:06 am	Leo
23rd 8:37 am	Taurus	23rd 8:56 pm	Cancer	23rd 2:28 am	Cancer	23rd 3:32 pm	Virgo
25th 12:04 pm	Gemini	25th 11:13 pm	Leo	25th 5:44 am	Leo	25th 9:36 pm	Libra
27th 1:23 pm	Cancer	28th 1:52 am	Virgo	27th 9:43 am	Virgo	28th 5:36 am	Scorpio
29th 2:05 pm	Leo			29th 2:52 pm	Libra	30th 3:46 pm	Sagittarius
31st 3:48 pm	Virgo			31st 10:02 pm	Scorpio		

May 1991		June 1991		July 1991		August 1991	
3rd 3:56 am	Capricorn	1st 11:42 am	Aquarius	1st 5:48 pm	Pisces	2nd 4:29 pm	Taurus
5th 4:50 pm	Aquarius	4th 11:34 am	Pisces	4th 3:31 am	Aries	4th 8:53 pm	Gemini
8th 4:01 am	Pisces	6th 8:22 am	Aries	6th 9:48 am	Taurus	6th 10:48 pm	Cancer
10th 11:29 am	Aries	9th 1:12 am	Taurus	8th 12:38 pm	Gemini	8th 11:10 pm	Leo
12th 3:03 pm	Taurus	11th 2:35 am	Gemini	10th 1:02 pm	Cancer	10th 11.36 pm	Virgo
14th 3:50 pm	Gemini	13th 2:16 am	Cancer	12th 12:37 pm	Leo	13th 1:54 am	Libra
16th 4:16 pm	Cancer	15th 2:12 am	Leo	14th 1:17 pm	Virgo	15th 7:39 am	Scorpio
18th 5:35 pm	Leo	17th 4:05 am	Virgo	16th 4:39 pm	Libra	17th 5:14 pm	Sagittarius
20th 9:02 pm	Virgo	19th 9:06 am	Libra	18th 11:41 pm	Scorpio	20th 5:34 am	Capricorn
23rd 3:10 am	Libra	21st 5:21 pm	Scorpio	21st 10:19 am	Sagittarius	22nd 6:27 pm	Aquarius
25th 11:44 am	Scorpio	24th 4:18 am	Sagittarius	23rd 10:57 pm	Capricorn	25th 5:49 am	Pisces
27th 10:21 pm	Sagittarius	26th 4:50 pm	Capricorn	26th 11:48 am	Aquarius	27th 2:59 am	Aries
30th 10:42 am	Capricorn	29th 5:46 am	Aquarius	28th 11:34 pm	Pisces	29th 10:00 pm	Taurus
				31st 9:18 am	Aries		

September 1991		October 1991		November 1991		December 1991	
1st 3:03 am	Gemini	2nd 2:50 pm	Leo	3rd 4:14 am	Libra	2nd 4:36 pm	Scorpio
3rd 6:19 am	Cancer	4th 5:46 pm	Virgo	5th 10:13 am	Scorpio	5th 1:34 am	Sagittarius
5th 8:14 am	Leo	6th 9:03 pm	Libra	7th 6:26 pm	Sagittarius	7th 12:45 pm	Capricorn
7th 9:39 am	Virgo	9th 2:03 am	Scorpio	10th 5:20 am	Capricorn	10th 1:28 am	Aquarius
9th 11:57 am	Libra	11th 10:03 am	Sagittarius	12th 6:08 pm	Aquarius	12th 2:18 pm	Pisces
11th 4:48 pm	Scorpio	13th 9:12 pm	Capricorn	15th 6:31 am	Pisces	15th 1:06 am	Aries
14th 1:17 am	Sagittarius	16th 10:04 am	Aquarius	17th 4:04 pm	Aries	17th 8:05 am	Taurus
16th 1:05 pm	Capricorn	18th 9:52 pm	Pisces	19th 9:49 pm	Taurus	19th 11:18 am	Gemini
19th 1:56 am	Aquarius	21st 6:30 am	Aries	22nd 0:23 am	Gemini	21st 11:54 am	Cancer
21st 1:17 pm	Pisces	23rd 11:53 am	Taurus	24th 1:26 am	Cancer	23rd 11:41 am	Leo
23rd 9:56 pm	Aries	25th 3:08 pm	Gemini	26th 2:38 am	Leo	25th 12:28 pm	Virgo
26th 3:59 am	Taurus	27th 5:37 pm	Cancer	28th 5:14 am	Virgo	27th 3:42 pm	Libra
28th 8:25 am	Gemini	29th 8:21 pm	Leo	30th 9:50 am	Libra	29th 10:05 pm	Scorpio
30th 11:57 am	Cancer	31st 11:48 pm	Virgo				

Appendix B: Rising Sign Tables

JANUARY 1

AM	Rising Sign	PM	Rising Sign
1	Libra	1	Taurus
2	Scorpio	2	Gemini
3	Scorpio	3	Gemini
4	Scorpio	4	Cancer
5	Sagittarius	5	Cancer
6	Sagittarius	6	Cancer
7	Capricorn	7	Leo
8	Capricorn	8	Leo
9	Aquarius	9	Virgo
10	Aquarius	10	Virgo
11	Pisces	11	Virgo
12 noon	Aries	12 midnight	Libra

JANUARY 4

AM	Rising Sign	PM	Rising Sign
1	Libra	1	Taurus
2	Scorpio	2	Gemini
3	Scorpio	3	Gemini
4	Scorpio	4	Cancer
5	Sagittarius	5	Cancer
6	Sagittarius	6	Leo
7	Capricorn	7	Leo
8	Capricorn	8	Leo
9	Aquarius	9	Virgo
10	Pisces	10	Virgo
11	Pisces	11	Virgo
12 noon	Aries	12 midnight	Libra

JANUARY 7

AM	Rising Sign	PM	Rising Sign
1	Libra	1	Taurus
2	Scorpio	2	Gemini
3	Scorpio	3	Gemini
4	Scorpio	4	Cancer
5	Sagittarius	5	Cancer
6	Sagittarius	6	Leo
7	Capricorn	7	Leo
8	Capricorn	8	Leo
9	Aquarius	9	Virgo
10	Pisces	10	Virgo
11	Aries	11	Libra
12 noon	Aries	12 midnight	Libra

JANUARY 10

AM	Rising Sign	PM	Rising Sign
1	Libra	1	Taurus
2	Scorpio	2	Gemini
3	Scorpio	3	Gemini
4	Sagittarius	4	Cancer
5	Sagittarius	5	Cancer
6	Sagittarius	6	Leo
7	Capricorn	7	Leo
8	Capricorn	8	Leo
9	Aquarius	9	Virgo
10	Pisces	10	Virgo
11	Aries	11	Libra
12 noon	Taurus	12 midnight	Libra

JANUARY 19

AM	Rising Sign	PM	Rising Sign
1	Scorpio	1	Gemini
2	Scorpio	2	Gemini
3	Scorpio	3	Cancer
4	Sagittarius	4	Cancer
5	Sagittarius	5	Leo
6	Capricorn	6	Leo
7	Capricorn	7	Leo
8	Aquarius	8	Virgo
9	Pisces	9	Virgo
10	Pisces	10	Virgo
11	Aries	11	Libra
12 noon	Taurus	12 midnight	Libra

JANUARY 22

AM	Rising Sign	PM	Rising Sign
1	Scorpio	1	Gemini
2	Scorpio	2	Gemini
3	Scorpio	3	Cancer
4	Sagittarius	4	Cancer
5	Sagittarius	5	Leo
6	Capricorn	6	Leo
7	Capricorn	7	Leo
8	Aquarius	8	Virgo
9	Pisces	9	Virgo
10	Aries	10	Libra
11	Aries	11	Libra
12 noon	Taurus	12 midnight	Libra

JANUARY 25

AM	Rising Sign	PM	Rising Sign
1	Scorpio	1	Gemini
2	Scorpio	2	Gemini
3	Sagittarius	3	Cancer
4	Sagittarius	4	Cancer
5	Sagittarius	5	Leo
6	Capricorn	6	Leo
7	Capricorn	7	Leo
8	Aquarius	8	Virgo
9	Pisces	9	Virgo
10	Aries	10	Libra
11	Taurus	11	Libra
12 noon	Taurus	12 midnight	Libra

JANUARY 28

AM	Rising Sign	PM	Rising Sign
1	Scorpio	1	Gemini
2	Scorpio	2	Gemini
3	Sagittarius	3	Cancer
4	Sagittarius	4	Cancer
5	Capricorn	5	Leo
6	Capricorn	6	Leo
7	Aquarius	7	Virgo
8	Aquarius	8	Virgo
9	Pisces	9	Virgo
10	Aries	10	Libra
11	Taurus	11	Libra
12 noon	Taurus	12 midnight	Libra

JANUARY 31

AM	Rising Sign	PM	Rising Sign
1	Scorpio	1	Gemini
2	Scorpio	2	Cancer
3	Sagittarius	3	Cancer
4	Sagittarius	4	Cancer
5	Capricorn	5	Leo
6	Capricorn	6	Leo
7	Aquarius	7	Virgo
8	Aquarius	8	Virgo
9	Pisces	9	Virgo
10	Aries	10	Libra
11	Taurus	11	Libra
12 noon	Gemini	12 midnight	Scorpio

FEBRUARY 3

AM	Rising Sign	PM	Rising Sign
1	Scorpio	1	Gemini
2	Scorpio	2	Cancer
3	Sagittarius	3	Cancer
4	Sagittarius	4	Leo
5	Capricorn	5	Leo
6	Capricorn	6	Leo
7	Aquarius	7	Virgo
8	Pisces	8	Virgo
9	Pisces	9	Virgo
10	Aries	10	Libra
11	Taurus	11	Libra
12 noon	Gemini	12 midnight	Scorpio

FEBRUARY 6

AM	Rising Sign	PM	Rising Sign
1	Scorpio	1	Gemini
2	Scorpio	2	Cancer
3	Sagittarius	3	Cancer
4	Sagittarius	4	Leo
5	Capricorn	5	Leo
6	Capricorn	6	Leo
7	Aquarius	7	Virgo
8	Pisces	8	Virgo
9	Aries	9	Libra
10	Aries	10	Libra
11	Taurus	11	Libra
12 noon	Gemini	12 midnight	Scorpio

FEBRUARY 9

AM	Rising Sign	PM	Rising Sign
1	Scorpio	1	Gemini
2	Sagittarius	2	Cancer
3	Sagittarius	3	Cancer
4	Sagittarius	4	Leo
5	Capricorn	5	Leo
6	Capricorn	6	Leo
7	Aquarius	7	Virgo
8	Pisces	8	Virgo
9	Aries	9	Libra
10	Taurus	10	Libra
11	Taurus	11	Libra
12 noon	Gemini	12 midnight	Scorpio

FEBRUARY 12

AM	Rising Sign	PM	Rising Sign
1	Scorpio	1	Gemini
2	Sagittarius	2	Cancer
3	Sagittarius	3	Cancer
4	Capricorn	4	Leo
5	Capricorn	5	Leo
6	Aquarius	6	Virgo
7	Aquarius	7	Virgo
8	Pisces	8	Virgo
9	Aries	9	Libra
10	Taurus	10	Libra
11	Taurus	11	Libra
12 noon	Gemini	12 midnight	Scorpio

FEBRUARY 15

AM	Rising Sign	PM	Rising Sign
1	Scorpio	1	Cancer
2	Sagittarius	2	Cancer
3	Sagittarius	3	Cancer
4	Capricorn	4	Leo
5	Capricorn	5	Leo
6	Aquarius	6	Virgo
7	Aquarius	7	Virgo
8	Pisces	8	Virgo
9	Aries	9	Libra
10	Taurus	10	Libra
11	Gemini	11	Scorpio
12 noon	Gemini	12 midnight	Scorpio

FEBRUARY 18

AM	Rising Sign	PM	Rising Sign
1	Scorpio	1	Cancer
2	Sagittarius	2	Cancer
3	Sagittarius	3	Leo
4	Capricorn	4	Leo
5	Capricorn	5	Leo
6	Aquarius	6	Virgo
7	Pisces	7	Virgo
8	Pisces	8	Virgo
9	Aries	9	Libra
10	Taurus	10	Libra
11	Gemini	11	Scorpio
12 noon	Gemini	12 midnight	Scorpio

FEBRUARY 21

AM	Rising Sign	PM	Rising Sign
1	Scorpio	1	Cancer
2	Sagittarius	2	Cancer
3	Sagittarius	3	Leo
4	Capricorn	4	Leo
5	Capricorn	5	Leo
6	Aquarius	6	Virgo
7	Pisces	7	Virgo
8	Aries	8	Libra
9	Aries	9	Libra
10	Taurus	10	Libra
11	Gemini	11	Scorpio
12 noon	Gemini	12 midnight	Scorpio

FEBRUARY 24

AM	Rising Sign	PM	Rising Sign
1	Sagittarius	1	Cancer
2	Sagittarius	2	Cancer
3	Sagittarius	3	Leo
4	Capricorn	4	Leo
5	Capricorn	5	Leo
6	Aquarius	6	Virgo
7	Pisces	7	Virgo
8	Aries	8	Virgo
9	Taurus	9	Libra
10	Taurus	10	Libra
11	Gemini	11	Scorpio
12 noon	Gemini	12 midnight	Scorpio

FEBRUARY 27

AM	Rising Sign	PM	Rising Sign
1	Sagittarius	1	Cancer
2	Sagittarius	2	Cancer
3	Capricorn	3	Leo
4	Capricorn	4	Leo
5	Aquarius	5	Virgo
6	Aquarius	6	Virgo
7	Pisces	7	Virgo
8	Aries	8	Libra
9	Taurus	9	Libra
10	Taurus	10	Libra
11	Gemini	11	Scorpio
12 noon	Gemini	12 midnight	Scorpio

MARCH 2

AM	Rising Sign	PM	Rising Sign
1	Sagittarius	1	Cancer
2	Sagittarius	2	Cancer
3	Capricorn	3	Leo
4	Capricorn	4	Leo
5	Aquarius	5	Virgo
6	Aquarius	6	Virgo
7	Pisces	7	Virgo
8	Aries	8	Libra
9	Taurus	9	Libra
10	Gemini	10	Scorpio
11	Gemini	11	Scorpio
12 noon	Cancer	12 midnight	Scorpio

MARCH 5

AM	Rising Sign	PM	Rising Sign
1	Sagittarius	1	Cancer
2	Sagittarius	2	Cancer
3	Capricorn	3	Leo
4	Capricorn	4	Leo
5	Aquarius	5	Virgo
6	Pisces	6	Virgo
7	Pisces	7	Virgo
8	Aries	8	Libra
9	Taurus	9	Libra
10	Gemini	10	Scorpio
11	Gemini	11	Scorpio
12 noon	Cancer	12 midnight	Scorpio

MARCH 8

AM	Rising Sign	PM	Rising Sign
1	Sagittarius	1	Cancer
2	Sagittarius	2	Leo
3	Capricorn	3	Leo
4	Capricorn	4	Leo
5	Aquarius	5	Virgo
6	Pisces	6	Virgo
7	Aries	7	Libra
8	Aries	8	Libra
9	Taurus	9	Libra
10	Gemini	10	Scorpio
11	Gemini	11	Scorpio
12 noon	Cancer	12 midnight	Scorpio

MARCH 11

AM	Rising Sign	PM	Rising Sign
1	Sagittarius	1	Cancer
2	Sagittarius	2	Leo
3	Capricorn	3	Leo
4	Capricorn	4	Leo
5	Aquarius	5	Virgo
6	Pisces	6	Virgo
7	Aries	7	Libra
8	Taurus	8	Libra
9	Taurus	9	Libra
10	Gemini	10	Scorpio
11	Gemini	11	Scorpio
12 noon	Cancer	12 midnight	Sagittarius

MARCH 14

AM	Rising Sign	PM	Rising Sign
1	Sagittarius	1	Cancer
2	Sagittarius	2	Leo
3	Capricorn	3	Leo
4	Aquarius	4	Leo
5	Aquarius	5	Virgo
6	Pisces	6	Virgo
7	Aries	7	Libra
8	Taurus	8	Libra
9	Taurus	9	Libra
10	Gemini	10	Scorpio
11	Gemini	11	Scorpio
12 noon	Cancer	12 midnight	Sagittarius

MARCH 17

AM	Rising Sign	PM	Rising Sign
1	Sagittarius	1	Cancer
2	Capricorn	2	Leo
3	Capricorn	3	Leo
4	Aquarius	4	Virgo
5	Aquarius	5	Virgo
6	Pisces	6	Virgo
7	Aries	7	Libra
8	Taurus	8	Libra
9	Gemini	9	Scorpio
10	Gemini	10	Scorpio
11	Cancer	11	Scorpio
12 noon	Cancer	12 midnight	Sagittarius

MARCH 20

AM	Rising Sign	PM	Rising Sign
1	Sagittarius	1	Cancer
2	Capricorn	2	Leo
3	Capricorn	3	Leo
4	Aquarius	4	Virgo
5	Pisces	5	Virgo
6	Pisces	6	Virgo
7	Aries	7	Libra
8	Taurus	8	Libra
9	Gemini	9	Scorpio
10	Gemini	10	Scorpio
11	Cancer	11	Scorpio
12 noon	Cancer	12 midnight	Sagittarius

MARCH 23

AM	Rising Sign	PM	Rising Sign
1	Sagittarius	1	Leo
2	Capricorn	2	Leo
3	Capricorn	3	Leo
4	Aquarius	4	Virgo
5	Pisces	5	Virgo
6	Aries	6	Libra
7	Aries	7	Libra
8	Taurus	8	Libra
9	Gemini	9	Scorpio
10	Gemini	10	Scorpio
11	Cancer	11	Scorpio
12 noon	Cancer	12 midnight	Sagittarius

MARCH 26

AM	Rising Sign	PM	Rising Sign
1	Sagittarius	1	Leo
2	Capricorn	2	Leo
3	Capricorn	3	Leo
4	Aquarius	4	Virgo
5	Pisces	5	Virgo
6	Aries	6	Libra
7	Taurus	7	Libra
8	Taurus	8	Libra
9	Gemini	9	Scorpio
10	Gemini	10	Scorpio
11	Cancer	11	Sagittarius
12 noon	Cancer	12 midnight	Sagittarius

MARCH 29

AM	Rising Sign	PM	Rising Sign
1	Sagittarius	1	Leo
2	Capricorn	2	Leo
3	Aquarius	3	Leo
4	Aquarius	4	Virgo
5	Pisces	5	Virgo
6	Aries	6	Libra
7	Taurus	7	Libra
8	Taurus	8	Libra
9	Gemini	9	Scorpio
10	Gemini	10	Scorpio
11	Cancer	11	Sagittarius
12 noon	Cancer	12 midnight	Sagittarius

APRIL 1

AM	Rising Sign	PM	Rising Sign
1	Capricorn	1	Leo
2	Capricorn	2	Leo
3	Aquarius	3	Virgo
4	Aquarius	4	Virgo
5	Pisces	5	Virgo
6	Aries	6	Libra
7	Taurus	7	Libra
8	Gemini	8	Scorpio
9	Gemini	9	Scorpio
10	Cancer	10	Scorpio
11	Cancer	11	Sagittarius
12 noon	Cancer	12 midnight	Sagittarius

APRIL 4

AM	Rising Sign	PM	Rising Sign
1	Capricorn	1	Leo
2	Capricorn	2	Leo
3	Aquarius	3	Virgo
4	Pisces	4	Virgo
5	Pisces	5	Virgo
6	Aries	6	Libra
7	Taurus	7	Libra
8	Gemini	8	Scorpio
9	Gemini	9	Scorpio
10	Cancer	10	Scorpio
11	Cancer	11	Sagittarius
12 noon	Cancer	12 midnight	Sagittarius

APRIL 7

AM	Rising Sign	PM	Rising Sign
1	Capricorn	1	Leo
2	Capricorn	2	Leo
3	Aquarius	3	Virgo
4	Pisces	4	Virgo
5	Aries	5	Libra
6	Aries	6	Libra
7	Taurus	7	Libra
8	Gemini	8	Scorpio
9	Gemini	9	Scorpio
10	Cancer	10	Scorpio
11	Cancer	11	Sagittarius
12 noon	Leo	12 midnight	Sagittarius

APRIL 10

AM	Rising Sign	PM	Rising Sign
1	Capricorn	1	Leo
2	Capricorn	2	Leo
3	Aquarius	3	Virgo
4	Pisces	4	Virgo
5	Aries	5	Libra
6	Taurus	6	Libra
7	Taurus	7	Libra
8	Gemini	8	Scorpio
9	Gemini	9	Scorpio
10	Cancer	10	Sagittarius
11	Cancer	11	Sagittarius
12 noon	Leo	12 midnight	Sagittarius

APRIL 13

AM	Rising Sign	PM	Rising Sign
1	Capricorn	1	Leo
2	Capricorn	2	Leo
3	Aquarius	3	Virgo
4	Pisces	4	Virgo
5	Aries	5	Libra
6	Taurus	6	Libra
7	Taurus	7	Libra
8	Gemini	8	Scorpio
9	Gemini	9	Scorpio
10	Cancer	10	Sagittarius
11	Cancer	11	Sagittarius
12 noon	Leo	12 midnight	Capricorn

APRIL 16

AM	Rising Sign	PM	Rising Sign
1	Capricorn	1	Leo
2	Aquarius	2	Virgo
3	Aquarius	3	Virgo
4	Pisces	4	Virgo
5	Aries	5	Libra
6	Taurus	6	Libra
7	Gemini	7	Scorpio
8	Gemini	8	Scorpio
9	Cancer	9	Scorpio
10	Cancer	10	Sagittarius
11	Cancer	11	Sagittarius
12 noon	Leo	12 midnight	Capricorn

APRIL 19

AM	Rising Sign	PM	Rising Sign
1	Capricorn	1	Leo
2	Aquarius	2	Virgo
3	Aquarius	3	Virgo
4	Pisces	4	Virgo
5	Aries	5	Libra
6	Taurus	6	Libra
7	Gemini	7	Scorpio
8	Gemini	8	Scorpio
9	Cancer	9	Scorpio
10	Cancer	10	Sagittarius
11	Cancer	11	Sagittarius
12 noon	Leo	12 midnight	Capricorn

APRIL 22

AM	Rising Sign	PM	Rising Sign
1	Capricorn	1	Leo
2	Aquarius	2	Virgo
3	Pisces	3	Virgo
4	Aries	4	Libra
5	Aries	5	Libra
6	Taurus	6	Libra
7	Gemini	7	Scorpio
8	Gemini	8	Scorpio
9	Cancer	9	Scorpio
10	Cancer	10	Sagittarius
11	Leo	11	Sagittarius
12 noon	Leo	12 midnight	Capricorn

APRIL 25

AM	Rising Sign	PM	Rising Sign
1	Capricorn	1	Leo
2	Aquarius	2	Virgo
3	Pisces	3	Virgo
4	Aries	4	Libra
5	Taurus	5	Libra
6	Taurus	6	Libra
7	Gemini	7	Scorpio
8	Gemini	8	Scorpio
9	Cancer	9	Sagittarius
10	Cancer	10	Sagittarius
11	Leo	11	Sagittarius
12 noon	Leo	12 midnight	Capricorn

APRIL 28

AM	Rising Sign	PM	Rising Sign
1	Aquarius	1	Leo
2	Aquarius	2	Virgo
3	Pisces	3	Virgo
4	Aries	4	Libra
5	Taurus	5	Libra
6	Taurus	6	Libra
7	Gemini	7	Scorpio
8	Gemini	8	Scorpio
9	Cancer	9	Sagittarius
10	Cancer	10	Sagittarius
11	Leo	11	Sagittarius
12 noon	Leo	12 midnight	Capricorn

MAY 1

AM	Rising Sign	PM	Rising Sign
1	Aquarius	1	Virgo
2	Aquarius	2	Virgo
3	Pisces	3	Virgo
4	Aries	4	Libra
5	Taurus	5	Libra
6	Taurus	6	Scorpio
7	Gemini	7	Scorpio
8	Cancer	8	Scorpio
9	Cancer	9	Sagittarius
10	Cancer	10	Sagittarius
11	Leo	11	Capricorn
12 noon	Leo	12 midnight	Capricorn

MAY 4

AM	Rising Sign	PM	Rising Sign
1	Aquarius	1	Virgo
2	Aquarius	2	Virgo
3	Pisces	3	Virgo
4	Aries	4	Libra
5	Taurus	5	Libra
6	Gemini	6	Scorpio
7	Gemini	7	Scorpio
8	Cancer	8	Scorpio
9	Cancer	9	Sagittarius
10	Cancer	10	Sagittarius
11	Leo	11	Capricorn
12 noon	Leo	12 midnight	Capricorn

MAY 7

AM	Rising Sign	PM	Rising Sign
1	Aquarius	7	Virgo
2	Pisces	2	Virgo
3	Aries	3	Libra
4	Aries	4	Libra
5	Taurus	5	Libra
6	Gemini	6	Scorpio
7	Gemini	7	Scorpio
8	Cancer	8	Scorpio
9	Cancer	9	Sagittarius
10	Leo	10	Sagittarius
11	Leo	11	Capricorn
12 noon	Leo	12 midnight	Capricorn

MAY 10

AM	Rising Sign	PM	Rising Sign
1	Aquarius	1	Virgo
2	Pisces	2	Virgo
3	Aries	3	Libra
4	Aries	4	Libra
5	Taurus	5	Libra
6	Gemini	6	Scorpio
7	Gemini	7	Scorpio
8	Cancer	8	Sagittarius
9	Cancer	9	Sagittarius
10	Leo	10	Sagittarius
11	Leo	11	Capricorn
12 noon	Leo	12 midnight	Capricorn

MAY 13

AM	Rising Sign	PM	Rising Sign
1	Aquarius	1	Virgo
2	Pisces	2	Virgo
3	Aries	3	Libra
4	Taurus	4	Libra
5	Taurus	5	Libra
6	Gemini	6	Scorpio
7	Gemini	7	Scorpio
8	Cancer	8	Sagittarius
9	Cancer	9	Sagittarius
10	Leo	10	Sagittarius
11	Leo	11	Capricorn
12 noon	Leo	12 midnight	Aquarius

MAY 16

AM	Rising Sign	PM	Rising Sign
1	Aquarius	1	Virgo
2	Pisces	2	Virgo
3	Aries	3	Libra
4	Taurus	4	Libra
5	Taurus	5	Scorpio
6	Gemini	6	Scorpio
7	Cancer	7	Scorpio
8	Cancer	8	Sagittarius
9	Cancer	9	Sagittarius
10	Leo	10	Capricorn
11	Leo	11	Capricorn
12 noon	Virgo	12 midnight	Aquarius

MAY 19

AM	Rising Sign	PM	Rising Sign
1	Aquarius	1	Virgo
2	Pisces	2	Virgo
3	Aries	3	Libra
4	Taurus	4	Libra
5	Gemini	5	Scorpio
6	Gemini	6	Scorpio
7	Cancer	7	Scorpio
8	Cancer	8	Sagittarius
9	Cancer	9	Sagittarius
10	Leo	10	Capricorn
11	Leo	11	Capricorn
12 noon	Virgo	12 midnight	Aquarius

MAY 22

AM	Rising Sign	PM	Rising Sign
1	Pisces	1	Virgo
2	Pisces	2	Libra
3	Aries	3	Libra
4	Taurus	4	Libra
5	Gemini	5	Scorpio
6	Gemini	6	Scorpio
7	Cancer	7	Scorpio
8	Cancer	8	Sagittarius
9	Leo	9	Sagittarius
10	Leo	10	Capricorn
11	Leo	11	Capricorn
12 noon	Virgo	12 midnight	Aquarius

MAY 25

AM	Rising Sign	PM	Rising Sign
1	Pisces	1	Virgo
2	Aries	2	Libra
3	Aries	3	Libra
4	Taurus	4	Libra
5	Gemini	5	Scorpio
6	Gemini	6	Scorpio
7	Cancer	7	Sagittarius
8	Cancer	8	Sagittarius
9	Leo	9	Sagittarius
10	Leo	10	Capricorn
11	Leo	11	Capricorn
12 noon	Virgo	12 midnight	Aquarius

MAY 28

AM	Rising Sign	PM	Rising Sign
1	Pisces	1	Virgo
2	Aries	2	Libra
3	Taurus	3	Libra
4	Taurus	4	Libra
5	Gemini	5	Scorpio
6	Gemini	6	Scorpio
7	Cancer	7	Sagittarius
8	Cancer	8	Sagittarius
9	Leo	9	Sagittarius
10	Leo	10	Capricorn
11	Leo	11	Aquarius
12 noon	Virgo	12 midnight	Aquarius

MAY 31

AM	Rising Sign	PM	Rising Sign
1	Pisces	1	Virgo
2	Aries	2	Libra
3	Taurus	3	Libra
4	Taurus	4	Scorpio
5	Gemini	5	Scorpio
6	Cancer	6	Scorpio
7	Cancer	7	Sagittarius
8	Cancer	8	Sagittarius
9	Leo	9	Capricorn
10	Leo	10	Capricorn
11	Virgo	11	Aquarius
12 noon	Virgo	12 midnight	Aquarius

JUNE 3

AM	Rising Sign	PM	Rising Sign
1	Pisces	1	Virgo
2	Aries	2	Libra
3	Taurus	3	Libra
4	Gemini	4	Scorpio
5	Gemini	5	Scorpio
6	Cancer	6	Scorpio
7	Cancer	7	Sagittarius
8	Cancer	8	Sagittarius
9	Leo	9	Capricorn
10	Leo	10	Capricorn
11	Virgo	11	Aquarius
12 noon	Virgo	12 midnight	Pisces

JUNE 6

AM	Rising Sign	PM	Rising Sign
1	Pisces	1	Libra
2	Aries	2	Libra
3	Taurus	3	Libra
4	Gemini	4	Scorpio
5	Gemini	5	Scorpio
6	Cancer	6	Scorpio
7	Cancer	7	Sagittarius
8	Leo	8	Sagittarius
9	Leo	9	Capricorn
10	Leo	10	Capricorn
11	Virgo	11	Aquarius
12 noon	Virgo	12 midnight	Pisces

JUNE 9

AM	Rising Sign	PM	Rising Sign
1	Aries	1	Libra
2	Aries	2	Libra
3	Taurus	3	Libra
4	Gemini	4	Scorpio
5	Gemini	5	Scorpio
6	Cancer	6	Sagittarius
7	Cancer	7	Sagittarius
8	Leo	8	Sagittarius
9	Leo	9	Capricorn
10	Leo	10	Capricorn
11	Virgo	11	Aquarius
12 noon	Virgo	12 midnight	Pisces

JUNE 12

AM	Rising Sign	PM	Rising Sign
1	Aries	1	Libra
2	Taurus	2	Libra
3	Taurus	3	Libra
4	Gemini	4	Scorpio
5	Gemini	5	Scorpio
6	Cancer	6	Sagittarius
7	Cancer	7	Sagittarius
8	Leo	8	Sagittarius
9	Leo	9	Capricorn
10	Leo	10	Capricorn
11	Virgo	11	Aquarius
12 noon	Virgo	12 midnight	Pisces

JUNE 15

AM	Rising Sign	PM	Rising Sign
1	Aries	1	Libra
2	Taurus	2	Libra
3	Taurus	3	Scorpio
4	Gemini	4	Scorpio
5	Gemini	5	Scorpio
6	Cancer	6	Sagittarius
7	Cancer	7	Sagittarius
8	Leo	8	Capricorn
9	Leo	9	Capricorn
10	Virgo	10	Aquarius
11	Virgo	11	Aquarius
12 noon	Virgo	12 midnight	Pisces

JUNE 18

AM	Rising Sign	PM	Rising Sign
1	Aries	1	Libra
2	Taurus	2	Libra
3	Gemini	3	Scorpio
4	Gemini	4	Scorpio
5	Cancer	5	Scorpio
6	Cancer	6	Sagittarius
7	Cancer	7	Sagittarius
8	Leo	8	Capricorn
9	Leo	9	Capricorn
10	Virgo	10	Aquarius
11	Virgo	11	Aquarius
12 noon	Virgo	12 midnight	Pisces

JUNE 21

AM	Rising Sign	PM	Rising Sign
1	Aries	1	Libra
2	Taurus	2	Libra
3	Gemini	3	Scorpio
4	Gemini	4	Scorpio
5	Cancer	5	Scorpio
6	Cancer	6	Sagittarius
7	Leo	7	Sagittarius
8	Leo	8	Capricorn
9	Leo	9	Capricorn
10	Virgo	10	Aquarius
11	Virgo	11	Pisces
12 noon	Libra	12 midnight	Aries

JUNE 24

AM	Rising Sign	PM	Rising Sign
1	Aries	1	Libra
2	Taurus	2	Libra
3	Gemini	3	Scorpio
4	Gemini	4	Scorpio
5	Cancer	5	Sagittarius
6	Cancer	6	Sagittarius
7	Leo	7	Sagittarius
8	Leo	8	Capricorn
9	Leo	9	Capricorn
10	Virgo	10	Aquarius
11	Virgo	11	Pisces
12 noon	Libra	12 midnight	Aries

JUNE 27

AM	Rising Sign	PM	Rising Sign
1	Taurus	1	Libra
2	Taurus	2	Libra
3	Gemini	3	Scorpio
4	Gemini	4	Scorpio
5	Cancer	5	Sagittarius
6	Cancer	6	Sagittarius
7	Leo	7	Sagittarius
8	Leo	8	Capricorn
9	Leo	9	Capricorn
10	Virgo	10	Aquarius
11	Virgo	11	Pisces
12 noon	Libra	12 midnight	Aries

JUNE 30

AM	Rising Sign	PM	Rising Sign
1	Taurus	1	Libra
2	Taurus	2	Scorpio
3	Gemini	3	Scorpio
4	Gemini	4	Scorpio
5	Cancer	5	Sagittarius
6	Cancer	6	Sagittarius
7	Leo	7	Capricorn
8	Leo	8	Capricorn
9	Virgo	9	Aquarius
10	Virgo	10	Aquarius
11	Virgo	11	Pisces
12 noon	Libra	12 midnight	Aries

JULY 3

AM	Rising Sign	PM	Rising Sign
1	Taurus	1	Libra
2	Gemini	2	Scorpio
3	Gemini	3	Scorpio
4	Cancer	4	Scorpio
5	Cancer	5	Sagittarius
6	Cancer	6	Sagittarius
7	Leo	7	Capricorn
8	Leo	8	Capricorn
9	Virgo	9	Aquarius
10	Virgo	10	Aquarius
11	Virgo	11	Pisces
12 noon	Libra	12 midnight	Aries

JULY 6

AM	Rising Sign	PM	Rising Sign
1	Taurus	1	Libra
2	Gemini	2	Scorpio
3	Gemini	3	Scorpio
4	Cancer	4	Scorpio
5	Cancer	5	Sagittarius
6	Leo	6	Sagittarius
7	Leo	7	Capricorn
8	Leo	8	Capricorn
9	Virgo	9	Aquarius
10	Virgo	10	Pisces
11	Virgo	11	Aries
12 noon	Libra	12 midnight	Aries

JULY 9

AM	Rising Sign	PM	Rising Sign
1	Taurus	1	Libra
2	Gemini	2	Scorpio
3	Gemini	3	Scorpio
4	Cancer	4	Sagittarius
5	Cancer	5	Sagittarius
6	Leo	6	Sagittarius
7	Leo	7	Capricorn
8	Leo	8	Capricorn
9	Virgo	9	Aquarius
10	Virgo	10	Pisces
11	Libra	11	Aries
12 noon	Libra	12 midnight	Aries

JULY 12

AM	Rising Sign	PM	Rising Sign
1	Taurus	1	Libra
2	Gemini	2	Scorpio
3	Gemini	3	Scorpio
4	Cancer	4	Sagittarius
5	Cancer	5	Sagittarius
6	Leo	6	Sagittarius
7	Leo	7	Capricorn
8	Leo	8	Capricorn
9	Virgo	9	Aquarius
10	Virgo	10	Pisces
11	Libra	11	Aries
12 noon	Libra	12 midnight	Taurus

JULY 15

AM	Rising Sign	PM	Rising Sign
1	Taurus	1	Scorpio
2	Gemini	2	Scorpio
3	Gemini	3	Scorpio
4	Cancer	4	Sagittarius
5	Cancer	5	Sagittarius
6	Leo	6	Capricorn
7	Leo	7	Capricorn
8	Virgo	8	Aquarius
9	Virgo	9	Aquarius
10	Virgo	10	Pisces
11	Libra	11	Aries
12 noon	Libra	12 midnight	Taurus

JULY 18

AM	Rising Sign	PM	Rising Sign
1	Gemini	1	Scorpio
2	Gemini	2	Scorpio
3	Cancer	3	Scorpio
4	Cancer	4	Sagittarius
5	Cancer	5	Sagittarius
6	Leo	6	Capricorn
7	Leo	7	Capricorn
8	Virgo	8	Aquarius
9	Virgo	9	Aquarius
10	Virgo	10	Pisces
11	Libra	11	Aries
12 noon	Libra	12 midnight	Taurus

JULY 21

AM	Rising Sign	PM	Rising Sign
1	Gemini	1	Scorpio
2	Gemini	2	Scorpio
3	Cancer	3	Scorpio
4	Cancer	4	Sagittarius
5	Leo	5	Sagittarius
6	Leo	6	Capricorn
7	Leo	7	Capricorn
8	Virgo	8	Aquarius
9	Virgo	9	Pisces
10	Virgo	10	Pisces
11	Libra	11	Aries
12 noon	Libra	12 midnight	Taurus

JULY 24

AM	Rising Sign	PM	Rising Sign
1	Gemini	1	Scorpio
2	Gemini	2	Scorpio
3	Cancer	3	Sagittarius
4	Cancer	4	Sagittarius
5	Leo	5	Sagittarius
6	Leo	6	Capricorn
7	Leo	7	Capricorn
8	Virgo	8	Aquarius
9	Virgo	9	Pisces
10	Libra	10	Aries
11	Libra	11	Aries
12 noon	Libra	12 midnight	Taurus

JULY 27

AM	Rising Sign	PM	Rising Sign
1	Gemini	1	Scorpio
2	Gemini	2	Scorpio
3	Cancer	3	Sagittarius
4	Cancer	4	Sagittarius
5	Leo	5	Sagittarius
6	Leo	6	Capricorn
7	Leo	7	Capricorn
8	Virgo	8	Aquarius
9	Virgo	9	Pisces
10	Libra	10	Aries
11	Libra	11	Taurus
12 noon	Libra	12 midnight	Taurus

JULY 30

AM	Rising Sign	PM	Rising Sign
1	Gemini	1	Scorpio
2	Gemini	2	Scorpio
3	Cancer	3	Sagittarius
4	Cancer	4	Sagittarius
5	Leo	5	Capricorn
6	Leo	6	Capricorn
7	Virgo	7	Aquarius
8	Virgo	8	Aquarius
9	Virgo	9	Pisces
10	Libra	10	Aries
11	Libra	11	Taurus
12 noon	Scorpio	12 midnight	Taurus

AUGUST 2

AM	Rising Sign	PM	Rising Sign
1	Gemini	1	Scorpio
2	Cancer	2	Scorpio
3	Cancer	3	Sagittarius
4	Cancer	4	Sagittarius
5	Leo	5	Capricorn
6	Leo	6	Capricorn
7	Virgo	7	Aquarius
8	Virgo	8	Aquarius
9	Virgo	9	Pisces
10	Libra	10	Aries
11	Libra	11	Taurus
12 noon	Scorpio	12 midnight	Gemini

AUGUST 5

AM	Rising Sign	PM	Rising Sign
1	Gemini	1	Scorpio
2	Cancer	2	Scorpio
3	Cancer	3	Sagittarius
4	Leo	4	Sagittarius
5	Leo	5	Capricorn
6	Leo	6	Capricorn
7	Virgo	7	Aquarius
8	Virgo	8	Pisces
9	Virgo	9	Pisces
10	Libra	10	Aries
11	Libra	11	Taurus
12 noon	Scorpio	12 midnight	Gemini

AUGUST 8

AM	Rising Sign	PM	Rising Sign
1	Gemini	1	Scorpio
2	Cancer	2	Sagittarius
3	Cancer	3	Sagittarius
4	Leo	4	Sagittarius
5	Leo	5	Capricorn
6	Leo	6	Capricorn
7	Virgo	7	Aquarius
8	Virgo	8	Pisces
9	Libra	9	Aries
10	Libra	10	Aries
11	Libra	11	Taurus
12 noon	Scorpio	12 midnight	Gemini

AUGUST 11

AM	Rising Sign	PM	Rising Sign
1	Gemini	1	Scorpio
2	Cancer	2	Sagittarius
3	Cancer	3	Sagittarius
4	Leo	4	Sagittarius
5	Leo	5	Capricorn
6	Leo	6	Capricorn
7	Virgo	7	Aquarius
8	Virgo	8	Pisces
9	Libra	9	Aries
10	Libra	10	Taurus
11	Libra	11	Taurus
12 noon	Scorpio	12 midnight	Gemini

AUGUST 14

AM	Rising Sign	PM	Rising Sign
1	Gemini	1	Scorpio
2	Cancer	2	Sagittarius
3	Cancer	3	Sagittarius
4	Leo	4	Capricorn
5	Leo	5	Capricorn
6	Virgo	6	Aquarius
7	Virgo	7	Aquarius
8	Virgo	8	Pisces
9	Libra	9	Aries
10	Libra	10	Taurus
11	Libra	11	Taurus
12 noon	Scorpio	12 midnight	Gemini

AUGUST 17

AM	Rising Sign	PM	Rising Sign
1	Cancer	1	Scorpio
2	Cancer	2	Sagittarius
3	Cancer	3	Sagittarius
4	Leo	4	Capricorn
5	Leo	5	Capricorn
6	Virgo	6	Aquarius
7	Virgo	7	Aquarius
8	Virgo	8	Pisces
9	Libra	9	Aries
10	Libra	10	Taurus
11	Scorpio	11	Gemini
12 noon	Scorpio	12 midnight	Gemini

AUGUST 20

AM	Rising Sign	PM	Rising Sign
1	Cancer	1	Scorpio
2	Cancer	2	Sagittarius
3	Cancer	3	Sagittarius
4	Leo	4	Capricorn
5	Leo	5	Capricorn
6	Virgo	6	Aquarius
7	Virgo	7	Pisces
8	Virgo	8	Pisces
9	Libra	9	Aries
10	Libra	10	Taurus
11	Scorpio	11	Gemini
12 noon	Scorpio	12 midnight	Gemini

AUGUST 23

AM	Rising Sign	PM	Rising Sign
1	Cancer	1	Sagittarius
2	Cancer	2	Sagittarius
3	Leo	3	Sagittarius
4	Leo	4	Capricorn
5	Leo	5	Capricorn
6	Virgo	6	Aquarius
7	Virgo	7	Pisces
8	Libra	8	Aries
9	Libra	9	Aries
10	Libra	10	Taurus
11	Scorpio	11	Gemini
12 noon	Scorpio	12 midnight	Gemini

AUGUST 26

AM	Rising Sign	PM	Rising Sign
1	Cancer	1	Sagittarius
2	Cancer	2	Sagittarius
3	Leo	3	Sagittarius
4	Leo	4	Capricorn
5	Leo	5	Capricorn
6	Virgo	6	Aquarius
7	Virgo	7	Pisces
8	Libra	8	Aries
9	Libra	9	Taurus
10	Libra	10	Taurus
11	Scorpio	11	Gemini
12 noon	Scorpio	12 midnight	Gemini

AUGUST 29

AM	Rising Sign	PM	Rising Sign
1	Cancer	1	Sagittarius
2	Cancer	2	Sagittarius
3	Leo	3	Capricorn
4	Leo	4	Capricorn
5	Virgo	5	Aquarius
6	Virgo	6	Aquarius
7	Virgo	7	Pisces
8	Libra	8	Aries
9	Libra	9	Taurus
10	Libra	10	Taurus
11	Scorpio	11	Gemini
12 noon	Scorpio	12 midnight	Gemini

SEPTEMBER 1

AM	Rising Sign	PM	Rising Sign
1	Cancer	1	Sagittarius
2	Cancer	2	Sagittarius
3	Leo	3	Capricorn
4	Leo	4	Capricorn
5	Virgo	5	Aquarius
6	Virgo	6	Aquarius
7	Virgo	7	Pisces
8	Libra	8	Aries
9	Libra	9	Taurus
10	Scorpio	10	Gemini
11	Scorpio	11	Gemini
12 noon	Scorpio	12 midnight	Cancer

SEPTEMBER 4

AM	Rising Sign	PM	Rising Sign
1	Cancer	1	Sagittarius
2	Cancer	2	Sagittarius
3	Leo	3	Capricorn
4	Leo	4	Capricorn
5	Virgo	5	Aquarius
6	Virgo	6	Pisces
7	Virgo	7	Pisces
8	Libra	8	Aries
9	Libra	9	Taurus
10	Scorpio	10	Gemini
11	Scorpio	11	Gemini
12 noon	Scorpio	12 midnight	Cancer

SEPTEMBER 7

AM	Rising Sign	PM	Rising Sign
1	Cancer	1	Sagittarius
2	Leo	2	Sagittarius
3	Leo	3	Capricorn
4	Leo	4	Capricorn
5	Virgo	5	Aquarius
6	Virgo	6	Pisces
7	Libra	7	Aries
8	Libra	8	Aries
9	Libra	9	Taurus
10	Scorpio	10	Gemini
11	Scorpio	11	Gemini
12 noon	Scorpio	12 midnight	Cancer

SEPTEMBER 10

AM	Rising Sign	PM	Rising Sign
1	Cancer	1	Sagittarius
2	Leo	2	Sagittarius
3	Leo	3	Capricorn
4	Leo	4	Capricorn
5	Virgo	5	Aquarius
6	Virgo	6	Pisces
7	Libra	7	Aries
8	Libra	8	Taurus
9	Libra	9	Taurus
10	Scorpio	10	Gemini
11	Scorpio	11	Gemini
12 noon	Sagittarius	12 midnight	Cancer

SEPTEMBER 13

AM	Rising Sign	PM	Rising Sign
1	Cancer	1	Sagittarius
2	Leo	2	Capricorn
3	Leo	3	Capricorn
4	Leo	4	Aquarius
5	Virgo	5	Aquarius
6	Virgo	6	Pisces
7	Libra	7	Aries
8	Libra	8	Taurus
9	Libra	9	Taurus
10	Scorpio	10	Gemini
11	Scorpio	11	Gemini
12 noon	Sagittarius	12 midnight	Cancer

SEPTEMBER 16

AM	Rising Sign	PM	Rising Sign
1	Cancer	1	Sagittarius
2	Leo	2	Capricorn
3	Leo	3	Capricorn
4	Virgo	4	Aquarius
5	Virgo	5	Aquarius
6	Virgo	6	Pisces
7	Libra	7	Aries
8	Libra	8	Taurus
9	Scorpio	9	Gemini
10	Scorpio	10	Gemini
11	Scorpio	11	Cancer
12 noon	Sagittarius	12 midnight	Cancer

SEPTEMBER 19

AM	Rising Sign	PM	Rising Sign
1	Cancer	1	Sagittarius
2	Leo	2	Capricorn
3	Leo	3	Capricorn
4	Virgo	4	Aquarius
5	Virgo	5	Pisces
6	Virgo	6	Pisces
7	Libra	7	Aries
8	Libra	8	Taurus
9	Scorpio	9	Gemini
10	Scorpio	10	Gemini
11	Scorpio	11	Cancer
12 noon	Sagittarius	12 midnight	Cancer

SEPTEMBER 22

AM	Rising Sign	PM	Rising Sign
1	Leo	1	Sagittarius
2	Leo	2	Capricorn
3	Leo	3	Capricorn
4	Virgo	4	Aquarius
5	Virgo	5	Pisces
6	Libra	6	Aries
7	Libra	7	Aries
8	Libra	8	Taurus
9	Scorpio	9	Gemini
10	Scorpio	10	Gemini
11	Scorpio	11	Cancer
12 noon	Sagittarius	12 midnight	Cancer

SEPTEMBER 25

AM	Rising Sign	PM	Rising Sign
1	Leo	1	Sagittarius
2	Leo	2	Capricorn
3	Leo	3	Capricorn
4	Virgo	4	Aquarius
5	Virgo	5	Pisces
6	Libra	6	Aries
7	Libra	7	Taurus
8	Libra	8	Taurus
9	Scorpio	9	Gemini
10	Scorpio	10	Gemini
11	Sagittarius	11	Cancer
12 noon	Sagittarius	12 midnight	Cancer

SEPTEMBER 28

AM	Rising Sign	PM	Rising Sign
1	Leo	1	Capricorn
2	Leo	2	Capricorn
3	Leo	3	Aquarius
4	Virgo	4	Aquarius
5	Virgo	5	Pisces
6	Libra	6	Aries
7	Libra	7	Taurus
8	Libra	8	Taurus
9	Scorpio	9	Gemini
10	Scorpio	10	Gemini
11	Sagittarius	11	Cancer
12 noon	Sagittarius	12 midnight	Cancer

OCTOBER 1

AM	Rising Sign	PM	Rising Sign
1	Leo	1	Capricorn
2	Leo	2	Capricorn
3	Virgo	3	Aquarius
4	Virgo	4	Aquarius
5	Virgo	5	Pisces
6	Libra	6	Aries
7	Libra	7	Taurus
8	Scorpio	8	Gemini
9	Scorpio	9	Gemini
10	Scorpio	10	Cancer
11	Sagittarius	11	Cancer
12 noon	Sagittarius	12 midnight	Cancer

OCTOBER 4

AM	Rising Sign	PM	Rising Sign
1	Leo	1	Capricorn
2	Leo	2	Capricorn
3	Virgo	3	Aquarius
4	Virgo	4	Pisces
5	Virgo	5	Pisces
6	Libra	6	Aries
7	Libra	7	Taurus
8	Scorpio	8	Gemini
9	Scorpio	9	Gemini
10	Scorpio	10	Cancer
11	Sagittarius	11	Cancer
12 noon	Sagittarius	12 midnight	Leo

OCTOBER 7

AM	Rising Sign	PM	Rising Sign
1	Leo	1	Capricorn
2	Leo	2	Capricorn
3	Virgo	3	Aquarius
4	Virgo	4	Pisces
5	Libra	5	Aries
6	Libra	6	Aries
7	Libra	7	Taurus
8	Scorpio	8	Gemini
9	Scorpio	9	Gemini
10	Scorpio	10	Cancer
11	Sagittarius	11	Cancer
12 noon	Sagittarius	12 midnight	Leo

OCTOBER 10

AM	Rising Sign	PM	Rising Sign
1	Leo	1	Capricorn
2	Leo	2	Capricorn
3	Virgo	3	Aquarius
4	Virgo	4	Pisces
5	Libra	5	Aries
6	Libra	6	Taurus
7	Libra	7	Taurus
8	Scorpio	8	Gemini
9	Scorpio	9	Gemini
10	Sagittarius	10	Cancer
11	Sagittarius	11	Cancer
12 noon	Sagittarius	12 midnight	Leo

OCTOBER 13

AM	Rising Sign	PM	Rising Sign
1	Leo	1	Capricorn
2	Leo	2	Aquarius
3	Virgo	3	Aquarius
4	Virgo	4	Pisces
5	Libra	5	Aries
6	Libra	6	Taurus
7	Libra	7	Taurus
8	Scorpio	8	Gemini
9	Scorpio	9	Gemini
10	Sagittarius	10	Cancer
11	Sagittarius	11	Cancer
12 noon	Capricorn	12 midnight	Leo

OCTOBER 16

AM	Rising Sign	PM	Rising Sign
1	Leo	1	Capricorn
2	Virgo	2	Aquarius
3	Virgo	3	Aquarius
4	Virgo	4	Pisces
5	Libra	5	Aries
6	Libra	6	Taurus
7	Scorpio	7	Gemini
8	Scorpio	8	Gemini
9	Scorpio	9	Cancer
10	Sagittarius	10	Cancer
11	Sagittarius	11	Cancer
12 noon	Capricorn	12 midnight	Leo

OCTOBER 19

AM	Rising Sign	PM	Rising Sign
1	Leo	1	Capricorn
2	Virgo	2	Aquarius
3	Virgo	3	Pisces
4	Virgo	4	Pisces
5	Libra	5	Aries
6	Libra	6	Taurus
7	Scorpio	7	Gemini
8	Scorpio	8	Gemini
9	Scorpio	9	Cancer
10	Sagittarius	10	Cancer
11	Sagittarius	11	Cancer
12 noon	Capricorn	12 midnight	Leo

OCTOBER 22

AM	Rising Sign	PM	Rising Sign
1	Leo	1	Capricorn
2	Virgo	2	Aquarius
3	Virgo	3	Pisces
4	Libra	4	Aries
5	Libra	5	Aries
6	Libra	6	Taurus
7	Scorpio	7	Gemini
8	Scorpio	8	Gemini
9	Scorpio	9	Cancer
10	Sagittarius	10	Cancer
11	Sagittarius	11	Leo
12 noon	Capricorn	12 midnight	Leo

OCTOBER 25

AM	Rising Sign	PM	Rising Sign
1	Leo	1	Capricorn
2	Virgo	2	Aquarius
3	Virgo	3	Pisces
4	Libra	4	Aries
5	Libra	5	Taurus
6	Libra	6	Taurus
7	Scorpio	7	Gemini
8	Scorpio	8	Gemini
9	Sagittarius	9	Cancer
10	Sagittarius	10	Cancer
11	Sagittarius	11	Leo
12 noon	Capricorn	12 midnight	Leo

OCTOBER 28

AM	Rising Sign	PM	Rising Sign
1	Leo	1	Aquarius
2	Virgo	2	Aquarius
3	Virgo	3	Pisces
4	Libra	4	Aries
5	Libra	5	Taurus
6	Libra	6	Taurus
7	Scorpio	7	Gemini
8	Scorpio	8	Gemini
9	Sagittarius	9	Cancer
10	Sagittarius	10	Cancer
11	Sagittarius	11	Leo
12 noon	Capricorn	12 midnight	Leo

OCTOBER 31

AM	Rising Sign	PM	Rising Sign
1	Virgo	1	Aquarius
2	Virgo	2	Aquarius
3	Virgo	3	Pisces
4	Libra	4	Aries
5	Libra	5	Taurus
6	Scorpio	6	Gemini
7	Scorpio	7	Gemini
8	Scorpio	8	Cancer
9	Sagittarius	9	Cancer
10	Sagittarius	10	Cancer
11	Capricorn	11	Leo
12 noon	Capricorn	12 midnight	Leo

NOVEMBER 3

AM	Rising Sign	PM	Rising Sign
1	Virgo	1	Aquarius
2	Virgo	2	Pisces
3	Virgo	3	Pisces
4	Libra	4	Aries
5	Libra	5	Taurus
6	Scorpio	6	Gemini
7	Scorpio	7	Gemini
8	Scorpio	8	Cancer
9	Sagittarius	9	Cancer
10	Sagittarius	10	Cancer
11	Capricorn	11	Leo
12 noon	Capricorn	12 midnight	Leo

NOVEMBER 6

AM	Rising Sign	PM	Rising Sign
1	Virgo	1	Aquarius
2	Virgo	2	Pisces
3	Libra	3	Aries
4	Libra	4	Aries
5	Libra	5	Taurus
6	Scorpio	6	Gemini
7	Scorpio	7	Gemini
8	Scorpio	8	Cancer
9	Sagittarius	9	Cancer
10	Sagittarius	10	Leo
11	Capricorn	11	Leo
12 noon	Capricorn	12 midnight	Leo

NOVEMBER 9

AM	Rising Sign	PM	Rising Sign
1	Virgo	1	Aquarius
2	Virgo	2	Pisces
3	Libra	3	Aries
4	Libra	4	Taurus
5	Libra	5	Taurus
6	Scorpio	6	Gemini
7	Scorpio	7	Gemini
8	Sagittarius	8	Cancer
9	Sagittarius	9	Cancer
10	Sagittarius	10	Leo
11	Capricorn	11	Leo
12 noon	Capricorn	12 midnight	Leo

NOVEMBER 12

AM	Rising Sign	PM	Rising Sign
1	Virgo	1	Aquarius
2	Virgo	2	Pisces
3	Libra	3	Aries
4	Libra	4	Taurus
5	Libra	5	Taurus
6	Scorpio	6	Gemini
7	Scorpio	7	Gemini
8	Sagittarius	8	Cancer
9	Sagittarius	9	Cancer
10	Sagittarius	10	Leo
11	Capricorn	11	Leo
12 noon	Aquarius	12 midnight	Leo

NOVEMBER 15

AM	Rising Sign	PM	Rising Sign
1	Virgo	1	Aquarius
2	Virgo	2	Pisces
3	Libra	3	Aries
4	Libra	4	Taurus
5	Scorpio	5	Gemini
6	Scorpio	6	Gemini
7	Scorpio	7	Cancer
8	Sagittarius	8	Cancer
9	Sagittarius	9	Cancer
10	Capricorn	10	Leo
11	Capricorn	11	Leo
12 noon	Aquarius	12 midnight	Virgo

NOVEMBER 18

AM	Rising Sign	PM	Rising Sign
1	Virgo	1	Pisces
2	Virgo	2	Pisces
3	Libra	3	Aries
4	Libra	4	Taurus
5	Scorpio	5	Gemini
6	Scorpio	6	Gemini
7	Scorpio	7	Cancer
8	Sagittarius	8	Cancer
9	Sagittarius	9	Cancer
10	Capricorn	10	Leo
11	Capricorn	11	Leo
12 noon	Aquarius	12 midnight	Virgo

NOVEMBER 21

AM	Rising Sign	PM	Rising Sign
1	Virgo	1	Pisces
2	Libra	2	Aries
3	Libra	3	Aries
4	Libra	4	Taurus
5	Scorpio	5	Gemini
6	Scorpio	6	Gemini
7	Scorpio	7	Cancer
8	Sagittarius	8	Cancer
9	Sagittarius	9	Leo
10	Capricorn	10	Leo
11	Capricorn	11	Leo
12 noon	Aquarius	12 midnight	Virgo

NOVEMBER 24

AM	Rising Sign	PM	Rising Sign
1	Virgo	1	Pisces
2	Libra	2	Aries
3	Libra	3	Taurus
4	Libra	4	Taurus
5	Scorpio	5	Gemini
6	Scorpio	6	Gemini
7	Sagittarius	7	Cancer
8	Sagittarius	8	Cancer
9	Sagittarius	9	Leo
10	Capricorn	10	Leo
11	Capricorn	11	Leo
12 noon	Aquarius	12 midnight	Virgo

NOVEMBER 27

AM	Rising Sign	PM	Rising Sign
1	Virgo	1	Pisces
2	Libra	2	Aries
3	Libra	3	Taurus
4	Libra	4	Taurus
5	Scorpio	5	Gemini
6	Scorpio	6	Gemini
7	Sagittarius	7	Cancer
8	Sagittarius	8	Cancer
9	Sagittarius	9	Leo
10	Capricorn	10	Leo
11	Capricorn	11	Leo
12 noon	Aquarius	12 midnight	Virgo

NOVEMBER 30

AM	Rising Sign	PM	Rising Sign
1	Virgo	1	Pisces
2	Libra	2	Aries
3	Libra	3	Taurus
4	Scorpio	4	Gemini
5	Scorpio	5	Gemini
6	Scorpio	6	Cancer
7	Sagittarius	7	Cancer
8	Sagittarius	8	Cancer
9	Capricorn	9	Leo
10	Capricorn	10	Leo
11	Aquarius	11	Virgo
12 noon	Aquarius	12 midnight	Virgo

DECEMBER 3

AM	Rising Sign	PM	Rising Sign
1	Virgo	1	Pisces
2	Libra	2	Aries
3	Libra	3	Taurus
4	Scorpio	4	Gemini
5	Scorpio	5	Gemini
6	Scorpio	6	Cancer
7	Sagittarius	7	Cancer
8	Sagittarius	8	Cancer
9	Capricorn	9	Leo
10	Capricorn	10	Leo
11	Aquarius	11	Virgo
12 noon	Pisces	12 midnight	Virgo

DECEMBER 6

AM	Rising Sign	PM	Rising Sign
1	Libra	1	Aries
2	Libra	2	Aries
3	Libra	3	Taurus
4	Scorpio	4	Gemini
5	Scorpio	5	Gemini
6	Scorpio	6	Cancer
7	Sagittarius	7	Cancer
8	Sagittarius	8	Leo
9	Capricorn	9	Leo
10	Capricorn	10	Leo
11	Aquarius	11	Virgo
12 noon	Pisces	12 midnight	Virgo

DECEMBER 9

AM	Rising Sign	PM	Rising Sign
1	Libra	1	Aries
2	Libra	2	Taurus
3	Libra	3	Taurus
4	Scorpio	4	Gemini
5	Scorpio	5	Gemini
6	Sagittarius	6	Cancer
7	Sagittarius	7	Cancer
8	Sagittarius	8	Leo
9	Capricorn	9	Leo
10	Capricorn	10	Leo
11	Aquarius	11	Virgo
12 noon	Pisces	12 midnight	Virgo

DECEMBER 12

AM	Rising Sign	PM	Rising Sign
1	Libra	1	Aries
2	Libra	2	Taurus
3	Libra	3	Taurus
4	Scorpio	4	Gemini
5	Scorpio	5	Gemini
6	Sagittarius	6	Cancer
7	Sagittarius	7	Cancer
8	Sagittarius	8	Leo
9	Capricorn	9	Leo
10	Capricorn	10	Leo
11	Aquarius	11	Virgo
12 noon	Pisces	12 midnight	Virgo

DECEMBER 15

AM	Rising Sign	PM	Rising Sign
1	Libra	1	Aries
2	Libra	2	Taurus
3	Scorpio	3	Gemini
4	Scorpio	4	Gemini
5	Scorpio	5	Cancer
6	Sagittarius	6	Cancer
7	Sagittarius	7	Cancer
8	Capricorn	8	Leo
9	Capricorn	9	Leo
10	Aquarius	10	Virgo
11	Aquarius	11	Virgo
12 noon	Pisces	12 midnight	Virgo

DECEMBER 18

AM	Rising Sign	PM	Rising Sign
1	Libra	1	Aries
2	Libra	2	Taurus
3	Scorpio	3	Gemini
4	Scorpio	4	Gemini
5	Scorpio	5	Cancer
6	Sagittarius	6	Cancer
7	Sagittarius	7	Cancer
8	Capricorn	8	Leo
9	Capricorn	9	Leo
10	Aquarius	10	Virgo
11	Aquarius	11	Virgo
12 noon	Pisces	12 midnight	Virgo

DECEMBER 21

AM	Rising Sign	PM	Rising Sign
1	Libra	1	Aries
2	Libra	2	Taurus
3	Scorpio	3	Gemini
4	Scorpio	4	Gemini
5	Scorpio	5	Cancer
6	Sagittarius	6	Cancer
7	Sagittarius	7	Leo
8	Capricorn	8	Leo
9	Capricorn	9	Leo
10	Aquarius	10	Virgo
11	Pisces	11	Virgo
12 noon	Aries	12 midnight	Libra

DECEMBER 24

AM	Rising Sign	PM	Rising Sign
1	Libra	1	Taurus
2	Libra	2	Taurus
3	Scorpio	3	Gemini
4	Scorpio	4	Gemini
5	Sagittarius	5	Cancer
6	Sagittarius	6	Cancer
7	Sagittarius	7	Leo
8	Capricorn	8	Leo
9	Capricorn	9	Leo
10	Aquarius	10	Virgo
11	Pisces	11	Virgo
12 noon	Aries	12 midnight	Libra

DECEMBER 27

AM	Rising Sign	PM	Rising Sign
1	Libra	1	Taurus
2	Libra	2	Taurus
3	Scorpio	3	Gemini
4	Scorpio	4	Gemini
5	Sagittarius	5	Cancer
6	Sagittarius	6	Cancer
7	Sagittarius	7	Leo
8	Capricorn	8	Leo
9	Capricorn	9	Leo
10	Aquarius	10	Virgo
11	Pisces	11	Virgo
12 noon	Aries	12 midnight	Libra

DECEMBER 30

AM	Rising Sign	PM	Rising Sign
1	Libra	1	Taurus
2	Scorpio	2	Taurus
3	Scorpio	3	Gemini
4	Scorpio	4	Cancer
5	Sagittarius	5	Cancer
6	Sagittarius	6	Cancer
7	Capricorn	7	Leo
8	Capricorn	8	Leo
9	Aquarius	9	Virgo
10	Aquarius	10	Virgo
11	Pisces	11	Virgo
12 noon	Aries	12 midnight	Libra

ABOUT THE AUTHOR

ROBIN MacNAUGHTON is the author of twelve books, including the best-selling *Robin MacNaughton's Sun Sign Personality Guide, Robin MacNaughton's Moon Sign Personality Guide, How to Transform Your Life Through Astrology, Power Astrology,* and *How to Seduce Any Man in the Zodiac.* A professional astrologer for twenty-nine years, she has also extensively studied Jungian psychology, Buddhism, Hinduism, the Tarot, the Kabbalah, and Taoism. She maintains a private practice in Avon, Connecticut, where she also works as an astrological consultant for several psychologists and a Jungian analyst.